Time Out

Bangkok

timeout.com/bangkok

D0066773

Published by Time Out Guides Ltd, a wholly owned subsidiary of Time Out Group Ltd.
Time Out and the Time Out logo are trademarks of Time Out Group Ltd.

© Time Out Group Ltd 2007
Previous editions 2003, 2005.

10 9 8 7 6 5 4 3 2 1

This edition first published in Great Britain in 2007 by Ebury Publishing
A Random House Group Company
20 Vauxhall Bridge Road, London SW1V 2SA

Random House Australia Pty Limited 20 Alfred Street, Milsons Point, Sydney, New South Wales 2061, Australia
Random House New Zealand Limited 18 Poland Road, Glenfield, Auckland 10, New Zealand
Random House South Africa (Pty) Limited Isle of Houghton, Corner Boundary
Road & Carse O'Gowrie, Houghton 2198, South Africa

Random House UK Limited Reg. No. 954009

For details of distribution in the Americas, see www.timeout.com

ISBN 10: 1-84670-021-3
ISBN 13: 978184670 0217

A CIP catalogue record for this book is available from the British Library

Printed and bound by Firmengruppe APPL, aprinta druck, Wemding, Germany

The Random House Group Limited makes every effort to ensure that the papers used in our books are made from trees
that have been legally sourced from well-managed and credibly certified forests. Our paper procurement policy can be
found on www.randomhouse.co.uk.

Time Out Guides Limited
Universal House
251 Tottenham Court Road
London W1T 7AB
Tel + 44 (0)20 7813 3000
Fax + 44 (0)20 7813 6001
Email guides@timeout.com
www.timeout.com

Editorial

Editor Philip Cornwel-Smith
Deputy Editor Stuart Sumner
Listings Editors Ruayporn Nophananthanaporn, Chanitra Akjiratikarl
Proofreader Patrick Mulkern
Indexer Sally Davies

Managing Director Peter Fiennes
Financial Director Gareth Garner
Editorial Director Ruth Jarvis
Deputy Series Editor Dominic Earle
Editorial Manager Holly Pick

Design

Art Director Scott Moore
Art Editor Pinelope Kourmouzoglou
Senior Designer Josephine Spencer
Graphic Designer Henry Elphick
Junior Graphic Designer Kei Ishimaru
Digital Imaging Simon Foster
Ad Make-up Jodi Sher

Picture Desk

Picture Editor Jael Marschner
Deputy Picture Editor Tracey Kerrigan
Picture Researcher Helen McFarland

Advertising

Sales Director Mark Phillips
International Sales Manager Fred Durman
International Sales Consultant Ross Canadé
International Sales Executive Charlie Sokol
Advertising Sales (Bangkok) Splash Communications
Advertising Assistant Kate Staddon

Marketing

Group Marketing Director John Luck
Marketing Manager Yvonne Poon
Sales and Marketing Director North America Lisa Levinson

Production

Group Production Director Mark Lamond
Production Manager Brendan McKeown
Production Coordinator Caroline Bradford

Time Out Group

Chairman Tony Elliott
Financial Director Richard Waterlow
Time Out Magazine Ltd MD David Pepper
Group General Manager/Director Nichola Coulthard
Time Out Communications Ltd MD David Pepper
Time Out International MD Cathy Runciman
Group Art Director John Oakey
Group IT Director Simon Chappell

Contributors

Introduction Philip Cornwel-Smith. **History** Anon Nakornthab (*Siam or Thailand?* & *The Yellow Coup* Philip Cornwel-Smith). **Bangkok Today** Philip Cornwel-Smith. **Arts & Architecture** Alex Kerr. **Belief** Mettanando Bhikku (*Buddha embodied* Alex Kerr). **Bangkok by Design** Brian Mertens. **Where to Stay** Korakot Punlopruksa. **Sightseeing Introduction** Philip Cornwel-Smith. **Phra Nakorn** Philip Cornwel-Smith, Steven Pettifor. *Banglamphu* Jim Algie. **Thonburi, River & Canals** Stirling Silliphant (*Kred ability* Philip Cornwel-Smith). **Dusit** Jim Algie. **Chinatown** Jennifer Gampell. **Downtown & Suburbs** Philip Cornwel-Smith, Steven Pettifor. **Further Afield** Philip Cornwel-Smith. **Restaurants** Howard Richardson, Korakot Punlopruksa. **Bars & Pubs** Karuna Gurung & Laurie Osborne of *Bangkok Recorder*. **Markets & Vendors** Korakot Punlopruksa. **Shops & Services** Anon Nakornthab. **Festivals & Events** Philip Cornwel-Smith, Brian Mertens. **Children** Andrea Francis. **Film** Philip Cornwel-Smith (*A big leap* Anchalee Chaiworaporn). **Galleries** Philip Cornwel-Smith (*Curate expectations* Phattarawadee Phattarawanik). **Gay & Lesbian** Robin Newbold (*How-dee!* Karuna Gurung). **Mind & Body** Chamsai Jotisalikorn (*Suite retreat* Philip Cornwel-Smith). **Music** Tim Carr (*Jazz* Howard Richardson). **Nightlife** Karuna Gurung & Laurie Osborne of *Bangkok Recorder* (*Adult nightlife* & *Go-go going… gone?* Thomas Schmid). **Performing Arts** Pichayanund Chindahporn (*Dramas about drama* Philip Cornwel-Smith). **Sport & Fitness** Howard Richardson. **Beach Escapes** Terry Blackburn, Philip Cornwel-Smith (*Hua Hin* Dennis Duncan, *Ko Chang* Jo Smith). **Directory** Kathareeya Jumroonsiri, Philip Cornwel-Smith.

Maps john@jsgraphics.co.uk. Map data supplied by Bangkok Co Part (www.bangkokguide.homepage.com).

Photography Heloise Bergman, except: page 12 Sotheby's/akg-images; pages 18, 159 REUTERS/Chaiwat Subprasom; page 22 ABACA/EMPICS; page 101 Mark Parren Taylor; page 162 REUTERS/Sukree Sukplang; page 167 SAHAMONGKOLFILM INTERNATIONAL CO LTD; page 168 Jan Tao; page 174 John Goss; page 188 (left) GMM Grammy; page 188 (right) Jesper Haynes; pages 184, 185 Click Radio Co Ltd; page 205 Photolibrary.com.

The following images were provided by the featured establishment/artist: pages 48, 207, 210, 214, 220.

The Editor would like to thank Navamintr Vitayakul of Rose Hotel, Rungsaeng Sripaoraya of TAT, Bangkok Tourist Bureau, Tim Carr, *Bangkok Recorder*, Anucha Thirakanont, Nilobol Phanichkarn, Ian Stewart, Yvan van Outrive, and all contributors to previous editions of *Time Out Bangkok*, whose work forms the basis for this book.

Contents

THE JIM THOMPSON
ART CENTER

Located in the heart of Bangkok, The Jim Thompson Art Center is situated in the same compound as the unique and famous Jim Thompson House Museum. Serving as a haven for Bangkok's local and international arts communities, the Center is gaining a reputation as a place to mingle, interact, and exchange dialogues. In conjunction with its exhibitions, the Center activities include parties, events, seminars, lectures and workshops.

6 Kasemsan Soi 2, Rama 1 Road, Patumwan, Bangkok 10330 Thailand
Tel. 662 612 6741, 662 219 2911 Fax. 662 219 2911
Access : BTS National Stadium Station, towards Jim Thompson House
Open Hours : 9 – 5 pm. Daily / Office Hours : 11 – 8 pm. Daily

Introduction

Bangkok is many things – wonderful, wayward and contradictory – but always interesting. And this is an especially rewarding time to visit the Thai capital. Relics of history litter the concrete city, and communities retain historic traditions amid new cosmopolitan lifestyles. But at this pivotal time there's a sense of seeing history in action. Millions wear yellow on Mondays to honour the King. Contemporary design remodels the city's skyline and details. A fresh indie mindset inspires the young to the chagrin of prudish elders. And everyone is so polite, even when there's a coup. It's quite a place.

Raised as Buddhists to live in the moment, the Thais calmly moved on from ructions like the 2004 tsunami, the 2006 putsch and the New Year 2007 bombings. Bangkok remains safer than most world cities, and street activity hasn't lost its kaleidoscopic charm under increased security. And people maintain their trademark sensibilities: *sanuk* (fun), *sabai* (relaxation), *sa-ngob* (serenity), *metta* (compassion) and *mai pen rai* (never mind).

Tourism has proved so resilient that Thais are getting more selective about quality. This can mean higher standards in spas and toilets, or stricter rules on visas, property and investment. As the country upgrades, so vacationers shift from backpackers to flashpackers, from so-called 'zero-dollar' Chinese package tours to 25,000-dollar dinners for tycoons.

Such lures to the fickle super-rich contrast with crackdowns on independent young Westerners who worked un-permitted, often making 'tourist visa runs' for years. Ironically, many of those dismissed as 'low quality visitors' (usually affluent, but budgeting long-term) are among Thailand's most loyal foreign advocates. Countless visa run veterans have contributed needed skills or founded businesses. Aside from teaching English, they have played significant developmental roles, from arts, media and modelling to diving, DJ-ing and design. Though things have got more formalised, *farang* (Westerners) continue to settle here because Bangkok inhabits a mind-boggling dimension unlike anywhere else.

Evoked by writers from Conrad and Maugham to Garland (*The Beach*), Thailand has for centuries beguiled Asiaphiles seeking oriental exotica. Constant festivities pepper the bewildering blend of ancient, modern and eternal. From the 1960s onwards, Bangkok gained specialist appeal among foodies, pilgrims, gays and denizens of its ribald nightlife. Meanwhile thousands have come here to learn massage and meditation, gemology and boxing. Now the city also delivers in designer travel niches: boutique hotels, holistic retreats, haute cuisine, superstar clubbing, voluntourism. However international it seems, Bangkok has absorbed such globalised waves before, digested them, and created something distinctly its own.

ABOUT TIME OUT CITY GUIDES

This is the third edition of *Time Out Bangkok*, one of an expanding series of Time Out guides produced by the people behind the successful listings magazines in London, New York and Chicago. Our guides are all written by resident experts who have striven to provide you with all the most up-to-date information you'll need to explore the city or read up on its background, whether you're a local or a first-time visitor.

THE LIE OF THE LAND

To make the book (and the city) easier to navigate, we have divided Bangkok into areas, which are reflected in the chapters and headings in our Sightseeing section, starting on p54. Although these areas are a simplification of Bangkok's geography,

they follow official districts and local terms where possible. These areas are used in addresses throughout the guide and in the series of fully indexed colour street maps at the back of the guide, starting on p248.

Though signs in English are a common sight in tourist areas, addresses nationwide can often be confusing, with imprecision, variable spellings and inconsistent numbering. In those cases, we've noted landmarks for orientation. All bus destination boards are in Thai, though airports, the BTS SkyTrain, MRT subway, trains and taxis have wording in English. For more guidance on getting around, *see p224*.

ESSENTIAL INFORMATION

For all the practical information you might need for visiting the area – including visa and customs information, details of local transport,

a listing of emergency numbers, information on local weather and a selection of useful websites – turn to the Directory at the back of this guide. It begins on page 224.

THE LOWDOWN ON THE LISTINGS

We have tried to make this book as easy to use as possible. Addresses, phone numbers, opening times and admission prices are all included in the listings. However, businesses can change their arrangements at any time. Before you go out of your way, we'd strongly advise you to phone ahead to check opening times and other particulars. While every effort and care has been made to ensure the accuracy of the information contained in this guide, the publishers cannot accept responsibility for any errors it may contain.

PRICES AND PAYMENT

We have listed prices in Thai baht (B) throughout. In cases where rates are in US dollars ($), payment is accepted in baht. We have noted whether venues such as shops, hotels and restaurants accept credit cards or not, but have only listed the major cards: American Express (AmEx), Diners Club (DC), MasterCard (MC) and Visa (V). Many businesses and ATMs will also accept other cards, including Switch/Maestro or Delta, JCB, Discover and Carte Blanche. Beyond major hotels, banks and exchange booths, extremely few venues will accept travellers' cheques.

Advertisers

We would like to stress that no establishment has been included in this guide because it has advertised in any of our publications and no payment of any kind has influenced any review. The opinions given in this book are those of Time Out writers and entirely independent.

The prices we've listed in this guide should be treated as guidelines, not gospel. Some rates are seasonal. If prices vary wildly from those we've quoted, ask whether there's a good reason. If not, go elsewhere. Then please let us know. We aim to give the best and most up-to-date advice, so we want to know if you've been badly treated or overcharged.

TELEPHONE NUMBERS

All Thailand's phone numbers incorporate the former area code in a system of eight digits plus an initial 0, even when you're phoning from within the same area. Mobile phones are common in Thailand, with numbers that start 08 before an eight-digit number; they cost more than land lines, but are cheaper long-distance.

To dial numbers as given in this book from abroad, use your country's exit code (00 in the UK, 01 in the US), followed by the country code for Thailand (66), then omit the initial 0 before dialing the eight-digit number. For more details of phone codes and charges, *see p234*.

MAPS

We've provided map references for most places listed in central Bangkok, indicating the page and grid reference at which an address can be found on our street maps. These are located at the back of the book on pp246-252. The maps also now pinpoint the specific locations of hotels (❶), restaurants (❶), and bars and pubs (❶). There's a street index on pp253-4.

LET US KNOW WHAT YOU THINK

We hope you enjoy *Time Out Bangkok*, and we'd like to know what you think of it. We welcome tips for places that you consider we should include in future editions and take note of your criticism of our choices. You can email us your comments at guides@timeout.com.

There is an online version of this book, along with guides to over 100 international cities, at **www.timeout.com**.

www.**bangkokair**.com

Guilin Xi'an Jinghong

Shenzhen

Ho Chi Minh City

Hong Kong

Luang Prabang

Pakse

Hiroshima

Siem Reap

Fukuoka

Bangkok

Phnom Penh

Yangon

Maldives

Trat (Koh Chang)

Chiang Mai

Singapore

Sukhothai

Pattaya (U-Tapao)

Phuket

Samui

Flying to more exotic gems of Asia
Bangkok Airways - Your airline

In Context

Wat Suthat. *See p70.*

The visit of the French ambassador in 1750.

History

The never-ending struggle for power.

The Thai term for history derives from *prawat* (biography), hence the focus on nationalistic heroes in archives, official literature and state-funded movies like the 2007 trilogy *King Naresuan*. Royal manuscripts serve as the official record, while the 'father of Thai history', Prince Damrong Rajanupharb, provided the framework that Oxbridge-trained historians – notably Damrong's half-brother, King Rama VI, Prince Chula Chakrabongse and ML Manich Jumsai – shaped into the national narrative.

'Thai Studies' now, however, encompass economic, social and geo-political factors, thanks to generations of revisionists, from DGE Hall (*A History of South-east Asia*) to the late David Wyatt (*Thailand: A Short History*) and Thongchai Winichakul (*Siam Mapped*), who charts the fluidity of borders and allegiances before the 19th-century unitary state. Currently, Pasuk Pongpaichit and Chris Baker (*A History of Thai Land*) show how official 'Thainess' is as much a product of policy as historiography. While experts split over the origins of Thai ethnicity, adequate records document the Thai domain and its peoples. So then, how did Siam start?

FROM SEA BED TO SUKHOTHAI

When present-day Bangkok was under the sea a few millennia ago, early South-east Asians fashioned some of civilisation's earliest bronze axes, invented the outrigger canoe and seemingly initiated wet rice cultivation. By the time that Prince Sitthatha Gotama (who became the Buddha) was wandering northern India six centuries before Christ, merchants from the subcontinent had established trading posts in Suwannaphum. They traded and intermarried with indigenous farmers around the Gulf of Siam. Suwannaphum became important enough that in the third century BC it received two monks dispatched by Emperor Asoka of India, a Buddhist convert.

Meanwhile, over millennia, tattooed Tai clans (tribal ancestors of Thais) migrated through Yunnan in southern Han-dynasty China, into lowland South-east Asia. Living in stilt houses, they tended rice in water-filled fields using buffaloes, a status symbol until recent times. Subduing earlier settlers, they carved a pastoral society out of forest in what became upper-central Siam. Some spread as far as Assam in India and upper Vietnam.

From the sixth century Suwannaphum was supplanted by Dvaravati, a little-known Mon civilisation of devout Therevada Buddhists with centres at Suphanburi, Nakhon Ratchasima (formerly Khorat) and Nakhon Pathom, near Bangkok. The sole evidence of Dvaravati's name is a clay inscription found hereabouts. From the eighth to 13th centuries Southern Thailand was part of the equally elusive Mahayana Buddhist empire of Srivijaya, centred in Sumatra.

Dvaravati eventually succumbed to ninth century Khmers of Angkor, from whom the Tais adopted the Hindu concept of *devaraja* – divine kingship. Some Dvaravati fringes like Lavo (now Lopburi) defied Khmer overlords for two more centuries, sending diplomats to China and becoming heavily populated by Tais – whom the Khmer called Syam (Sanskrit for 'swarthy').

'At the Battle of Nong Sarai, waged on war elephants, Naresuan slew the crown prince of Burma, restoring Thai freedom.'

By Angkor's decline around 1220, a Tai-Mon-Khmer blend in the Chao Phraya basin gelled into a Siamese ethnicity. Power then shifted northwards when King Sri Indraditya (c1240-70) established a Tai kingdom at Sukhothai ('Dawn of Happiness'). During Ramkhamhaeng's reign (c1279-98), Sukhothai blossomed into a powerful federation of Buddhist states, including Si Satchanalai and Kamphaengphet. Wielding influence more through *dhammaraja* (Buddhist kingship) than military might, Sukhothai reached west to the Indian Ocean, east to Lao Vientiane and south to Nakhon Si Thamarat in the Malay peninsula, though skirting the Lopburi-run lower plains. To the north, he forged an alliance in 1287 with Phayao and Lanna (literally 'One Million Rice Fields') to repel raids by Mongol China.

The court supported a stylised Buddhist aesthetic most celebrated in the world's first statues of the Buddha walking. In the first script to distinguish Thai's five tones, Sukhothai left royal engravings including a still quoted line on self-sufficiency: 'Fish are in the rivers, rice is in the fields.'

THE RISE AND FALL

While Sukhothai declined, Suphanburi and Lopburi vied over the central plains. During a cholera outbreak, the Lopburi aristocrat U Thong (conveniently wed to a noblewoman

from each ruling house) fled south to a river island. There on 4 March 1351 he founded a new kingdom: Ayutthaya (named after the Indian city of Rama, hero of the Ramayana epic). As King Ramathibodi (1351-69), U T hong sent his relatives to rule Suphanburi and Lopburi, thus pitting the two dynasties to squabble over Ayutthaya's throne – a spat that went on for generations.

Already busy with Asian merchants, Ayutthaya quickly grew, while the rivermouth trading post of Bang Makok ('Village of Plum Olives'; aka Bangkok) became a strategic gateway. The first of several canals to bypass Bangkok's river meanders was cut by King Baromtrailokanart (1448-88). On the west bank, Thonburi gained a fortress just before the Burmese sacked Ayutthaya in the reign of King Chakkrapat (1548-69).

Ayutthaya reasserted its independence through King Naresuan (1590-1605), hero of the eponymous new Thai movie, who'd grown up as a hostage at the Burmese court. At the Battle of Nong Sarai, waged on war elephants, Naresuan slew the crown prince of Burma, restoring Thai freedom. In the 17th century Ayutthaya prospered into a trading hub with over a million people, then larger than London. As a duty port, Bangkok received European ships, while myriad nations were granted quarters around Ayutthaya. Visiting traders, explorers, writers and engravers attested to Ayutthaya's gilded opulence and magnificent rituals, such as presentations of white elephants and the royal barge processions that still grace the Chao Phraya river.

Under the diplomatic King Narai (1656-88) and his lead minister, the Greek adventurer Constantine Phaulkon, Ayutthaya became an international power. In 1687 Narai invited Louis XIV of France to establish a military mission in the southern port of Songkhla. Secretly hoping to control trade and to convert King Narai to Christianity, the French occupied a fort in Bangkok. Siamese xenophobia at foreign influence swept the court as Narai lay dying. A conspiracy installed as regent his foster brother, Phra Phetracha, who eliminated Narai's heirs, had Phaulkon executed, and usurped the throne. Phetracha (1688-1703) then exchanged cannon fire with the French in Bangkok before negotiating the French exit.

Siam was effectively closed to *farang* (foreigners) for two centuries, though Asian contacts flourished. Theravada Buddhism had been introduced from Sri Lanka in the 13th century via Nakhon Sri Thammarat. In 1751 Sri Lanka asked King Barommakot (1733-58) to help restore waning Sinhalese Buddhism. Meanwhile, Ayutthaya's treasury had swelled

Siam or Thailand?

People and publications often erroneously refer to Sukhothai, Ayutthaya, Thonburi and Bangkok as successive capitals of Thailand, when the country's name, Prathet Thai (Thailand), dates only from 1939. For eight centuries before that, the multi-ethnic land was widely known as Siam, a term for 'swarthy' that Khmers used to denote Thais. King Rama IV formally called his realm Siam when staving off colonialists and required territories to have fixed borders, a name and a national flag. The flag he devised depicted a royal white elephant upon a red standard, until King Rama VI switched to a modern, Westernised tricolour: red (nation), white (religion) and blue (monarchy).

During the ultra-nationalist mid 20th century, the dictator Plaek Phibunsongkhram made Thai ethnicity key to the identity of the nation he had renamed Thailand. Influenced by the ideologue Luang Wichit Wathakarn, he told Thais that they needed 'national traditions', such as standing for an anthem that opens with the line 'Thailand embodies

the blood and flesh of the Thai race'. Yet, his 'cultural mandates' often favoured modern Western traits over authentic Thainess. Phiphat music was suppressed in favour of big band jazz, while government offices wouldn't serve people in traditional clothing, to encourage adoption of Western suits, dresses, shoes and hats, regardless of the climate. He even instructed husbands to kiss their wives on the cheek when leaving home.

Though some feel Siam embraces more ethnic and regional diversity, Phibun's Thailand concept still pervades daily life, media and identity. Informally, though, Thais talk of their country as 'Meuang Thai'. Historically this was a land of *meuang* ('city states'), focused on the power centre rather than the amorphous jungle frontiers. Hence many old maps labelled the kingdom 'Ayutthaya', rather than Siam, and provinces are still named after their *meuang* capital district. Today most of those people longing for Siam are foreigners, for whom the word casts such an exotic spell.

through rice exports to China, and come under the administration of newly arrived Chinese and descendants of Persians and Indian Brahmins, who had entered service under Narai – notably, the still influential Bunnag family.

> **'In keeping with an edict that no royal blood should touch the ground, Taksin was bound in a sack and struck above the neck.'**

During dynastic power struggles, the spectre of Burma reappeared. They besieged Ayutthaya in 1766 until famine, disease and fires prompted King Ekatat (1758-67) to surrender. The Burmese refused concessions and systematically razed the city.

TAKSIN GETS THE SACK
In October 1767 a fleet commanded by Chaophraya (Lord) Taksin landed at Thonburi as dawn light bathed Wat Makok (now Wat Arun, the 'Temple of Dawn'). Having escaped from Ayutthaya, Taksin's forces had taken Chantaburi on the Gulf then doubled back by sea up the Chao Phraya. With Ayutthaya reduced to anarchy, they started anew at Thonburi.

On being crowned, Taksin (1767-82) invited the old nobility to help restore order. He subdued Phimai, where Ekatat's half-brother had set up court, then travelled to Fang and Phitsanulok, both run by red-robed renegade monks. By annexing Battambang and Siem Reap, Taksin ended any threat from Cambodia and reacquired all Ayutthayan territory. The campaign required the support of the Teochiu Chinese in strategic trading posts. After all, the new king of Siam was a son of China, a fact not lost on the court's public relations people, who advertised his ancestry in bids to improve trade with the Chinese.

Burma largely withdrew and Lanna joined Siam as a buffer against its former Burmese oppressors. With Taksin's authority, Chaophraya Chakri and his brother Chaophraya Surasi then moved on Lao, returning with spoils including the Emerald Buddha. Enshrined in Thonburi, and later at Wat Phra Kaew in Bangkok, the jadeite image remains a palladium of Thai independence.

By 1779 Taksin's aberrant behaviour, religious visions and arbitrary lashing out puzzled visitors and alienated the old nobility. In April 1782 rebels opposing a tax official were urged to march on Thonburi, and enthrone Chakri. In keeping with a 15th-century edict that no royal blood should touch the ground,

Taksin was bound in a sack and struck above the neck with a sandalwood club, then secretly buried in the capital he had founded.

THE BANGKOK PERIOD

Chakri returned from quelling a Cambodian revolt to become King Ramathibodi, aka Rama I (1782-1809), thereby founding the current Chakri dynasty. While keeping Thonburi as a fort, he moved the capital to the river's more defensible east bank at Bangkok.

The Bangkok period often gets dubbed 'Rattanakosin', after the royal island formed by a girdle of canals on the model of Ayutthaya. Its walls reused bricks from the former capital, leaving little to be seen at Ayutthaya. Additional canals were dug and the so-called 'Venice of the East' soon swelled into a vibrant, cosmopolitan city. Princes and officials erected stately homes on the central canals. Displaced from Rattanakosin, Chinese merchants scrambled for sites along the river, founding Sampaeng (Chinatown). Indians, Muslims and Catholics, too, formed communities.

> ### 'One of Rama I's 40-odd children succeeded him as Rama II and sired 73 offspring.'

Rama I's Three Seals Laws underpinned justice for a century, and his Buddhist reforms included compilation of the Tipitaka scriptures. To ensure manpower and to prevent private armies, peasants had to serve *corvée* (forced labour) for four months per year, and be tattooed with the names of their masters and locality. In his year of coronation, 1785, Rama I faced Burma's last major attack. He defeated 100,000 men in nine armies, though skirmishes continued (and still occur today). Rama I further secured Siam's borders through relationships with Lanna and Lao, and imposition over Malay states including Pattani, which remains a restive region.

One of Rama I's 40-odd children succeeded him as Rama II (1809-24) and sired 73 offspring – a testament to the stability of his 15-year reign. The first two Chakri reigns entertained a literary revival, restoring the chronicles and dramatic works lost at Ayutthaya. Each country's adaptation of the Indian epic *Ramayana* reflects its culture. Rama I's translation, the *Ramakien*, has a Siamese resonance; its kings are named after the hero, Rama, while monkey general Hanuman brims with *sanuk* (fun). Scribes also translated foreign classics like the Javanese *Inao* and the Chinese *Sam Kok* ('Romance of Three Kingdoms').

A notable poet himself, Rama II sponsored the star of this renaissance, the UNESCO-recognised poet Sunthorn Phu.

In the early 1820s Burma's constant will to attack proved less concerning than tussles with Vietnam over Cambodia, which they divided. Siam got Angkor and parts of Lao, which then turned aggressor. Feeling slighted by Rama III (1824-51) on a visit to Bangkok, the Lao ruler of Vientiane, Chao Anuwong, marched troops towards Bangkok in 1827. Chaophraya Bodindecha soon sent the Lao scattering, occupied Vientiane, withdrew and then returned to raze Vientiane. So many Lao were brought over the Mekong river to Isaan that today 17 million of the 21 million Lao live in Thailand.

South-east Asian warfare has been as much about populations as territory, resulting in a cultural cross-fertilisation, with Siam a receptive crossroads of cultures and ethnicities. For example, Siamese dance was influenced by performers captured from Angkor, Burma seized Ayutthayan troops to enrich its own court arts, and Siam reinfluenced Khmer dance and culture after further campaigns by Bodindecha reoccupied Cambodia. By Rama III's passing in 1851, Bangkok ran the biggest Siamese empire yet.

Statue of **King Rama V**. *See p16.*

RETAINING INDEPENDENCE

When Europeans intensified imperialism after the Napoleonic Wars, Siam was the region's leading power. By the time King Mongkut (Rama IV, 1851-68) ascended the throne after 27 years as a Buddhist monk, Britain and France had encroached upon Burma and Vietnam respectively. In 1855 former Hong Kong governor Sir John Bowring forced the king and his cabinet, led by the powerful Chaophraya Si Suriyawong, into an unequal agreement that dismantled state monopolies, restricted duties and limited Siam's judicial power over British subjects. The following decade the French seized Siamese Cambodia and swept up the Mekong river.

> **'Rama V's visits to Europe influenced Bangkok's layout and architecture – and his courtiers' hairstyles.'**

During the reign of King Chulalongkorn (aka Rama V, 1868-1910) a crisis erupted when French agents in Laos were expelled and one was killed. French gunboats invaded the Chao Phraya river, forcing Siam to concede Laos and western Cambodia to French Indochina. Britain later received four Malay states after relinquishing legal jurisdiction over its subjects and agreeing to provide a loan for building a railway. Siam lost territories it had annexed or reclaimed over the past century, but was the only South-east Asian country to remain independent.

Western colonialists trumpeted the rationale that they brought civilisation, a pretext that was deftly undermined by the modernisation of Siam by Rama IV and his son. Rama IV published a government gazette, initiated educational reforms and eased laws on slavery and *corvée*. Foreign tutors hired to educate the king's children included Anna Leonowens, whose famous memoirs are as inaccurate and self-aggrandising as her job application. Hence Thai distaste for the subsequent musical and film *The King and I* that exaggerated her faulty depiction of Rama IV. Newly discovered letters by the king, however, reveal his discussion of state matters with Anna.

King Chulalongkorn continued his father's reforms, establishing the civil service, abolishing slavery and modernising the army. He became the first Thai monarch to travel abroad. After visits to British Singapore and Dutch Java in 1871, he conformed the court dress and hairstyles to European trends. Several princes were sent to study in Europe.

In 1897 Rama V's visits to Europe influenced Bangkok's layout and architecture, especially in the new royal district of Dusit.

POWER STRUGGLE

In November 1911 the 13-day coronation of King Vajiravudh (Rama VI, 1910-25) cost almost ten per cent of the state budget. Three months later some military officers were arrested for conspiring to mount a coup. It was Siam's first test of absolute monarchy.

As Bangkok spread eastwards, Rama VI donated Lumphini Park and expressed his love of theatre. He translated classics, acted in plays and installed theatres in his palaces. Meanwhile, nationalism was on the rise, encouraged by Western trade restrictions and Chinese dominance of the Thai economy. Rama VI's concept of the Thai nation called for a homogenous society rallying under a new flag (*see p14* **Siam or Thailand?**), compulsory education and, for the first time, surnames.

The capital then became the stage for a succession of power struggles. On 4 June 1932 the self-dubbed 'People's Party' – principally, young officials and officers who had studied in Europe – seized the city in a quiet, bloodless coup that installed a constitutional monarchy and parliament. King Prajadhipok (Rama VII, 1925-35) abdicated while in England three years later, and the cabinet invited his nephew

History recreated at the **Central World Plaza**. *See p154.*

Ananta Mahidol, who was at school in Switzerland, to reign. As Rama VIII (1935-46), he did not return for another ten years, while the 1932 coup promoters squabbled over power.

A coup leader, Plaek Phibunsongkhram, twice assumed the prime ministership (1938-44 and 1948-57). Styling himself on fascist leaders, Phibun renamed the country Thailand and propagated an ideal of the ethnically Thai nation (see p14 **Siam or Thailand?**). He established paramilitary troops, expanded the military and, during World War II, reclaimed disputed parts of Laos and Cambodia. With Japan occupying Thailand in 1942, Phibun's regime declared war on the Allies. Regent Pridi Banomyong refused to endorse the declaration, and helped found the Seri Thai ('Free Thai') covert network to resist Japanese occupation. Co-ordinated by ambassador Seni Promoj in Washington, Seri Thai saved the country from post-war reparations.

'Risking fortunes on dubious stocks caught on in a town where gambling, although illegal, is endemic.'

On becoming new peacetime prime minister, Pridi was preparing Thailand for democracy when, in June 1946, King Ananta was found dead in his royal chamber with a gunshot wound to his head. The death, never fully explicated, was used as a pretext for branding Pridi a communist. A military coup in 1947 then forced Pridi – who many call the 'father of Thai democracy' – into permanent exile. In a strange twist, Phibun, who had declared war on the Allies, returned in 1948 to head a regime that received economic and military aid from the US.

PROTESTS AND BLOODSHED

For the next quarter-century, military strongmen staged coups and counter-coups while young King Bhumibol Adulyadej (Rama IX, 1946-present) was confined to ceremonial duties. For three days in February 1949 the capital shut down as the navy and marines unsuccessfully battled the army- and police-led government in a failed attempt to restore Pridi to power. But the army and police couldn't quell a two-day naval uprising two years later. The air force settled it by bombing the royal flagship *Sri Ayudhya* in the river, allowing the captured Phibun to swim to safety. More than 1,000 soldiers and civilians were killed, and 2,000 wounded. Eight years later Phibun's protégé, General Sarit Thanarat, staged a bloodless overnight coup that drove his mentor into a final exile.

A semblance of order at the expense of democracy buoyed economic fortunes, while US aid poured in to prevent Thailand becoming the next communist domino to fall. Demand for rice and other commodities saw Bangkok's port expand, while highways and airports eclipsed the railways, trams and increasingly paved over canals. With more electrification, consumer goods poured in.

As the Vietnam War intensified, Thailand became the centre of US operations. With over 40,000 US troops stationed here in the 1960s, parts of Bangkok, Pattaya and other cities turned into R&R playgrounds. Hostess bars opened along Patpong Road and sleepy Petchaburi Road reinvented itself as a neon-lit strip of massage parlours and hotels. The capital's population expanded even faster than the national average, as migrants left no-longer-bucolic rural life in search of service and construction jobs. New infrastructure also supported the crucial tourist industry – though the environment suffered alarming degradation.

Arbitrary abuse of power by the 'Three Tyrants' – Prime Minister Thanom Kittikachorn, his son Colonel Narong Kittikachorn, and Field Marshal Prapas Charusathien, Narong's son-in-law – finally proved too much for a new generation of educated Thais raised on Pridi's ideals. On 14 October 1973 more than half a million students, workers and merchants gathered at Thammasat University to demand a constitution. Protestors and troops were locked in a stand-off when an unidentified commando unit opened fire. Bloodshed ensued and the Three Tyrants were forced into exile.

After an interval of turbulent democracy Thanom returned in September 1976, prompting another protest at Thammasat that snowballed into a mass demonstration. The right wing struck back, identifying the students with communist China. On 6 October the police opened fire on demonstrators, killing hundreds, while quasi-military units took special glee in lynching, beating and even burning some alive. Their hopes crushed, many of the students joined rural communist insurgents. This brutal suppression left a scar on the national psyche that has yet to heal.

In the 1980s the nation slowly eased into a new rhythm. Moderate military rule under General Prem Tinsulanond allowed a degree of stability, political participation and media comment, while insurgents were persuaded to rejoin society. The groundwork for democracy was laid and the economy boomed under Prime Minister Chatichai Choonhavan's elected government. His 'buffet cabinet' swelled with industry captains who scrambled for lucrative ministerial portfolios.

The yellow coup

Few in the world media grasped why Bangkok generally welcomed the coup of 19 September 2006 that deposed PM Thaksin Shinawatra, who had the biggest electoral majority in Thai history. Reared on avoidance of confrontation, Thais were aghast at the growing disparities between town and country,

even dividing families. So they looked to the embodiment of their unity, King Bhumibol, symbolised by the colour of his birthday: yellow for Monday.

Yellow became the colour of the zeitgeist. At the anti-Thaksin rallies of 2005-6, demonstrators donned yellow caps and shirts, waved yellow banners. They also displayed folk imagery showing Thaksin as an unlucky lizard or as the god of eclipses, Rahu, eating not the sun or moon, but Thailand. Effigies and cartoons exaggerated Thaksin's angular head as a cube, nicknaming him 'Na Liam' (squareface) after a northern phrase for an untrustworthy person.

In the run-up to the King's Diamond Jubilee in June 2006, and ever since, a majority of the public started to wear yellow on formal occasions and on Mondays, in shirts, ties and rubber wristbands, sometimes entire outfits. Come the coup, soldiers tied yellow ribbons around their epaulettes, guns and tank barrels. Citizens wearing yellow posed for photographs by tanks and handed flowers to soldiers in hope of social peace.

Nationwide, fashion hues gave way to the ancient birthday-colour themes that originated in Hindu astrology and then battlefield tunics and royal insignia before infusing popular culture. Pink (for Tuesday) recalls King Chulalongkorn, pale blue (Friday) signifies Queen Sirikit and lilac (Saturday) Princess Sirindhorn. Thais literally wear their loyalties on their sleeve.

THE BUBBLE BURSTS

Double-digit growth ushered in the 1990s. Farmers and orchard owners became millionaires as developers snapped up land for condominiums, hotels, offices, factories and housing. Expressways barely kept pace with Bangkok's traffic, swelled by luxury cars and the world's second biggest market for pick-up trucks. The affluent new middle classes shopped with a vengeance, showing off imported labels and mobile phones at grand malls and giant discos. The elite developed a taste for wine, though the tipple of choice remained Scotch whisky. Students clamoured for the high-tech trappings and manga taste of Japan – the bubble-era model of the Asian 'tiger economy'. Risking fortunes on dubious stocks caught on in a town where gambling, although illegal, is endemic.

The party was briefly interrupted when Chatichai and his 'unusually rich' ministers

were toppled in a bloodless military coup in February 1991 by the National Peace-Keeping Council (NPKC). Respected diplomat Anand Panyarachun was installed as interim prime minister to appease the public until the intended NPKC-backed premier was linked to alleged drug trading. NPKC leader General Suchinda Kraprayoon then took the top job.

This time the middle classes rallied for his removal, led by the ascetic vegetarian General Chamlong Srimuang, an ex-governor of Bangkok. Protests climaxed in 'Black May' 1992, when the Democracy Monument again witnessed the killing and 'disappearance' of dozens of protestors. Suchinda was forced to resign and Anand led again until September elections brought in a coalition under the modest, principled Chuan Leekpai.

Order was restored and serious urban planning and mass transit finally got under way, but influential figures continued to enrich themselves, and the buying of votes accelerated, prompting a new liberal constitution of 1997, drafted under Anand. Speculation and market manipulation peaked under the governments of Banharn Silpa-archa and Chavalit Yongchaiyudh until the baht crashed in June 1997, dragging the Asian economy down with it. The bubble had vaporised, leaving a Bangkok skyline scarred with half-built concrete eyesores.

In the aftermath came denial. Many were quick to blame foreigners, notably George Soros and the IMF. A second Chuan administration steadied the economy, but failed to invigorate it. Few conceded that the boom had been one big pyramid scheme. Fortunately, the response was practical subsistence not social upheaval. Rolex watches were sold by weight in plastic bags in the 'Market for the Former Rich' and traffic eased due to vehicles getting repossessed. Car boot sales became a short-lived phenomenon, but because selling belongings involves a loss of face, middlemen surreptitiously traded many luxury used goods abroad.

As in Japan, recovery was stifled by rich debtors not being held accountable. Saving face and corrupt networks meant that 'influential transgressors, the 'unusually rich' or the merely incompetent rarely get punished – they're typically transferred to an inactive post'. Finally, in 2003 an ex-minister was jailed, though scandals continually get reburied.

REFORM AND REFORM AGAIN

The constitution envisaged both more stable governments and decentralisation, yet power got concentrated to an unparalleled degree in billionaire Thaksin Shinawatra. Under his Thai Rak Thai ('Thais Love Thais', TRT) Party, this telecom tycoon swept to Thailand's first absolute parliamentary majority in 2000, completed the first full government term, and in 2004 led the first one-party cabinet. Having narrowly escaped conviction in a constitutional court trial, Thaksin consolidated his self-styled CEO authority in most national institutions, appointing his cousin to head the army, treating non-governmental organisations as foreign-funded subversives, and subduing academics and constitutional watchdogs.

Echoing Phibun's social engineering, Thaksin pledged to transform Thailand drastically. His populist policies included universal healthcare, bureaucracy reform, a new moral order, cheap credit for entrepreneurs, and poverty alleviation through handouts and grassroots development. Support for these redistributive aims among academics, progressives and the middle class then dwindled due to fear of a bubble in household

debt, and revulsion at human and civil rights violations. Numerous activists and protestors disappeared, and a drugs crackdown claimed over 2,500 suspected extrajudicial killings. Bloodshed in the Muslim deep south has reached crisis levels since 2004, when dozens of suspected insurgents died in clashes with the military in April and again in October.

Meanwhile, the businesses of Thaksin's family and cabinet cronies outpaced the wider economy in wealth generation. Accusations of 'policy corruption' peaked in early 2006 with the Shinawatras selling their Shin Corp and its nation's security concessions to a Singapore state firm for US$2 billion – tax free.

Middle class outrage swelled protests that had gathered since late 2005 under firebrand media baron Sondhi Limthongkul, shouting 'Ork Pai' (get out!). Treating democracy as a numbers game, Thaksin called an early election in April 2006, declaring he'd take a 'political break'. Though TRT would have won anyway, an opposition boycott, electoral irregularities, paralysis of state mechanisms, multiple accusations of *lèse-majesté*, and Thaksin's quick resumption of power undermined its legitimacy. The king asked judges to untangle the 'mess', and a political truce took effect during the king's diamond jubilee that June. Amid rumours of renewed confrontation, the army chief General Sonthi Boonyaratglin led a peaceful coup on 19 September 2006 while most ministers were abroad. Thaksin languished in exile.

Calling itself the Council for National Security, the junta abolished the constitution and appointed a civilian government within two weeks. The modest, respected new PM, retired General Sarayud Chulanont, ironically had once been hailed by *Time* as an 'Asian hero' for having removed the military from politics. Matching the conservative appointed assembly, Sarayud's elderly cabinet of bureaucrats, officers and academics was considered decent, if undynamic, and dubbed 'old ginger'. Their one-year agenda included rooting out corruption, reforming the police and following the king's concept of 'sufficiency economics'.

Foreign confidence, which wavered after the coup, again slipped following currency controls, restrictions on globalised business, and multiple bombings at Bangkok's New Year celebrations. Blame fell variously on southern insurgents, Thaksin sympathisers or rival power cliques. With elections under a new constitution promised by 2008, it remains to be seen whether the 'Silk Revolution' will upgrade or unravel Thai democracy. Or whether Thaksin will engineer another comeback.

Bangkok Today

With chic modernity masking an ancient heart, the Thai capital is a crucible of change.

Bangkok stands at a crossroads. Not normally given to navel-gazing, Thais are publicly pondering what kind of society they want. Long open to outside influences, fashion and unrestrained commerce, the city faces social and cultural dilemmas as it hurtles towards the future while grappling for anchors from a somewhat imagined past. The impact of Thaksin addressing poverty means that the public and officialdom alike now recognise that the country needs to reconcile the growing gulf between the capital and the countryside.

Thaksin had also encouraged a second consumer boom of materialism, personal debt, entrepreneurial zeal, mega-projects and social welfare. He proclaimed Bangkok the 'world-class hub' – or wannabe hub – of no fewer than 30 industries, from cars to spas, from 'Bangkok Fashion City' to 'Kitchen of the World'. In several of these sectors, especially design (*see p34* **Decrees of chic**) the potential remains real, if premature. But holding everything back is a legendary resistance to planning.

ORDERING CHAOS

Bangkok has been a byword for unplanned metropolitan sprawl. The surplus of over-priced, time and money wasting vanity projects typically shrouds deficient focus on the fundamentals of development and management, and worsening disasters like the floods of 2006. Continuity suffers when office holders scupper integrated schemes in favour of their own pet projects, or to repay voters and cronies. Grand claims to air-hub status withered once the long-suspected flaws of the new Suvarnabhumi Airport came to light (*see p22* **Landing in Cobra Swamp**). Still, the BTS SkyTrain and MRT Subway have shown that Bangkok can have good infrastructure, and several new lines are due to be completed between 2008 and 2012.

If mass transit had started in the 1970s, as intended, suburbs would have grown around it, as is now happening, instead of spreading horizontally into an endless plain. Mass transit has made downtown apartments hip. One reason for Bangkok's notorious traffic jams lies in its unusually small road area for a city its size, while also being riddled with dead ends, bottlenecks and zigzags. The car is not only a status symbol and a reflection of prosperity, but necessary to access *moo baan* (housing estates) located down alleys with insufficient transit or amenities.

Following the tree-planting, air-cleaning and pedestrianised festivals achieved under Governor Bhichit Rattakul (1996-2000), Bangkok stagnated under hot-tempered Governor Samak Sundaravej (2000-04). Optimism about City Hall revived on the election of Governor Apirak Kosayothin. An earnest young executive, he advocates micro-reforms to improve the quality of life, from safety and recycling to reviving the Bangkok Metropolitan Art Museum that Samak had tried to turn into a car park. But the BMA's inertia continue to thwart conservation, management of vendors, and Apirak's 'smart' traffic schemes, like taxi ranks, signs indicating jams, and Bus Rapid Transit (BRT) lanes. The first of five BRT lines is due by early 2008.

Bangkok tries to do too much. It's the focus of almost all national life: royalty, government, finance, commerce, tourism, nightlife, shopping, entertainment, industry, the military, universities, transport, and ceremony. Decentralisation is, however, the new mantra, and even the parliament may move out.

When a series of bombs scuppered the Bangkok's New Year 2006-7 celebrations, Aprirak removed wastebins and pledged to install CCTV, London-style, while security has been tightened citywide. 'Thai' means 'free', and Bangkokians feel rattled by these cramps on their easy-going liberty.

Meanwhile, long-term problems persist. Due partly to groundwater pumping, Bangkok is gradually sinking. Moreover it's built on a once expanding delta that has started to erode. Given global warming, the erstwhile 'Venice of the East' may yet need to redig the canals it has paved over. Architect Sumet Jumsai even advocates amphibious construction principles. While Thai buildings no longer stand on stilts, the expressways invariably do. Compounding the car's primacy, many roads get raised above shop and house doorsteps so that residents, not drivers, suffer during floods.

HERITAGE AT RISK

Thais still emulate the Japanese focus on state-subsidised mega-projects. Whatever the benefits, the losses include destruction of landscapes and cityscapes that lend a place character and identity. The authorities cling to outmoded ideas of modernisation; hence the proliferation of wires, pipes, jarring signage and noise pollution, while trees get hacked, pavements encroached upon, parks concreted and heritage destroyed. At last some wires are now being buried.

A royal city

It's hard to imagine any world city as avowedly royalist as this capital of a constitutional monarchy. Millions wear yellow on Mondays in tribute to the king's birthday colour, and every day don yellow rubber wristbands bearing the statement: 'We Love Our King'. When the king's anthem plays, (which it does before cinema screenings), all must stand in silence. Thai Olympians donate their medals to their monarch. Money is handled respectfully because it bears at least one regal head.

The love and respect Thais have for King Bhumibol Adulyadej (1946-present) – the world's longest reigning monarch – stems partly from his development work and diverse talents. He is a sailor and boat-builder, writer and photographer, painter and jazz composer (see p186), as well as the world's first monarch to earn a patent (for a water aerator). These deeds are recorded in photographic museums at Dusit Park (see p80). The king's powers may be constitutionally limited, like Britain's Queen, but he remains central to the culture. Thai tabloids don't erode royal mystique; they uphold taboos about commenting upon the 'highest institution'. Lèse-majeste is a crime.

There is a pervasive belief that Thai kings are semi-divine. In ancient Ayutthaya, Thai Buddhist and animist faith acquired the Hindu *devaraja* (god-king) cosmology, which still infuses royal decorations, festival rites and the traditional arts. King Bhumibol is also known as Rama IX, since each king of the Chakri dynasty is named after Rama, an avatar of Vishnu and the hero of the Indian Ramayana epic. That's why Vishnu's vehicle, the bird-man Garuda, became the royal insignia adorning highway signs, power poles, government documents, and companies trading 'by royal appointment'.

Monarchy also acts as role model for righteous behaviour and good governance. Under King Bhumibol's guidance, dozens of royal projects aid development, such as regenerating land, preserving crafts, managing water sources and mentoring sustainable agriculture (see p81 Chitrlada). Thais bathe the country in candles and fairylights on his birthday, 5 December, which in 2008 marks his 80th year.

Landing in Cobra Swamp

The new Suvarnabhumi Airport (*see p224*) epitomises Bangkok in both its good qualities and its equally spectacular flaws. Misleadingly pronounced Soo-wan-na-poom, its title (Sanskrit for 'Golden Land') may sound more auspicious than its ominous location, Nong Ngu Hao (Cobra Swamp), but it conjures an apt image for the whole enterprise: a gold-plated swamp.

Under construction for four decades, it was fast-tracked by Thaksin to become a regional air hub, a symbol of modern Thailand and – boasting the world's tallest control tower – a monument to himself. It may be no coincidence that he was ousted just days before its rushed, lucrative completion. Though blamed for its physical problems and suspected corruptions, Thaksin escaped having to solve them,

a process so chaotic that 'the Nation' headlines its daily coverage 'Airport Fiasco'.

All new airports have teething troubles, here including too few toilets, signs or fire escapes. In some ways Suvarnabhumi is state-of-the-art. Flights proceed safely. It's easy to reach and will link to the BTS by late 2008. However, dubious deals plague its operation. A scanner scandal prompted a no-confidence motion in parliament. Duty free shops mysteriously doubled, blocking passengers and signs. In an unworkable plot favouring solely the limousine concession, passengers originally had to go by bus to a distant taxi rank, and then had to change floors to exit at non-monopoly prices.

More fundamentally, Suvarnabhumi suffers built-in design faults. The 70-year-old airport at Don Muang on the city heights

could have been expanded, but its replacement was laid on top of a low-level tidal marsh used for flood diversion. Long before Thaksin, graft allegations dogged the landfill project. Therein lies a clue to the taxiway cracks and rumpled runways. The glass-and-strut design looks modern, if rather severe, but is unsuited to the tropics. Users complain it overheats, leaks and defies cleaning. Having the world's biggest single terminal seems prestigious, but multiple smaller terminals would have shortened the treks passengers must endure. Yet, dumbfoundingly, it is already at capacity, feels cramped and requires buses to reach many planes.

For its future, Thaksin envisaged a surrounding 'aeropolis' as a new province. The coup regime then dithered over reviving Don Muang for some flights during repairs – or permanently. Eventually, Suvarnabhumi will likely attain normality, if not regional hub status. When it opened, Thais flocked to sightsee this icon of national pride. Now they cringe at this lesson in how not to manage the country's gateway.

Conservation tends to focus on landmark buildings, while threatening viable ancient neighbourhoods like those around Mahakan Fort (*see p57*), Tha Tien, Wat Kalaya (for both, *see p75*) and Wat Yannawa (*see p74*). On behalf of Wat Yannawa, a developer demolished some of historically important Soi Wanglee at 3am the night before New Year 2007, in the middle of negotiations with official heritage bodies about a viable restoration plan.

Bangkok continues to erase or standardise such subtle, fragile assets as markets, old communities, greenery, cultural diversity and the laid-back lifestyle. Highways now fragment Bangkok's last expanse of boat-accessed canal at Bang Kruay, ruining an irreplaceable asset for the coming post-industrial era. At least some original buildings survive through conversion into restaurants, spas, bars and museums. This tends to delight foreigners more than Thais, who often assume old houses will be haunted.

> **'Highways now fragment Bangkok's last expanse of boat-accessed canal at Bang Kruay.'**

GOING INTER OR INWARD?

The market value of what Thais had long taken for granted came firmly into focus in 2002, when international companies tried to patent Thai jasmine rice and *tuk-tuks*. It wasn't long before potential indigenous brands were classified as 'Thai Wisdom' and marketed under the state's OTOP scheme, or inspired new industries like spas (*see p178* **Mind & body**) and design (*see pp33-35* **Bangkok by design**). Foreign store buyers routinely scour Bangkok for ideas and products, sometimes to copy – an ironic reversal of the pirates who still operate here with seeming impunity.

Thai films, fashion and music are also 'going inter' (breaking out internationally). Many of the creators and fans are a young, globalised generation who identify as indie (independent; *see p67* **Flashpacker meets indie)**. An earlier cadre that resisted dictatorship in the 1970s maintain their radicalism through protest art (*see pp169-172* **Galleries**) and 'Songs for Life' (*see p188* Pleng Puer Cheewit).

In the face of this cultural and economic flowering, the old guard fears non-conformists and their outlets in fashion, digital media and nightlife (see p132 Drink up!). Campaigns of prudery, prohibition, and censorship since 2001 have stifled values like tolerance, *sanuk* (fun) and *mai pen rai* (never mind), that historically balanced hierarchical discipline. Few countries

block more websites. Priggish officials go apoplectic about spaghetti straps, yet as historians point out, until the influence of missionaries and Western education, it was authentically Thai to bare shoulders. Raiding nightclubs has been an easy target, since drugs are far harder to confiscate from taxi drivers, school crammers, untouchable rich kids and those who take *yaa baa* (the 'crazy drug' amphetamine) to work harder. The nanny-state hectoring also reflects the application of industrious immigrant Chinese values upon an easygoing South-east Asian culture.

AT A CROSSROADS

Bangkok's ambitions to be the hub of myriad industries benefit from location, location, location. Long a crossroads of commerce and culture, it could become the fulcrum of a region bigger than the EU, a feat that the kingdom of Ayutthaya once managed. With the opening up of formerly closed neighbours, a transcontinental transport network will emanate from Bangkok. Aside from the many budget airlines, the city will handle increasing road and rail traffic with India and China via Myanmar; with Vietnam via Laos and Cambodia; and with Singapore via Malaysia.

Development also brings risks. China is busy reducing the Mekong into a shipping conduit and hydroelectric exhaust duct that overrides natural flows to downstream countries. Calls for an industrialised Kra Canal or 'land bridge' across the southern isthmus would foul the environment on which tourism relies.

> **'Officials go apoplectic about spaghetti straps, yet until the influence of missionaries, it was authentically Thai to bare shoulders.'**

Much else depends on China, as well. Commerce, diplomacy, tourism, fashion and entertainment are all orienting northwards (*see pp84-89* **Chinatown**), in the same deft way that Thailand has repeatedly kept its independence from overarching powers – by interacting with them. Decades – indeed centuries – of relentless hospitality have taken their toll, but the city has also benefited. In upgrading its amenities, cultivating cosmopolitan tastes, showcasing its culture and continuing to smile, Bangkok has compromised many things, but not its essence. By embracing every onslaught so warmly, Bangkok remains steadfastly Thai.

Belief

Monk columnist **Mettanando Bhikkhu** places Thai Buddhism in its modern context.

The centenary in 2006 of the late Buddhadasa Bhikku rekindled interest in the accessible way this influential monk expressed Buddhism's relevance to the modern Thai. In writings like *A Handbook for Mankind*, he explained Buddhism could infuse economics, environmentalism and urban life through mindfulness and meditation. People from around the world still head for his temple to de-stress (for meditation retreats, *see p181*). The detachment behind such calming Thai concepts as *jai yen* (keep cool) and *mai pen rai* (never mind) helps explain how Bangkok residents can maintain their tolerant, light-hearted serenity in the midst of such an essentially hard-edged city.

This is the wisdom of Siddhartha Gautama, a sixth-century BC Indian prince who only became a Buddha ('awakened one') after rejecting first his privileged upbringing, then ascetic hermithood. Finally, through meditation he achieved enlightenment as the 'Middle Way' between luxury and austerity. Buddhism doesn't require a belief in Buddha as a god; it's a practical technique to liberate one's self from conditioning, dealing more with the here and now than metaphysical meanderings or moralistic judgement.

Finding that path has become increasingly challenging as industrialisation has exposed Thais to new ideas, activities, possessions and temptations. Yet the past two decades have seen great spiritual energy, with temples being built, modern Buddhist communities organised, massive social projects undertaken and missions overseas growing. Headlines, however, often dwell on tabloid scandals about dubious fundraising, charismatic sects and monks dabbling in worldly pleasures. Calls for reform also spark controversy. Coupled with a perceptible slipping in Buddhist practice, this has created what some call a crisis of faith. Still, the *Dharma* (teachings) reassuringly stress that everything is ultimately subject to change.

BORN AGAIN (AND AGAIN)

Buddhism is big on numerical lists. The Three Marks of Existence (*anicca*, impermanence; *dukkha*, unsatisfactoriness; and *anatta*, absence of self) describe how everything arises and passes away, moment to moment. The Four Noble Truths help us see that dissatisfaction is caused by craving (*tanha*), which can never be permanently satisfied. The way to end craving (and hence suffering) is explained in the Noble Eightfold Path and elaborated upon by the Thirty-Seven Factors of Enlightenment. These labels describe a progression in the mind when meditating. Apply it to favourite foods or seeking the perfect beach, and cravings fade with ease. Entrenched lust or anger are tougher to rid.

The ultimate aim is attaining nirvana, a final disengaging from the birth-death-rebirth cycle. One's degree of suffering depends on *karma* (action) earlier in this life or a previous existence. In Buddhism, time is cyclic and endless, unlike the linear, finite human life of monotheistic Judaism, Christianity and Islam. The Buddhist cosmos is eternal and houses innumerable world systems, in which Gautama was the fourth Buddha, and Lord Maittreya the future fifth.

Before this land became Siam, Buddhism here was of the Mahayana school prevalent in northern Asia, which embraces *bodhisattva* (enlightened beings delaying nirvana in order to help others). Some Mahayana customs remain, like statue worship, though almost all Thai Buddhists follow stricter Theravada doctrine.

Reincarnation was part of Indian belief at the foundation of Buddhism, but direct Hindu influences remain visible throughout Thai culture, in a complex fusion with spirit beliefs. The **Erawan Shrine** (*see p98* **Shop and pray**) is one of countless Thai shrines to Brahma, while ministry logos depict the elephant-headed Ganes, Garuda bird-men adorn banks, the City Pillar is partly a phallic Shiva lingam, and the *Ramayana* epic permeates all the arts. The Chakri kings (the current line) are considered emanations of Rama, an incarnation of Vishnu, while Brahmin priests conduct royal rites.

Religion sits on a high social pedestal alongside monarchy and nation, so visitors should show respect to all three. Thailand's tricolour flag signifies royalty (blue), religion (white) and people (red). Therevada Buddhism, enshrined in the 1997 constitution, has been

Buddha embodied

Buddhist sculpture is very stylised. Early prohibition of a human likeness left a legacy of abstract icons that Thais revere: the wheel of law, the footprint or the bodhi tree (under which Buddha was enlightened). It was the ancient Greek-influenced Gandhara sculpture in today's Afghanistan/Pakistan that first gave form to the Buddha attributes listed in scriptures, such as curly hair, broad shoulders, a clinging robe and the *ushnisa* (bulge on the head). Over time, distinct styles emerged. The *ushnisa* rose to resemble a flame, then a spire. Dvaravati Buddhas feature thick lips, heavy lidded eyes and sweet smiles. Sukhothai statues have rounded, androgynous faces and bodies, with long pointy noses. In affluent Ayutthaya, Buddha images with crowns, jewels and elongated faces express the hauteur of a powerful court. Bangkok Buddhas verge on the baroque, with robes and pedestals profuse with minute detail. Framing the Buddha is the *mandorla*, a flame-like vortex of light similar to the halo in Christian iconography.

The Buddha's postures and *mudra* (gestures) convey philosophical principles and incidents in his life. Oft-seen sets of eight postures denote each weekday (Wednesday is halved), and are worshipped according to one's day of birth. In the most common *mudra* Bhumisparsa ('calling the earth to witness'), the Buddha sits in lotus position, right fingers pointing downward 'touching the earth' to resist the temptations of Mara, the devil. Standing with one or both hands held up, palm frontward, the Buddha reassures or calms; when the thumb and forefinger touch, he is teaching, or 'turning the wheel of law'. In culmination, the 'reclining Buddha' shows the moment of final release: nirvana.

the official religion since the time of Sukhothai.

Many consider being Thai synonymous with being Buddhist, and often refer to those of Muslim, South Asian or Middle Eastern origin as *khaek* (guests). This unsurprisingly grates with the four per cent of Thais who follow Islam. Since 2004, sectarian (and seemingly separatist) violence in the mostly Muslim southernmost provinces escalated to include attacks on monks as symbols of central Thai hegemony, shocking the wider population.

MAKING MERIT

Most Thais try to accrue positive karmic points through *tham boon* (making merit). This encompasses offerings (from standard lotus buds, candles and incense sticks to elaborate assemblages), donations, charity, putting food in monks' alms bowls at daybreak, and acts of kindness like freeing caged birds.

Formally, making merit involves revering the *trirattana* (triple gems): Buddha, *Dharma* and *Sangha* (the monkhood). Essentially, the public subsidises Thailand's 270,000 *bhikkhu* (monks) and 90,000 *samaneras* (novices) to live a life of moral example at more than 30,000 *wat* (monasteries), by donating food, clothing and money for necessities like shelter. Wat are not just a symbolically designed place of worship, meditation and scripture (*see p31* **What makes a wat?**), but may serve as a community centre, orphanage, hospital,school, market, playground, crematorium, fairground, museum, theatre, garden, zoo and morgue.

The high number of monks derives from the convention that all men (typically before marriage) briefly ordain, and may do so up to

High spirits

The Buddhist canon rejects faith in rituals and the supernatural, yet animist heritage infuses each Buddhist country. With organised Buddhism resistant to change, modern Thais remain drawn to alternative beliefs old and new, from the Chinese cult of Kuan Yin to luck propitiation. Most Thais believe in ghosts, omens, mediums, astrology and amulets. Pervasive numerology (nine is especially lucky) means that many shrines are busiest ahead of lottery draws.

Animism is most evident in the white wrist thread (*sai sin*) – tied by monks or elders to keep a person's 32 bodily spirits from wandering – and the spirit house.

Installed at most building plots at an auspiciously divined location and time, spirit houses typically come as a pair. The higher one (*saan phra phum*) resembles a mini-temple on a pedestal for the Hinduised 'spirit of the land', sometimes sheltering a Hindu statue, especially of Brahma. The lower, simpler shrine (*phra phum chao thii*) resembles a stilt house for the indigenous 'spirit of the place', akin to spirits that guard domains like forests, fields, waterways, mountains and vehicles.

Spirits must be appeased with daily offerings and a staff of model servants and dancers, as a spirit's personality is apparently won over by offering its favourite food, drinks, habit or mantra. Delays at Bangkok's new airport were blamed on late installation of a spirit house.

Less benign are the restless spirits of the dead (*phii*), who suffer in our midst until dispatched by exorcism or karma to heaven or hell, before eventual rebirth. Thai ghosts tend to be generic: elongated *phii phraet* (hungry ghosts) suffer pin-hole mouths due to greed; elderly *phii bhop* witches scoff raw chicken entrails; and disembowelled *phii kraseu* trail their innards while seeking rotten food. With *phii* so prevalent, Thais often shun big trees, old houses, antique furniture and developments built on cemeteries. Many drivers garland shrines at accident black spots. Unsurprisingly, ghost stories dominate movies, comics and soap operas, especially classics like **Nang Nak** (*see p101* **Wat Maha But**).

three times. Considered the most noble way to honour to one's parents, and to generate them great merit, ordination must, like conscription, be accommodated by employers. Historically, this lasted one *phansaa* – the three-month rainy season retreat – or perhaps just for the day of an elder relative's cremation. Strangely, Thailand is the only Buddhist country where study of the Tripitaka (canonical literature) is not included in formal monastic training. Thai Buddhists are trained to be faithful to their tradition more than their canon.

Aside from meditation and scholarship, monks perform rites at weddings, funerals, installations of spirit houses and anointings. Less orthodox monks may also read fortunes, inscribe protective tattoos or issue lottery numbers. Ideally, it's a life of peace and renunciation, free from harm to fellow beings. Through 227 restrictive precepts (which preclude sex, soft bedding, entertainment, possessions and female contact) a Theravadin monk learns to recognise and then relinquish his attachments in order to free his mind.

Modern distractions and compulsions mean that young men increasingly can't – or won't – find the time. Hence the suggestion of mass ordination for students during vacations. While some inspired initiates stay on, a shortage of those with long-term commitment has caused a sixth of all wat to be abandoned. By contrast, some disreputable types don the robes to gain lenience and have reoffended while ordained.

Nevertheless, the *Sangha* refuses to ordain devout *mae chi*: white robed women who follow fewer precepts. Buddha founded an order of yellow-robed *bhikkuni* (nuns), but the line faded out before Buddhism arrived in Siam. In February 2001 Chatsumarn Kablisingh – ex-professor and daughter of a Buddhist nun ordained in Taiwan – became a nun in Sri Lanka, intensifying an already heated debate.

CONTROVERSY AND CHANGE

Within the brotherhood of *bhikkhus*, successive scandals have tarnished public faith, which faltered most noticeably on disclosure that two monks with large followings had had affairs with female disciples and patronised prostitutes. One of them, Phra Yantra Amaro, escaped to lead a Buddhist community in San Diego. Meanwhile, the abbot of Wat Dhammakaya – a temple north of Bangkok with aggressive fundraising tactics, hundreds of thousands of followers and a B500 million *chedi* (reliquary) – was arrested. His embezzlement case lasted years until dismissed in 2006 to maintain 'national unity', an exoneration that coincided with a massive rally held by Thaksin Shinawatra shortly before the coup against him.

Both monks and lay people have called for stricter screening and supervision of monks, plus reform of the *Sangha*, a largely self-governing body headed by the royally appointed Supreme Patriarch. Administered under semi-democratic structures in 1941, it was placed under a hierarchical bureaucracy by Sarit's dictatorship in 1962. The Ecclesiastical Council doesn't recognise monks' rights as citizens, such as having ID cards, passports or the right to vote. Some factions suggest that the hierarchy might have become overly preoccupied with ritual, purity and amulet mass production, rather than social problems. As the Supreme Patriarch recedes into his dotage, renewed rivalry between the mainstream Thammayut order and the Maha Nikaya order founded by King Rama IV has prompted more calls for the reform of monastic management.

'Two monks with large followings had had affairs with female disciples.'

State involvement in teaching and welfare has deprived wat of their social and educative role. A consequence, suggested by the respected monk and scholar Phra Phromgunaporn (PA Payutto), is that some of the *Sangha* have developed a 'habit of idleness', subsisting on the patronage system. However, certain monks are far from idle, such as the Buddhadasa disciple Phra Payom Kalyano, an outspoken social activist who has initiated large projects for the poor. In the early 1990s Phra Alongkot converted his wat in Saraburi into Thailand's first AIDS hospice, receiving support from the king, the princess mother, the WHO and the UN.

Female ordination is supported by a prominent group, Santi Asok, advocating veganism, austerity and sharing of property. Its founder, Phra Phothirak, a former TV announcer, declared himself independent of the *Sangha* and was arrested, tried and lightly punished in 1988, though the community and its vegetarian restaurants continue. Its most famous adherent, General Chamlong Srimuang, was governor of Bangkok, founded a political party and led demonstrations against dictatorship in 1992 and against Thaksin in 2006.

Ultimately, though, Theravada Buddhism places responsibility on the individual to overcome conditioning, become enlightened and act with compassion. For lay practitioners, Sulak Sivaraksa – Thai Buddhism's sharpest-tongued commentator and a past Nobel Prize nominee for his human rights work – advocates 'engaged Buddhism': active, reflective practice for the benefit of individuals and society.

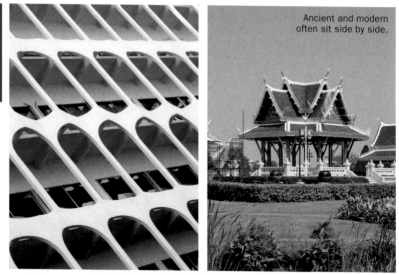

Ancient and modern often sit side by side.

Art & Architecture

Asia cultural expert **Alex Kerr** on the divine fusions that inspire Thai crafts.

If minimalism is the mark of modern style, then Thailand belongs to a bygone era. But if, as some predict, glamorous theme parks are to be the wave of the future, then Thailand is already there. Nothing makes such an impact on a visitor as the sheer dazzle of temples and palaces. Façades and pilasters shimmer with inset glass and mirrors. Surfaces dance with multicoloured paintings and statues of deities, demons and heroes.

The dazzle is deliberate. It has deep religious and political significance (reflection, the light of paradise, majesty) and has been refined over centuries. Thai art absorbed streams of influence from China, India, Sri Lanka, Cambodia, Java and the Malay peninsula. As in Japan, most of the culture can be traced to some outside source, yet the Thais have moulded all

these imports into something distinctively their own. Copying (and thus honouring) a master has long been the ideal of Thai artisans, so the aesthetic adapts incrementally.

Thai art's beginnings lie in the Baan Chiang pottery left by Neolithic peoples. By the fifth to eighth centuries the Mon Dvaravati culture combined Theravada Buddhism with animism, giving rise to sacred *bai sema* (boundary stones) and stone sculptures so realistic their features resemble Thais today. Under Khmer sway from the ninth to the 13th centuries, Siam inherited massive temple complexes, stone satellites of Angkor evoking a Hindu cosmology by way of India and Java.

Khmer temples were microcosms of heaven. Surrounded by moats and sub-temples symbolising the seas and continents, they centred on a scripture vault beneath a *prang* (tower) representing sacred Mount Meru, axis of the universe, and the home of Indra (King of the Gods), represented by a trident. Such references to the gods served to reinforce the powers of empire and divine kingship.

Although Thailand is devoutly Buddhist, an enduring faith in Hinduism means that spires are capped with Indra's trident; pediments feature Vishnu (the creator) mounted on the man-bird Garuda, Indra riding the multi-headed elephant Erawan, and elephant-headed Ganesha, remover of obstacles, god of the arts (and logo of the government's Fine Arts Department). Thailand, it's said, boasts far more shrines to Brahma than India. Also from the Khmers came an architectural vocabulary, including the *prang*, multi-stepped altars with redented corners, and relief carvings of intertwining vines and flame motifs.

DEVELOPING STYLE

By the 13th century Tai tribes had founded the Lanna and Sukhothai kingdoms. Hailing from northern forests, the Tai came from a tradition of wood, not stone. They brought Chinese-influenced house and temple forms, distinguished by long sloping roofs.

> ### 'Erected with elaborate rites, houses embody ancient animist symbolism about earth and heaven, fire and water.'

From India, Thais took the visual language of the Buddha image's features and postures, as well as *stupa* (towers holding relics of the Buddha or a revered person). *Stupa* evolved into Thai *chedi* (a type of pagoda) by way of the bell-shaped Sri Lankan *dagoba*. Subsequent changes could be called 'Thai grace', elongating *stupa* into elegant bud-shaped *chedi* and being the first to portray the Buddha walking (descending from heaven). In contrast to solemn Khmer art, the walking Buddhas of Sukhothai are flowing, rounded and almost appear to float.

As power moved south to Ayutthaya from the 14th century, this elongation and 'etherealisation' stretched the *dagoba* into a soaring spire, its deep indentations reduced to the semblance of ribs. The rounded Khmer *prang* lengthened into a lofty corn cob; walls and columns extended, lifting the multi-tiered roofs high into the heavens.

Statues acquired crowns and jewellery, while inset glass glowed from elaborately tiered palaces. By the 17th century Ayutthayan art was heavily preoccupied with light: gleam and sparkle were exaggerated by enclosing open temple pavilions, allowing only slits to let in light. By the Bangkok period every surface had become encrusted with gilding, filigree and a mosaic of glass and ceramic.

The trapezoid added the final touch. The walls of ancient Tai houses leaned slightly for stability, outward in the north, inward in the south. This tapering increased to impart elegance. Doors and windows tilted too. Chests and boxes became trapezoids, and bases of temples and thrones swooped like boats. This merging of styles, eras and peoples continues today, resulting in art that is recognisably Thai. The epitome of this eclectic style remains the temple (*see p31* **What makes a wat?**).

ABSOLUTELY PREFABULOUS

The archetypal Thai house is comprised of hardwood modular components, raised on stilts, with high peaked roofs. It belongs to a domestic architectural style that originated in the Asian tropics and spans from Indonesia to Japan. The stilts raised homes above flooding, and multiple eaves allowed ventilation while protecting from fierce rain and sun. It's not all just about function, though. Erected with elaborate rites, houses also embody ancient animist symbolism about earth and heaven, fire and water. Hence the fish, bird, *naga* and flame imagery upon gables, eaves and ridgelines.

A defining feature of Thai design, the elegant rooflines vary by region. Earlier designs swept low and wide, as visible up north. Central Thai roofs pitch steeper, their end bargeboards curving down from sharp points, rising again with *ngao* (a flame-like flick). More elaborate home and temple roof ridges end in upward bird-like finials called *chofa*. Plainer houses are thatched with leaves; grander roofs are tiled with teak shingles or glazed ceramic.

MR Kukrit Pramoj's Heritage Home (*see p99*), **Jim Thompson's House** (*see p97* **The silk root**), **Suan Pakkard Palace** and **Thai House** (*see p99*) cooking school are prime examples. Interiors are sparsely furnished, *tang* (low seat/bed/table with hoof or claw legs) being a constant, along with triangular *maun khwan* (axe pillows).

Though now both rare and expensive, the practise of Thai house building remains a living art. You can buy a new house in old style in

> ▶ Many of the buildings mentioned here are covered in more detail in other sections, notably **Sightseeing** and **Beach Escapes**.

Jim Thompson's House. See p97.

Ang Thong province, or even **Chatuchak Market** (*see p138* **Market forces**). Craftsmen carve modular units like stepped wall-panels to be reassembled to enable future moves.

DANCING ON ICE

In Thailand painting is frozen dance. Whether flying or seated quietly, *thep* (angels) and heroes in murals typically appear in the posed attitudes of dance: fingers bent, elbows arched back, legs splayed apart. Conversely, classical dance is painting come to life. Dancers wear costumes and masks inspired by murals, and pose in ensemble tableaux.

> ### 'Costumes heavy with gold thread and beaded with reflective glass gleam like temple walls.'

Thai dance is rooted in the ancient Indian concept that it was the gods who were doing the dancing. A performer's repertoire of poses and *mudra* are designed to evoke the divine in the mind of the spectator. The courts of Java and Cambodia modified these moves, with an emphasis on outward curving fingers and strident heroic stances. Movements in *khon*

and *lakhon* – traditional Thai performing arts – are clearly recognisable from 12th-century bas-reliefs at Cambodia's Angkor Wat.

Thais elaborated on Angkorean dance, adding stylisation and sparkle. Fingernails (often with metal extensions) twist backwards at impossible angles; *chadaa* (headdresses) rise into sleek spires like those crowning temples; shoulder finials curve upwards. Costumes heavy with gold thread and beaded with reflective glass gleam like temple walls.

Pivotal to painting and dance is the *Ramakien*, the Thai version of India's *Ramayana* saga. Painting and dance part company, however, when it comes to foreign influence. Classical dance, centred on the court until very recently, remained conservative (though modern troupes now reinterpret it). But painting embraced China and the West with the same gusto as did architecture. Painters place Thai temples within natural landscapes resembling Western paintings and among figures with dynamic movement, notably at **Wat Suwannaram** (*see p76*). These stand beside Chinese panels depicting fretwork, antiques and the surreal Thai bonsai: globular *mai dut* bushes. Masterpieces of this merger include the *Ramakien* murals at **Wat Phra Kaew** (*see p59*). Other attempts, as at **Wat Bowoniwet** (*see p71*), result in a bizarre, Dali-esque fusion. This coded religious heritage remains a vibrant force in Thai arts.

CREATIVE FLAME

Contemporary Thai design products – from cushions to cutting-edge spas – manage to distil an essence of Thainess. They achieve this in part by applying elements of *lai thai*, a language of design derived from ancient patterns. These involve the geometric repetition of certain forms in countless variations; these patterns adorn traditional crafts in profusion, from wood carvings and mother-of-pearl inlay to *benjarong* (five-colour) ceramics. Hints, outlines and fractions of these patterns are now often used as postmodern motifs in architecture, decor and clothing.

The swirls and geometry on neolithic pottery from Ban Chiang recur today, though more widespread are the natural shapes traced from Khmer lintels and 13th-century BC Chinese pottery, such as the distinctive *lai kranok* (a twirling flame). True to form, the Thais stretched and elaborated *kranok* until they became long, sinewy and pointy. *Kranok* merge with other forms into hybrids; leaves and flowers, even animals and gods flow into rhythms of flame that curl delicately like the fingers of classical dancers. The huge *lai Thai* lexicon also includes *lai bua* (lotus forms), *lai krajang* (pointed leaf forms), interlocking

What makes a wat?

The focus of every village, and many urban communities, the *wat* (Thai Buddhist monastery), plays many secular roles and even offers entertainment. Still the *wat* compound is sacred ground, removed from the mundane world by walls beyond an initial gate or fortified moat. To the Khmer cosmological plan, Thais added *chedi* (pointed reliquary towers) and their ancestral rooflines, the eaves chiming with brass bells.

The key building is the *bot* (or *ubosot*), the ordination hall rarely open to the public and demarcated by eight *bai sema* (which inspired Thai Airways' logo). Often leaf-shaped, these flat standing monoliths may be sheltered in miniature shrines. Most temples have one or more *vihaan* (assembly halls). Lacking *bai sema*, but resembling *bot* in their decorative gables, crown-like window frames, raised terrace and roofs of green and orange tiles, *vihaan* usually host the principal Buddha images and public worship.

Thai motifs also embellish other temple structures. The cubic *mondop*, with complex cruciform roof, houses a Buddha footprint or scriptures. *Hor trai* (libraries) sit upon a pedestal or stilts over water to protect against fire and insects. Sometimes Buddha

images line a cloister. And as in secular spaces, *sala* (elevated open pavilions) can shelter any activity, from resting, eating or meeting, to music, dance or massage.

Chedi, however, are usually the dominant structures. Beside the massive *prang* at **Wat Arun** in Bangkok or record-breaking **Phra Pathom Chedi** in Nakhon Pathom, the surrounding buildings are merely grace notes.

Inside temple halls, complex symbolism infuses murals, lacquer work and carved wooden doors, lintels, walls, furniture and ceilings. Attending Hindu gods are lesser deities, like *thep*, *apsara* (heavenly dancers) and the half-woman, half-bird *kinnaree*. The focus of all this decoration is the image of Lord Buddha, in which every variation of detail, posture or gesture carries meaning (*see p25* **Buddha Embodied**). He sits on a throne built up of complex, boat-contoured angles, or fringed with lotus petal patterns. The ubiquitous lotus, rising from the mud to bloom in purity, is Buddhism's favoured symbol. The faith's supreme protector, the aquatic serpent *naga* shelters the Buddha under his multi-headed hood, curves round walls and through decorative panels and slithers along bridges to holy ground.

rectangles and diamonds, floral scrolls, vines, hexagons, octagons, roundels, trefoil and quatrefoil lozenges, and 'animal interlace' (snake tails, Naga heads, bird beaks, fishtails and lions). Figures of dancers, warriors, Garuda, *thep*, *apsara* (heavenly dancers), the masked pantheon of the Ramakien epic, and even cumbersome elephants – all melt and merge into the *lai thai* interlace.

'More than to any other style, the Thais took to Greco-Roman classicism with a vengeance.'

Architecture and crafts mirror each other, with spires, redented corners, incisions and trapezoid lines scaling up or down, so that, for example, lacquer boxes take the shape of altar bases, *hor trai* (libraries) or lotus buds. In garlands and offerings, flowers and leaves are folded and threaded into shapes themselves inspired by flowers and leaves. The effect is of art folded back upon itself, combining complex detail with seamless finishing.

The origins of *lai thai* can be seen in rustic patterns applied to practical village handicrafts from basketry to textiles. Handwoven cloth is unique to each village, most ambitiously in *mudmee* images woven from pre-tie-dyed thread. Simple natural materials – bamboo slivers, weathered wood, interwoven reeds – give texture to much of the nation's new craftwork. Contemporary Thai design is a continuing outgrowth of both classic and rustic traditions, while also drawing on a well of international influences.

MIX AND MATCH

All Asian cultures experimented with foreign modes, but none mixed styles with such breathtaking abandon as the Thais. In 17th-century Ayutthaya and Lopburi Persian windows, Chinese gardens and French mirrored wall panels were in vogue. Countless examples reflect the visions of Kings Rama IV, V and VI, notably the interior of **Wat Ratchabophit** and the kaleidoscope of Thai, Chinese, Gothic and baroque at **Bang Pa-in Palace**.

More than to any other style, the Thais took to Greco-Roman classicism with a vengeance. The archetypal example, **Chakri Maha Prasat Throne Hall** in the Grand Palace, caps a Renaissance-style marble edifice with Thai roofs rising up to three soaring spires. Its English architect, John Chinitz, had originally planned for a dome, but Chao Phraya Srisuriyawongse, the former regent, persuaded King Rama V to inject a unique Thai accent.

Dubbed 'a *farang* in a Thai hat', this odd hybrid grew to become a 20th-century institutional template visible in the **National Museum**, **National Library** and myriad ministries.

Urban architecture has otherwise been dominated by the Chinese shophouse. As in the Peranakan Sino-Malay culture, Sino-Thai *hong taew* (literally, 'row house') blend the crowded mercantile streets of old China – where people live above trading premises – and colonial Portuguese masonry terraces, with shutters and colonnades. Prime examples adorn old Bangkok, especially **Tha Chang**, while wooden shophouses survive in pockets in Bangkok and at **Nakorn Chaisri Market** and Chachoengsao's **Baan Talad Mai**. The part-timber mansions of nobility and Chinese merchants also borrowed tropical colonial devices such as porches, verandas and fretworked vents. Many are now restaurants, like **Café Siam**, **China House**, and **Starbucks** on Thanon Khao San.

The love affair with Western classicism proved enduring. Today countless shophouses, mansions and offices still boast Roman columns, balustrades and sculptures – in white concrete. Even temples aren't immune. Extreme examples are the domed, porticoed skyscrapers **State Tower** and **Chatpetch Tower** along the river. Others co-opt Gothic windows and spires, or even pharaonic pilasters (**Grand Hyatt Erawan Hotel**).

Modernism and postmodernism also made inroads, especially in skyscrapers, with novelty excesses like the 'Robot Building' (**Bank of Asia**) and **Elephant Building**. For those with retro taste, Chinatown is a trove of art deco, the **Atlanta Hotel** a 1950s diorama, while modernist remnants from the 1960s and '70s include Silom's **Dusit Thani Hotel**, the multi-cylinder **Fifty-nine Condo** off Witthayu, and motel-esque Sukhumvit inns. 'Ranch-style' homes in compounds also line many residential *soi*, some converted into bars or restaurants (**Spring Summer, Pickle Factory**).

Among attempts at Thai modernism, the best example, the Siam InterContinental Hotel (styled after a royal hat), was demolished in 2002, though Thai accents continue in the elegant gilded peaks of **SCB Park Plaza**, Ratchayothin and on Sathorn Road, with the cascading slopes of **Harindhorn Tower**, the reflecting pools of the **Sukhothai Hotel**, and the trapezoids of **Sathorn City Tower** and the **Diamond Tower**.

This gleeful fusion is so sustained it could be considered inherently Thai. Whether you think it kitsch or innovative, globalised Thai architecture has produced some of the world's most surprising buildings.

Bangkok by Design

How Krung Thep became a style city.

Thailand's rise in design since the mid 1990s – charted by international exhibitions, awards and commercial success – is exceptional for a developing country. Indeed, Thai designers have turned this outsider status into an asset, innovating in fields like furnishings, fashion and graphics. They practise a winning contrarianism, in ways both deliberate and innate. In our techno age of globalised mega-production, Bangkok designs tend to be hand-crafted, made of natural materials, inherently sustainable, and produced by small enterprises run by the designers themselves.

They're strongly committed to their own individual styles and to certain principles. One is 'let it be Thai'. That doesn't mean Buddhist imagery or kitschy ethnicity, but freer evocations of a Siamese essence, like the irrepressible spirit of *sanuk* (fun). Many modern designs employ sinuous forms, trapezoids,

strong hues or animal motifs that echo traditional crafts, yet without aping the past. Thailand's design, like its cuisine, continues to embody the local culture – refined but unfussy, appropriate, inventive, and often intensely pleasurable.

The *sanuk* impulse in so much of the design is governed by a rule of Thai social life: don't be boring. The **Propaganda** (*see p153*) brand has won a worldwide cult following for products that are not just housewares, but also veritable works of pop art. One floor lamp takes the form of a giant, glowing matchstick. Another

▶ Many of the examples given here are detailed in other sections, notably **Where to Stay** (*see pp38-52*), **Eat, Drink, Shop** (*see pp109-156*) and **Mind & Body** (*see pp177-181*)

Decrees of chic

Bureaucrats and politicians tend to be ungainly players in design, but in Bangkok they've scored points with initiatives in capacity building and marketing. The royal family, among other groups, sponsored rural development to improve communities.

The go-getting administration of Thaksin Shinawatra cooked up an alphabet soup of new projects targeting design as a tool for national competitiveness: TCDC, BFC, FTC, OTOP. The rationale was sound; Thai firms can't attain prosperity without originating their own products and intellectual property.

TCDC (Thailand Creative & Design Center) demonstrated that a local project billed as 'world class' could truly be world class. With exhibitions, seminars, a manufacturing materials consultancy and a 15,000 book library, this resource centre has impressed experts from around the globe. During its maiden year (2005-6), it hosted first-rate exhibitions on Islamic architectural space, Vivienne Westwood, the DNA of Japanese product design, Marimekko and the unsung culture of Thailand's northeast, Isaan. However, the old-guard, post-coup government made the decision to trim TCDC's funding heavily. As the brainchild of chief Thaksin advisor Pansak Vinyaratn, it became politically vulnerable, but with 7,000 members and a constituency in industry, TCDC should endure.

Its smaller counterpart, FTC (Fashion Trend Center), lent young couturiers the books and periodicals they need to succeed but can little afford. It was part of the Bangkok Fashion City project (BFC), which overshot the runway when the interim government ended its three-year spree. While BFC included practical elements like technical training, fluff such as advertising that rashly declared Bangkok a global fashion capital indicated more hype than sustainable foundations.

At the grass roots level, Thaksin's One Tambon One Product (OTOP) programme got the nation's 70,000-plus *tambon* (villages) to identify and better market its speciality foods or crafts. However, too many villages made too many of the same things, much of it kitsch. Already successful products and firms were simply grandfathered. But local pride, quality and expertise grew. The coup regime kept the scheme and name, but redefined it as 'community and local products'.

Before Thaksin, the Department of Export Promotion had boosted design via its workshops and trade fairs like the annual Thailand International Furniture Fair (TIFF).

The royal family has played a leading role in design for decades. Queen Sirikit's SUPPORT Foundation has helped sustain handicrafts nationwide, keeping alive skills and materials now put to use by design firms. The late Princess Mother's Mae Fah Luang Foundation has enriched hilltribe handicrafts with marketable designs. King Bhumibol, in addition to being a musician, painter and photographer, is a designer. Written into the public's memory is a photo of the young king working on a yacht of his own design, still in commercial production today.

Yet one government effort is missing – a programme or fund to protect the unique Bangkok markets where budding craftspeople and designers first take root. Rents at Siam Square have skyrocketed, and so will those at Chatuchak once the impossibly charming Suan Loom Night Bazaar, home to hundreds of indie designers, gets replaced by a skyscraper and mall. Sometimes the ambition to upgrade undermines the very entrepreneurs responsible for Thailand's design revolution.

appears to be a light bulb frozen in the act of melting surreally into a puddle.

Boredom-defying fashion includes work by **Headquarter** (*see p147*) designer Chai Jeamamornrat. His collection for Mae Fah Luang in 2002 was inspired by Bangkok street life, and the bangles, straps and pantaloons sported by backpacking *farangs* on Khao San Road. Chai also played socio-political commentator; his motorcycle taxi vests assembled from mobile phone holsters tweaked both a Thai fetish and the then political hegemony of telecoms tycoon Thaksin Shinawatra.

In jewellery, a sense of fun and invention inspires work such as Kit-ti's bead designs, made of disparate materials like Venetian glass, coloured pencils and bottle caps.

Trippy Thai interiors are exemplified by **Reflections Rooms in Bangkok** (*see p50*), a funhouse-mirror rendition of the 'design hotel'. Innkeeper Anusorn Ngernyuang joined a camp of 28 artistically inclined friends to each do up a room. One subverts a modernist icon – Eero Saarinen's 1957 Tulip chair – turning it into a washbasin. Another room posits a beach in the city, with a hammock slung over a sandbox.

Unusually for a design movement, it's possible to pinpoint the exact moment this one began: 2 July 1997, when the baht's peg to the dollar fell, collapsing the economy. Out-of-work interior stylists, architects and ad professionals started making housewares and fashions. Most of the products were hand-made, but the cheaper baht made them affordable overseas.

Indigenous inspirations and resources proved a vast, untapped asset, illustrated by woven designs in rattan or novel materials like water hyacinth, liana, plastic, even metal. The new weaving goes far beyond familiar 'colonial' styles, ranging from Udom Udomsrianan's bio-sculptural seating for **Planet 2001** (*see p153*), to Suwan Khongkhunthian's sinuous, pared-down pieces at **Yothaka** (*see p153*). And Thai ergonomics are less stilted. The convention of floor seating led designers to create low-slung chairs as broad platforms. Investigating other directions, floral designer Sakul Intakul creates bronze and ceramic bud vessels inspired by tropical seeds, while Angus Hutcheson, a Bangkok-based English architect, makes super-organic lighting out of silk cocoons and sculpted latex for his brand **Ango** (*see p153*).

The best collections go for export only, but ever more items appear in Bangkok malls and at the Chatuchack Weekend Market, at half what you'd pay overseas. The trend towards branding began in textiles, thanks to Jim Thompson's pioneering efforts from the late 1940s. The American entrepreneur disappeared in 1967, but his Thai Silk Co has carried on

Home decor at **Panta**. *See p153.*

innovating, through interior textiles designer Tinnart Nisalak. New names like the **Mae Fah Luang Foundation's Doi Tung** (*see p146*) brand specialise in handwoven cotton and hemp, rich in both texture and neo-Thai style.

Graphic design also reflects young Thais' whole-hearted embrace of global pop culture, as seen in ads, packaging and magazines. Thai classical art may aid this creativity; temple murals and *lai thai* motifs are graphic.

However, heavy industry has so far had little input, since factories here tend to be either foreign-owned, or on foreign contract. But multinationals are starting to set up their own R&D centres here staffed by Thais.

Thai flair need not come from a factory, brand or studio. Throughout the world design is all around us, complicit in the pervasive corporatisation of our lives. Enter Thailand, and its amazing world of everyday innovation: sidewalk vending, hand-decorated trucks, shophouse signage, shrine-like taxi interiors, temple fairs, all distinct in their own originality. In Bangkok's folk realm of impromptu wit, colour and disarming ingenuity, there's rarely a dull moment.

● *Brian Mertens is the author of* Bangkok Design.

Where to Stay

Reflections Rooms in Bangkok.
See p50.

Where to Stay

Quirky guesthouses, boutique chic, deluxe splurges – Bangkok hotels offer soul for a song.

For decades Bangkok's lodgings excelled at both budgetry extremes, but it's only recently that the mid market has been treated to such attentive hospitality. Of course, the city still boasts a fair number of impeccable grand hotels with great vistas, which cater to every whim, and at bargain rates by global standards. And budget quarters proliferate in well-serviced ghettos that support floating communities of travellers. But now, at long last, the moderately affluent traveller – previously faced with mostly tired shophouse digs, past-their-prime hotels or ho-hum inns above tailors – is being treated to a new breed of boutique hotels and designer guesthouses that is turning this segment of the market into a headline-grabbing phenomenon (*see p49* **Luxe goes local**).

The best Beds

For quiet urban refuge
Sukhothai (*see p51*).
Baan Thai Wellness Retreat (*see p47*).
Marriott Bangkok Resort & Spa (*see p40*).

For dramatic skyline views
Peninsula (*see p41*).
LeBua at State Tower (*see p44*).
Banyan Tree Bangkok (*see p50*).
Dusit Thani (*see p44*).
Millennium Hilton (*see p41*).

For maximum minimalism
Metropolitan (*see p51*).
Luxx (*see p45*).

For one-of-a-kind rooms
Reflections Rooms in Bangkok (*see p50*).
La Résidence (*see p46*).
Shanghai Inn (*see p43*).
Phra Nakorn Norn Len (*see p43*).

Low cost, highly desirable
Arun Residence (*see p40*).
Suk11 Guesthouse (*see p50*).

For the ghost with the most
Peachy Guesthouse (*see p40*).

When the likes of Joseph Conrad and Somerset Maugham steamed in a century ago there was only one place to stay: the **Oriental**. Some present-day literati may still drop the name with a certain hauteur, yet this institution has now been rivalled – many say overtaken – by several world-class hotels. It's not just plush properties on the river – the **Shangri-La, Peninsula** and **Marriott Bangkok Resort & Spa** – there are many devotees of the **Four Seasons (Regent), Grand Hyatt Erawan, Sheraton Grande Sukhumvit** and, especially, the suavely chic **Sukhothai**. Even dated dames like the **Dusit Thani** and **Nai Lert Park** (formerly the Hilton) have had facelifts to counter swish, youthful arrivistes such as the Conrad, the Metropolitan and the posh new Thai chain LeBua.

At the cheap end, too, upgrading has changed the face of the world's most famous flophouse, Thanon Khao San (*see p67* **Flashpacker meets indie**). Now gap-year lawyers-to-be wheel their backpacks into modish lodges and chic guesthouses in Banglamphu, Phra Nakorn, Dusit and even Chinatown.

Handy for mass transit, **Downtown** offers the most rooms, with higher (but reasonable) prices and better services, plus shopping, dining and nightlife. Rooms in **Bangrak** cost a bit more due to their business and nightlife convenience. Visitors prioritising shopping and dining settle in **Patumwan** or **Sukhumvit**, which has plenty of mid range options, thanks to the Indian-run inns around Nana. Throughout the city, faded, no-frills, no-smiles Chinese hotels offer shelter for just a few red notes.

ROOMS AND RATES
Single rooms can often sleep two, while doubles may have two double beds. Some beds could even sleep three, within communal rooms tailored to Thai group-travel tastes. So ask to view rooms first. In guesthouses and cheap Chinese hotels, rates can vary widely by the room's size, or whether it has a fan or air-

> ❶ Green numbers given in this chapter correspond to the location of each hotel as marked on the street maps. See pp248-252.

Chakrabongse Villas.

conditioning and en suite or shared bathrooms. Bangkok has a habit of snaring visitors, and monthly rates start as low as B10,000, with studios and apartments from B13,000. At the other extreme, discreet motels charge by the hour. Thailand's ban on smoking in all public buildings includes hotels, but permits hotels to have some guest rooms that allow smoking.

We have divided areas by price category, according to the cost of a standard double room: **deluxe** (from B6,000), **expensive** (B3,000-B5,999), **moderate** (B1,000-B2,999), **budget** (under B1,000). Note: big hotels add service and VAT (known as 'plus plus' or '++'). Rates given are for high season (November-March), but off-season discounts can be huge. 'Family' means a multi-bed room. Some hotels list their rates in dollars (in which case we have done so here), but you can pay in baht. All hotels below have air-conditioning, unless we mention fan-cooled rooms. Breakfast is included in the rates.

BOOKINGS AND BACKGROUND

Booking in advance avoids traipsing around suitcase-unfriendly Bangkok streets. The better hotels fill up at busy times, but you can always find a room, with thousands more coming on stream in 2007. Rates at major hotels may be higher if booked within Thailand.

The **Thailand Hotels Association** (www.thaihotels.org) offers information and reservations, and has a stall at the airport. The best website for cheaper prices is **www.hotelsdirect.com**, while other recommended online booking sites are **www. asia-hotels.com/thailand**, **www.asiarooms. com**, **www.bookingthaihotel.com**, **www.hotelthailand.com**,**www.sawadee.**

com and **www.siam.net**. For hostels run to IYHA standards, contact the **Thai Youth Hostels Association** (0 2628 7415, www.tyha.org) and check **www.hostelworld. com**, which also lists good guesthouses.

Phra Nakorn & Banglamphu

A backpacker enclave since the early 1980s, **Thanon Khao San** has grown from rabbit-hutch guesthouses (immortalised on page and screen in *The Beach*) to embrace more modern comfort. But as this 'Freak Street' gets more cacophonous, many travellers opt for quieter **Thanon Rambuttri**, **Thanon Phra Arthit** and the *sois* off **Thanon Samsen**.

Deluxe

Chakrabongse Villas

396 Thanon Maharat (0 2622 3356-8/fax 0 2622 1900/www.thaivillas.com). Tha Ratchinee. **Rooms** 3. **Rates** $190-$230 double. **Credit** MC, V. **Map** p248 B5 ❶
A jewel set on the river, this 19th-century mansion built by Prince Chakrabongse Bhuvanath has three Thai-style villas. Exquisitely furnished with teak, silk and modern amenities, they offer seclusion, a garden pool and views of Wat Arun across the river from the boardwalks and dining pavilion. Expect a warm welcome and Thai meals bought and cooked to order. Outside the gate lies the Bangkok of the imagination, with Wat Pho, the flower market, the apothecaries of Tha Tien and Expressboat piers (although the villas also have their own boat). Book well in advance.
Internet (wireless). Parking (free). Pool. Restaurant. Smoking rooms. TV (music/widescreen/DVD).

Expensive

Aurum: The River Place

Soi Pansook, 394/27-29 Thanon Maharat (0 2622 2248/www.aurum-bangkok.com). Tha Tien. **Rooms** 12. **Rates** B3,500-B4,500. **Credit** MC, V. **Map** p248 B5 ❷

Opened in September 2006, this three-storey corner landmark affords guaranteed views: three rooms overlook the old town, nine the adjacent river. Its stuccoed Parisian feel continues inside, with floor-to-ceiling windows, dark floorboards and white marble bathrooms in rooms that make up in practical, tasteful touches what they lack in size. *Concierge. Internet (wireless). Parking (free). TV.*

Old Bangkok Inn

607 Thanon Phra Sumen (0 2629 1787/www.old bangkokinn.com). **Rooms** 10. **Rates** B4,000-B6,000 double; B6,000-B12,000 suite. **Credit** MC, V. **Map** p248 C3 ❸

This charming boutique hostelry was named one of the world's hottest new hotels by Condé Nast Traveler, so it books out fast. Beside the Queen's Gallery and the Golden Mount, it occupies a shophouse on the site of a palace that has been in the Tulyanond family for seven generations. Beyond the lobby, compact colour-themed rooms (Lemongrass, Jasmine, Rice, Orchid) and suites recreate a bygone Thai/Burmese urban ecology, matching salvaged-wood bathrooms and fittings with modern functionality in the form of in-room computers and CFC-free coolers. A dollar a night goes to community charity. *Concierge. Gym. Internet (wireless). Parking (street). Restaurant. Room service. TV (widescreen/DVD).*

Moderate

Arun Residence

36-38 Soi Pratoo Nok Yoong, Thanon Maharat (0 2221 9158/www.arunresidence.com). **Rooms** 5. **Rates** B2,950 double; B4,700 suite. **Credit** AmEx, MC, V. **Map** p248 B4 ❹

Facing Wat Arun from its superb Franco-Italian-Thai bistro the Deck, its riverbank patio and some of its rooms, this old corner shophouse has been sleekly converted but reflects the homely retro charms of its old neighbourhood. The loftiest room includes a chill-out roof garden and so fills up fast. *Bar. Internet (high-speed, wireless). Restaurant. Smoking rooms. TV (DVD).*

Buddy Lodge

265 Thanon Khao San (0 2629 4477/fax 0 2629 4744/www.buddylodge.com). **Rooms** 76. Rates B2,000-B2,600 double. **Credit** MC, V. **Map** p248 B3 ❺

Buddy Lodge's red brick façade hides modern rooms with ace wooden floors, writing desks, old-fashioned lamps and white timber walls. The balconies in the deluxe rooms are bigger than the standard rooms, and are nice spots for a nightcap. *Bar. Business centre. Concierge. Internet (high-speed). Pool. Restaurant. Room service. Spa. TV.*

Budget

My House

37 Soi Chanasongkhram (0 2282 9263-4). **Rooms** 60. **Rates** B350 double with fan; B500 double with air-con. **No credit cards.** **Map** p248 B2 ❻

The area behind Wat Chanasongkhram risks becoming a cheap drinking substitute for Khao San refugees, but its old tranquillity remains intact at this tidy, five-storey guesthouse. The Thai-style entrance and lounge/restaurant give way to rooms that are a touch generic, but perfectly clean and comfy. *Internet (pay terminal). Restaurant.*

Nakorn Pink Hotel

9/1 Samsen Soi 6 (0 2281 6574/fax 0 2282 3727). **Rooms** 118. **Rates** B390 double with fan; B490 double with air-con. Hot water B80 supplement. **No credit cards.** **Map** p248 C2 ❼

Of the many old Chinese-style hotels off Thanon Samsen, this pastel-coloured one is the plum. Rooms are well decked out, with clunky old wooden furniture and small fridges. There's no restaurant, but the *soi* mouth has a fine seafood eaterie. *Internet (high-speed). Parking (free). TV (pay movies).*

Peachy Guesthouse

10 Thanon Phra Arthit (0 2281 6471/6659). **Rooms** 56. **Rates** B160 double with fan & shared bathroom; B200 double with air-con & shared bathroom; B400 double with air-con & en suite. **No credit cards.** **Map** p248 B2 ❽

This converted school offers large double beds, wardrobes and a beer garden/restaurant serving breakfasts, crêpes and real coffee. If that seems homely, remember that it's rumoured to be haunted by the spirits of an old lady and a handyman. *Internet (pay terminal). Restaurant. TV room.*

Deluxe

Marriott Bangkok Resort & Spa

257/1-3 Thanon Charoen Nakorn (0 2476 0022/ fax 0 2476 1120/www.marriotthotels.com/bkkth). *Saphan Taksin BTS then hotel boat.* **Rooms** 413. **Rates** $170-$240 double; $300-$1,800 suite. **Credit** AmEx, DC, MC, V.

Situated downstream from the other river five-stars, this unpretentious resort attractively frames a verdant pool area and canal. The facilities include the excellent Mandara Spa, a mini-mall and several dining options such as Trader Vic's, renowned for its Sunday jazz brunch. It may be a trek to shops and nightlife, but guests relish the shuttle boat trip to the Saphan Taksin BTS/Pier and River City. The teak barge, Manohra, hosts dinner and overnight cruises. *Bar. Business centre. Concierge. Disabled-adapted rooms. Gym. Internet (high-speed, wireless, pay terminal). Parking (free). Pool. Restaurants (4). Room service. Smoking rooms. Spa. TV.*

Millennium Hilton Bangkok

123 Thanon Charoen Nakorn (0 2442 2086/
2000/www.hilton.com). Hilton ferry from
Tha Saphan Thaksin or Tha River City. **Rooms** 543.
Rates $170-$210 double; $230-$1,570 suite.
Credit AmEx, DC, MC, V. **Map** p250 D6 ❾

This distinctive white river landmark opened as the Hilton in early 2006. It was worth the long wait: breathtaking spaces abound. The Thai modernist-style lobby soars eight storeys high. The excellent café/buffet Flow looks over the Chao Phraya through vast windows and from its deck. At the pool, loungers rest in the water, and on a sandy beach, several floors up. Reached by glass elevator, Three Sixty bar (*see p130*) surveys the city from the discus-shaped penthouse. All rooms have panoramas of river life, open-plan bathrooms and Thai accents like golden lacquer. Other amenities include a resort-like spa, Zeta Bar (*see p130*), impressive steakhouse Prime and Cantonese restaurant Yuan, which excels at dim sum and rare teas. With Khlong San Market on its doorsteps, the Hilton has a sleek ferry serving River City and the BTS at Tha Sathorn.
Bars (2). Business centre. Concierge. Disabled-
adapted rooms. Gym. Internet (high-speed, wireless,
pay terminal). Parking (free). Pool. Restaurants (3).
Room service. Smoking rooms. Spa. TV (pay
movies/music/suites: widescreen/DVD).

Peninsula

333 Thanon Charoen Nakorn (0 2861 2888/fax 0
2861 1112/http://bangkok.peninsula.com). Saphan
Taksin BTS then shuttle boat. **Rooms** 370. **Rates**
$240-$340 double; $500-$3,000 suite. **Credit** AmEx,
DC, MC, V. **Map** p250 D7 ❿

This stylish modern tower in many ways outdoes the ageing (and pricier) Oriental. The interior exudes sophistication, with contemporary Thai art in the large, well-equipped rooms, each with both river and Downtown panoramas. Restaurants Mei Jiang (Cantonese) and Jester's (Pacific Rim fusion; *see p112*) are the city's best in their categories, while Thip Thara combines healthy Thai cuisine within an authentic-feeling teak courtyard on the water's edge. Beyond a canal, a five-pool deck cascades towards the river from the colonial-styled new ESPA spa (*see p178* **Suite retreats**). Shuttleboats serve the BTS pier and River City. Meticulous service throughout.
Bar. Business centre. Concierge. Disabled-adapted
rooms. Gym. Internet (high-speed). Parking (free).
Pool. Restaurants (5). Room service. Smoking rooms.
Spa. TV (music/DVD).

Expensive

Ibrik Resort

256 Soi Wat Rakang, Thanon Arun-Amarin (0 2848
9220/fax 0 2411 1183/www.ibrikresort.com). Boat
from Tha Chang or Tha Prachan Pier to Tha Wat
Rakang. **Rooms** 3. **Rates** B4,000 double. **Credit**
AmEx, MC, V. **Map** p248 A3 ⓫

This trio of unique balconied rooms – River, Sunshine and Moonlight – features pared-down design and oriental touches. With boats functioning as the main transport, this retreat boasts unmatched riverscapes of the Grand Palace.
Restaurant. TV (widescreen).
Other locations: 235/16 Thanon Sathorn,
South (0 2211 3470).

Where to Stay

A beach in the sky, at the **Millennium Hilton Bangkok**.

Dusit

Moderate

Phra Nakorn Norn Len
46 Thewet Soi 1 (0 2628 8188-9/www.phranakorn-nornlen.com). **Rooms** 35. **Rates** B2,100. **Credit** AmEx, MC, V. **Map** p248 C2 ⑫

The owners of this cosy guesthouse refashioned an old building to meld together bygone styles of Thai wooden-house living with art and a sense of community. In the tranquil garden, an art terrace sells products from their Rabbit in the Moon foundation, which teaches arts and nature appreciation to children. They encourage guests to support the locals, by breakfasting in the market instead of the hotel's (albeit lovely) coffee corner, say, or taking washing to a nearby laundry. Every room has its own character, differentiated by paintings, colour schemes and details like a bathroom mosaic, or an outsize window that was once an old door. A top-floor room looks out at the giant Buddha of Wat In.
Internet (wireless).

Budget

Budget options line Thanon Si Ayutthaya beyond the National Library, with shops, a temple, bar/restaurants and Kaloang riverside restaurant (*see p114*) adding to the charm and amenities of the area.

Baan Phiman Resort
123 Samsen Soi 5 (0 2282 5594). **Rooms** 19. **Rates** B200-B400 double with fan; B500 double with air-con; B100 tent. **No credit cards.** **Map** p248 B2 ⑬

At this curious complex, which is set within an old community, you can choose between riverside bungalows, small rooms in a traditional house, or two tents, functionally equipped with a mattress, fan and light. It also includes a garden, sun deck and very cheap restaurant.
Bar. Business centre. Concierge. Internet (pay terminal). Restaurant. Room service. TV room.

Sri-Ayuthaya Guesthouse
23/11 Sri Ayutthaya Soi 14 (0 2282 5942/0 2281 6829). **Rooms** 16. **Rates** B350-B450 double with fan; B500 double with air-con. **No credit cards.** **Map** p248 C1 ⑭

With traditional touches such as wooden angels set in the brick walls and a restaurant full of handicrafts and old photos of Bangkok, this three-floor guesthouse is one of the area's classiest acts. The small rooms have rustic decor and stone-walled bathrooms with saloon doors.
Internet (high-speed, pay terminal). Restaurant. Room service. TV room.
Other locations: Tawee Guesthouse, 83 Sri Ayutthaya Soi 14, Dusit (0 2280 1447).

Chinatown

Moderate

Grand China Princess
215 Thanon Yaowarat (0 2224 9977/fax 0 2224 7999/www.grandchina.com). **Rooms** 165. **Rates** B2,600 double; B3,500-B8,000 suite. **Credit** AmEx, DC, MC, V. **Map** p248 C5 ⑮

A great base for exploring the old town, these large rooms, some with balconies, overlook the city and river. The top floor has Bangkok's only revolving club lounge (open in the evenings). Facilities are a bit worn and the decor rather haphazard, but it rewards those who are after some chaos and character.
Bars (2). Business centre. Concierge. Disabled-adapted rooms. Gym. Internet (high-speed, wireless, pay terminal). Parking (free). Pool. Restaurants (3). Room service. Smoking rooms. TV (pay movies).

Shanghai Inn
479-481 Thanon Yaowarat (0 2221 2121/fax 0 2221 2124/www.shanghai-inn.com). **Rooms** 55. **Rates** B2,200 double; B3,400 suite. **Credit** AmEx, DC, MC, V. **Map** p250 D5 ⑯

It's no overstatement to say this boutique hotel electrifies – and it's not just the acidic colour scheme: it has a real buzz. The rooms are beautiful but come with mod cons. Oriental kitsch at its best. **Photo** *p44.*
Business centre. Concierge. Internet (wireless). Parking (free). Restaurant. TV (pay movies/music/widescreen/DVD).

Budget

Baan Hualampong
336/20 Chalong Krung Soi 21 (0 2639 8054/www.baanhualampong.com). Hualamphong MRT. **Rooms** 14. **Rates** B270 single; B500 double; group B200 per person. **No credit cards.** **Map** p250 E5 ⑰

Basic but delightful, this semi-wooden guesthouse near the main station has a friendly atmosphere and a comfortable lounge, kitchen and laundry. The owner speaks English and German.
Internet (high-speed, pay terminal). Parking (street). TV room.

New Empire Hotel
57 Thanon Yaowarat (0 2234 6990-6/fax 0 2234 6997/www.newempirehotel.com). **Rooms** 130. **Rates** B650-B720 double. **No credit cards.** **Map** p249 D5 ⑱

At the very top of Chinatown's main drag, the Empire is clean, cheap and comfortable, with well-equipped rooms, and carpets and wallpaper straight out of a Wong Kar Wai movie. The staff speak just enough English for essential exchanges.
Concierge. Disabled-adapted rooms. Parking (free). Restaurant. Room service. Smoking rooms. TV.

Riverview Guesthouse
768 Thanon Songwad (0 2235 8501/fax 0 2237 5428). **Rooms** 40. **Rates** B200-B450 double with fan; B690 with air-con. **Credit** AmEx. **Map** p250 D6 ⑲

Very basic, but great value and quiet, clean and friendly, the Riverview offers a chance to experience 'old' Bangkok. The higher rooms do indeed overlook the Chao Phraya, as does the top-floor restaurant. The largest air-con room has a fridge and (Thai) TV. *Internet (pay terminal). Restaurant. Room service. Smoking rooms. TV room.*

Train Inn

428, Thanon Rong Meuang (0 2215 3055/08 1819 5544/www.thetraininn.com). Hualamphong MRT. **Rooms** 40. **Rates** B600-B700 double; B900 suite. **No credit cards. Map** p249 E5 ⑳
Next to the Italianate terminus, this simple shop-house plays with the idea of staying aboard a train with rooms classified as First, Second and Third Class. Touches of bright colour and nicely arranged furniture make for an enjoyable stay. *Bar. Concierge. Disabled-adapted rooms. Internet (high-speed, dataport). Parking (free). Restaurant. Room service. Smoking rooms. TV.*

Bangrak

Deluxe

Dusit Thani

946 Thanon Rama IV (0 2236 9999/fax 0 2236 6400/www.dusit.com). Saladaeng BTS/Silom MRT. **Rooms** 517. **Rates** $185-$300 double; $400-$2,500 suite. **Credit** AmEx, DC, MC, V. **Map** p251 G6 ㉑

Dignitaries and royalty favour this triangular, spired institution, which soars imperiously above Lumphini Park, Patpong and a BTS/MRT interchange. Its angular 1970 architecture has been stripped of its old dowdy trappings and artfully re-lit, from the chic MyBar, offering garden views and jazz in the lower lobby, via nice-enough rooms, to the haute cuisine D'Sens (*see p115*) in the penthouse. Ringing the waterfall courtyard and pool, Deverana Spa is perhaps Bangkok's most meditative holistic haven. *Bars (3). Business centre. Concierge. Disabled-adapted rooms. Gym. Internet (high-speed). Parking (free). Pool. Restaurants (9). Room service. Smoking rooms. Spa. TV (pay movies/widescreen).*

LeBua at State Tower

1055 Thanon Silom (0 2 624 9555/www.lebua.com). Saphan Taksin BTS/Pier. **Rooms** 325. **Rates** B8,360 1 bedroom; B17,100 2 bedrooms; B24,320 3 bedrooms. **Credit** AmEx, DC, MC, V. **Map** p250 E7 ㉒
The latest Thai hotel brand targets the same posh market as its world-famous restaurants Sirocco, Breeze and Mezzaluna (*see p116*), and bar Distil (*see p132*), which top this golden-domed, pseudo-Roman skyscraper. The rooms above the 50th floor give similarly awesome views over city and river. All rooms are spacious, contemporary-styled suites, while the lobby disguises its low ceilings with a modern Victorian air, and the outdoor poolside feels like a secret corner. Service is meticulous, and if you really want to splurge, a Condé Nast Traveler award-winning chef will cook in your suite. It's a hike to the BTS, though.

Colour, style and convenience at the **Shanghai Inn**. *See p43.*

Bars (3). Business centre. Concierge. Gym. Internet (high-speed, dataport). Parking (free). Pool. Restaurants (4). Room service. Smoking rooms. Spa. TV (music/DVD).

Oriental

48 Charoen Krung Soi 38 (0 2659 9000/fax 0 2659 0000/www.mandarinoriental.com). Saphan Taksin BTS. **Rooms** 396. **Rates** $370-$440 double; $510-$2,550 suite. **Credit** AmEx, DC, MC, V. **Map** p250 D7 ㉒

One of the world's grandest hotels, this river landmark started as a lodge for European traders, which burnt down in 1865. Two Danish naval captains, Jarck and Salje, rebuilt it 11 years later and soon attracted the cultured guests for which it's famed. In 1887 another Dane, HN Anderson, upgraded the hotel with what is now the Authors' Wing, containing suites named after writer-guests from an unknown Joseph Conrad to Somerset Maugham, Noel Coward, Graham Greene, John le Carré and, er, Barbara Cartland. No sandals allowed, so dress up for this piece of living history, with staff who recall your every taste. Although the Oriental feels a tad dated, little beats its superior venues, from Le Normandie (see p115), China House (see p117) and the jazzy Bamboo Bar (see p186), to sublime seafood at Lord Jim's, high tea in the Author's Lounge, and cocktails to relish on the riverbank terrace. Ferries shuttle you to the BTS, River City and the Oriental Spa (see p178 **Suite retreats**) and Sala Rim Nam restaurant (see p199) on the Thonburi side. **Photo** p46.

Bar. Business centre. Concierge. Disabled-adapted rooms. Gym. Internet (high-speed, wireless, pay terminal). Parking (free). Pools (2). Restaurants (7). Room service. Smoking rooms. Spa. TV (pay movies/music/suites: widescreen/DVD).

Shangri-La

89 Soi Wat Suan Plu, Thanon Charoen Krung (0 2236 7777/fax 0 2236 8579/www.shangri-la.com). Saphan Taksin BTS. **Rooms** 799. Rates $260-$320 double; $400-$2,500 suite. **Credit** AmEx, DC, MC, V. **Map** p250 D7 ㉓

Bangkok's largest river hotel, with two wings, two pools and leafy grounds, this Singapore-owned landmark has won many awards. Adjacent to the BTS and Expressboats, it has first-rate service, facilities and dining options, including Italian at Angelini (see p115), Thai at the palatial teak Sala Thai, family Sunday brunch at refurbished NEXT2, and river cruises on its luxury yacht. The modern rooms, with oriental accents, overlook either the city or the river. The hotel's CHI Spa specialises in Himalayan healing arts (see p178 **Suite retreats**). **Photo** p48.

Bars (4). Business centre. Concierge. Disabled-adapted rooms. Gym. Internet (high-speed, wireless). Parking (free). Pools (2). Restaurants (5). Room service. Smoking rooms. Spa. TV (pay movies/suites: music/widescreen/DVD).

Sofitel Silom

188 Thanon Silom (0 2238 1991/fax 0 2238 1999/ www.sofitel.com). Chong Nonsi BTS. **Rooms** 454.

Rates $180-$220 double; $320-$550 suite. **Credit** AmEx, DC, MC, V. **Map** p250 E7 ㉕

The first hotel in Bangkok to decorate in contemporary Thai design, this business high-rise also exudes a French 'art de vivre' feel. It is a stimulating place, with beautifully harmonised hues, smart furnishings and flamboyant artwork. The refreshment options excel, too, notably the Parisian patisserie LeNôtre (see p119) and the panoramic penthouse wine bar V9 (see p133).

Bars (2). Business centre. Concierge. Disabled-adapted rooms. Gym. Internet (high-speed, wireless). Parking (free). Pool. Restaurants (4). Room service. Smoking rooms. Spa. TV (pay movies/music/widescreen/suites: DVD).

Expensive

Luxx

6/11 Thanon Decho (0 2635 8800/ www.staywith luxx.com). **Rooms** 13. **Rates** B3,300-B3,800 double; B4,300-B6,200 suite. **Credit** MC, V. **Map** p250 E7 ㉖

Tucked away off busy Silom, this slim five-floor boutique hotel keeps things Zen, with refreshing scents, wooden floors, reclining Japanese bath tubs and bathroom partitions that can move to extend the rooms. The modern design is enhanced through the intriguing use of space.

Bar. Concierge. Internet (high-speed, wireless). Pool. Restaurant. Room service. Smoking rooms. TV (music/DVD).

Tarntawan Place Hotel

119/5-10 Thanon Surawong (0 2238 2620/fax 0 2238 3228/www.tarntawan.com). Saladaeng BTS/Silom MRT. **Rooms** 75. Rates B2,500 double; B4,000-B6,000 suite. **Credit** AmEx, DC, MC, V. **Map** p250 F6 ㉗

Right beside Patpong, yet quiet, this small hotel forgoes chic for other qualities: cosiness, convenience and efficiency. It's particularly gay-friendly.

Bar. Business centre. Concierge. Internet (high-speed, wireless). Parking (free). Restaurant. Room service. Smoking rooms. TV (pay movies/music/suites: widescreen/DVD).

Triple Two Silom

222 Thanon Silom (0 2627 2222/fax 0 2627 2300/www.tripletwosilom.com). Saladaeng BTS/Silom MRT. **Rooms** 75. **Rates** B5,900 double; B6,900 suite. **Credit** AmEx, DC, MC, V. **Map** p250 E7 ㉘

Bangkok's first boutique hotel (2002) hit just the right attitude and service to earn that mantle. The vibrant mixture of colours and textures involves unusual materials: marble floor mosaics, striking woven rugs on wooden boards, collaged panels of old photos. Some of the finely appointed rooms overlook a garden. The pool, fitness facilities and new Dalah Spa are in the drab adjoining parent hotel, the Narai.

Bar. Business centre. Concierge. Disabled-adapted rooms. Gym. Internet (high-speed, wireless, dataport). Parking (free). Pool. Restaurant. Room service. Smoking rooms. Spa. TV (DVD).

Oriental. *See p45.*

Moderate

La Résidence

*173/8-9 Thanon Surawong (0 2266 5400-2/
fax 0 2237 9322). Saladaeng BTS/Silom MRT.*
Rooms 26. **Rates** B1,200-B2,000 double; B3,000-
B3,800 suite. **Credit** AmEx, MC, V. **Map** p250 F6 ❷
Gleaning much repeat business, this small modern
hotel is out of earshot of Patpong. Each room has its
own theme, with colour schemes, wallpaper and art
conjuring up different moods, whether cosy living
room, grand European salon or dramatic red-walled
suite. It's clean and friendly, and fairly good value,
but has no leisure facilities save for a small library.
*Concierge. Internet (high-speed, wireless, pay
terminal). Restaurant. Room service. TV (TV
room/suites: pay movies).*

Rose Hotel

*118 Thanon Surawong (0 2266 8268-72/
fax 0 2266 8096).* **Rooms** 70. **Rates** B1,850 double.
Credit AmEx, DC, MC, V. **Map** p250 F6 ❸
A long-time favourite, this handy hotel has had an
urban retro facelift while retaining its atmosphere and
friendly staff. Each room feels and smells brand new,
and comes with a generously sized bath. Just don't
expect a view. A new pool abuts the recently opened
Thai restaurant in a teak stilt house. **Photo** *p50.*
*Concierge. Internet (pay terminal). Parking (free).
Restaurant. Room service. Smoking rooms. TV.*

Pathumwan

Deluxe

Conrad Bangkok

*All Seasons Place, 87 Thanon Witthayu (0 2690
9999/fax 0 2690 9980/www.conradbangkok.com).
Ploenchit BTS.* **Rooms** 392. **Rates** B6,000-B9,000
double; B16,000-B78,200 suite. **Credit** AmEx, DC,
MC, V. **Map** p251 H5 ❸
This elegant tower hotel wears its chic attitude on
its sleeves, literally: the staff all have designer
uniforms. The warm, luxurious decor features creative touches such as vibrant carpets, and backlit
silk and flower installations by Sakul Intakul, but
the window-walled bathrooms may not appeal to all.
The Diplomat Bar (*see p133*) sets a suave jazzy note,
and Liu Chinese restaurant was designed by Zhang
Jin Jie of Beijing's hot eaterie, Green T House. The
spa/pool/gym has extensive roof gardens. The
nightclub 87-Plus, Italianate restaurant, ballroom
and adjoining All Seasons Place shopping centre
have extra entrances on Soi Ruam Rudee.
*Bars (2). Business centre. Concierge. Disabled-
adapted rooms. Gym. Internet (high-speed, wireless).
Parking (free). Pool. Restaurants (4). Room service.
Spa. TV (pay movies/music/widescreen/suites: DVD).*

Four Seasons

*155 Thanon Ratchadamri (0 2254 9999/0 2251
6127/fax 0 2254 5390/www.fourseasons.com).
Ratchadamri BTS.* **Rooms** 353. **Rates** $230-$300
double; $250-$2,200 suite. **Credit** AmEx, DC, MC, V.
Map p251 G5 ❷
The former Regent incorporates Thai crafts into its
furnishings, while still retaining its contemporary
style and functionality. An impressive spot for meetings, the lobby wows with its murals and backlit marble columns. The rooms offer generous bathrooms
and separate dressing areas, while i.sawan spa villas
crown the roof (*see p178* **Suite retreats**). The Tony
Chi-designed restaurants are impeccable and among
the city's best – notably, Biscotti (Italian; *see p119*),
Madison (grill) and Shintaro (Japanese) – and the
suave Aqua bar shares the shopping atrium with a
pâtisserie, photo exhibitions and a water garden.
*Bar. Business centre. Concierge. Disabled-adapted
rooms. Gym. Internet (high-speed, shared terminal).
Parking (free). Pool. Restaurants (7). Room service.
Spa. TV (pay movies/music/widescreen/DVD).*

Grand Hyatt Erawan

*494 Thanon Ratchadamri (0 2254 1234/fax
0 2253 5856/www.bangkok.hyatt.com). Chidlom
BTS.* **Rooms** 380. **Rates** B11,600-B17,200 double;
B19,400-B72,000 suite. **Credit** AmEx, DC, MC, V.
Map p251 G5 ❸

Behind the brash neo-Egyptian façade, welcoming, business-like rooms offer spacious, elaborate marble bathrooms, modern Thai art and sleek furnishings of hardwood and silk. Many locals frequent the Spasso music/pizza venue (*see p189*), You & Mee noodle shop, cavernous ballroom, and the Chinese Restaurant, which makes dramatic use of crackled glass. The hotel connects to the Erawan mall, where it runs the refined Erawan Tea Room.
Bars (3). Business centre. Concierge. Disabled-adapted rooms. Gym. Internet (high-speed, dataport, shared terminal). Parking (free). Pool. Restaurants (6). Room service. Smoking rooms. Spa. TV (pay movies/widescreen/suites: music/DVD).

Nai Lert Park Hotel

2 Thanon Witthayu (0 2253 0123 /www.nailert park.swissotel.com). Ploenchit BTS. **Rooms** 338. **Rates** $200-$230 double; $350-$1,500 suite. **Credit** AmEx, DC, MC, V. **Map** p251 H4 ㉞
One of the few Bangkok hotels with expansive grounds, the refurbished former Hilton is managed as a Swissôtel by Raffles of Singapore. All rooms have private balconies overlooking the lush canalside garden, and the bathrooms are bright and airy. Among the hotel's assets are the free-form swimming pool, the artsy arcade Promenade Decor and a trendy bar, Cyn, where hi-sos lounge in suspended globular seats. At the Soi Somkid entrance stands the phallic Chao Mae Tubtim Shrine.
Bars (2). Business centre. Concierge. Disabled-adapted rooms. Gym. Internet (high-speed, wireless). Parking (free). Pool. Restaurants (6). Room service. Smoking rooms. Spa. TV (pay movies/music/widescreen/suites: DVD).

Expensive

Pathumwan Princess

444 Thanon Phayathai (0 2216 3700-29/fax 0 2216 3730-3/www.pprincess.com). National Stadium BTS. **Rooms** 462. **Rates** $175-$475 double. **Credit** AmEx, MC, V. **Map** p249/p250 F5 ㉟
Connected to MBK mall and the BTS, this family-friendly hotel is hardly a retreat, but with all conceivable facilities, it's certainly convenient. Even the cheaper rooms are generously proportioned and comfortable. The Olympic Health Club is famed for its gym and 25m saltwater pool, while the Korean restaurant comes well rated. The numerous staff are extremely helpful.
Bar. Business centre. Concierge. Disabled-adapted rooms. Gym. Internet (high-speed, wireless, pay terminal). Parking (free). Pool. Restaurants (4). Room service. Smoking rooms. Spa. TV (pay movies/suites: music/DVD).

Budget

Between Jim Thompson's House and Siam Square, **Kasemsan Soi 1** is a friendly spot for budget travellers, with the functional, good-value **White Lodge**, clean, basic **A-1 Inn** and the **Reno**.

Golden House

1025/5-9 Thanon Phloenchit (0 2252 9535-7/fax 0 2252 9538/www.goldenhouses.net). Chidlom BTS. **Rooms** 26. **Rates** B1,650-B1,800 double. **Credit** AmEx, MC, V. **Map** p251 H4 ㊱
Hidden in a quiet yet ultra-convenient *soi*, this guesthouse offers bright and clean standard-sized rooms.
Business centre. Concierge. Internet (high-speed). Restaurant. Room service. Smoking rooms. TV.

Reno Hotel

40 Kasemsan Soi 1, Thanon Rama I (0 2215 0026-7). National Stadium BTS. **Rooms** 57. **Rates** B890-B1,080 double; B1,490 suite. **Credit** MC, V. **Map** p250 F4 ㊲
The makeover of the crisply styled lobby and hip Reno Café hangout hasn't yet reached most of the dowdy rooms. But they're still clean and great value.
Bar. Business centre. Concierge. Internet (high-speed, pay terminal). Parking (free). Pool. Restaurant. Room service. TV.

Sukhumvit

Deluxe

Baan Thai Wellness Retreat

7 Sukhumvit Soi 32 (0 2258 5403/fax 0 2259 0076/www.thebaanthai.com). Thonglor BTS. **Rooms** 21. **Rates** $350-$460 double; $960-$1,300 suite. **Open** Spa 8am-8pm daily. Restaurant 8am-10pm daily. Main course B180-B290. **Credit** AmEx, DC, MC, V. **Map** p252 L7 ㊳
First opened as a Thai restaurant in 1965, this teak garden compound founded by aristocrats was recently augmented with more old stilt houses to create a hotel-cum-spa that truly beds retreat from the city bustle. Each room and suite is individually styled with antiques, plush fittings and mod cons, and many come with private treatment rooms (rates include a daily massage). A meandering pool enhances the resemblance to an old canal village; the quaint meeting room and library are typically thoughtful touches. The public has other rooms for massage (Thai, Ayurvedic, Tibetan, Swedish, lymphatic or sport), wraps, baths, scrubs, acupuncture, colonics, rebirthing and other holistic therapies, as well as a gym, sauna, juice bar, aerobics studio and meditation sala. The covered terrace restaurant lists fat and calorie counts as well as dairy, wheat and chilli content on its fine menu. Thai with western options, it caters superbly for vegetarians, with wine the only alcohol.
Concierge. Gym. Internet (high-speed, wireless). Parking (free). Pool. Restaurant. Room service. Smoking rooms. Spa. TV (music).

JW Marriott Bangkok

4 Sukhumvit Soi 2 (0 2656 7700/ www.marriott. com). Ploenchit/Nana BTS. **Rooms** 441. **Rates** B7,000-B60,000 double/suite. **Credit** AmEx, DC, MC, V. **Map** p251 J5 ㊴
This business hotel won no fewer than four Best Business Hotel awards in 2006 for its full-facility

Oriental opulence: the seriously swish **Shangri-la**. *See p45.*

rooms and levels of hospitality. When Dubya visited it served as the temporary White House (well, it is white). The health club has superb equipment and sauna facilities, plus a spa, but the pool is small and shallow. Designed by modernist Thai architect Sumet Jumsai, the hotel has finally made good use of its Sukhumvit frontage with the superb Bangkok Baking Company café and an entrance to – brace yourself – a Japanese restaurant by the name of Tsu Nami, which kept its wave-cascading-into-the-basement concept even after the 2004 disaster. Meanwhile, New York Steakhouse (*see p124*) remains a key place to broker deals.

Bars (2). Business centre. Concierge. Disabled-adapt rooms. Gym. Internet (high-speed, wireless, dataport, pay terminal). Parking (free). Pool. Restaurants (7). Room service. Smoking rooms. Spa. TV (pay movies/music/widescreen).

Sheraton Grande Sukhumvit

250 Sukhumvit Soi 12 (0 2649 8888/fax 0 2649 8000/www.starwoodhotels.com/bangkok). Asok BTS/Sukhumvit MRT. **Rooms** 429. **Rates** B13,500 double; B18,700-B55,000 suite. **Credit** AmEx, DC, MC, V. **Map** p251 J5 ㊽

Despite the prices and the haughty 'e' on the name, this deeply impressive hotel earns loyalty through charming service, large luxurious rooms, a delightfully private pool with attached spa and uniformly great eating and drinking outlets. Basil (contemporary Thai) and Rossini (Italian) maintain impeccable food and mood, the Living Room (*see p186*) hosts

the city's best jazz, and all three combine in an awesome Sunday brunch. Bar Su regales drink aficionados with themed music. Owing to the hotel's year-round popularity, booking is essential and there are no low-season discounts.

Bar. Business centre. Concierge. Disabled-adapted rooms. Gym. Internet (high-speed, wireless). Parking (free). Pool. Restaurants (5). Room service. Smoking rooms. Spa. TV (pay movies/widescreen/TV room).

Expensive

Eugenia

267 Sukhumvit Soi 31 (0 2259 90179/www.the eugenia.com). **Rooms** 12. **Rates** B5,800-B7,200 double. **Credit** AmEx, MC, V. **Map** p252 K5 ㊶

This stuccoed colonial mansion dates from, oh… 2006. Taiwanese interior designer Eugene Yu-Cheng Yeh blended French Indochinoise with British Burma tiffin-ness throughout the bright, massive bedrooms, as well as the living room, lounge, comfortable reading room and lucious emerald-green pool in the lawn. Every corner oozes plush individuality, emphasised by soft Belgian linens on dark wood four-poster beds. Compounding the sense of being in the midst of a BBC costume drama, the limousine service features a Daimler 1970 DS420, a Jaguar 1965 S-Type and a Mercedes 220 S Ponton.

Bar. Concierge. Internet (wireless). Parking (free). Pool. Restaurant. Room service. Smoking rooms. TV.

Moderate

Majestic Suites

110 Thanon Sukhumvit, between Sois 4 & 6 (0 2656 8220/fax 0 2656 8201/www.majesticsuites.com). Nana BTS. **Rooms** 55. **Rates** B1,350-B2,050 double. **Credit** AmEx, DC, MC, V. **Map** p251 J5 ㊷

This small, friendly, Indian-run inn next to Nana Post Office offers great value, especially the comfy deluxe double. It includes breakfast in the lobby bar and free use of the pool and parking at the owners' luxury, 251-room Majestic Grande nearby.

Bar. Business centre. Concierge. Internet (high-speed, wireless, dataport). Restaurant. Room service. Smoking rooms. TV.

Other locations: Majestic Grande, 12 Sukhumvit Soi 2 (0 2262 2999).

Budget

The area around Sukhumvit Soi 11/1 is crammed with similar inns. All offer cheap, but rather sparse rooms with phones, air-con, cable TV and clean en suite bathrooms. The **Bangkok Inn** (155/12-13 Sukhumvit Soi 11/1, 0 2254 4834, www.bangkok-inn.com, double B1,266) and the **Business Inn** (155/4-5 Sukhumvit Soi 11, 0 2255 7155-8, www.awgroup.com, double B800-B990) are among the better ones.

Atlanta Hotel

78 Sukhumvit Soi 2 (0 225 21650 /6069/ www.the atlantahotel.bizland.com). Nana BTS. **Rooms** 49. **Rates** B481-B642 double with fan; B850-B7,000 double with air-con; B1,552 family. **No credit cards. Map** p251 J5 ㊸

Founded in 1952, this one-time beau monde haunt has hosted the likes of Jim Thompson and Scandinavian royalty and, under Charles Henn, it's enjoying a new golden age. With moralistic literary notices dotting the bookshelves, walls and even the menu at its superb, mainly vegetarian Thai restaurant, the Atlanta boasts a cult following among a new generation of writers, photographers, producers and Asia obsessives. Its concrete exterior may be crumbling and the bathrooms basic, but it retains a charming style (check out the vintage 1950s lobby). There's a 24-hour pool, writing desks in the garden and Thai dancing on Saturdays, yet one night's stay costs the same as lunch at the nearby Marriott (*see p48*).

Gym. Pool. Restaurant. Smoking rooms. TV room.

Honey Hotel

31 Sukhumvit Soi 19 (0 2253 0646-9). Asoke BTS/Sukhumvit MRT. **Rooms** 75. **Rates** B800-B1,000 double; B1,500-B1,700 suite. **Credit** MC, V. **Map** p251 J5 ㊹

Superbly kitsch, the Honey's long, low, black granite foyer and aqua pool will suit anyone who thinks

Luxe goes local

When Bangkok bought into the boutique hotel boom, upmarket uncluttered sleekness was the order of the day. The first to open, **Triple Two** (*see p45*), echoed in miniature both the modern Asian aesthetics that Ed Tuttle pioneered at the **Sukhothai** (*see p51*) and Phuket's **Amanpuri** (*see p218*), and the minimalism of Singaporean Christina Ong's **Metropolitan** in London, which opened its über-chic sibling in Bangkok (*see p51*) in 2003. The compact **Luxx** (*see p45*) perpetuates that pared-down look.

The trend, however, is now starting to draw upon local character, with many small to midsized hotels starting to open in historic neighbourhoods rather than anonymous Downtown avenues. Some, such as Thonburi's microscopic **Ibrik Resort** (*see p41*), are little more than views with a room. Across the river at Tha Tien, three new hotels epitomise efforts to offer a fuller experience: timber houses, neo-colonial fantasy and evocations of everyday Thainess. **Chakrabongse Villas** (*see p39*) provides a rare opportunity to stay in a teak

stilt house (which just happens to be in a palace garden), as do **Baan Thai Wellness Retreat** (*see p47*) and the **Thai House** in a distant Thonburi canal (*see p128 Pan handling*). Right at Tha Tien pier, **Aurum** (*see p40*) goes for the Parisan-slash-Victoriana touches that are also found at **The Eugenia** on Sukhumvit (*see p48*). Finally, **Arun Residence** (*see p40*) makes charming use of old wood and ordinary retro objects in a down-to-earth manner akin to **Old Bangkok Inn** (*see p40*), **Phra Nakorn Norn Len** (*see p43*), **The Train Inn** (*see p44*), **Baan Hualumphong** (*see p43*) and **Suk11 Guesthouse** (*see p50*).

In contrast to such subtleties, electric hues emanate from the kitsch boudoirs of **Shanghai Inn** (*see p43*) and the artist-created interiors at **Reflections Rooms** (*see p50*). Here, once over the threshold, guests enter the realms of pure imagination; from romance to sexiness, running water to recycled materials, pop art to radical cartoons.

Bangkok has gone beyond boutique – its mid range hotels now reflect the city's soul.

crimplene and cocktail frankfurters are 'faaabulous'. Rooms are unglamorous and slightly musty, but good value. Honey has tons of atmosphere, plus a cast of generic middle-aged white men and Thai girls lounging poolside.
Parking (free). Pool. Restaurant. Room service. Smoking rooms. TV.

Miami
2 Sukhumvit Soi 13 (0 2253 0369). Nana BTS. **Rooms** 132. **Rates** B800 double; B1,000-B1,200 suite. **No credit cards. Map** p251 J5
The Miami has seen better days, but it's worth going just for its retro motel feel (check out the pale blue pool in the courtyard). Rooms may be plain and rather old-looking, but they are also large and functional. There are quieter rooms away from the non-stop street bustle, and the friendly *kathoey* staff will cut the rates for long stays.
Business centre. Concierge. Internet (high-speed). Parking (free). Pool. Restaurant. Room service. Smoking rooms. TV.

Suk11 Guesthouse
1/33 Sukhumvit Soi 11 (0 2253 5927-8/fax 0 2253 5929/www.suk11.com). Nana BTS. **Rooms** 67. **Rates** B600 double; B800 family; B250 dorm. **No credit cards. Map** p251 J5
Guesthouses are sparse in Sukhumvit, but in a sub-soi near Cheap Charlie's (*see p134*) this rare find spreads charmingly over four shophouses disguised in old wooden fittings. Rooms are smallish, but pleasant, clean and new-looking, while dorm beds cater to the most frugal travellers. All rooms have air-con and come with breakfast in a café sala you can't help lingering in. Its spa displaces you to an imagined village apothecary.
Internet (high-speed, wireless). Restaurant. Spa. TV room.

North

Moderate

Reflections Rooms in Bangkok
81 Soi Phaholyothin 7 (Soi Aree) (0 2270 3343-4/ fax 0 2617 0484/www.reflections-thai.com). Ari BTS. **Rooms** 32. **Rates** B2,850-B3,600 double. **Credit** AmEx, MC, V.
Created by Thailand's guru of kitsch, Anusorn 'Nong' Ngernyuang, this hotel dares to think differently. For a start, it's raspberry pink. Co-ordinated by celebrated Czech architect Borek Sipek, each room has a different concept. The Taj Mahal room employs the intense oranges and pinks of India and has a Moorish doorway. Thaiwijit Puangkasemsomboon created the oddly shaped Post Industrial room using his trademark recycled props. Meanwhile, in the Crystal Spectrum room, one wall is a fish tank. Fabulously camp products from Nong's decor business are also fittings in the hotel's Japanese and Thai seafood restaurants. Though not central, Reflections is connected by the BTS and close to expressways and vibrant streetlife and stalls. **Photo** *p51.*
Bars (3). Internet (high-speed). Parking (free). Pool. Restaurant. Room service. Spa. TV (DVD).

South

Deluxe

Banyan Tree Bangkok
21/100 Thanon Sathorn Tai (0 2679 1200/fax 0 2679 1199/www.banyantree.com). **Rooms** 216. **Rates** $330-$1,000 suite. **Credit** AmEx, DC, MC, V. **Map** p251 G7
Better known for its award-winning Phuket spa resort, this Singaporean chain also offers its signature spa treatments (*see p178* **Suite retreats**) at this all-suite luxury hotel. Located in a distinctive, wafer-thin tower with an enormous hole through the middle, it offers every form of relaxation that the spoilt international exec could desire, including six levels of spa facilities, an outdoor 'sky deck' and two pools. Saffron serves contemporary Thai food from the penthouse, while rooftop alfresco grill Vertigo and its Moon Bar (*see p135*) offer great views and high prices. The rooms are stylish and the service great.
Bars (2). Business centre. Concierge. Disabled-adapted rooms. Gym. Internet (high-speed, wireless, dataport). Parking (free). Pool. Restaurants (6). Room service. Smoking rooms. Spa. TV (pay movies/music/DVD).

Quirky design at the **Rose Hotel**. *See p46.*

Reflections Rooms in Bangkok.
See p50.

Metropolitan

27 Thanon Sathorn Tai (0 2625 3333/fax 0 2625 3300/www.themetropolitan.com). **Rooms** 171. **Rates** $240-$300 double; $340-$2,000 suite. **Credit** AmEx, DC, MC, V. **Map** p251 G7 ㊽

Since opening in late 2003, this sister hotel to London's pioneering minimalist icon has set the benchmark in Bangkok for design-led hospitality. Owner and Singapore-based interior designer Christina Ong forged a sleek, modern oriental look from the former YMCA, while London lighting architects Isometrix enabled the concrete shell to glow softly at night. Staff in casual uniforms by Yohji Yamamoto whisk guests off to a lofty reception where iMacs offer free internet access. Also pared down in style, though not in texture, the rooms have been so well thought out as to include a full desk set from highlighters to metal rulers. By far the biggest in Bangkok, the standard rooms still pale in comparison with the two-storey suites, which come complete with kitchenette and floor-to-ceiling windows, while the terrace rooms have a balcony shower (fortunately for non-exhibitionists, it's not overlooked). Top chef Amanda Gale directs thrilling cuisine down at the poolside Cy'an (*see p127*) and health-orientated Glow café. Only guests and members – including the city's creative cream – can enter the exclusive Met Bar. For the spa, see p178 **Suite retreats**. **Photo** *p52*.

Bar. Business centre. Concierge. Disabled-adapted rooms. Gym. Internet (high-speed, wireless, shared terminal). Parking (free). Pool. Restaurants (2). Room service. Smoking rooms. Spa. TV (music/ widescreen/DVD).

Sukhothai

13/3 Thanon Sathorn Tai (0 2344 8888/ www.sukhothai.com). **Rooms** 210. **Rates** B12,000-B14,000 double; B17,200-B86,000 suite. **Credit** AmEx, DC, MC, V. **Map** p251 G7 ㊾

Designed by Ed Tuttle in an influential Siamese minimalist fashion, which showcases exquisite artefacts and floral installations by engineer-turned-florist Sakul Intakul, the Sukhothai is arguably Bangkok's most beautiful hotel. Set in six acres of gardens modelled on Sukhothai, with pools containing brick chedi, this is a classy retreat, with exquisite service. Most rooms look out on to the peaceful grounds, although they'll be impaired shortly by the massive tower the owners are currently in the process of erecting behind. Locals love the food and design at Celadon (Thai; *see p128*), the infamously indulgent champagne brunch at the Colonnade, and Italian restaurant La Scala (*see p128*). The health club and sublime pool are included in the price; tennis, squash and massages cost extra.

Bar. Business centre. Concierge. Disabled-adapted rooms. Gym. Internet (high-speed, wireless, dataport). Parking (free). Pool. Restaurants (3). Room service. Smoking rooms. Spa. TV (widescreen/suites: music/DVD).

Budget

The **Soi Ngam Duphlee/Soi Sri Bumphen** area became a pre-Khao San backpacker scene. Now it's more a hub for long-stayers, who enjoy its frisson and tolerance for night guests.

Malaysia Hotel

54 Soi Ngam Duphli, Thanon Rama IV (0 2679 7127-36/fax 0 2287 1457/www.malaysia hotelbkk.com). **Rooms** 119. **Rates** B818-B888 double. **Credit** AmEx, DC, MC, V. **Map** p251 H7 ⑤⓪

An old GI R&R joint, this block became Bangkok's first backpacker hotel in the 1970s. Today it receives a lot of return business due to its value and people-watching quotient. The owners charge ten per cent service, but you do get a lot: a pool, travel booking facilities, and rooms with phones, air-con and private bathrooms with hot showers; some come with a TV, video and fridge. The notorious 24-hour coffeeshop is a morning clearing house for creatures of the night.
Internet (high-speed). Parking (free). Pool. Restaurant. Room service. Smoking rooms. TV (DVD).

Sala Thai Daily Mansion

15 Soi Sri Bamphen, Thanon Rama IV (0 2287 1436). Lumphini MRT. **Rooms** 16. **Rates** B200-B400 double with fan; B450 double with air-con. **No credit cards. Map** p251 H7 ⑤①

Tucked away in the quiet, snail shaped *soi* off Sri Bamphen, this guesthouse remains popular with journalists and English teachers, and refuses night visitors. The rooms are all clean, basic and small, with shared bathrooms, a rooftop garden and a communal TV/reading area. The staff are lovely and if you sport the right look, owner Khun Anong may even turn you into a local star (she scouts for *farang* to model in brochures and adverts).
Smoking rooms. TV room.

Metropolitan. *See p51.*

Serviced apartments

Many residential blocks let rooms short-term at very good rates. Hotels have won a restriction on apartment stays under a week, despite the evident demand from families, business travellers, self-caterers and long-stay visitors for domestic ambience, kitchenettes and multi-room layouts. Apartments are coy about mentioning daily rates, but may quote them if asked. Alternatively,compare and reserve apartments online at www.sabaai.com.

Ascott Sathorn

187 Thanon Sathorn Tai, South (0 2676 6868/fax 0 2676 6888/www.the-ascott.com). Chong Nonsi BTS. **Rooms** 177. **Rates** B4,600-B6,600 double; B7,300-B11,000 suite; B90,000 suite monthly. **Credit** AmEx, DC, MC, V. **Map** p250 F7 ⑤②

Ringed by bank towers, this fabulous new block caters to expats and upmarket Thais who require a certain cachet. Stimulating interior design graces rooms that are flush with modern comforts. The Cascade Club fitness centre boasts the latest gym equipment and a spa. Aldo's Café and Wine Bistro has served the rich and famous, while a branch of Singapore's Hu'u Bar (*see p135*) suits deals and dates.
Bar. Business centre. Concierge. Gym. Internet (wireless). Parking (free). Pool. Restaurant. Room service. Smoking rooms. Spa. TV (music/DVD).

Chateau de Bangkok

29 Ruamrudee Soi 1, Thanon Ploenchit, Pathumwan (0 2651 4400/www.chateaudebangkok.com). Ploenchit BTS. **Rooms** 137. **Rates** B3,200-B7,400 apartment. **Credit** AmEx, DC, MC, V. **Map** p251 H5 ⑤③

Located on a residential soi, this refurbished block run by hoteliers Accor gets much repeat business. The apartments have luxury furnishings, daily cleaning (including linen and towel changes), king-size beds and full kitchens. All but the smallest studios have jacuzzis. There's also a deli/café, an Italian restaurant and a small rooftop pool/gym.
Bar. Business centre. Concierge. Gym. Internet (high-speed, wireless). Parking (free). Pool. Restaurant. Spa. TV (DVD).

Natural Ville

61 Thanon Lang Suan, Lumphini, Pathumwan (0 2250 7000/www.naturalville.com). **Rooms** 150. **Rates** (monthly) B55,000-B200,000 apartment. **Credit** AmEx, MC, V. **Map** p251 H5 ⑤④

These serviced apartments are spacious, with clear lines and natural materials. All have a pantry and king-size bed. The amenities match the best hotels and include a business centre, self-service laundry and a gym with classes in aerobics, yoga and muay Thai boxing. The pool adjoins the gorgeous Nipana Spa on the roof. Café LeNôtre (*see p119*) provides a perfect Parisian breakfast or nightcap.
Business centre. Concierge. Gym. Internet (high-speed, wireless). Parking (free). Pool. Restaurant. Room service. Smoking rooms. Spa. TV (music/DVD).

Sightseeing

Introduction

Tactics for exploring this tropical urban maze.

A multi-polar metropolis, Bangkok often bewilders the newcomer, though deploying some strategy and tactics can soften the hard edges from what is actually a fluid, easy-going city. Most hotels sit in modern downtown, though sights congregate in the old town. The original centre of gravity, **Phra Nakorn**, contains the regal landmarks of **Rattanakosin Island** and the backpacker enclave **Banglamphu**. 'Venice of the East' remnants riddle the canals of the former capital, **Thonburi** (here taken as the entire west bank of the Chao Phraya river up to Nonthaburi province). While **Dusit**'s boulevards access grand institutions, **Chinatown**'s capillary-like lanes exude the chaos of raw business.

West of the elevated expressway, **Downtown** lies within the BTS skytrain and MRT subway loops. It comprises **Bangrak**, a core of finance and nightlife; **Pathumwan**, the shopping nexus; **Sukhumvit**, an avenue of drinking, dining and entertainment; **North**, a diverse area leading to Chatuchak Weekend Markets; and **South**, a developing zone fringed by commerce along the river.

Expressways make the suburbs quite reachable. Development is booming to the **East**, including the new Suvarnabhumi Airport in Samut Prakarn province, while **Outer North** encompasses old Don Muang Airport and parts of Nonthaburi and Pathum Thani provinces. In between, the residential **North-east** is also a nightlife zone.

While the opening of the BTS in 1999 felt like the end of a war, traffic skirmishes still make it wise to focus on only one or two areas per day. The elevated BTS is a tour in itself, revealing hidden gardens and mansions behind forbidding walls and shophouses. Even more fun, **Expressboats** link the BTS to the old town along Bangkok's original highway, the river. Bangkok's flat floodplain now bristles with skyscraper reference points, though one-way systems and zigzagging *soi* (side roads, often numbered) can be circuitous and cause some confusion. For transport options, *see pp224-27*. For the **Bangkok Tourist Bureau** and **Tourism Authority of Thailand (TAT)**, *see p235*.

TIPS FOR TOURISTS
● Treat etiquette and dress codes seriously (*see p228* **Attitude & etiquette**).
● Non-Thais are often charged much more than locals. Argument is futile.
● Many establishments close over Thai and Chinese New Years.
● State museums open early, shut around 4pm and close on Mondays, Tuesdays and holidays. Private museums usually keep office hours daily (including holidays), but may close on Sundays. Many have compulsory tours. Non-TAT guides may get ejected.
● Most temples are free, and *bot* (ordination halls) might be unlocked on request.
● Many signs are in English, which is spoken widely in tourist centres, but, given differing accents, writing things down may clarify confusions. Transliterations into English vary.
● Cameras are banned from inside museums, malls and official places, but are permitted in most temples. Some places charge a camera fee. Thais (with the exception of Muslims and members of hill tribes) generally like being snapped, but prefer to compose themselves. Smile through any awkwardness, but remember that 'No photo' means just that – though hill tribes may pose for a fee.

● Late shop hours mean shopping can be saved for the evenings (or afternoons in the rainy season).

TOUTS AND SCAMS

Aside from the pushers of porn, sex shows and massage in Patpong, touts plague major sights and piers. Ignore touts or *tuk-tuk* drivers saying 'it's closed today', 'festival across town', 'craft demonstration' or 'one-day tax break', and prevent them 'guiding' you to the sight.

Touts are paid out of overcharging at the bar or shop they take you to (tours may do this too). They're rarely dangerous, but proffered food and drink might be doped. Don't believe promises of sudden wealth through gem dealing (*see p149* **Cutting edge**), but since touts are just opportunists making a living, politely say *mai ow khrub/kha* ('don't want', said by male/female) or *mee laew khrub/kha* ('have already').

Specialist tours

The **Bangkok Tourist Bureau** (*see p235*) offers canal tours of Bangkok Noi; cycling tours of Rattanakosin (6.30-9pm Sat) or Thonburi to Phutthamonthon (8am-4.30pm Sat, Sun); occasional bus tours of Rattanakosin; and four good walking tours (8am-noon, 1-5pm Wed-Sun) of Thonburi (Kudi Jeen), Sam Praeng, Wang Lang, Banglamphu and Bangrak. Numbers limited; book 3 days ahead (1 week for bus); prices vary. For specifically gay-friendly tours, *see p174.*

ETC (Educational Travel Centre)

Room 318, Royal Hotel, 2 Thanon Ratchadamnoen Avenue, Phra Nakorn (0 2224 0043/fax 0 2622 1420/www.etc.co.th). Tha Saphan Phan Fah. **Open** 8.30am-5pm Mon-Sat. **Credit** AmEx, DC MC, V. **Map** p248 B3.
Various trips from culture and cooking to canal homestays and eco-adventures. Its Thanatharee river barge/bicycling trips won a TAT award, though rooms are simple.
Other locations: 180 Thanon Khao San, Phra Nakorn (0 2282 7823)

Oriental Escape

187 Soi Riverside, Thanon Ratchavithi, Dusit (0 2883 1219/www.orientalescape.com). **Open** 9am-5pm Mon-Fri. **Credit** MC, V.
Professional travel agency covering Thailand with tailored guiding option for sights, shopping, nightlife, specific interests and local insight.

Origin Cultural Programs

(0 2259 4896-7/www.alex-kerr.com/www.origin-asia.com). **No credit cards**.
Authentic cultural experiences of one day or longer, with Thai experts offering a hands-on insight into arts like dance, floral offerings, *lai Thai* design, cooking and martial arts. The programmes are held in English at a teak compound in Bangkok, with alents in Chiang Mai and Japan. No skills req but your understanding of things Thai will flou

Real Asia

10, 5/7 soi Ari, Sukhumvit 26, Sukhumvit (0 2665 6364/08 1812 9641/www.realasia.net). Thonglor BTS. **Open** 9am-6pm daily. **No credit cards**. **Map** p252 L5.
Runs daily cycling tours (10am-3pm and 1-5pm) to rural riverside Bang Kra Jao. Their canal/walking tour (9.30am-4.30pm Sat & Sun) incorporates boats, market and community walk. A fish market features in train tours to Mahachai village (8.15am-3.30pm daily, B1,800).

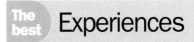

The best Experiences

Peoplewatching

Morning mayhem in **Lumphini Park** (*see p93*), **Thonburi** canal lifestyles (*see p72*), youth tribes in **Siam Square** (*see p141*).

Templespotting

The dazzling **Grand Palace** (*see p59*); **Wat Pho** reclining Buddha (*see p65*).

Teak house style

Cultural discovery at **Origin** (*see above*), neo-Thai chic at **Jim Thompson's House** (*see p97*), refresh at **Baan Thai Wellness Retreat** (*see p47*), dine at **Ruen Mallika** (*see p127*), stay at **Chakrabongse Villas** (*see p39*).

Embrace the modern

Sample **Thai Design** (*see p33*), ride the **SkyTrain & Subway** (*see pp225-26*) party at **Bed Supperclub** (*see p191*).

Buy everything

Shop global in the **Malls** (*see p141*), local in **Chatuchak Weekend Market** (*see p138*).

Eye-popping pop

Wear **Kit-ti** jewellery (*see p150*), eat or stay at **Reflections Rooms** (*see p150*).

Street culture

Explore **Chinatown** lanes (*see p84*), see **Luuk Thung** music live (*see p182*), visit **Erawan Shrine** (*see p98*).

Succumb to luxury

High tea at the **Oriental** (*see p45*), pampering at **i.sawan Residential Spa** (*see p179*), dine in the sky at **Sirocco** (*see p116*).

Sightseeing

r skills

...d seaside, people
...to study. To hone the
...self, some train in **massage** (see
p180) or **meditation** (see p181). Many get
internationally certificated in **diving** (see
p201), **muay Thai** kickboxing (see p203)
or **gemology** (see p149 **Cutting edge**), while
cooking schools reveal the secrets of Thai
food (see p128 **Pan handling**). Somewhat
less handy are courses in piloting a jumbo
– that is, becoming an elephant *mahout*.
For a hands-on grounding in Thai culture,
Origin Cultural Programs (see p55) impart
easily understood 'keys' to the traditional
threads running through Thai arts, design
and everyday ritual that beguile but often
baffle outsiders. You'll never look at
Thailand in the same way again.

River & canal tours

If you hire a longtail boat, two hours minimum
are needed to explore the canals properly.
Sights like Wat Arun are better (and more
cheaply) seen separately. At piers like Oriental,
Chang and Nonthaburi, tour routes and prices
vary (B300-B700 per hr). For **Bang Sai**, **Bang
Pa-In** and **Ayutthaya**, see pp103-107; for
nearer river sights, see p74 **Quays to the
city**; for tours by Chao Phraya **Expressboat**,
see p229.

Aggressive touts may try illegally to bar non-
Thais from cramped longtail buses plying canal
routes for B8-B40. Hiring a small, bumpy *rua
song torn* speedboat taxi gets you into minor
khlongs (canals) amid orchards, temples and
stilt houses. They cost B300-B500 per hour,
from piers at **Nonthaburi**, or the **Southern
Bus Terminal**.

Among hotel cruises, the **Oriental** (see
p45) holds dinner aboard the *Maeyanang*
(7.30-10pm Tue-Sun, B1,850, B1,000 under-
10s), while **Marriott Bangkok Resort
& Spa** (see p40) runs the *Manohra* for
evening cocktails or Bang Pa-In tours,
overnighting in teak berths (0 2476 0021-2,
www.manohracruises.com, three days two
nights $1,265++ for two people, single
$935++; dinner cruise 7.30-10pm daily,
B1,700 adults, B850 under-12s).

Asian Oasis also runs two-day jaunts
to Bang Pa-In/Ayutthaya on the exquisite
Mekhala teak barge (0 2655 6245, www.asian-
oasis.com): Up-trip package B25,760 per two
people (by barge from Bangkok, stay in a

hotel then return by bus); Down-trip package
B22,060 per two persons (by bus from
Bangkok, spend a night on the barge
returning from Autthaya).

Mit Chao Phraya Travel Service

*Tha Chang, Thanon Na Phra Lan, Phra Nakorn
(0 2225 6179/02221 2297).* **Open** *Office* 9am-5pm
daily. **Rates** B900 1hr; B1200 90mins; B1,500 2hrs.
No credit cards. **Map** p248 4B.
From Tha Chang they run three daily river and
Thonburi canal tours over 60 or 90 minutes, plus
weekend trips to Koh Kred via Khlong Om (9am-
4pm Sat, Sun, B250).

Si Phraya Boat Trip & Travel

*Soi Captain Bush, Charoen Krung Soi 30, Bangrak
(0 2235 3108). Tha Si Phraya.* **Open** *Office* 7am-
8pm daily. **Rates** B1,000 1hr; B1,200 1.5hrs; B1,500
2hrs. **No credit cards**. **Map** p250 D7.
River and canal tours leave River City (7am-6pm
daily), often combining longtail, *tuk-tuk* and
Expressboat. A two-hour dinner cruise (6pm, 8pm
daily) costs B1,300. Book a day ahead for the Bang
Pa-In/Ayutthaya trip (7.20am-5pm, B1,600).

Yok Yor Marina & Restaurant

*885 Somdet Chao Praya Soi 17, Thonburi (0 2863
0565-6/www.yokyor.co.th).* **Open** *Restaurant* 11am-
midnight daily. *Tours* 8am-10pm daily. **Credit**
AmEx, DC, MC, V. **Map** p250 6D.
A dinner tour on the double-decker steel boat comes
with a live band and a taped guide in Thai and
English (B140 plus food). The pier seafood restau-
rant has a dance stage.
Other locations: 885 Thanon Somdetchaophraya,
Thonburi (0 2439 3477).

Eco-tours & 'voluntourism'

Intrusive activities abuse the label ecotourism,
but responsible operators do exist. **Friends
of Nature** (0 2642 4426-7, www.friendsofnature
93.com) runs trips to natural, historical and
cultural sites for various interests. **Nature
Trails** (0 2735 0644, www.naturetrailsthailand.
com) organises weekend birdwatching.

Some eco-tours incorporate voluntary work,
a trend boosted by improptu tsunami aid by
tourists. One result was **North Andaman
Tsunami Relief** (NATR, 08 1787 7344/
www.northandamantsunamirelief.com),
which helps villages recover. **Lost Horizons**
(0 2860 3936, www.losthorizonsasia.com) offers
cultural and turtle conservation projects as well
as rafting, diving, trekking and island life.

In remotest Isaan, **North by North East
Tours** (0 4251 3572/www.north-by-north-
east.com) holds culinary, canoeing, cycling
and cultural trips, and 'voluntourism' in
development, conservation, education
and health. Which all just goes to show:
philanthropy can be fun.

Phra Nakorn

Where the grandest sights and oldest communities reveal the true essence of Bangkok.

Map p248

Set within the remnants of walls that held the capital for the first of its two centuries, Phra Nakorn ('Holy City') boasts most of Bangkok's must-see landmarks. It's also one of the few world cities where the centre retains vibrant original communities. However, there are plans to evict them and turn Phra Nakorn into a historical park that repackages 'Thainess' for tourist consumption. The immediate threat ebbed with the fall of Thaksin and his dream of turning the Ratchadamnoen processional avenue into a boutique-lined Thai version of the Champs-Elysées. But the bureaucrat's fetish for monuments never dies. A philistine, decades-old plan would bulldoze the historic neighbourhoods north and south of the Grand Palace into a sterile riverside promenade. Although the plan also restricts the height and design of new construction, residents and architects must continually fight to preserve pockets of living history like **Tha Tien, Tha Phra Chan** and **Mahakan Fort** (*see pp20-23* **Bangkok Today**).

You need at least a couple of days to visit the many well- and less-known gems within Phra Nakorn. At its core is **Ko Rattanakosin**, a conch-shaped island bounded by the Chao Phraya river and **Khlong Lord** (the first of three concentric canals girdling it to the east). The axial Thanon Ratchadamnoen Klang leads east past the **Democracy Monument** to Khlong Ong Ang, and effectively includes the **Golden Mount** just beyond. To the avenue's north lies **Banglamphu**, which gained notoriety as an international backpacker ghetto – and is now rediscovering its initial identity as a fount of Thai arts. Phra Nakorn's commercial areas, south of Thanon Charoen Krung, are basically a continuation of Chinatown (*see*

pp84-89). Although royalty has moved to Dusit, Phra Nakorn still hosts frequent pageantry, such as the Royal Ploughing Ceremony.

The old town is unusually suited to pedestrians (*see p58* **Community values** and *p61* **Grand canal**) and is sprouting many characterful hotels (*see p49* **Luxe goes local**). Moreover, until the MRT Subway extends along Charoen Krung (set to happen by 2010), the quickest way to reach it from Downtown remains by water, either via river Expressboat piers or canal boat to Golden Mount.

Entry to sights listed in this chapter is free and 24-hour unless otherwise noted.

Rattanakosin Island

When King Rama I moved the capital to the more defensible east-bank settlement of Bangkok in 1782, he modelled this artificial island on the auspicious layout of lost

The best Views

For a historic panorama
Once Bangkok's highest point, the **Golden Mount** still puts old and new in 360° context. *See p70.*

For skyscraper rooftop restaurants
Sirocco (*see p116*) and **Vertigo** (with its Moon Bar, *see p50*) thrill diners and drinkers from over 60 storeys up.

For (just about) seeing the sea
Peer to beyond Bangkok's fringes from its loftiest lookout, **Baiyoke II Tower**. *See p96.*

For remarkable riverscapes
Supatra River House (*see p199*) and the **Millennium Hilton Bangkok** (*see p41*) trace the Chao Phraya's curves.

For low-altitude cruising
The **BTS SkyTrain** affords glimpses behind walls and across rooftops. *See p225.*

Sightseeing

Walk 1 Community values

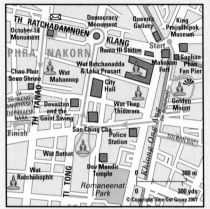

Wandering the fringes of Rattanakosin leads you through pockets of traditional craft workshops, canal life, intact communities and temples. Including refresher stops, this walk can take the best part of a day.

To get your bearings, begin at the top of the **Golden Mount** (*see p70*). If you don't relish climbing, start at the north-west of the mount at Maha Uthit Bridge, famous for its bas-reliefs, and head down **Thanon Boriphat**, a street lined by timber merchants. The first left beyond Thanon Bumrung Muang is **Soi Ban Baat** – known as the **Monk's Bowl Village** – where descendants of Ayutthayan refugees keep alive a Khmer method of beating out alms bowls from eight strips of metal, representing the eight spokes of the Dharma wheel. The community leader's workshop is at 71 Soi Ban Baat (0 2621 2635, open 8am-5pm daily, admission free). When decorated and lacquered, the bowls are prized by collectors – despite their function being a symbol of non-attachment.

Backtrack and head along **Thanon Bamrung Muang**, an elephant trail that became one of the city's first paved streets. Its shopfronts gleam with Buddha images, regalia and ritual

accoutrements. Passing the **Giant Swing** and **Wat Suthat** (*see p70*), head along **Thanon Dinso**, past the imposing **City Hall**, which will eventually become a museum documenting Bangkok. On reaching the **Democracy Monument**, turn left past the **Rim Khob Fah** shop of books on Thailand (*see p144*) and left again at the **14 October Monument** (*see p69*) into **Thanon Tanao**.

South along Tanao, at the tranquil Rama III-era **Wat Mahanopharam** (0 2224 4675, open 8am-5pm daily, *bot* 7am-5pm daily) offerings include *takraw* balls, their tightly woven rattan representing group unity and strength. Further down and across Tanao, the **Chao Poh Seua Shrine** (0 2224 2110, open 6am-5.30pm daily) honours the Chinese tiger god. It's guarded by two golden tigers, with vendors selling tiger-appeasing offerings like pork, rice and eggs – and the inevitable lottery tickets. Couples place sugar tigers here in hope of pregnancy. Looming ahead on the right, **Phraeng Sanphasat Palace Gate** is a neo-classical remnant of Prince Sanphasart Supakit's long-razed 1901 residence. To the east is narrow **Trok Chang Thong**, a goldsmiths' quarter destroyed by fire (prompting scavengers to dig for treasure) and the former home of wartime dictator Phibunsongkhram.

To glimpse the lifestyle of a (somewhat self-conscious) old community, nip into **Thanon Phraeng Nara**, the middle lane of **Samphraeng** ('three Phraeng streets'). Here a surviving part of the palace of Prince Narathip (Rama IV's son) is now a lawyer's office, but the quaintly shuttered shophouses and cottage industries here and around the square on **Thanon Phraeng Poothon**, parallel to the south, offer authentic produce and unadulterated local cuisine. Government workers from nearby offices relish the toothsome home-made ice-cream (topped with corn, nuts and red beans) and pig's brain noodles (said to improve the intellect).

Ayutthaya – both aesthetically and symbolically. Its 64-syllable name, the world's longest, means: 'Great city of angels, the supreme repository of the divine jewels (the Emerald Buddha), the supreme unconquerable land of the immortal divinity (Indra) endowed with the nine noble gems, the delightful capital

city abounding in royal palaces, which resemble paradises for the reincarnated deities, granted by Indra for Vishnu to create.' Or Krung Thep ('City of Angels'), for short.

The architectural glorification likewise announced that the reunified kingdom was growing strong and independent. At its centre stand the **Grand Palace** and its astonishing temple, **Wat Phra Kaew** (for both, *see below*), home of the Emerald Buddha. It faces **Sanam Luang** (*see p64*), the royal field that dominates the island's north, while to the south is **Wat Pho** and its ethereal Reclining Buddha.

Grand Palace & Wat Phra Kaew

Thanon Na Phra Lan (0 2222 8181). Tha Chang. **Open** 8.30am-3.30pm daily. **Admission** (incl access to Dusit Park & either Ananta Samakhom Throne Hall or Sanam Chan Palace in Nakhon Pathom) B250; free children under 120cm/47in. **No credit cards.** **Map** p248 B4.

There are no two ways about it: you must see this exquisite architectural and spiritual treasure (preferably early on a sunny morning, when it's at its most dazzling). Ignore the gem touts claiming 'it's shut today', and immerse yourself in the palace's palpable dignity (while observing the stringent dress code that bans sandals, shorts and bare shoulders). Nearly 2km (1.5 miles) of walls with lotus-shaped crenellations enclose what was once a 65-acre self-contained city, comprising ceremonial buildings, royal chambers, servants' quarters, ministerial offices and a small prison. Begun in 1782, the palace was modified by each Chakri king. Laid out similarly to Chinese imperial palaces, it has a reception zone, followed by a royal audience zone (the interiors of which are open on National Children's Day; *see p160*). But the public isn't permitted to view even the exteriors of the inner chambers that lie beyond, where the kings' wives used to live. Disused once Rama VI had only one wife, those quarters now house a finishing school for upper-class girls. Since the royals moved to Dusit, the Grand Palace gets used only for ceremonies and state visits, but it remains Thailand's proudest and holiest landmark.

Visitors entering Wat Phra Sri Rattana Sasadaram – better known as Wat Phra Kaew, the temple of the Emerald Buddha (Thailand's most sacred image) – are greeted by a statue of Buddha's physician, Shivaka Kumar Baccha, before being swamped by a kaleidoscope of forms and colours. Modelled on royal chapels in Sukhothai and Ayutthaya, and embellished to an astonishing degree, the temple omits monastic living quarters, since there are no resident monks.

The circular, Sri Lankan-style Phra Si Rattana Chedi, tiled in gold, enshrines a piece of the Buddha's breastbone. It stands on the upper terrace beside the Phra Mondop (library of palm-leaf scriptures), a columned cube of green and blue glass mosaic under a tiered spire; and the cruciform, *prang*-roofed Royal Pantheon, where on Chakri Day (*see p161*) the king honours statues of his forebears. Monuments to each Chakri reign stud the terrace, along with gilded statues of creatures from the mythical Himaphan Forest such as the *apsarasingha* (lion-woman) and *kinnorn* (bird-man), with multicoloured guardians supporting a pair of small gold *chedi* to the east. To the north, Ho Phra Nak (the royal mausoleum) and Hor Phra Monthien Tham (a library) flank porcelain-clad Vihaan Yod and a sandstone model of Angkor Wat temple in Cambodia (a vassal state when King Rama IV commissioned this carving).

On the temple's eastern side loom eight porcelain-covered pastel *prang* (representing Buddhism's eightfold path). Two stand within a notch in the cloister, which stretches 2km (1.5 miles), its walls adorned with 178 murals painted in Thai-Western

Sightseeing

Grand Palace.

National Museum.
See p63.

style of the entire *Ramakien* epic. In the south-east corner, the shrine of the Gandharara Buddha in rain-summoning posture is used in the Royal Ploughing Ceremony (*see p161*). Six pairs of towering stone *yaksha* (demons) guard the bot, which has mosaics in gold and glass and is ringed by 112 *garuda* holding *naga* snakes. From a public altar you enter the bot's murralled interior on your knees, facing a lofty gilded altar topped by the Emerald Buddha. Carved from solid jade, this statue is 66cm (26in) tall and dressed by the king in one of three seasonal robes: cool, hot or rainy. Of mysterious origin, but in late Lanna style, this palladium of Thai independence was discovered in Chiang Rai in 1434 and arrived here via Lampang, Chiang Mai, Vientiane in Laos and Wat Arun in Thonburi.

Visitors may rest at one of the *sala* (pavilions) before entering the palace precinct. The halls make for a curious medley of each Thai period, alongside European classicism, Chinese sculpture and globular *mai dut* topiary. Visible through railings on the left, the belle époque Borom Phiman Mansion was built in 1903 for the future King Rama VI. Now a state guest house, it has hosted Queen Elizabeth II and Bill Clinton. Its Sivalai Gardens contain the Phra Buddha Ratana Sathan (Rama IV Chapel).

Next, the Phra Maha Montien Buildings include Amarin Winitchai Hall, where esteemed guests such as the 19th-century ambassador Sir John Bowring were received by the king upon the boat-like throne. The main focus, however, is Chakri Maha Prasat Hall, a celebrated architectural fusion built (1876-82) by the Englishman John Chinitz. He had planned for

a dome, but Chao Phraya Srisuriyawongse, the former regent, convinced King Rama V to add a Thai roof. This odd combination was dubbed 'a *farang* in a Thai hat'. Beneath its chamber for banquets and state visits is a public Weapons Museum; the top floor houses the ashes of Chakri kings.

To its west stand Aphonphimok Pavilion and Dusit Throne Hall. The Pavilion was built by Rama IV for changing gowns en route via palanquin to the cruciform Throne Hall, which contains the throne of Rama I and is still used for coronations and lying-in-state. Beyond these, a restored building will house the new Queen's Textile Museum from late 2007.

Expect to stay at least two hours, perhaps hiring an audio guide (B100 with a passport/credit card deposit) or a guide (B300). **Photo** *p59*.

Sanam Luang & around

A broad field used for anything from royal ceremonies to public recreation, Sanam Luang is ringed by institutions. Clockwise from the Grand Palace are **Silpakorn University** (*see p64*); a Buddhist University at **Wat Mahathat** (*see p65*); **Thammasat University** (*see p65*); the **National Museum** (*see p63*); and the **National Theatre**. North of Phra Pinklao Bridge lies the **National Gallery** (*see p63*), then east along Sanam Luang stand the Royal Hotel; the Mae Toranee Fountain; **Lak Muang** (the City Pillar; *see p63*) and the **Ministry of Defence** (*see p65* **National Discovery Museum**).

The Rattanakosin waterfront was once reserved for minor palaces, but the tone is now set by the charming Phra Chan community between Tha Phra Chan and Tha Chang piers. The shophouses here burgeon with cultural regalia, traditional massage and herbal preparations, alongside outlets for local students, selling indie music, concert tickets, art-house film rentals and artists' materials. Fortune-tellers gather on the pedestrianised forecourt of Tha Phra Chan, while trinket stalls spread out from **Amulet Alley** market (*see p137*).

Flanked by 33 classically stuccoed shophouses (dating from the fifth reign) on land that once belonged to the poet Sunthorn Phu, Tha Chang's forecourt has also been paved, and food vendors shelter under its frangipani trees and in shacks behind the pier where the touts flog canal tours to passing tourists. It is named 'Elephant Pier' because the palace pachyderms once bathed here. The landscaped embankment beside the Grand Palace, which houses both the Ratchaworadit Royal Pier and Ratchakitwinitchai Throne Pavilion, is reserved for royal occasions.

Walk 2 Grand Canal

Dug as a defence for Rattanakosin Island, this tree-shaded canal carried produce from the river to the Weekend Market when it was at Sanam Luang. Lined with timber lampposts shaped like Thonburi's old wooden city wall pillars, it offers a tranquil hour's stroll.

The western bank, **Thanon Ratchinee**, starts at Thailand's fanciest drinking fountain. Erected in 1872, it encloses a sculpture of Mae Phra Thorani, the Earth Goddess, who wrung water from her hair to wash away the demons trying to corrupt the Buddha. Heading south, you pass the Civil Court, the Department of Public Prosecutions and the **Ministry of Defence**. These look across the canal to Thanon Atsadang, where fifth-reign shophouses with crumbling European detailing peddle musical instruments, clocks and military uniforms. One of the canal's many interesting spans is **Charoensri 34 Bridge**. Built to withstand an elephant, it's named for the 34th birthday of the fourth Chakri King, and hence decorated with Thai number fours.

Just beyond, floral garlands hang from the snout of a gilded **Pig Memorial**, erected in 1913 to honour Rama VI's mother, who was born in the Year of the Pig. Donations for this monument also paid for **Saphan Pee Goon** ('pig year bridge'), which you can cross to reach the Euro-classical Ministry of the Interior on Atsadang and **Wat Ratchabophit** (*see p67*). Then dart back via **Saphan Hok**, a 1982 reconstruction amalgamating four similar footbridges that used to traverse the canal, to reach **Wat Ratchapradit** (*see p67*) and **Saranrom Park**. A gay cruising beat by night, the park offers walkers a verdant breather and fruit juice vendors the chance to hawk their wares.

Finally, cross once more to Atsadang for some even finer, even more crumbling shophouses, and **Baan Mor Market** (*see p139*), named after its hidden, still used private palace. Around here you can dine and drink at **Café Today** (0 2222 5531, open 6pm-1am daily), then turn left into Thanon Chakphet to wade through orchids in **Pak Khlong Talad** flower market (*see p140*).

Lak Muang

Thanon Sanam Chai (0 2222 9876). Tha Chang.
Open 6.30am-6pm daily. **Map** p248 B3/4.

Thais believe the guardian spirits of a Thai town reside at its foundation pillar. Bangkok's birth (and horoscope) thus dates from the auspicious time on 22 April 1782 when Rama I installed this bud-tipped wooden pillar, now housed in a Khmer-revival cruciform tower. Some claim it's a Shiva *lingam* – the phallic form of the Indian god; others trace its origins to the Tai tribal adoption of an animistic southern Chinese tradition of placing a phallus on a town crossroads. And Bangkok's laburnum-wood Lak Muang – 274cm (108in) above ground, 201cm (79in) below – is an infinite crossroads since all metropolitan distances are measured from it. Shellacked and gilded, it is accompanied by the taller Lak Muang of Thonburi, moved here when the former capital joined greater Krung Thep. Spirits of the city and country are embodied in statues housed in a pavilion to the east of this compound. Those whose wishes have been granted by these spirits pay *lakhon chatri* dancers to perform at a *sala* (pavilion).

National Gallery

5 Thanon Chao Fa, nr Sanam Luang (0 2282 2639). Tha Phra Arthit. **Open** 9am-4pm Wed-Sun.
Admission B10 Thais; B30 foreigners. **No credit cards. Map** p248 B3.

Most Thai artists dream of exhibiting at this high-ceilinged institution, established in 1977 in the neo-classical former Royal Mint. The shows tend to be excellent, but the small permanent collection hasn't kept pace with contemporary art. It includes work by such modernist notables as the Impressionist painter Fua Haripitak, sculptor Misiem Yipintsoi, portraitist Chamrus Khietkong and watercolourist Sawasdi Tantisuk.

National Museum

4 Thanon Na Phra That (0 2224 1333/www. thailandmuseum.com). Tha Chang/Tha Prachan.
Open 9am-4pm Wed-Sun (last entry 3.30pm).
Admission B20 Thais; B40 foreigners. **No credit cards. Map** p248 B3.

Holding the largest museum hoard in South-east Asia, the capital's first public museum originated in 1874 as King Rama IV's collection of regalia within the Grand Palace. With branches countrywide, it went on to become a refuge for antiquities from gangs of smugglers, and is only now starting to address signage and display to fulfil its educative role. It occupies part of the former Wang Na ('front palace') of the 'deputy king', a shortlived office held by Rama IV's brother Phra Pinklao. Most unmissable is the Buddhaisawan Chapel, whose exquisite murals focus attention on the revered Phra Buddha Sihing, an image that is seven centuries old.

In the Gallery of Thai History stands the Ramkhamhaeng Stone, claimed to be the earliest inscription of tonal Thai lettering. The central audience hall contains rooms of such varied treasures as a life-size model elephant in battle armour, *khon* masks, and the Viceregal Puppets, restored by artist Chakraphan Posyakrit. Temporary shows fill the front Throne Hall. Front, left and right are small

Sightseeing

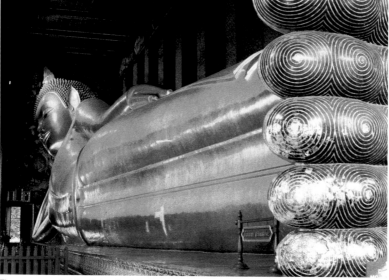

The monumental Reclining Buddha at **Wat Pho**. *See p66.*

Wat a welcome: **Wat Ratchabophit**. *See p67.*

royal pavilions, including Baan Daeng, an Ayutthayan house with Rattanakosin furnishings and a rare early indoor toilet.

Shaded courtyards enable you to recharge before tackling the north and south wings. These hold a badly lit, ill-placed bombardment of religious iconography, running chronologically from Rooms S1-9, spanning the Dvaravati and Lopburi periods, and continuing (Rooms N1-10) with Sukhothai, Ayutthaya, Lanna and Bangkok styles. But persevere: masterpieces await. Languishing at the back on a nondescript plinth, the world-renowned Sukhothai walking Buddha faces arrestingly stylised Hindu bronzes on a stair landing, with a Dvaravati figure and a striking Ayutthayan Buddha head hidden under the steps.

The gilded funerary chariots from the first Chakri reign receive more appropriate display. Their sheer scale and the glass-inlaid wood carving leaves are breathtaking. Moving these teak structures requires 300 men – a feat last carried out in 1996 for King Bhumibol's mother. Although the labelling lacks context or flair, the museum still provides a good grounding in Thai artistic and cultural history (and its guidebook fills in many of the blanks). The National Museum Volunteers offer tours (9.30am-noon Wed, Thur, or by appointment) in English, German, French and Japanese. Disabled access has improved. Thai tours (10am, 1.30pm). **Photo** *p60.*

Sanam Luang

Tha Chang. **Map** p248 B3.

Fringed by handsome tamarind trees, this large oval lawn is one of the city's few truly open spaces. Here elaborate pyres are constructed for royal cremations to resemble sacred Mount Meru, its Thai pronunciation giving rise to the park's alternative name, the *pramane* ground. Among its annual ceremonies are the bathing of the Phra Buddha Sihing statue at Songkran (*see p161*), the Royal Ploughing Ceremony (*see p161*), and the King's and Queen's Birthday celebrations (*see p159 & p162*). In decades past, Bangkok's elite came here for horse racing, bird hunting and golf. Until 1982 it hosted the Weekend Market (now at Chatuchak; *see p138* **Market forces**), with produce arriving via Khlong Lord. Current diverse uses include folk entertainments, festivals, concerts and informal recreation, notably kite flying (February-April).

Silpakorn University & Gallery

31 Thanon Na Phra Lan (0 2623 6115-21/ www.su.ac.th/art centre 0 2221 3841/www.art-centre.su.ac.th). Tha Chang. **Open** 8.30am-4.30pm Mon-Fri. *Art centre* 9am-7pm Mon-Fri; 9am-4pm Sat. Closed hols. **Map** p248 B3/4.

Thailand's oldest and most venerable fine art university, Silpakorn contains a small museum and a courtyard sculpture dedicated to its founder (Silpa Bhirasri, aka Corrado Feroci, an Italian commissioned in the 1920s to sculpt such landmarks as the Rama I statue and the Democracy Monument). Hosting regular exhibitions by students, masters and foreign artists-in-residence, the serene Silpakorn Art Centre Gallery was once part of Tha Phra Palace. There are specialist galleries in the faculties of architecture, decorative arts (products and textiles), and painting, sculpture and graphic arts.

Thammasat University

*2 Thanon Phra Chan (0 2221 6111/www.tu.ac.th).
Tha Chang/Tha Prachan.* **Open** 8.30am-4.30pm
Mon-Fri. **Map** p248 A3/B3.

The country's second most prestigious university
(after Chulalongkorn) dates from 1932. A statue of
its founder, statesman Pridi Bhanomyong, sits in
front of its drill bit-shaped tower, near a Chinese
stone lion bedecked with animalian offerings.
Thammasat students are known for dissent and
were the leading demonstrators (and victims) of the
14 October 1973 and 6 October 1976 incidents,
recorded on two memorials inside the gate on
Thanon Deuan Tula (October Road). In 2002 all but
postgraduates were shifted to the distant Rangsit
campus, despite protests about the loss of the
activist spirit of this political crucible.

Wat Mahathat

3/5 Thanon Maharat (0 2222 6011). Tha Chang.
Open 7am-6pm daily. **Map** p248 B3.

Less handsome than its neighbours, this large
monastery is nonetheless important. All Thai capitals have ritually required a royal temple of a holy
relic (*maha that*), though the public cannot see the
interior of this one. It's also the first of Thailand's
two Buddhist universities, founded in the 18th century. Later, Rama V donated a library. This feels
more like a working temple than many Rattanakosin
wats and its International Buddhist Meditation
Centre runs English-language meditation classes,
Dhamma talks and retreats. From Sanam Luang,
you enter through the gates of the imposing
Thawornwatthu Building, an East-meets-West
architectural fusion designed by Prince Naris as a
royal funerary hall.

Wat Pho & around

Bangkok's oldest and largest temple, **Wat Pho**
(*see p66*), spreads out behind the Grand Palace.
To its east stand ministries, **Saranrom Park**

(*see p66*), **Wat Ratchapradit** (*see p67*) and,
across Khlong Lord, the marvellous **Wat
Ratchabophit** (*see p67*). Flanking the western
side, Tha Tien has ferries to Wat Arun and
offers a rare glimpse of early Bangkok market
life. Dandied up with pilasters, pediments and
stucco akin to Tha Chang's, its shophouses still
function authentically. Aromas emanate from
herbal apothecaries, dried fish stalls, cafés
and warehouses. Shockingly, this historic
neighbourhood is under threat from zealous
planners. From 9pm until 11pm daily, Thanon
Maharat becomes the city's largest wholesale
market for Thai *khanom* (sweets). At
Rattanakosin's southern tip, the future
National Discovery Museum (*see below*)
and the 1914 Phra Ratchawong police station
face across the Charoenrat 31 Bridge over
Khlong Lord to **Pak Khlong Talad** flower
market (*see p140*).

National Discovery Museum

*Former Commerce Ministry, behind Ratchawong
Police Station, Thanon Sanam Chai (0 2357
3999). Tha Ratchinee.* **Open** call for details.
Map p248 B5.

A B3.7-billion Siamese 'Smithsonian' was conceived
by Thaksin to occupy former ministries down Sanam
Luang's east side to educate Thais, demonstrate
Thailand's modernity and bolster Rattanakosin's
status as a museum centre. The Museum of Thai
History will open by 2008 at the old Commerce
Ministry, with an emphasis on interactive exhibits.
As this guide went to press, however, the Museum
of Natural History of SE Asia, the Museum of History
of the People and the Land of SE Asia, and the
Museum of Science and Technology were facing both
political and physical uncertainties.

A report revealed the structural unsuitability of
one planned venue, the 1885 classical edifice of the
Defence Ministry. Since the dictatorship era, the 40

Sightseeing

Democracy Monument. *See p68.*

historic cannons at the Ministry (all honorifically named) have been on public display, their barrels notoriously pointing at the Grand Palace until reversed in 2004. Uneasy facing the barrels of the guns, the generals then turned them sideways towards the City Pillar and Wat Pho, in other words facing civilians and monks. The neutral solution of moving them to the new defence HQ seems likely.

Saranrom Park

Thanon Charoen Krung, at Thanon Rachini (0 2221 0195). Tha Tien. **Open** 5am-9pm daily. **Map** p248 B4.

This picturesque former garden of Saranrom Palace has been public since the 1960s and, like all Thai parks, is liveliest around dawn and dusk. Expect loud music as mass aerobics classes step to the beat and joggers thud by the ponds, cherub fountain, Chinese pagoda (at the rear) and central memorial from King Rama V to his wife Queen Sunanda (who drowned in a boating accident in 1880). It hosts an increasing number of cultural events.

Wat Pho

2 Thanon Sanam Chai (0 2226 0335). Tha Tien. **Open** 8am-6pm daily. **Admission** B50. **No credit cards**. **Map** p248 B4.

Formally called Wat Phra Chetuphon, this mellow compound rewards wandering around, despite some touristy aspects. Its popular name derives from the 16th-century Wat Photharam, which was rebuilt as part of Rama I's grand Rattanakosin scheme. In one of several restorations, Rama III added its monumental Reclining Buddha in 1832. Rama III also turned Wat Pho into Thailand's 'first university', ordering that the walls be inscribed with lessons in astrology, history and literature. It remains a core repository of traditional medicine, meditation and traditional massage – the perfect resting spot for weary sightseers.

Made from brick and gilded plaster, the Reclining Buddha is an awesome 46m (151ft) long and 15m (49ft) high. With pillars of the *vihaan* built around it obscuring a full view, the head and feet capture the photographer's focus. A picture of serenity, this recumbent position illustrates the Buddha passing into nirvana. Visitors linger over its large, flat-footed soles, where mother-of-pearl inlay (an early Rattanakosin speciality) depicts 108 auspicious signs. The mystical number 108 recurs in the quantity of bowls spanning the chapel wall, with a coin dropped in each bringing luck and longevity.

Wat Pho is also a refuge for antique Buddha images rescued by Rama I's brother from Ayutthaya and Sukhothai, with a major Ayutthayan image in the *bot*. (The ashes of Rama I were interred in its pedestal base by Rama IV.) Protecting the inner sanctuary are large pairs of stone guards with Western features. Wat Pho houses a staggering 99 *chedi* (nine is another lucky number to Thais), the main four being the colour-themed Phra Maha Chedi, signifying the first four Chakri reigns. In Rattanakosin style, they resemble a square bell, with

Flashpacker meets indie

Banglamphu has two separate scenes – foreign and Thai – but they overlap more than you'd think. Until the late 1990s the Thai press referred to Bangkok's backpacker central, **Thanon Khao San** (see p71), as a slum. Meanwhile, *farang banglamphu* (a variant of *farang kii nok* – 'birdshit foreigner') became shorthand for the cliché of the decadent, hygienically challenged travellers who crashed here, demanding discounts then splurging the savings on Beer Chang. Even before the book and film *The Beach* made Khao San a pop icon, the TAT promoted the road as a sight, and tourists duly flock here to snap its dreadlocked, batik-trousered habitués.

But with the 'flashpacker' phenomenon of travellers morphing from professional hippies to hip professionals, the area has gentrified. It started with the rebuilding of Buddy Lodge as a boutique hotel (see p40). Then coffeeshops blaring pirate VDOs of Hollywood movies turned into designer bars. The monthly magazine for travellers, *Untamed Travel* (formerly *Farang*), both records and symbolises the upgrade, and has since been joined by free mags like the *Khaosaner*. Eventually the authorities saw the potential and initiated the country's first attempt at permanent pedestrianisation. Now Khao San has some of Bangkok's priciest real estate.

It used to be a semi-scary adventure for moneyed young Thais to visit here, but once that exotic frisson became hip, a parallel Thai nightlife culture sprang up. Curiously, the Thai side of Banglamphu mirrors the flashpacker ethic. The frisson of entering a foreign space appealed to educated, open-minded, party-oriented Thais, particularly those who identify as indie.

The Bangkok indie scene is like the Bauhaus, the 1960s sexual revolution, psychedelia, punk, postmodernism, the internet and mass consumerism all happening at once, with a strong dose of Japanese 'cute' thrown into the mix. Raised under democracy, open to outside influences and often foreign-educated, these *dek naew* (trend kids) seek stimulation and self-discovery in underground music, avant-garde movies, art installations, extreme sports, provocative art plays and radical fashion.

Originating with fans of independent British music labels, the indie movement has diversified to encompass fans (and makers) of handmade books, short films, diary-like art work, lomography, alt rock, modern dance and, yes, independent travel – something group-oriented Thais have generally shunned in the past. Though locals and foreigners occupy different scenes within Banglamphu – the Thais gather mainly at neighbouring Phra Arthit and the Fat Festival (see p158) – their mutual interest in the 'other' cross-fertilises both cultures and keeps the neighbourhood vibrant.

indented corners and floral ceramic cladding. Two hold the remains of Ramas II and III, while another enables slim sightseers to climb inside and enjoy a unique viewpoint. The *kuti* (monks' quarters) lie south of Thanon Chetuphon, where the main entrance is less tout-ridden than the gate by the Reclining Buddha. **Photo** *p63*.

Wat Ratchabophit
2 Thanon Fuang Nakhon (0 2221 1888). **Open** *Temple* 5am-8pm daily. *Bot* 9-9.30am, 5.30-6pm daily; 8.45am-3.30pm religious hols. **Map** p248 B4.
With a fruit market at the side and schoolchildren playing in its grounds, this seldom-visited but fabulously ornate temple is most lively in late afternoon. Begun in 1869, its structure encloses the main *chedi* with a unique circular cloister encased in pastel Chinese porcelain, from which other buildings protrude. The small inner chapel feels European thanks to its Gothic columns, with mother-of-pearl doors. The doors bear toy-like carvings of soldiers. The *wat* also has a cemetery for Rama V's family. **Photo** *p64*.

Wat Ratchapradit
2 Thanon Saran Rom (0 2223 8215). **Open** *Temple* 9.30am-6pm daily. *Bot* 9.30-10am, 5.30pm-6pm daily; 9am-6pm religious hols. **Map** p248 B4.
Less grandiose than its neighbours, this pretty little grey marble temple has an inviting, contemplative atmosphere. Another amalgam of East and West, it was begun in 1864 on what was then a coffee plantation bought for the Thammayut Nikai sect by Rama IV (who is depicted observing a lunar eclipse in the murals focusing on Thai festivals). His ashes are contained under a replica of the Phra Buddha Sihing in a *vihaan* flanked by two *prang*.

Ratchadamnoen Klang

Once the city limit, this fascinating area was formally planned around **Thanon Ratchadamnoen Klang**, the 'royal passage' linking the Grand Palace and King Rama V's residences at Dusit Park. Lit by lamps in the shape of mythical *kinnaree/kinnon* (half-bird, half-woman/man), this broad, tree-lined middle (*klang*) section has become a traffic artery flanked by identical rows of sleek buildings designed by Jitsen Aphaiwong under the Phibunsongkhram regime in 1939. Plans to upgrade these rather dowdy terraces into a commercial showcase are in hiatus. Elaborate decorations bathe the road in fairylights for royal birthdays.

The avenue features two political landmarks: the **14 October Monument** (*see p69*) at the corner of Thanon Tanao, and the **Democracy Monument** (see *below*). The latter's ringed by **Café Democ** dance bar (*see p130*), **Rim Khob Fah** specialist Bangkok bookshop (*see p144*) and a branch of McDonald's that won an award for architectural sensitivity.

To the south, a pleasantly walkable network of streets (*see p58* **Community values**) surrounds the City Hall and the **Sao Ching Cha** (Giant Swing) of **Wat Suthat** (*see p70*), one of the country's six principal temples. East of the *wat* is the Brahmin temple of **Devasathan** and **Rommaninat Park** (for both, *see p69*). Another smaller Vishnu shrine stands west of Wat Suthat.

A cluster of sights rings Phanfa Bridge, which crosses Khlong Ong Ang at the point where Ratchadamnoen bends north towards Dusit. A park affords a view of **Wat Ratchanadda** and its one-of-a-kind **Loha Prasat** (for both, *see p69*). Beside it, another park may be created behind a remnant of the city wall at **Mahakan Fort**. It seems the canalside community here will, after a long fight, now be accommodated in the landscaping, not evicted. The fort's cannons were disarmed in 2002, amid concern they might be fired in a terrorist plot. Out of 14 original watchtowers, the only other survivor is Phra Sumen Fort. Continuing anti-clockwise are **King Prajadhipok Museum** (*see p69*) and the **Queen's Gallery** (*see p69*). Looming over the scene beyond Mahakan Fort, the peaceful **Golden Mount** of **Wat Saket** (for both, *see p70*) offers a fine panorama.

Democracy Monument

Thanon Ratchadamnoen Klang. **Map** p248 C3.
Designed by Italian sculptor Corrado Feroci (founder of Silpakorn University; *see p64*), this icon to the 1932 end of absolutism pointedly sits in a traffic circle interrupting the royal processional avenue.

Taking liberties

Achieving Thai democracy has been a tortuous path, one littered with coups, crackdowns and umpteen constitutions along the way. Memorialising the struggle has proved just as fraught. Textbooks and histories allude to massacres as 'incidents', although monuments do at least now mark the martyrs.

Inlaid in Royal Plaza, east of the King Rama V statue, the small brass People's Party Plaque reads: 'At this spot, the People's Party has introduced a constitution for the advancement of the nation at dawn on June 24, BE 2475 (1932).' The end of absolute monarchy is a delicate matter finessed by official phraseology, as related in the King Prajadhipok Museum (*see p69*).

The museum's corner location is pivotal. It looks north up Thanon Ratchadamnoen Nok to Royal Plaza's plaque, Ananta Samakhom Throne Hall, where the first assembly convened, and behind it Parliament House. And it faces west down Thanon Ratchadamnoen Klang towards sites of anti-authoritarian resistance.

Marking the end of absolutism, the Democracy Monument (*see below*) provides

the default rallying point, most recently against the 2006 coup regime. It was here that anti-dictatorship crowds were mown down by the military on 14 October 1973.

It took until 2002 for the state to allow a 14 October Monument, and it's even more reticent to recall those murdered by troops and paramilitaries when the generals retook power on 6 October 1976, branding the demonstrators communists. So Thammasat University, where many of the student protestors died, unveiled a 6 October Monument. Images of the fallen scream in marble inside the gate on Thanon Deuan Tula (October Road). To remember the middle-class ralliers shot at the Democracy Monument in 'Black May' 1992, a memorial foundation stone has been laid nearer Sanam Luang, where the demonstrators had razed a government building.

The struggles have entered popular culture, with *pleng puer cheewit* ('songs for life'), preserving the principles through music. However, the 2006 coup saw so-called 'October People' divided between those supporting Thaksin's liberal side and those despising his rights violations.

The date infuses the design. Around a sculpted constitution upon a three-metre (ten-foot) tall tray (June was then the third Thai month) array 75 cannons (for year 2475BE) and four vertical wings (24 metres high for June 24) symbolising soldiers, police, officials and civilians. Instead of royal or Buddhist imagery, bas-reliefs depict armed revolution, the People's Party and labourers, all in the muscular, 'heroic worker' style typical of mid 20th-century monuments worldwide. **Photo** *p65*.

Devasathan & the Giant Swing

268 Thanon Dinso (0 2222 6951). **Open** *Chapel* 10am-4pm Thur, Sun. *Swing* 24hrs daily. **Map** p248 C3.

Standing in City Hall square, the Giant Swing (Sao Ching Cha) was originally built in 1784 as part of the adjacent Devasathan, a Brahmin compound of shrines to Shiva, Ganesha and Vishnu. The Bramin priests based here still officiate at royal and other ceremonies (although no longer the Brahmin New Year rite conducted at the swing). Symbolising an exploit of the god Shiva, four brave men swung from this lofty red structure to grab pouches of coins with their mouths. Due to fatal casualties the ritual was banned in the 1930s. The poles had been erected in 1919 by the Louis T Leonowens Company in honour of their namesake, the son of Anna Leonowens (the contentious governess of *The King and I*). In 2006 the rickety timbers were replaced by new ones (the search to find teak trees big enough took months); the old ones will go to a museum.

14 October Monument

14/16 Thanon Ratchadamnoen Klang, at Thanon Tanao (0 2622 1013-5/www.14tula.com). **Map** p248 C3.

A granite spire bears the names of 73 victims killed by the military during the 1973 overthrow of the dictatorship, though an accurate toll still awaits investigation. The surrounding galleries will become a museum to inform later generations. Survivors and relatives maintaining the site are keen to talk about their experiences. It also hosts other rights protests.

King Prajadhipok Museum

2 Thanon Lanluang (0 2280 3413-4). Tha Saphan Phan Fah. **Open** 9am-4pm Tue-Sun. **Admission** *Thais* B20; free Sat, Sun, hols. *Foreigners* B40. **No credit cards. Map** p248 C3.

Relocated from Parliament, memorabilia pertaining to King Rama VII's reign (1925-35) now enjoys state-of-the-art audio-visual displays at the graceful former Public Works Building. Coverage of his youth, Eton schooling, marriage to Queen Rambai Barni, unanticipated crowning, constitutional challenges, abdication and last years in England provide insights into early 20th-century Siamese society. Text panels, also in English, handle the delicate issue of democracy replacing absolutism with aplomb.

Queen's Gallery

101 Thanon Ratchadamnoen Klang (0 2281 5360-1/www.queengallery.org). Tha Saphan Phan

Wat Suthat. *See p70.*

Fah. **Open** 10am-7pm Mon, Tue, Thur-Sun. **Admission** B20; free concessions. **No credit cards. Map** p248 C3.

Dedicated to Queen Sirikit, this major multi-floor space offers world-class exhibitions by leading Thai and foreign artists. Selections by top-line alumni from owner Bangkok Bank's prestigious art prize are often on show. The café's gift shop has a rare stock of monographs and retrospective tomes, although catalogues soon sell out.

Rommaninat Park & Corrections Museum

Thanon Maha Chai (0 2226 1704). **Open** *Park* 5am-9pm daily. *Museum* 9am-4pm Mon-Fri. **Admission** free. **No credit cards. Map** p248 C4.

In former prison buildings on the site of this park a small penal museum displays instruments of punishment. Amid the gardens' ponds, fountains and a large bronze of a conch shell, locals exercise in the cool hours, including at an alfresco gym.

Wat Ratchanadda & Loha Prasat

2 Maha Chai Road (0 2224 8807). Tha Saphan Phan Fah. **Open** *Temple* 9am-5pm daily. *Bot* 8-9am, 4-5pm daily; 8.30-10am religious days. **Map** p248 C3.

The only version of this style of spiritual architecture still standing, the step-pyramidal Loha Prasat ('Metal Palace') is modelled on a Sri Lankan metal temple from the third century BC, which was in turn based on an Indian original of 2,500 years ago. Built

Sightseeing

by Rama III in 1846, it has 37 spires, each symbolising the virtues needed to attain enlightenment. On every level a labyrinth of passages leads to meditation cells (closed to visitors), with a spiral staircase to rooftop views. In order to reveal the Prasat, the art deco Chalerm Thai Theatre was controversially demolished in the early 1990s to create a park containing a statue of Rama III and the Mahachesdabodin Royal Pavilion for official receptions. Behind the *wat*, a market sells amulets.

Wat Saket & Golden Mount

344 Chakkraphatdiphong (0 2223 4561). Tha Saphan Phan Fah. **Open** *Temple* 8am-9pm daily. *Golden Mount* 7.30am-5.30pm daily. **Admission** *Temple* free. *Golden Mount* free Thais; B10 foreigners. **No credit cards. Map** p248 C3/D3.
Assembled from canal diggings, the Golden Mount (Phu Khao Thong) was intended by Rama III to be clad as a giant *chedi*. Proving unstable, the rubble was instead reinforced with trees and plants to prevent erosion. Shrines dot the two spiral paths to the summit, where a gilded *chedi* contains Buddha relics from India and Nepal. Its breezy, bell-chiming concrete terrace offers a wonderful 360° panorama of both old and modern Bangkok. Phu Khao Thong belongs to Wat Saket, which spreads eastward with handsome *kuti* (monks' quarters), fine murals and a peaceful atmosphere. This *wat* was where the bodies of people who died from epidemics were once brought for cremation. **Photo** *p66.*

Life's a beach on **Khao San**. See p71.

Wat Suthat

146 Thanon Bamrung Muang (0 2224 9845/ www.watsuthat.org). **Open** 8.30am-9pm daily. **Admission** B20. **No credit cards. Map** p248 C4.
Looming behind the Giant Swing, Bangkok's tallest *vihaan* houses the awe-inducing 8m (26ft) Phra Sri Sakyamuni Buddha. One of the largest surviving bronzes from Sukhothai, it was brought south by boat, and its base contains the ashes of King Rama VIII. Begun by Rama I in 1807, the temple took three reigns to complete, though its mesmerising murals are now decaying (despite restoration). Rama II himself started the carving of its elaborate teak doors. Numerous Chinese stone statues (found in several Rattanakosin temples) served as both tributes to the king and as valuable ballast for Chinese junks collecting rice. **Photo** *p69.*

Banglamphu

The old neighbourhood around **Thanon Khao San** may be famous worldwide as a backpacker ghetto (*see p71*), but Banglamphu has clung to its roots. Descendants of palace dancers and artisans still live here and **Banglamphu Market** (*see p140*) remains a labyrinthine local bazaar. Behind **Wat Chana Songkhram** (*see p71*), **Thanon Phra Arthit** midwifed the new indie generation through arty venues and cultural events at the riverside **Santichaiprakarn Park** (*see below*). Between the park and the Bangkok Tourist Bureau under Phra Pinklao Bridge, a walkway on stilts in the river offers front views of Phra Arthit's mansions and accesses the Expressboat landing where Old Phra Arthit Pier is a retro spot to take refreshment.
    The park contains **Phra Sumen Fort**, part of the old city wall that ran between Thanon Phra Sumen and Khlong Banglamphu until it was demolished by King Rama V. Another remnant stands opposite **Wat Bowoniwet** (*see p71*), while the stretch at Mahakan Fort faces the **Queen's Gallery** (*see p69*) at Saphan Phanfah. North of Khlong Banglamphu, which was dug two centuries ago by Lao POWs, you'll find **Wat Tri Thosathep** (*see p71*) and Thanon Samsen, which leads to Dusit and the elevated approach above Thanon Visut Kasat to the **Rama VIII Bridge**.
    A slog to reach by road, Banglamphu is easily accessed by river Expressboat to Tha Phra Arthit or by canal boat to Tha Saphan Phan Fah.

Santichaiprakarn Park & Phra Arthit

Thanon Phra Arthit. Tha Phra Arthit. **Map** p248 B3.
Unusually, this multi-tiered riverside park caters for the blind with Braille-marked paths and maps of attractions, such as the district's last *lamphu* trees,

after which Banglamphu is named, and the octagonal Phra Sumen Fort, one of only two city wall watchtowers to survive. Late afternoon on weekends, especially Sunday, the park brims with non-mainstream activity, from fire juggling and breakdancing to jams of classical *phiphat* music.

The park and Phra Arthit community's bohemian bar-restaurants play HQ to the indie generation, an influential subculture of contrarian youth in a deeply conformist society. They hawk self-made books, postcards, music and artwork here, especially at the Indy Festival (*see p159*) and Bangkok Theatre Festival (*see p158*). The park also hosts official events like Loy Krathong (*see p158*).

Several mansions line Thanon Phra Arthit. The classical Baan Chao Phraya faces art nouveauish Baan Phra Arthit, which housed the Goethe Institut (1962-86), then the publishers Manager Group and its swish Coffee & More café. Others are visible only from the river walkway between the park and the Bangkok Tourist Bureau. From the south end, these include the UNICEF offices in a former home of the queen consort to Rama IV; a home of the late prime minister, novelist and cultural pundit, Kukrit Pramoj; and the UN-FAO building at Baan Maliwan, where Pridi Bhanomyong lived as regent for Rama VIII and also directed the anti-fascist wartime Seri Thai Movement.

Thanon Khao San

www.khaosanroad.com. Tha Phra Arthit.
Map p248 B3.
The opening scene of Alex Garland's 1997 novel *The Beach* unravels in a Khao San guesthouse, immortalising in literature the world's most infamous haunt for budget travellers. Now Khao San ('street of uncooked rice') has gentrified due to social changes among both Thais and travellers (*see p67* **Flashpacker meets indie**). Flophouses are being gentrified into chainstores, trendy bar-restaurants and boutique hotels. The first guesthouses opened in 1982 to soak up the human flotsam spilling over from the city's bicentennial celebrations. Glimpses of the road's past can still be seen in the wooden shophouses just past Khao San Center, and in the restored mansions that now house the Sidewalk Café and the Sunset Street branch of Starbucks.

For many young travellers the road is just one long bucket shop, where they can purchase bus and ferry tickets to the islands, or plane tickets to Indochina, not to mention fake student ID cards. It also plays bargain basement for discounted clothes, beachwear and sandals – and services to 'buy anything'. The many second-hand bookshops have the best selection of contemporary fiction in Thailand. Meanwhile, costumed Akha tribesfolk pester everyone to buy silverware.

Khao San remains a party madhouse, though 'packers now venture beyond Gulliver's Traveller's Tavern to the trendy new bars (*see p130*). Young Thais prefer Suzie Pub (*see p130*), or bars in quieter Thanon Rambuttri. **Photo** *p70*.

Wat Bowoniwet's intricate designs.

Wat Bowoniwet

248 Thanon Phra Sumen (0 2281 6411). **Open** *Temple* 8.30am-5pm daily. *Bot* 8.30am-5pm Sat, Sun, religious hols. **Map** p248 C3.
Home to both the city's second Buddhist university and the Supreme Patriarch (leader) of Thai Buddhism, this temple is a major focus on Buddhist holidays. Founded in 1826, it melds Thai and Chinese designs, with gilded *naga* balustrades and windows adorning the main chapel. Kings Rama IV and Rama IX were both ordained here, the former becoming its abbot before his reign.

Wat Chana Songkhram

77 Thanon Chakrabong (0 2280 4415). Tha Phra Arthit. **Open** 6am-6pm daily. **Map** p248 B3.
Originally built in Mon style – because Rama I got many Burmese to lay the groundwork for the fledgling city – this great monastery was renovated and renamed the 'winning the war temple' after the sovereign's brother's victory against the Burmese. Most of the 300 monks here study Pali (the ancient Sanskrit derivative in which the Buddhist scriptures were first written down) at the temple school.

Wat Tri Thosathep

Thanon Prachatipathai (0 2282 4453). **Open** 6am-9pm daily. *Murals* 9am-4pm Mon-Sat. **Map** p248 C3.
At this relatively recent temple, national artist Chakraphan Posyakrit is due to finish in 2007 one of the most ambitious murals of our times.

Sightseeing

honburi, River & Canals

See the 'Venice of the East' before it sinks beneath rising development.

Maps p248 & p250

When the Mae Nam Chao Phraya ('River of Kings') overflowed in 2006 it only did what comes naturally. Draining a basin the size of Britain into a narrow funnel through Bangkok, the Chao Phraya instinctively wants to flood. Though visitors typically find the waterways their most rewarding city experience, the 'Venice of the East' label barely still applies. Thais have forgone their ancient aquatic culture of adaptation for attempted containment. The pockets of *khlongs* (canals) and teak stilt houses continue to be destroyed. Meanwhile, roads, cement walls and developments like the new Suvarnabhumi Airport (built on a drainage swamp) prevent the absorption of rains and run-off from the north. As in the 1995 inundation, outlying areas like Nonthaburi were drowned to spare Bangkok. Currently 30 kilometres (18 miles) to the south, the sea once lapped north of Bangkok, with fertile, flood-borne silt expanding the delta five metres (16 feet) a year. Ominously, that coast is eroding – and much of Bangkok is sinking.

The force of tide and current is apparent watching cross-river *kham fahk* ferries wallowing through the ochre eddies, black *khlong* outflows and carpets of water hyacinths (a Brazilian plague that clogs waterways, but can be woven into furniture). Other vessels range from commuter expressboats, pleasure cruisers and longtails, to canoe vendors, floating banks and dainty tugs pulling beetle-shaped barges. Vertical embankments make waves choppier for small craft, which still remain in more intact canal areas southwest of Bangkok.

Mae Nam literally translates as 'mother of waters' and traditional Thai culture centres on

water's maternal power and benevolence, whether for fish or *padi* (rice fields), transport or trade, ritual or play. Mythically, it's home to *naga* – wrathful serpents seen in temple decor, tattoos and other iconography. *Kwetiao reua* (boat noodles) still get served from boat-shaped stalls today and events like Loy Krathong and Royal Barge processions recall the riverine past. Since the city was originally built to face the water, boats (*see p74* **Quays to the city**) aren't only quicker, but reveal beautiful frontages that neglect has helped preserve, though condominium builders have other plans.

FANG THON

Despite its size and significance as the previous capital, *fang thon* ('Thonburi side') gets dismissed as the 'other' bank of the river. Many sights lie between **Bangkok Noi** and **Khlong San**, but even Thonburi's prime tourist fetcher, **Wat Arun**, is usually visited on Bangkok tours. Yet the canals of Thonburi, Bang Khunthien, Bang Kruay and Nonthaburi still harbour a residual canal life. Looping through Khlong Om and Khlong Bangkok Noi by longtail or tour boat, you pass wooden stilt house, served by ancient *wats*, pierside stores and boat vendors selling to residents lounging on their flower-decked verandas. At dawn monks paddle for alms through the mist; come late afternoon families bathe and boys dive-bomb off bridges. Now new highways scar this idyll, opening it to inappropriate development.

Around Khlong San

Facing the Bangrak finance hub, Khlong San has spawned three top hotels. Best reached by ferry, the **Marriott Bangkok Resort** (*see p40*) is like staying upcountry, while the equally luxurious Peninsula (*see p41*) soars beside the **Oriental Spa**. Abandoned for a decade, the white saucer-topped edifice nearby has opened as the **Millennium Hilton** (*see p41*). It faces River City and flanks the lively, commuter-jammed Khlong San Market and **Yok Yor** (*see p56*), one of many riverside restaurants that run dinner cruises.

The SkyTrain will soon extend to Thailand's main southbound artery, Phetkasem Highway, which heads for Malaysia from just east of the equestrian statue of **King Taksin the Great** at the Wong Wien Yai intersection. The statue – brandishing a sword and wearing a stetson-esque hat – directs a vehicular armada through Thonburi's daunting gridlock. From adjacent **Wong Wien Yai station** a railway heads south-west to Mahachai seafood market, where Yaowarat restaurants buy their catch.

A cluster of low-key sights near the mouth of **Khlong Bangkok Yai** makes for a fetching three-hour walking tour – for which you can use signs from the Bangkok Tourist Bureau (*see p236*). Tours down Khlong Bangkok Yai often branch off south-west at Wat Paknam where *khlong* lifestyles may still be glimpsed along **Khlong Daokhanong, Khlong Bangkhuntien** and **Khlong Lart.** Sadly, **Wat Sai Floating Market** is a concrete and souvenir shadow of its past. The Ayutthayan-era **Wat Sai** (Thanon Thavorn-wattana, 0 2415 7173, open 6am-5pm daily, bot 8.30am-5pm daily, free) is noted for its circular belfry and *kanok* (flame) lacquer work on the Tamnak Thong monks' quarters.

Around Khlong Bangkok Yai

Seen on the TAT logo and B10 coin, the five-towered **Wat Arun** is an icon of Bangkok. King Taksin appended the temple to his new palace, **Wang Derm** (inside the Royal Thai Navy headquarters). Walking distance north, **Wat Rakhang** (Soi Wat Rakhang; open daily 6am-6pm) was restored by King Taksin and is famed for its red *hor trai*, comprising three teak scripture halls where Rama I stayed before his reign (his ashes are interred here). King Taksin replaced the melodious *rakhang* (bell) that he took to Wat Phra Kaew with the five bells that now hang in the belfry beside a perfectly proportioned *prang*.

Wat Rakhang can be combined with a weekend show at **Patravadi Theatre** (*see p198*) and/or the riverfront **Supatra River House restaurant** (*see p199*); they're run by daughters of the Expressboat founder. From there, an alley leads through **Prannok Market** to **Siriraj Hospital**, the world's fourth largest, which treats royalty and houses several museums (see below). Skirting its historic buildings and **Wat Amarin Market** you reach **Bangkok Noi train station**, a Western-style, Rama V-era brick building. It was used by the Japanese in World War II, hence the heavy Allied bombing of Bangkok Noi. Now a tourist centre, the station runs some Nakhon Pathom and Kanchanaburi services.

Siriraj Hospital Museums

Thanon Phrannok (0 2419 7000 ext 6363).
Tha Siriraj. **Open** Museums 9am-4pm Mon-Sat.
Admission B20 Thais; B40 foreigners; free students in uniform. **Map** p248 A3.
The six small museums here, dowdily displayed and aimed more at students, aren't for the squeamish, though some of their prize exhibits were briefly

Idyllic **Koh Kred**.
See p77.

Quays to the city

Bangkok and Thonburi were originally built to face the Chao Phraya River, the banks of which burgeon with evocative sights, whether you're aboard a longtail boat taxi, tour vessel (for both, *see p56*) or the 45-minute Expressboat route to Nonthaburi (*see p75*; piers noted below), some of which have English commentary. For details of sights mentioned, see the **Sightseeing** sections noted.

Pak Nam to Saphan Taksin

Piers *S3-S1 & Central; South and Thonburi.*
Pak Nam (the river mouth) is best seen from the hill in **Ancient City** (*see p100*). The furthest south that boat tours go is **Rama IX Bridge**, the suspension span beside the **Thai Farmer's Bank**'s slope-topped tower. Visible downstream, the stunning **Teepangkorn Rassameechote Bridge**, named after a new-born prince in 2006, uniquely crosses the river twice; suspended spans of 702m and 162m pass 50m above a narrow meander to the ring road. But hired longtail boats can zip around the ships between the forest of trees at **Bang Kra Jao** and the forest of cranes at **Khlong Toey port**. Or you can view the harbour traffic from the teak decks of **Baan Klang Nam** seafood restaurant (3792/160

Rama III Soi 14, 0 2292 2037-8, open 11am-10.15pm daily).

Expressboats terminate at **Wat Ratchasinghkorn**, but it's classier to start the upstream journey from the **Marriott Bangkok Resort** (*see p40)*, between **Krung Thep Bridge** and the white portico and campanile of the **First Presbyterian Church**, opposite early *godowns* (warehouses). The Marriott's free teak shuttleboats and luxury converted barge Manohra pass a 19th-century **Protestant Cemetery**, replete with Gothic tombs, beside the **Menam Hotel**. On the western bank, the pointy **Tridhos Marina** condo was designed by Mom Tri Devakul. Thonburi's **Chao Phraya River Cultural Centre** faces the **Fisheries Organisation**'s market, the **Royal Thai Naval Dockyard** and the ship-shaped *chedi* of **Wat Yannawa**, served by the busy, convenient Central Pier under Saphan Taksin BTS station.

Oriental Hotel to River City

Piers *N1-N3. Bangrak and Thonburi.*
The **Shangri-La** hotel (*see p45*) stands on the east bank beside the classical edifices of **Assumption College, EAC** (Eastern Asiatic Company) and the **Oriental hotel** (*see p45*) – which runs the **Oriental Spa** (*see p179*) and

Sala Rim Nam restaurant (*see p199*) on the western bank beside the soaring tower of the **Peninsula** hotel (*see p41*). Historic edifices continue on the east side with the restored **French Embassy** and mouldering Italianate **Customs House**, soon to be an Aman Resort hotel; and Wat Muang Khae, dwarfed by the green-glass slab of the **Communications Authority Tower**. Beyond the leaf-shaded **Portuguese Embassy** more concrete 'improvement' blights the mouth of Khlong Phadung Krung Kasem, between the overscaled **Royal Orchid Sheraton Hotel** and **River City** antiques mall (*see p142*), a major ferry terminus. The saucer-topped tower opposite has finally opened as the Millennium Hilton hotel.

River City to Bangkok Noi
Piers N4-N11; Chinatown, Phra Nakorn and Thonburi.
The dainty **Holy Rosary Church**, the classical **Siam Commercial Bank** (Thailand's first bank building) and an ancient Chinese temple precede a shambles of encroach-ment from Chinatown. So face west to admire the mural-rich temples **Wat Thong Noppakhun** and **Wat Thong Thammachat**. **Phra Pokklao Bridge** forms a double span with the river's first crossing, the obelisked **Rama I Memorial Bridge** (built in 1932). **Pak Khlong Market**'s emptied *godowns* are named after the mouth of Khlong Lord, which beyond which, on Rattanakosin Island, the pert classical edifice of **Ratchinee Girls School** was rebuilt after a recent fire. Beside it the lantern-towered **Wang Chakrabongse** palace is where Prince Chakrabongse's descendant now publishes 'River Books' in a compound that also houses **Chakrabongse Villas** hotel (*see p39*).

South of Thonburi's Khlong Bangkok Yai, **Santa Cruz Church** and its filigree jetty are flanked by the triple *chedis* of **Wat Prayoonwong** and outsized **Wat Kalayanimit**. The canal's north-bank fortress, **Vichai Prasit**, defends King Taksin's palace, **Wang Derm**, and **Wat Arun**'s crockery-covered *prang*.

To the east, **Wat Pho**'s spires peek above gabled shophouses at **Tha Tien**, where *wai roon* (trendies) frequent **Boh** bar (*see p130*) on the pier, after sunset. To enable clearer views of the **Grand Palace**, landscaping of an esplanade has begun, but many oppose its

plans to extend it by demolishing much of the ancient riverside communities, as well as parts of **Thammasat University** and the **National Theatre** (*see p197*), which rim the river towards **Phra Pinklao Bridge**.

On the Thonburi side, VIPs view royal barge processions from the Royal Navy's new pavilions. To its north, you pass **Wat Rakhang**, Patravadi Theatre's new riverside space (*see p198*), **Supatra River House** restaurant (*see p199*), **Prannok Market** and **Siriraj Hospital** before reaching **Bangkok Noi railway station** at the mouth of Khlong Bangkok Noi.

Pinklao Bridge to Nonthaburi
Piers N12-N30; Thonburi, Dusit and Outer North.
Under the Bangkok foot of Phra Pinklao Bridge, a stilted walkway from the **Bangkok Tourist Bureau HQ** passes mansions on **Thanon Phra Arthit** on its way to **Santichaiprakarn Park**'s lamphu trees and **Phra Sumane Fort**. The classical masterpiece across the river languishes unrestored as **Intara School**. North of Khlong Banglamphu lie numerous Dusit mansions, including the art nouveau **Wang Bangkhunprom**. Looming above, **Rama VIII Bridge** brandishes fussy gilded trimmings on a harp-like 2.1-kilometre long (1.3-mile) span suspended from one 300-metre (984-foot) high inverted-Y pillar standing in a park beside the **Bangyikhan Distillery** for Mekhong whisky.

On the Dusit bank, **Thewes Flower Market** flanks the mouth of Khlong Phadeung Krung Kasem, ahead of the **Royal Barge Dock**; just visible behind the dock is the childhood home of Queen Sirikit and **Kaloang Home Kitchen** seafood restaurant (*see p114*).

Beyond the green-shuttered royal pier Tha Vasukri, and **Wat Ratchathiwas**'s wooden *vihaan*, **St Francis Xavier Church** is the focus of a Vietnamese community. Most cruises turn back on themselves at the box-girder **Sang Hee (Krung Thon) Bridge**, the illuminated backdrop for **Khanab Nam** restaurant/boat, **River Bar Café** (*see p113*) and the **Royal River Hotel**.

Thereafter, amid traditional riverine communities you encounter the **Singha** and **Amarit** breweries, **Rama VI Bridge** (carrying the southern railway), the curious-looking **Wat Khien**, and **Rama V Bridge**, before disembarking at Nonthaburi terminus.

Sightseeing

stolen by a demented thief. The Si Ouey Forensic Medicine Museum (department of forensic medicine, 2nd floor, 0 2419 7000 ext 6547) contains skulls, pickled organs, stillborn babies, crime scene photos and the preserved body of murderer Si Ouey, the subject of a recent movie. The Congdon Anatomical Museum (anatomy department, 3rd floor, 0 2419 7035) displays human organs and bones from embryo to maturity, including Siamese twins (named after Thai-Chinese conjoined brothers Chang and Eng, born in 1811). Two floors down, the Sood Sangvichien Prehistoric Museum & Laboratory (0 2419 7029) looks at human and animal evolution.

The Ellis Pathological Museum (department of pathology, 2nd floor; 0 2411 2005) explains diseases, while the Parasitology Museum (parasitology department, 2nd floor, 0 2419 7000 ext 6488) preserves homelovin' hookworms, whipworms and tapeworms with the organs they've adopted. The Ouay Ketusingh Museum of History of Thai Medicine (department of pharmacology, 1st floor, 0 2411 5026) examines indigenous healing knowledge and the life cycle.

Wang Derm

Royal Thai Navy Headquarters, 2 Phra Ratcha Wang Derm, Thanon Arun Amarin (0 2475 4117/ f/www.wangdermpalace.com). **Open** 8.30am-4pm Mon-Fri by written appointment. **Admission** B60; B20 children. **No credit cards. Map** p248 A5.
Meaning 'original palace', King Taksin's compound of Chinese-influenced buildings orginally included Wat Arun, until Rama I reduced the palace grounds. Rama V gave the palace to the Thai navy with instructions to preserve the oldest buildings, which have won awards for their recent restoration, and display antique ceramics, paintings, old Thai currency and weaponry. A shrine to Taksin features a sword-wielding statue of the king in a century-old sala that fuses Thai and Western forms, while canons in Wichaiprasit Fort still guard Khlong Bangkok Yai. You must phone ahead, then fax/write two weeks before your visit enclosing your passport photocopy, and visit soberly dressed.

Wat Arun

34 Thanon Arun Amarin (0 2891 1149/0 2466 6752/www.watarun.org). Ferry from Tha Tien. **Open** 8am-6pm daily. **Admission** free Thais; B20 foreigners. **No credit cards. Map** p248 A5.
This landmark has been known as the 'Temple of Dawn' ever since Chaopraya Taksin landed by the then Wat Magog at sunrise in October 1767. Renamed Wat Jaeng when part of Taksin's palace, it became Wat Arunratchawararamat under Rama II, before being remodelled by Rama IV, who bestowed its present title, Wat Arunratchatharam Rajaworaramahavihara. The sundry Chinese-style structures pale before the iconic, 81m-high (266ft) Khmer-style *prang*, with four 'corncob' *prang* at the corners, all inlaid with polychromatic ceramic shards. Climbing the vertiginous *prang* is forbidden since a tourist fell to their death in 1998. Briefly home to the Emerald Buddha, Wat Arun features a

stunning statue pair of mythical *yaksa* (giants), ceramic gables on its *vihaan* and *bot*, and some 120 Buddha images. Instead of expensively visiting as part of a canal tour, go separately. It's just a B3 ferry ride from Tha Tien, where the pier becomes the studenty bar **Boh** (*see p130*) just as the *wat* is thrown into sunset silhouette.

Khlong Bangkok Noi

Khlong Bangkok Noi is the capital's most active canal. Now hemmed in by flood barriers, its wooden stilt houses have personal piers where residents hang out. Concrete walkways and humpback bridges allow for localised walks, but roads are scarce and boating is the norm here. Tours typically take in the **Royal Barge Museum**, **Wat Suwannaram** (for both, *see below*), **Bang Bu Village**, and fish feeding at **Wat Sisudaram** and **Taling Chan Floating Market**. The market (open 9am-4pm Sat & Sun) is mostly on land, but the food and souvenir vendors occupy semi-rural environs.

Royal Barge Museum

80/1 Rimkhlong Bangkok Noi, Thanon Arun Amarin (0 2424 0004). **Open** 9am-5pm daily. **Admission** B30; camera permit B100; video permit B200. **No credit cards. Map** p248 A2.
It's an unforgettable sight when dozens of slim, ornate boats carry the royal family from Vasukri Pier to Wat Arun, for a *kathin* ceremony; the most recent one marked King Bhumibol's diamond jubilee in 2006. You can see the craftsmanship of eight of the barges at dry berths in this canalside hangar. Bilingual displays of regalia, dioramas and barge lore add to the impact. Most impressive is the king's barge, Suphannahongse ('Golden Swan'), seen on the TAT logo. Carved from a single log and powered by 50 costumed, chanting oarsmen, the original of this 45.15m (148ft) long, 3.17m (10.5ft) wide vessel was destroyed at Ayutthaya. Rebuilt by Rama I and again by Rama V, its ageing woodwork is no longer risked much afloat. Second in importance is the 54-oar, Rama IV-era Anantanakaraj, its bow splayed with a seven-headed *naga*. The newest, Narai Song Suban, with Vishnu riding Garuda at its prow, was built for the king's golden jubilee in 1996. It's easiest to get to the museum by boat or canal tour, given the long trudge from the road via alleys with scant signposts.

Wat Suwannaram

33 Charan Sanit Wong Soi 32 (0 2433 8045). **Open** 8.30am-4.30 daily. **Admission** free.
Art students flock to the *wat's* Ayutthaya-era *bot* (ask a monk to open it) to sketch the Rama III-era murals by Thai artist Thongyu (primarily *jataka* tales of the Buddha's life). Chinese artist Kong Pae used slim brushes and shadows to accentuate motion. Look out for apocalyptic images of Buddha subduing Mara, and some racy erotic poses.

Kred ability

Imagine somewhere in Bangkok without cars – an idyllic green island dotted with temples, orchards and wooden cottages of villagers who maintain ancient crafts. Yes, it actually exists. Cut out of a river meander just north of Nonthaburi, **Koh Kred** has been settled by ethnic Mon since they populated the central plains over a millennia ago. Legend has it they can return to Burma when the tilting *chedi* of Wat Poramai finally collapses. This temple (aka **Wat Mon**) on the eastern side houses a small museum, and like another *wat* on the northern bank displays indicatively Mon banners shaped like millipedes. The lane between them serves the main settlement, though the path continues in a loop through plantations, taking two hours to stroll.

You can while away a half-day with a meal or a massage at converted waterside homes, and visits to low-tech pottery workshops. The potters throw and carve lidded jars of earthenware. They traditionally resemble a lotus bud, though newer designs can get mawkishly cute. Exemplars of the art gather dust in an endearingly haphazard museum.

The confident could take a B10 Laem Thong local boat from Nonthaburi to Pakkred and then cross by ferry to **Tha Pa Fai** pier on Koh Kred. Most brave the touts and take a longtail tour (around B300 a head for two hours) from Nonthaburi to another Kred pier. These conveniently take in a restaurant on stilts at the southwest end famed for intricate Thai *khanom* (sweets) topped with gold leaf, which make a tasty souvenir.

Nonthaburi

Suburbia extends 33 kilometres (20 miles) upriver to this province famous for its fruit, though flood damage and heedless building scar its semi-rustic charm. Fronting the sublime wooden fretwork of **Nonthaburi Provincial Office**, an esplanade (and impromptu skate park) links the expressboat terminal pier with **Rim Fang restaurant** (235/2 Thanon

Pracharat, 0 2525 1742, open noon-10pm daily). Most visitors take tours or hired longtail boats from the northern end of the pier to **Koh Kred** (*see p77* **Kred ability**) or make a two-hour loop back to Khlong Bangkok Noi via Khlong Om. This picturesque canal meets the river just north of **Wat Chaloem Prakiat**, a landscaped, Chinese-style temple dedicated by Rama III to his mother. Beside it is the culturally themed **Chaloem Kanchanaphisek Park**.

Walk 3 Old Thonburi

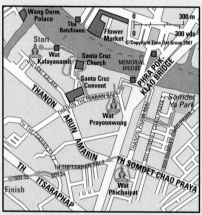

Winding through riverside alleys, this pleasant walk reveals a vibrant, 200-year-old Thonburi community; the **Bangkok Tourist Bureau** (*see p236*) also covers this route in a tour. Start at **Wat Kalayanamit**, near the mouth of Khlong Bangkok Yai. Founded in 1825 by a Chinese nobleman, the temple's huge *vihaan* boasts: Thailand's highest *chofa* (roof finial), biggest bell and largest indoor sitting Buddha (15 metres/49 feet high).

A new river walkway leads round via the Chinese shrine of **Kiang An Keng** to the maze of wooden houses in the Sino-Portuguese Kudee Jeen community around **Santa Cruz Church and Convent**, known as 'Wat Kudee Jeen'. Often rebuilt since King Taksin's time, the current pastel edifice topped by an octagonal dome dates from 1916. A ferry from Tha Rachini serves the church's pier.

A culinary legacy survives at **Khanom Farang Kudi Jeen**, a shophouse where pastries of apple and *jujube* are baked to the recipes of Portuguese mercenaries who

defended Ayutthaya from Burma. The powerful Persian-descended Bunnag clan, who helped administer Ayutthaya, built **Wat Prayurawongsawat** along Thanon Thetsaban Sai 1. Fenced in English cast iron, it features Bangkok's first Sri Lankan-style *chedi*, while across the road its verdant *Khao Mor* (artificial mountain) features Bunnag gravestones.

Turn left and curve round a garden under Memorial Bridge on Thanon Phaya Mai to Thanon Somdet Chaophraya. Take two lefts into Somdet Chaophraya Soi 3 to reach **Somdet Phra Srinagarinda Boromarajajonani Memorial Park**. The king's late mother, Somdet Ya, was born a commoner to goldsmiths and practised nursing. This memorial recreates her home on land donated by Daeng and Lek Nana, landlords of Sukhumvit's Soi Nana, in 1993. Amid mature trees, a museum documents Thonburi and royal family history (open 9am-4pm daily, admission B30), while a gallery holds exhibitions.

Cross Thanon Somdet Chaophraya and to your right is another Bunnag temple donated to Rama III, **Wat Pichayayatikaram Worawihan**, housing a Sukhothai-era Buddha image from Phitsanulok.

To extend the walk, cross thunderous Thanon Prachatipok into Thanon Thetsaban Sai 3, turn right then left into Itsaraphap Soi 24, then cross Thanon Itsaraphap into Soi 15 and **Baan Silpa Thai**, where the khon masks sold at Chatuchak Weekend Market have been made for two decades. The artisans may let you try crafting the gilded Ramayana characters (on sale for B1,000-B5,000; papier-mâché ones are B100). Nearby in **Baan Laos** (No 343, 0 2465 2880, open 10am-5pm daily by appointment) Jarin Klinbuppha now makes his *khlui* (bamboo flutes) in plastic.

Dusit

Palaces, parliament and urban planning grace this leafy monumental quarter.

Maps p248 & p249

During the 2006 coup, Dusit was the first district secured by tanks, as it houses the grand headquarters of monarchy, military and government, as well as major institutions and temples. Flanked by the river and the railway, it originated as a retreat of King Rama V, with greenery preserved in the grounds of palaces, a zoo and a horse-racing track. A lush break from Bangkok's congestion, Dusit was Siam's first attempt at a European-style urban planning grid and shows how Thai design meshed with the West. Its main boulevard, Thanon Ratchadamnoen is a processional avenue from the Grand Palace, with its outer stretch Thanon Ratchadmnoen Nok ending at Royal Plaza. This route and **Chitrlada Palace** are illuminated by fairylights for the King's and Queen's Birthdays (*see p159 and p162*). The ceremonial area is devoid of vendors and restaurants, but get sustenance around the Samsen riverside.

Royal Plaza & around

Modelled on the Champs-Elysées (seen by Rama V during a trip to Paris), Ratchadamnoen is a processional avenue in three parts. The inner section leads from the Grand Palace to a middle avenue of streamlined 1940s blocks (Thanon Ratchadamnoen Klang; *see p67*), then from Phanfa Bridge Thanon Ratchadamnoen Nok leads into Dusit. It focuses not on an arch, but on the Italianate, marble and copper-domed **Ananta Samakhom Throne Hall** (*see p81*). Behind it lies the modern **Parliament** (Thanon Uthong Nai) in democratically horizontal concrete, with a Brutalist-yet-breezy Brasilia aesthetic. It is open to the public only on Children's Day (*see p160*). In Parliament's forecourt stands a statue of King Rama VII, who granted the first constitution, explained in **King Prajadhipok Museum** (*see p69*) at Phanfa Bridge. The National Assembly itself may move to a new, bigger parliament in the suburbs. Also behind the Throne Hall, the wooden villas in **Dusit Park** (*see p80* **Angels in the clouds**) show the fretwork verandas and shutters of 'tropical European' taste. The park is home to **Wang Vimanmek**, the largest golden teak building in the world.

The **Royal Plaza** in front of the Throne Hall contains the equestrian statue of **King Chulalongkorn** (*see p81*). The plaza is flanked by the British-style former **Supreme**

Ananta Samakhom Throne Hall. *See p81.*

Angels in the clouds

The lush royal estate of **Dusit Park** is best known for **Wang Vimanmek**, the world's largest golden teak building. But there are plenty of other museums in this canal-laced compound offering insights into royalty and court life, as outlined in the continuous audio-visual displays at the **Slide Multivision Hall**.

Completed in 1901, **Vimanmek** – 'abode of the angels in the clouds' – was home to Rama V for five years. The free, compulsory guided tour (every 15 minutes, 9.45am-3.15pm daily) provides a chance to peek at regal domesticity; a winding staircase leads to the royal apartment, where such obscure items as a crystal chamber pot and Rama V's wooden wheelchair survive. Downstairs is the Throne Hall, with its four ornate thrones, while sublime panelled corridors connect yet more rooms filled with antiques. In the lakeside sala, dance and martial arts are performed at 10.30am and 2pm (free).

Other mansions contain carriages, clocks and ritual paraphernalia, such as palanquins, plus treasures from the prehistoric World Heritage Site of Baan Chiang in Udon Thani province. The **Ancient Cloth Museum** illustrates the diversity, meanings and status indicators of the patterns in Thai textiles, while upstairs are scenes from Rama V's trips to Europe. **King Bhumibol Photographic Museums I and II** show pictures by Rama IX, while images of his youth appear in **Suan Hong Royal Ceremonies Photography Museum**. Another fretwork fantasia, **Suan Si Reudu Hall**, has been reconstructed on its original site and displays Golden Jubilee gifts to Rama IX. The filigree **Hor Pavilion** was also moved here in 1998.

For her part, Queen Sirikit has been pivotal in preserving the exquisite court arts and other Thai crafts through the SUPPORT Foundation at **Bang Sai**; you can find some of these masterpieces in the **SUPPORT Museum**, which is housed within the **Abhisek Dusit Throne Hall** (a gem of wooden tracery), whose shop is better than the souvenir-lined entrance to Vimanmek. Often missed, the **Chang Ton National Museum** displays artefacts of the sacred white elephants (see p83 *Howdah* **you do?**) housed in one of their former stables.

Dusit Park & Wang Vimarnmek

16 Thanon Ratchawithi (0 2628 6300-9 ext 5119-5121). **Open** *9.30am-4pm daily.* **Admission** *Thais B75; B20 concessions. Foreigners B100. Free with Grand Palace ticket. Free compulsory guide (in English every 30 minutes from 9.45am).* **Map** p249 D1.

Abhisek Dusit throne.

Command building and to the west, **Amporn Gardens**, whose art deco pavilions host events, ranging from royal social events to a fair selling goods hand-made by Thailand's prisoners.

Bangkok is the United Nations' regional HQ, and the **UN ESCAP** (United Nations Economic & Social Commission for Asia & the Pacific, Thanon Ratchadamnoen Nok, 0 2288 1234, www.unescap.org, open by appointment) occupies a Thai modernist building that curves around one corner of the double bridge over Khlong Phadung Krung Kasem. Bisecting

Ratchadamnoen Nok and lined with flame trees, this majestic canal arcs west to **Thewet** flower market (*see p140*) and south-east to **Bo Bae** cloth market (*see p136*).

Further south down Ratchadamnoen Nok are a TAT office (*see p235*) and the art deco **Ratchadamnoen Boxing Stadium** (*see p204*). The Royal Thai Army headquarters opposite houses the **Royal Thai Army Museum** (*see below*) and exemplifies the work of Italian classical architects at the early 20th-century court.

Ananta Samakhom Throne Hall
Thanon Uthong Nai (0 2628 6300-9 ext 5119-5121). **Open** 9am-4pm daily. Closed 5, 10 Dec. **Admission** *Thais* B75; B10 concessions. *Foreigners* B100. Free with Grand Palace ticket. **Map** p249 D1.
Though clad in marble, this national icon was the first Thai building constructed (1908-16) on ferro-concrete pilings, a technique that Rama V saw in Europe. Its awesome cruciform interior – heavily gilded, with mosaic scenes of Chakri reigns I-IV lining the dome – convened the first Thai parliament, and still hosts state occasions. **Photo** *p79.*

Dusit Zoo
71 Thanon Rama V (0 2281 2000/www.zoothailand.org). **Open** 8am-9pm daily. **Admission** *Thais* B50; B10 concessions. *Foreigners* B100; B50 concessions. **No credit cards.** **Map** p249 D1/E1.
This state zoological park in Rama V's former botanical garden is one of Asia's best but keeps rare fauna in rather grim cement enclosures. Elephant rides and theme park attractions cater to the Thai families who dress up on weekends to visit its gardens, open-air restaurants and lake, where pedalos dodge the fountain. There had been talk of the park moving, but this plan may have been shelved.

King Chulalongkorn Statue
Royal Plaza. **Open** 24hrs daily. *Ceremonies* Tue eve, Thur eve, 23 Oct annually. **Map** p249 D1.
Devotees of King Chulalongkorn the Great (Rama V) gather on the anniversary of his death for rites at the six-metre (20-foot) equestrian statue he had cast in bronze during a 1907 visit to France. During his progressive reign (1868-1910; *see p16*), he learned about his subjects' concerns by disguising himself as a commoner. In gratitude, his portrait is widely venerated in homes, restaurants and workplaces, as well as on amulets, banknotes and busts used as talismans. Offerings are also made here on Tuesday and Thursday evenings, asking for luck in business, love or exams; they tend to include two of King Chula's favourite things: cognac and cigars.

Royal Thai Army Museum
Royal Thai Army HQ, 113 Thanon Ratchadamnoen Nok (0 2297 8121-2/www.rta.mi.th). **Open** 8.30am-2.30pm by written group appointment only. **Admission** free. **Map** p249 D2.
Models, weapons, flags, uniforms and insignia dominate this collection housed in the classical-style army headquarters and armoury of the Chulachomklao Royal Military Academy.

Chitrlada
King Bhumibol and Queen Sirikit reside behind a moated wall at verdant **Chitrlada Palace**. It faces the **Royal Turf Club** (*see p204*), founded by King Rama VI after his predecessor introduced horse racing to Siam following his European tour in 1897. Flanking **Dusit Zoo**,

Khlong Prem Prachakorn canal leads south past **Wat Benchamabophit** to **Government House**, a noble villa built in the sixth reign that now houses the Prime Minister's Office and is open only on Children's Day (*see p160*). It features suitably Byzantine detailing, with frescoed ceilings and a filigree stone frontage flanked by turrets. Further down Thanon Phitsanulok stands **Baan Phitsanulok**, the PM's residence since 1982. Legend has it that this 1925 Venetian Gothic confection is haunted.

Chitrlada Palace
Thanon Ratchavithi (0 2283 9145/booking 0 2282 8200). **Open** by written appointment only (7 days in advance) 8.30am-4.30pm daily. **Map** p249 E1.
Once a haven where King Rama VI wrote theatrical works and books on military history, Chitrlada Villa became a palace under Rama VII. As it is the king's residence, public access is restricted to tours of the Royal Projects (sustainable development schemes). Project and Support Foundation products are sold in Chitrlada Shops here and at the Grand Palace (*see p59*), Dusit Park (*see p80*), Oriental Hotel (*see p45*), Marriott Bangkok Resort (*see p40*), Suwannabuhmi Airport and near Chatuchak MRT. During royal birthday periods the moated perimeter is beautifully decorated. For an appointment, foreigners must apply with a copy of their passport/visa.

Wat Benchamabophit
69 Thanon Rama V (0 2282 7413). **Open** 8am-5pm daily. **Admission** B20. **No credit cards.** **Map** p249 D2.
Clad in Italian Carrara marble (left over from Ananta Samakhom Throne Hall), the 'marble temple' is a well-proportioned melding of East and West by Italian architect Hercules Manfredi. It was commissioned in 1899 by Rama V, who was a monk in the original Ayutthaya-era temple, and one room contains his ashes. The *bot* has stained-glass windows of Thai mythology and a replica of Thailand's most venerated Buddha image after the Emerald Buddha: the Phra Phutta Chinirat (the haloed Sukhothai-era original is in Pitsanulok). Lining the cloister, 53 Buddha images cover every era, style, *mudra* (gesture) and provenance. Wat Ben is a good spot to view Buddhist festivals and morning alms collection. **Photo** *p82.*

Samsen
Dusit's northern hinterland is a grid of tree-lined avenues containing the **Ratchabhat Institute** college and the exclusive **Vachirawut School**. Thanon Sukhothai, between Thanons Rama V and Nakhon Ratchasima, has a small northern Thai community selling the favourite Lanna lunch dish, *khao soi* (noodle curry). Branching off Sukhothai towards filthy Khlong Samsen, Thanon Suphan is a lovely, leaf-dappled street with some open-air food stalls and a sacred *bodhi* tree swathed in protective sashes and offerings.

Sightseeing

More hectic Thanon Samsen follows the river north past Samsen railway station, co-op housing and fine art at **Numthong Gallery** (*see p172*), and heads south towards Banglamphu. Down Samsen Soi 13 a riverside Vietnamese community surrounds **St Francis Xavier Church**, with **Wat Ratchathiwat** (*see p83*) nearby. Further south at the **National Library**, Thanon Sri Ayutthaya leads to **Kaloang** seafood restaurant (*see p114*). Take a breather in the little park on the corner of Uthong Nok Road or in **Thewet** flower market (*see p140*).

Finally, tucked behind shophouses on the east of Samsen, is **Wat Indrawihan** (*see p83*). Opposite stand the pleasingly modernist **Bank of Thailand** and its museum housed in **Wang Bangkhunprom**, a former palace best viewed from the dramatic new **Rama VIII Bridge**.

National Library
Tha Wasukri, Thanon Samsen (0 2281 5212/www.natlib.moe.go.th). **Open** 9am-7.30pm daily. **Admission** free. **Map** p248 C1.
Although Thais often regard reading as more chore than pleasure, this mid 20th-century, Thai-style structure is popular. This may, however, have something to do with the fashion and soap opera magazines, not to mention amulets, stored on the ground floor. The impressive lobby leads to upper storeys with limited volumes in English. The compound also contains the King Bhumibol Commemorative Library and the Princess Sirindhorn Music Library.

St Francis Xavier Church
94 Samsen Soi 13 (0 2243 0060-2). **Services** 6am, 7pm Mon-Sat; 6.30am, 8.30am, 10am, 4pm Sun. **Map** p248 C1.
A Vietnamese community surrounds this mid 19th-century church, where masses are held in Thai. Beyond the ornate gates it has a cheery Mediterranean feel, with a dainty shrine of its patron saint on the portico. Behind it, a statue of Christ healing a man attracts Thai garlands. Adjacent Soi 13 is quite picturesque.

Wang Bangkhunprom & Bank of Thailand Museum
273 Thanon Samsen (0 2283 5286/6723/www.bot. or.th). **Open** by written appointment only (7 days in advance) 9am-4pm Mon-Fri. **Admission** free. **Map** p248 C2.
The palace of Prince Baripatra until the end of absolutism in 1932, this baroque-cum-art nouveau edifice contains the Bank of Thailand's museum. It charts six centuries of Thai monetary evolution from glass beads to notes, via *pot duang* (bullet coins). The compound also contains the newly restored Wang Devavesm mansion. Women wearing trousers are not admitted. Foreigners must apply with a copy of their passport/visa.

Wat Indrawihan
144 Thanon Visut Kasat (0 2281 1406). **Open** 7am-midnight daily. **Admission** free. **Map** p248 C2.
Down an alley between shophouses, 'Wat In' is notable only for its standing Buddha. Eschewing

Scenes around **Wat Benchamabophit**. *See p81*.

Howdah you do?

Elephants never forget – and nobody forgets an elephant, especially one plodding through the Bangkok traffic fumes, its swaying rear light flashing red. Startled tourists reach for their cameras – and buy sugar cane from the *mahout* to feed the poor pachyderm. Thais pay to swoop under its belly for luck, but also wince at their national animal being reduced to begging. Much better to see them at **Dusit Zoo** (*see p81*), where you can ride on top of one in its *howdah* (saddle seat).

Formerly gracing the flag of Siam and carrying kings into battle, the elephant is lauded by all. When a rare *chang ton* (white elephant) is discovered it automatically belongs to the king. *Chang ton* must display distinguishing marks, such as pinkish-white skin and features, including its hair, tail hair, eyes, nails, palate and genitals. Since *chang ton* must not labour, the obligation of caring for one could drain a noble's finances (hence

the English phrase 'white elephant', denoting something prestigious yet impractical). At the **Chang Ton National Museum** (*see p80* **Dusit Park**) a model illustrates a Brahmin white elephant ceremony and displays tusks, ivory regalia and *mahout* charms alongside details of catching and corralling the beast.

Yet like so much traditional culture, the elephant is exploited to gain face and money, without sufficient long-term care and investment. From 20,000 in the mid 1980s, there are now fewer than 5,000. No more than 1,500 survive in the wild, from which babies still get snatched (usually requiring the protective mother's death), as captive breeding is rare. Farmers even kill them for eating their crops.

The 1988 logging ban left most domesticated elephants jobless. A few get used in illegal logging, sometimes being fed amphetamines to work longer. Meanwhile, southern Isaan's habitat has been so degraded, and the 125-kilogram (276-pound) daily diet so expensive, that the area's elephants beg in Bangkok, where there's better foraging in empty suburban lots. A Dusit Zoo vet estimated in 2000 that 30 elephants roamed Downtown, plus 20 in the suburbs. He treats injuries for free, since Thai roads can be hot, sharp and hazardous, with motorists fined only B500 for collisions, even if fatal. Elephants' use in post-tsunami clear-ups also exposed them to potential harm.

City authorities keep trying to ban elephant begging, threatening the *mahouts* with fines and dispossession, but viablesolutions lack funding. The only other options are tourist trekking, showbiz trips overseas, or their sometimes callous treatment as commodities by entertainment companies. The species' future depends on agencies like the **National Elephant Institute** in Lampang (www.thailand elephant.org), which houses many royal white elephants and has a hospital and orphanage.

normal proportions, this figure is a lofty 32m (105ft) tall – you can climb to its head for a so-so panorama – but unfeasibly thin and anchored by outsize feet. The adjacent *vihaan* (chapel) poignantly features jars of human ashes in its terrace walls.

Wat Ratchathiwat

3 Thanon Samsen Soi 9 (0 2243 2125). **Open** *Temple* 8am-9pm daily. *Bot* 9am-11am, 1-4pm Sat, Sun. **Admission** free. **Map** p248 C1.

Restored by Rama IV, this monastery contains a remarkable *bot* with a mural created by Italian professor C Rigoli behind a stone façade with Khmer accents by Prince Naris. Naris – evidently a busy man – also restyled the Ayutthayan Sala Karnparian, a sublime wooden pavilion with intricate relief panels and complex eaves. A new museum displays artefacts from the reigns of Kings Rama II-IV.

Chinatown

This lattice of lanes, shrines and stalls pulsates like a living museum.

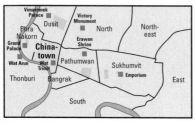

Maps p248 & p249

It may seem like a quaint enclave, but before Bangkok sprawled, Chinatown was its commercial heart. As late as the 1960s it sold goods unavailable elsewhere, was home to Bangkok's first department stores and cinemas, and became the crucible of Thai youth culture. Its neighbourhoods retain their maze-like character because no one can gather enough land to redevelop. That may change once the planned MRT subway extension burrows from Hualumphong to Thonburi. Although trains would improve access, residents protest that tunnelling would damage what is effectively a living museum. Chinatown embodies how Sino-Thais have shaped this city, both economically and physically, from market to shophouse to mall.

Bangkok may be the capital, but it has never been a quintessentially Thai town. Chinese lived here before Krung Thep existed. Originally invited from Southern China by King Taksin (himself half Teochew) to augment the workforce, they settled on the riverbank facing his capital, Thonburi. When King Rama I relocated to Bangkok, the Chinese were shifted south of the new city wall in 1782 to a dirt alley called Sampheng. From that nucleus grew today's Chinatown.

The expression 'to travel with a mat and a pot' sums up how little the waves of migrants brought. Mainly Teochew, with some Hainanese, Cantonese and Hokkien, they worked hard and saved even harder. Soon they were among the wealthiest commoners and were generally looked upon favourably by the authorities, despite discrimination in the mid 20th century. King Mongkut (Rama IV, 1851-68) apparently promoted immigration and intermarriage to imbue his subjects with that famous Chinese

work ethic. Until polygamy was abolished, wealthy Chinese families offered daughters as consorts, thus entering the blue bloodline.

Early settlers maintained ties with China, although they had to assimilate after World War II, due to controls on teaching Chinese languages and on immigration because of fears of communist infiltration. Given the scarcity of ethnic Chinese women, many took Thai wives and surnames (usually long compounds of auspicious words). The Chinese have integrated so well it's hard to gauge their magnitude. Some estimate that more than ten per cent of the population and more than half of all Bangkokians have Chinese genes.

Fewer Sino-Thais now live in Chinatown. Wealthier families have moved to suburban mansions, and many shophouses have become offices, warehouses or wholesalers for products no longer made within the community. Yet many people commute daily back to an air-conditioned cubicle in the back of their shop to have the final say, issue change and oversee a new migrant staff – from Thailand's north-east. Others run

Sightseeing

banks and businesses in Downtown founded by their industrious immigrant ancestors.

Thai-Chinese political and social influence reached a peak under Thaksin Shinawatra, who filled his cabinet with fellow Sino-Thai tycoons at a time when a resurgent China looked anew at its South-east Asian diaspora. Thailand's savvy approach to China echoes its successful policy towards European colonialism: remain independent by embracing attributes of the hegemon. Things Chinese have become hip, cultural exchanges are frequent, Chinese tourists are a huge and growing sector, and ASEAN proposes a China free trade zone. Sino-Thai firms have even invested in Shanghai malls. Surging confidence in Chinese cultural expression is focused on historical Chinatown. The formerly quiet, family-and-temple-oriented **Chinese New Year** (*see p160*) has become a state-sponsored street festival, led by the finance minister in Chinese costume. That is the only time the area's merchants shut, when Chinatown – indeed, the whole of Bangkok – suddenly empties.

LOSE YOURSELF

Bounded by Khlongs Ong Ang, Mahanak and Phadung Krung Kasem, Chinatown embraces the riverside district of Samphantawong and the less dense shophouse district of Pomprab. It can be divided into three swathes parallel to the river: **Thanon Yaowarat** and **Thanon Charoen Krung** are thoroughfares, while the lanes of **Sampeng Lane** and **Thanon Songwat** invite strolling (*see p86* **Walk 4**). For walking here you'll need a spirit of adventure, a tolerance for heat and crowds, light clothing, comfy shoes, plenty of fluids and the invaluably annotated *Nancy Chandler's Map of Bangkok*. Or you could follow two signposted walks from a booth dispensing maps at River City.

Depending on time and energy, there are many ways to 'do' Chinatown. You could focus on temples (Buddhist, Taoist, Chinese and Sikh). Or food (from stalls to fancy restaurants). Or markets, which are Bangkok's oldest and most diverse (*see pp136-40*). Or weird juxtapositions: casket makers near chicken hatcheries; mosquito coils beside cock rings. Or crane your neck up at the architecture, notably along Charoen Krung, Songwat and Ratchawong (although the classical columns, Sino-Portuguese detailing, sculpted shutters, tiered balconies and bursts of art deco are often partially obscured). There are details to relish on wooden shophouses in offshoots like Charoen Krung Sois 20 and 23.

Explore Chinatown logically, though, and you'll miss half the fun and many of the sights. It's better to follow your nose (both scents and stenches) down microscopic *trok* (paths) and risk getting lost until a landmark pops up. Confusingly, Chinese street names on rickety signs are giving way to Thai appellations on blue placards, hence **Soi Issaranuphap** is

Chinese lanterns.

Walk 4 Warehouse parties

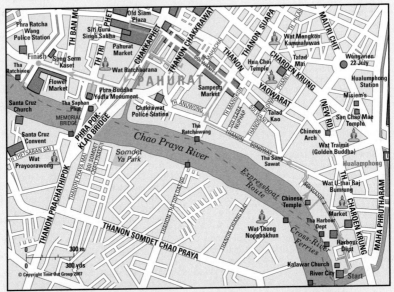

Chinatown's riverside is still cluttered with the *godowns* (warehouses) that were pivotal to Bangkok's aquatic trade. Weaving through the *godowns* on the city's first inland roads, Thanon Songwat and Sampeng Lane, this half-day walk encapsulates the multicultural, multi-faceted nature of the district perfectly.

Starting as an alley north of River City antiques mall, Wanit Soi 2 passes **Wat Kalawar** (Holy Rosary Church; 0 2266 4849) on the left, a Gothic riverside edifice built in 1787 on land given to the Portuguese for helping to fight the Burmese. On the path joining Soi Charoen Phanit, an ATM marks the gate of Thailand's first bank building (1904), a classical edifice that is still part of **Siam Commercial Bank**; you can then explore an architecturally interesting maze of lanes coated in oil from engine parts, the trade of this precinct named **Talad Noi**.

Down the left turn, follow signs to the **Riverview Guesthouse** (*see p44*) for a rooftop restaurant panorama. Secreted beyond is the 200-year-old **San Jao Sien Khong** (6am-6pm daily). Reputedly the oldest Chinese shrine in Chinatown, it's the only one facing the Chao Phraya river from this bank. During the **Vegetarian Festival** (*see p163*) in October, palm oil replaces engine grease as the lubricant of choice at stalls selling meat-free and spice-free dishes to white-clad devotees of the goddess Kuan Yin, while the temple features Chinese opera, and fairground games.

Return via narrow, barely signed Wanit Soi 2 to its end at Soi Phanu Rangsi. Turn right and immediately left on to **Thanon Songwat**, close to the river. Some time-warp alleys lead down to the river between *godowns* with deceptively modern frontages, where spice and rice merchants store gunny sacks or display

officially **Soi 16**, and **Wanit Soi 1** is actually **Sampeng**, Chinatown's first and foremost market (*see p138*). Once notorious for opium and gambling dens, brothels and pawnshops, it now teems with nothing more dangerous than roving snack merchants and motorbikes overloaded with bolts of fabric.

While some streets round her contain bits of everything, others have evolved specialisations. One-street wonders include herbalists (Thanon Rama IV west of Hualamphong station); stationery (Thanon Chakrawat between Sampeng and Yaowarat); metal cables (Thanon Songwat near Phanu

huge grandfather clocks and heavy mother-of-pearl-inlaid furniture. When the *soi* becomes one-way, gaze up at several beautiful but woefully unrestored Sino-European buildings on the right.

Where Songwat ends at **Thanon Ratchawong**, a famous vendor peddles *khanom jeeb* (Chinese minced pork dumplings) from a huge antique brass steamer in front of the 7-11 shop. Cross Ratchawong and head right (north), then go left at the crossroads marking **Sampeng Lane**. Off this chaotic market alley, narrow walkways (often obscured by racks of polyester clothes) lead left (south) to unexpected adventures. Sampeng emerges on to busy **Thanon Chakrawat**. Bear left to a large metal grille (with a 100-year-old Chinese herbalist on one side). This is the entrance to **Wat Chakrawat**, a peaceful temple with two tall *prang*, an artificial hill housing burial urns and a grotto with a supposed Buddha shadow on one wall and two ponds of large and languid crocodiles.

Back on Chakrawat, cross the footbridge, then turn left a few steps north on to **Soi Bhopit Phimuk**, an alley of shophouses redolent of spices. After crossing tree-lined **Khlong Ong Ang**, turn right back up to Sampeng Lane, where a left puts you on Thanon Chakraphet. Suddenly you're not in Chinatown any more, Dorothy. You're facing Little India (aka **Pahurat**; *see p89*).

Heading left towards the river, **Thanon Chakkaphet** leads on to Phra Pok Klao bridge, beside the elegant stone Saphan Phut, the 'Memorial Bridge' to King Rama I, whose statue commands its approaches in a small riverside park. Behind him, the royal temple of **Wat Ratchaburana** (119 Thanon Chakkaphet, 0 2221 9544), restored after bombing in World War II, was built as Wat Liab Jeen in Ayutthayan times by Liab, a Chinese trader. Come nightfall, stalls flood **Saphan Phut Market** (*see p136*) and **Pak Khlong Talad** flower market (*see p140*) west along Thanon Chakkaphet.

Rangsi); and plastic and jute rice sacks (Thanon Songsawat near Songwat). For more culturally interesting locales, try Thanon Phlubphlachai for paper funeral offerings and Thanon Plangnam, which stocks ritual paraphernalia, such as masks, swords and tea sets.

To locals, Yaowarat *is* Chinatown – an orientation word for taxi drivers. Synonymous with gold (*see p88* **Proven gilt**), this long road is also famed for its restaurants and food stalls, both relatively expensive; for reviews, *see pp110-128*. Between dusk and 9pm it becomes one huge night market, with vendors spreading into Soi Plaeng Nam and Soi Phadung Dao (aka Soi Texas Suki, after an exalted *sukiyaki* outlet). For respite, take Soi Issaranuphap south to **Talaat Kao** (Old Market) and **Sampeng Lane**, which have traded daily for two centuries, or north through **Talaat Mai** (New Market, a mere century old) to **Leng Noi Yee** temple (*see p88*).

Today's PR message is that Yaowarat has all along been shaped like a dragon – a lucky one, of course. This revelation accompanied the visit of Chinese President Jiang Zemin in 1999, who blessed the **Soom Pratu Chalerm Prakiat** – Chinatown's ceremonial arch, which commemorated King Rama IX's 72nd birthday in 1999, the illustrious sixth cycle of both Thai and Chinese 12-year calendars – at Odeon Circle, the dragon's eye. One of the creature's 'horns', tree-lined Thanon Traimit, boasts the solid gold Buddha at **Wat Traimit** (*see below*), beyond which there are old bamboo stores bristling with handcrafted baskets, utensils and brooms.

Traffic flows one way east up the dragon's mane (Charoen Krung) and west down its back (Yaowarat), with its forelegs supposedly Thanon Songwat. Another arch, **Pratu Sun Yat Sen**, stands near the top of Thanon Ratchawong, the purported hind legs. A century after China's nationalist revolutionary Sun Yat Sen fundraised in Bangkok (and was twice deported for anti-monarchical conduct), descendants of his supporters helped erect the memorial gate in 2004. Then dubbed Trok Sun (Sun Alley), the *soi* is today nicknamed **Trok Prasai** (Speechgiving Alley). Yaowarat's tail (lined with hardware shops) ends at **Merry King Department Store**.

Wat Traimit

661 Thanon Charoen Krung (0 2225 9775).
Open 9am-5pm daily. **Admission** *Temple* free.
Golden Buddha free Thais; B20 foreigners.
No credit cards. Map p249/p250 D5.
In drab surroundings, the world's biggest solid gold Buddha statue has an almost liquid lustre that's arguably less flattering than the usual gold leaf patina. The Sukothai-era image – 3m (10ft) high and 5.5 tonnes in weight – had been stuccoed to hide it from marauding Burmese and remained unrecognised until 1955, when its shell cracked on being dropped from a crane during its move here.

Sightseeing

w Road' because
d street (1861),
ins around **Baan**
runs one way
phan/Songsawat,
iver south through

Its first landmark is **Sala Chalermkrung** theatre (*see p198*), the last remnant of an art deco chain. With its well-restored wrought-iron detailing and sweeping red-carpeted staircase, it hosts everything from film premières to festivals to Thai classical dance and Bollywood screenings for the Indian community of Pahurat. Completing this block is **Old Siam Plaza**, a retro-styled mall stocking much that you'd find in Chinatown, only air-conditioned. Don't miss the Thai snacks and desserts. Using original recipes and equipment, costumed women create delicacies like *khanom krok* (coconut milk batter steamed in tiny iron moulds).

Beyond a block called Wang Burapha after a long-gone palace, stalls line both sides of Khlong Ong Ang at **Saphan Lek Market** (*see p140*), and **Woeng Nakhon Kasem** retains its nom de plume of 'Thieves' Market', though it's no longer fencing stolen goods (*see p140*). Before **Khlong Thom Market** (*see p139*), slip south down Thanon Chakrawat to **Wat Chai Channa Songkhram** (0 2221 4317), notable

Proven gilt

Stand on Thanon Yaowarat, where it meets Phadung Dao, and you can see why it's known as Thailand's gold street. You'll be dazzled by the garish red and gold frontages resembling art deco-era cinemas. Ubiquitous dragons adorn awnings over counters of jewellery, while guards lounge on their laps, outside, holding shotguns on their laps. The most famous gold merchant is **Tang Toh Kang** (345 Wanit Soi 1, 0 2225 2898). Other notable ones include **Hua Seng Heng** (332-334 Thanon Yaowarat, 0 2225 0202) and **Chin Hua Heng** (295-297 Thanon Yaowarat, 0 2224 0077).

Yaowarat gold is soft and yellow thanks to its 97.5 per cent purity. It's sold not in ounces, but in *baht* (different from the currency, one *baht* is 15.2 grammes, equalling four *saleung* of 25 *satang*). Gold is viewed as portable (and visible) wealth, and banks and pawnshops post buy/sell rates for those needing cash in a hurry.

both for its Khmer *prang* and its proximity to a night-time dessert vendor on Nakhon Kasem Soi 4 (create your own confection from ingredients in antique copper bowls).

Passing **Leng Noi Yee** temple (*see below*) are other entrances to Soi Issaranuphap and Talad Mai, before a left turn leads to **Thanon Phlubphlachai**, where dealers in funerary paraphernalia congregate around **Li Thi Miew Temple** (494 Thanon Phlubphlachai, 0 2221 6985), a small Taoist shrine. You can see satin banners and paper accoutrements – fake money, clothes, houses, cars – being made for burning with the deceased to provide for the soul. Some souls were doubtless handled by the **Poh Teck Tung** charity foundation (326 Thanon Chao Khamrob, 0 2226 4444-8, 8am-7pm daily), which collects accident victims and conducts funerals for unclaimed corpses.

North of Charoen Krung, Pomprab is known for **Talad Fai Chai** (Flashlight Market, 5pm Sat-6pm Sun), which sprawls around Central Hospital along Thanons Luang, Chakrawat, Charoen Krung and Suapa. Take a torch to sift treasures from all the dreck. At the bewildering Charoen Krung/Mitraphap/Rama IV junction, veer north up Thanon Mitraphap to the 22 July Circle (the date Thailand dispatched forces to help the Allies in World War I). Turning back southwards, toward Rama IV and Hualumphong Train Station, Thanon Maitreechit passes **Misiem's** sculpture gallery (*see p101* **New bronze age**) and **San Chao Mae Tubtim**, a joss house staging Chinese opera during October's **Vegetarian Festival** (*see p163*).

Leng Noi Yee
Thanon Charoen Krung, between Thanon Mangkorn & Soi Issaranuphap (0 2222 3975).
Bus 1, 16, 35, 36, 75, 93, 162. **Open** 6am-5.30pm daily. **Map** p249/p250 D8.
Set behind an imposing multi-tiered entrance, the 'Dragon Flower Temple' (aka Wat Mangkorn Kamalawat) is Chinatown's biggest. Several sermon halls ring a courtyard filled with statues of Mahayana Buddhist and Taoist deities. Dating from 1871, it takes on a livelier and folksier ambience during the Vegetarian Festival (*see p163*) in October.

Misiem's
402-408 Thanon Maitri Chit, Chinatown (0 2639 8057). Hualumphong MRT. **Open** 10am-7pm Sat, Sun. **Map** p249/p250 D5.
In the former About Café avant-garde gallery, owner/curator Klaomard Yipintsoi (*see p171* **Curate expectations**) displays bronzes and paintings by her late grandmother, National Artist Misiem Yipintsoi. Balletic full-size works by this pioneering, self-taught sculptress grace Benjasiri Park (*see p95*) and Misiem's Sculpture Garden (*see p101* **New bronze age**). A reading room downstairs has basic drinks.

Pahurat & Little India

From its inception, Chinatown was divided into ethnic trading areas. The block framed by Thanon Chakkaphet, Thanon Triphet and Thanon Pahurat was – and still is – Little India. On the east side of Chakkaphet huddle travel agents, seedy cafés blasting Punjabi rock and restaurants such as **Royal India** (*see p115*). Outside its ornately carved door, Indian sweet makers stir huge woks of confectionery. Cross Chakkaphet and turn right at the Chinese temple, passing the burnt-out **ATM Department**

Store, where Bangkok's first Indian themed mall will rise. Then dart left into 'ATM Alley', a funky passageway of open-air shops selling incense, Indian CDs and DVDs, Ganesh statues, saris, bangles, bindis and spiced *chai*.

The maze-like **Pahurat** cloth market (*see p137*) is similar to Sampeng, except it's in rows under one large roof. Inside (directions are hopeless) looms the yellow onion-domed **Sri Guru Singh Sabha**, a four-storey Sikh temple (0 2221 1011, 6am-5pm daily). The northern perimeter on Thanon Pahurat stocks Thai classical dancers' costumes.

Pahurat.

Sightseeing

Downtown

The focus of commerce, cuisine and clubbing hides a rich heritage.

Downtown is the most convenient place to stay, eat, shop and get things done in Bangkok. Driven by whim, rivalry, real estate and a legendary resistance to urban planning, its continually mutating skyline and streetscapes epitomise the juxtapositions of modern Thai life: faith versus materialism, tastefulness fending off vulgarity, extravagance skirting destitution. Amid the gleaming malls and mouldering slums you will find traditional houses, antiquities, parks and spiritual homes to Buddhism, Hinduism, animism and Christianity.

Downtown is broadly demarcated by the BTS SkyTrain and MRT Subway lines, but locating its centres of gravity depends on your criteria. The two BTS lines intersect at Siam in **Pathumwan**, the hub of shopping, fashion and youth culture. The Silom line heads south to the river via the nightlife focus of Patpong and financial CBD (Central Business District) of **Bangrak**. The Sukhumvit line accesses the hotels, restaurants, bars and shops of the expat and high-society nexus, **Sukhumvit**.

Between Khlong Saen Saeb and Chatuchak Weekend Market (see p138 **Market forces**), the BTS and MRT loop to form **North Bangkok**. This embraces the bus rider's epicentre, Victory Monument, plus two areas once planned as future CBDs: Makkasan swamp, where the Suvarnabhumi Airport rail terminus is due to open in 2008; and Ratchadaphisek ring road, where at last the culture centre will be enlarged.

Both BTS and MRT skirt Downtown's **South**, a semi-industrial port zone where yet another wannabe CBD was proposed for Thanon Rama III. Bisecting Downtown, canal boats on Khlong Saen Saep head west to Phra Nakorn and out to the suburban **East** (see pp57-71 and pp100-102).

Bangrak

Map p250

In the mid 19th century a new grid of canals defined the triangular Bangrak district – namely, Rama IV, Si Phraya, Surawong, Silom and Sathorn; all but the narrowed, polluted Khlong Sathorn were later paved as roads. Bisecting them, Thanon Narathiwat Ratchanakharin follows Khlong Chong Nonsi, and features a windmill sculpture at Thanon Silom (literally 'Windmill Road', as it was once a site of irrigation turbines).

Thanon Charoen Krung (nicknamed 'New Road' as it is Thailand's oldest paved road) hugs Bangrak's historic riverside between Sathorn Bridge and **River City** antiques mall (see p143). Here the lanes retain human-scale appeal (see p92 **Walk 5: Bangrak riverside**) amid antique and craft shops, tailors, restaurants and the animated **Bangrak Market**, around the toy-like Robinson's Bangrak department store. The quaint **Bangkokian Museum** (see p91) stands nearby. The elite dine at the top of the pastiche neo-classical State Tower, which dwarfs charming shophouses at the mouth of Thanon Silom.

A short stroll up Silom, three faux-heritage piazzas offer pleasant, traffic-free browsing. **Sun Square**'s fancified terraces hardly excite, although the excellent **Nicolie Asian Massage Centre** (see p180) displays a sublime collection of Asian antiques. Next up, the pretty, colonialesque façades of **Baan Silom**, some let to **B2S** bookshop (see p143) and **Kit-ti Gallery** jewellery (see p150), circle a lawn and a fine Italian restaurant. Just ahead, the original fairy-lit template, **Silom Village**, includes a seafood dinner theatre and souvenir arcades adapted from genuinely old houses.

This is also the gem-dealing district (see p149 **Cutting edge**) and above it looms the Jewelry Trade Centre, beneath which **Silom Galleria** is yet another art and antiques mall (see p143), containing the **Panorama Museum** (see p91) and **Tang Gallery** (see p172). Just beyond, **Kathmandu Photo Gallery** (see p172) nestles among the devotional stalls and curry shops flanking the elaborate Hindu **Maha Uma Devi** temple (see p91).

It's a bit of a hike past a half-demolished Chinese cemetery to Silom's busier northern end, where the BTS and MRT again meet. Siberian swallows flock here from October to March, but copping a dropping is, rationalise the Thais, good luck. That could explain the good fortunes of the corporate headquarters and the surrounding restaurants, shops, seafood stalls, **Silom Complex** mall, and hotels, including the spired, triangular **Dusit Thani** (*see p44*), which overlooks Lumphini Park. Off Silom towards Sathorn lie **Soi Convent** – a road of eating places as well as the Catholic St Joseph's Convent & School and the Gothic Anglican Christ Church – and **Soi Saladaeng**, a forked lane of restaurants ending in **Surapon Gallery** (*see p172*).

Bangrak means 'Village of Love' and love is pursued nightly in the go-go Neverland of **Patpong Sois 1** and **2**. The late Thai-Chinese millionaire Udom Patpongpanit turned a marshy banana plantation into this world-renowned fleshpot. Initially a recreation ground for wealthy locals and airline crews, Patpong went a-go-go in the late 1960s as American GIs flocked here on R&R from the Vietnam War. The 'Pong later blanded out into a Disneyfied coach party stop, flogging tit and tat to tourists. *See also pp129-40* **Bars** *and pp190-94* **Nightlife**. Also in the area are the bar strips of **Silom Soi 4** (beautiful people), **Silom Soi 2** (gay) and **Soi Thaniya** (a Little Tokyo).

Patpong and Thaniya link to slightly dingy Thanon Surawong, once Bangkok's tourist hub.

Halfway back to the river down Surawoi. the neighbouring **British Club** and **Neils Hays Library**, both social centres for expats housed in classical edifices.

Bangkokian Museum

273 Charoen Krung Soi 43 (0 2234 6741). **Open** 10am-4pm Wed-Sun. **Admission** free. **No credit cards. Map** p250 E6.

The Bangkokian is Bangrak's contribution to the plan to have a local museum in each city district; it is a charming residence kept in the decor of the owner's parents as a record of mid 20th-century bourgeois lifestyle. An Indian doctor's house in the grounds adds diversity.

Maha Uma Devi

2 Thanon Pan (0 2238 4007). **Open** 6am-8pm daily. **Admission** free. **Map** p250 E7.

Founded in the 1860s by the still-resident Tamil community, this Hindu temple is dubbed Wat Khaek ('guest temple') by Thais. It buzzes with Thais and Chinese making offerings to a small bronze statue of Uma Devi (Shiva's consort), and other images of Vishnu, Buddha and Uma's son, Ganesh. The multi-coloured walls, dome and tower bristle with sculptures. Rites of self-mortification take place here during October's Vegetarian Festival (*see p163*), and the temple observes Diwali (October/November).

Panorama Museum

4th floor, Silom Galleria, Jewelry Trade Center, 919/1 Thanon Silom (0 2235 4311/www.webmuseumof bangkok.pantown.com). Surasak BTS. **Open** 10am-5pm Mon-Fri. **Admission** free. **No credit cards. Map** p250 E7.

Maha Uma Devi.

Bangrak riverside

...as Bangkok's original ...ing centre. Its tranquil lanes ...nost foreign businesses, embassies, *godowns* (warehouses), mansions and hotels.

Start at **River City** antiques mall. Just beyond the **Royal Orchid Sheraton** hotel is the capital's oldest embassy, the 1820s **Portuguese Residence**. Take **Thanon Charoen Krung**, past the formidable art deco **Central Post Office**. Right, down Soi 34, you reach **Wat Muang Khae** and **Harmonique**, a shophouse terrace converted into a charming restaurant. Back on Charoen Krung, head past the **Rare Stone Museum** and into Soi 34. Perusing timber mansions to the right, you reach the **French Embassy** (best seen from the river). Beside it, the crumbling classical **Old Customs House** (a set in Wong Kar Wai's *In the Mood for Love*) is slate to become the jet-set, 33-room Aman Resort. Behind it, a path loops north then west past wooden houses to **Haroon Mosque** and back south across Soi 36 to the French Embassy.

Soi 38 leads to **OP Place**, a department store dating from 1905 that now houses antiques shops. A block south, Soi 40 features crafts workshops with temple-style roofs, and the dainty **China House** restaurant, though redevelopment has ruined its frontage and replaced its exquisite old timber neighbour with a boutique. Soi 40 is dubbed 'Oriental Lane', after the historic hotel. Its original river entrance (now the Authors' Wing) is visible from **Oriental Pier**, as is the neglected classical edifice of the **East Asiatic Company** (EAC, built in 1901) and **Chartered Bank**, now part of Assumption School. Through an arch behind the EAC an elegant tree-lined piazza links a Catholic

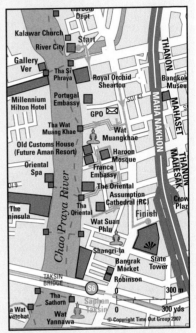

mission with **Assumption Cathedral**. Built in 1910, the red brick cathedral has twin towers and a fine marble altar. Soi 42 leads past wooden homes to the junction of Thanons Charoen Krung and Silom, where **LeBua at State Tower** hotel (*see p45*) offers views of your route from its rooftop restaurant (*Sirocco*; *see p116*).

A collection of stunning daguerrotype panoramas of Bangkok in 1865, photographed by Francis Chit. As well as the originals, a selection of prints are available to purchase.

Patpong & Silom Night Markets

Patpong Sois 1 & 2. Saladaeng BTS. **Open** *Night market* 6pm-2am daily. **Map** p250 F6.
Rows of guys gawp through doors at lacklustre pole-dancing and novelty sex shows in Soi 1, while their wives, kids and some Thais shop for copy watches, fake Levi's or pirate discs of music, movies, porn and games. Stalls flogging these and trendier clubwear and decor items spread along Silom between Silom Sois 2 and 8. Outdoor bars on Patpong Soi 2 tank up lonely booze-hounds.

Pathumwan

Map p251

Dug during the early 19th century for commerce and defence, Khlong Saen Saeb has become filthy, but offers glimpses of a bygone life at **Jim Thompson's House Museum** (*see p97* **The silk root**). East of Thanon Phayathai, it passes **Saprathum Palace**, an ochre edifice home to the king's late mother; her funerary tower is next door at **Wat Pathumwanaram** (*see p95*). Past the Pratunam canal boat interchange, the *khlong* skirts the phallic **Chao Mae Tubtim Shrine** (*see below*) in **Nai Lert Park Hotel** (*see p47*).

Parallel with the canal to the south, the contiguous avenues of Thanon Rama I and Thanon Ploenchit comprise Bangkok's main shopping area. East of the **National Stadium Pathumwan** (see p203) is the epicentre of Thai youth culture: an amalgam of things cute, cheap, arty, loud, colourful, slogan-clad and clued-into trends from the West, Japan and South Korea. Ground zero for teens is the tumultuous maze of shoplets, fast food and karaoke boxes at **MBK** (Mahboonkrong Centre; see p154) and **Siam Square** next door (see p141), which runs its own radio station and magazine, and is full of extra-study schools, such as the English courses at the **British Council** (see below). Though a timid scene by Western standards, Siam Square's subcultures prompt shrill denunciations by moralists. Get your T-shirt here at the **Hard Rock Café** (see p189).

Across the road, chic rules at the malls of **Siam Centre** and **Siam Discovery** (see p154) and **Siam Paragon** (see p154), which harbours **Siam Ocean World** (see below). These malls all join aerial walkways linking National Stadium, Siam and Chidlom BTS stations, the Royal Thai Police Headquarters and the vast **Central World Plaza** mall (see p154). Each cool season on its forecourt, rival beer gardens drown each other out in lager and live bands under the glow of South-east Asia's largest LCD screen. Across Thanon Ratchadamri stand the crafts mall of **Naranyaphand**, and the label havens of the **Gaysorn** (see p154) and **Erawan** malls. The latter looms behind the revered **Erawan Shrine** (see p98 **Shop and pray**). Further east lie Amarin Plaza and **Central Chidlom** department store (see p144), which faces the restaurant avenue of Soi Lang Suan.

Two entire blocks between Thanons Rama I and IV belong to Chulalongkorn University, Thailand's most prestigious. West of Thanon Phayathai is **Chulalongkorn Art Centre** (see below) and the **Snake Farm** (see p95), to the east the Khmer revival-style Chulalongkorn Auditorium sits amid park-like grounds. A block east, the BTS bisects greenery at the **Royal Bangkok Sports Club** (see p204), the refuge for old-money elites, and **Lumphini Park** (see below). The park will soon be bordered by huge towers. Soi Lang Suan will lose most of its famed restaurants when the soi's eastern side gets demolished to make condos. Across the embassy row of Thanon Witthayu the charming, popular **Suan Lum Night Bazaar** (see p140), once zoned as parkland, will be replaced by condos, a mall and Thailand's tallest skyscraper. The **Thai Traditional Puppet Theater** (see p198) can

remain, and **Lumphini Muay Thai Stadium** (see p204) might move, but the mega-project will evict 3,000 small businesses and deprive Bangkok of a precious asset.

British Council
254 Chulalongkorn Soi 64 (0 2652 5480-5/www. britishcouncil.or.th). **Open** 8.30am-7pm daily (9am-5pm for information). **Admission** free. **Map** p250 F5.
This language school and library brings touring promotions of 'cool Britannia' culture to Thailand, like artist Damien Hirst and designer Tom Dixon, plus a variety of DJs.

Chao Mae Tubtim Shrine
Soi Nai Lert, at service entrance of Nai Lert Park Hotel. Chidlom BTS. **Open** 24hrs daily. **Admission** free. **Map** p251 H4.
Hoping for fertility or prosperity, worshippers at this canalside shrine to the female deity Chao Mae Tubtim offer phallic offerings in every shape, size and material. They range from stylised Shiva lingams to realistic, red-tipped *palad khik* (animist phallic totems) and huge shafts swathed in sacred scarves. Some are planted like a picket fence, while others have legs (to make luck mobile).

Chulalongkorn Art Centre
7th Floor, Centre of Academic Resources, Chulalongkorn University, Thanon Phayathai, Pathumwan (0 2218 2964/5/www.car.chula.ac. th/art). **Open** *Term time* 9am-7pm Mon-Fri; 9am-4pm Sat. *Holidays* 9am-4pm Mon-Fri. **Admission** free. **Map** p249/p250 F5.
An important space that has hosted socially relevant shows by Sakharin Krue-on, Michael Shaowanasai, Navin Rawanchaikul, Pinaree Sanpitak, Chatchai Puipia and Vasan Sitthiket, plus top foreign names such as Yasumasa Morimura and Nobuyashi Araki.

Lumphini Park
192 Thanon Rama IV (0 2252 7006). Ratchadamri BTS/Saladaeng BTS/Silom MRT/Lumphini MRT. **Open** 4.30am-9pm daily. **Map** p251 G/H6.
Named after Buddha's birthplace in Nepal, the capital's best green enclave was donated by King Vajiravudh (Rama VI) in 1925, whose statue dominates the main (south-western) entrance. It's most interesting around dawn and dusk, when its pagoda and lakes (pedalos can be hired) are circled by joggers, its paths become t'ai chi classes, and others perform mass aerobics or play acrobatic *takraw*. There are even open-air gyms. Its shaded grounds also refresh lazier souls: there's a restaurant to the north-west, and even more picnickers than usual attend free Music in the Park concerts. By night, the perimeter becomes a soliciting ground: women on the east, men on the west.

Siam Ocean World & 4-D X-venture
Siam Paragon, Thanon Rama I, Pathumwan (0 2687 2000/0 2610 6603/www.siamparagon.co.th). Siam BTS. **Open** 9am-10pm daily. *X-venture* every 30mins 10.30am-8.30pm daily. **Admission** *Siam*

Sightseeing

Prime Privacy

Things are going swimmingly at **Siam Ocean World**. *See p93.*

Ocean World B450; B280 under 120cm/47in. *X-venture* B250. *Both* B690, B500 under 120cm/47in. **Credit** AmEx, DC, MC, V. **Map** p251 G4.
The largest aquarium in South-east Asia holds over 400 species, including penguins, giant crabs, sea horses and 30,000 fish. Zones include a simulated reef, an 'Amazon Rainforest'; at the main tank you can walk through a 270° acrylic tunnel, or pay extra to ride on a glass-bottomed boat or dive with sharks. The design is superb and interactive information excellent, allowing you to view shark eggs as they grow. You can even get married underwater. Co-ordinate your visit with feeding times and amusing multi-sensory simulator films at Sanyo 4-D X-venture.

Snake Farm
Queen Saovabha Memorial Institute, 1871 Thanon Rama IV (0 2252 0161-4/www.redcross.or.th). Saladaeng BTS. **Open** 8.30am-4.30pm Mon-Fri; 8.30am-noon Sat, Sun. *Shows* 10.30am, 2pm Mon-Fri; 10.30am Sat, Sun. Closed around 5 Dec holiday. **Admission** B20 Thais; B70 foreigners. **No credit cards. Map** p250 F6.
Run by the Thai Red Cross, this was the world's second snake farm (1922). It does research and treatment involving vaccinations, animal bites and antivenins. Since the serpents mostly doze, it's only worth going for the slideshow and demo, where the wisecracking hosts handle lethal snakes and milk venom from one of Thailand's six deadly species. Visitors can later wear a boa (yes, a live one).

Wat Pathumwanaram
969 Thanon Rama I (0 2254 2545). Siam BTS. **Open** 8.30am-6pm daily. **Admission** free. **Map** p251 G4.
Fronted by a terrapin pond, this tranquil, undervisited *wat* houses superlative murals and the ashes of Prince Mahidol, father of Kings Rama XIII and IX. In 1996 the ashes and elaborate crematorium of the king's mother were brought here from Sanam Luang.

Sukhumvit

Maps p251 & p252
Sukhumvit illustrates Bangkok's sprawl. The **Siam Society** (*see p96*) was built here in 1933 amid fields. Today it's suffocated by high-rises and packed with luxury condominiums, hotels, shops and hip spots to dine, drink and dance. Thai-Indian Sikhs own much of Sukhumvit between Sois 3-11, where their tailor shops, inns and restaurants proliferate. Other expatriate quarters include Arabs and Africans (Sois 3 and 3/1), Koreans (around Sukhumvit Plaza on Soi 12) and Japanese (Sois 31-53), with Westerners spread throughout.

The Nana area churns with souvenir stalls, travel agents, massage parlours (either healing or entrepreneurial) and hostess bars at **Nana Entertainment Plaza** on Soi 4, and further down at **Soi Cowboy** (Soi 23). **Benjasiri**

Sightseeing

Park and Benjakitti Park (for both, *see below*) offer much-needed green space.

The streets around **Emporium** mall (*see p153*), where you'll find the **Thailand Creative & Design Centre** (*see below*), shift upmarket. Branching off the 'green route' (a shortcut through back *sois*), expensive compounds and condos intersperse spas, boutiques, furniture showrooms, bars, restaurants, chintzy wedding plazas and complexes such as **H1** and **J Avenue** (*see p150* **Mini mall-ism**) catering to young hi-so (high society ingenues), especially around Thonglor (Soi 55) and Ekamai (Soi 63). The latter is also home to **Baan Chang Thai** (*see p203*), where you can study traditional arts; nearby is the **Eastern Bus Terminal** (*see p226*), from where coaches leave for the coast.

Benjakitti Park

Thanon Ratchadaphisek (0 2229 3000). Queen Sirikit Centre MRT. **Open** 5am-8pm daily. **Map** p252 J6/J7.

Surrounding Lake Ratchada, this park represents the first stage of the conversion of leafy Thailand Tobacco Monopoly into a park, and marked Queen Sirikit's sixth cycle (72nd) birthday in 2004. With circuits for jogging and cycling (with bike hire), it boasts water features, a playground, boat hire, an outdoor gym and a meditation zone, although its weedy saplings replaced shady mature trees during construction. You can explore this green zone on a Segway transporter: Thailand Segway Tours (Woraburi Hotel, end of Sukhumvit Soi 4, 0 2255 8463, www.thailandsegwaytours.com) runs glides for over-10s at 9am and 4pm daily (B1,800 for 90 minutes), including instruction.

Benjasiri Park

Thanon Sukhumvit, beside Emporium (0 2262 0810). Phrom Phong BTS. **Open** 5am-9pm daily. **Map** p252 K6.

Amid Benjasiri's fountains, ponds and pavilions stand sculptures by Thai artist Misiem Yipintsoi. The park hosts festivals, and exercisers relish the skate park, tiny pool and courts for basketball and *takraw*.

Siam Society & Baan Kamthieng

131 Sukhumvit Soi 21 (0 2661 6470-77/www.siam-society.org). Asoke BTS/Sukhumvit MRT. **Open** 9am-5pm Tue-Sat. **Admission** B100; B20-B50 concessions. **No credit cards. Map** p252 K5.

Situated in a 150-year-old northern Lanna wooden house, Baan Kamthieng museum has multimedia displays on Lanna culture, from courtship music and spirit dancing to spoken family histories. Set in a well-tended garden, it is said to be haunted by the spirits of three female former residents. The Siam Society Under Royal Patronage has a library with many rare books on Thailand as well as palm-leaf manuscripts and old maps. It holds Thursday lectures, exhibitions and study trips, mainly for members. **Photo** *p99*.

Thailand Creative & Design Centre (TCDC)

7th floor, Emporium, 622 Thanon Sukhumvit (0 2664 7667). **Open** 10.30am-9pm Tue-Sun. **Admission** free; some activities may charge. **No credit cards. Map** p252 K6.

One of the world's best design centres, this state enterprise (*see p34* **Decrees of chic**) inspires Thais with global design and showcases Thai creativity through superb exhibitions and talks. Accessed via this mall's cinema lobby, its stylish environs include a shop, an auditorium and a member's library of film, digital information and 15,000 publications.

North

The entire city is visible from its tallest structure, **Baiyoke II Tower** (*see below*), which soars out of congested **Pratunam Market** (*see p136*), with high-tech mall **Pantip Plaza** nearby (*see p145*). Other sights include the **Bangkok Dolls** museum (*see p164*), **Suan Pakkard Palace** (*see p98*) and **Phyathai Palace** (*see p98*) and **King Power Duty Free**'s puppet theatre (*see p197*), the last two a short walk from **Victory Monument**. Erected in 1941, this bayonet-like obelisk commemorates a dispute with France over Laos.

The BTS meets the MRT at the immense **Chatuchak Weekend Market** (*see p138* **Market forces**). It stands between the gay bars of Thanon Kamphaengphet and various **Chatuchak Park** attractions (*see below*).

Following the MRT clockwise, you skirt **Central Plaza Lad Prao** mall and arc down Ratchadaphisek Road, passing **Tadu Contemporary Art** (7th floor, Barcelona Motors (Yontrakit) Building, Thanon Thiem Ruam Mitr, 0 2645 2473, www.tadu.net, 9am-6pm Mon-Sat) – which presents visual arts, often in collaborations – the **Thailand Cultural Centre** (*see p198*), **Siam Niramit** show (*see p98*) and a nightlife zone of disco barns, beer halls and gaudy massage parlours, plus trendier bars at **Ratchada Soi 4** and **Royal City Avenue (RCA)**.

Baiyoke II Tower

84th floor, 22 Thanon Ratchaprarop, in sub-soi north of Indra Regent Hotel (0 2656 3000). **Open** 10am-10pm daily. **Admission** B200. **Credit** AmEx, MC, V. **Map** p251 G3/4.

This tower has an 84th-floor observation deck for vertiginous panoramas of the megalopolis and (on a clear day) the sea. There are also telescopic viewfinders, some drab displays and a bland restaurant.

Chatuchak Park, Rail Hall of Fame & Butterfly Garden

Thanon Phahon Yothin (0 2272 4575/01615 5776). Morchit BTS/Chatuchak Park MRT. **Open** *Park* 4.30am-9pm daily. *Rail Hall of Fame* 7am-3pm Sat,

The silk root

The current flowering of Thai contemporary design is one reason why devotees of Asian aesthetics ensure they visit the movement's birthplace, **Jim Thompson's House Museum** (*see also p33* **Bangkok by Design**). An architect by trade, American Jim Thompson (born 1906) volunteered for the army during World War II and was assigned to work in Bangkok with the OSS (now the CIA). He soon spotted the potential of the disappearing craft of silk weaving, which was then still practised in the Muslim Baan Khrua community facing his remarkable house across Khlong Saen Saeb. The silks' brilliant hues and shimmering textures soon became a sartorial trademark of the society figures he entertained at his home, and his successors have turned it into a global textiles and furnishing brand.

In 1959 Thompson reassembled six teak houses, some two centuries old, from Ayutthaya and Baan Khrua. Influencing all later adaptations of Thai houses to modern living, he turned the original multi-use rooms into a dining room, bedroom, bathroom, air-conditioned study and open-sided lounge. Now a museum, it looks much like it was when he went missing in Malaysia's Cameron Highlands in 1967. (As to his fate, conspiracy theories abound.)

The guided tour starts in the lush tropical gardens, where pavilions display more of Thompson's discerning collection of Asian arts and antiquities, including Khmer statuary, *bencharong* ceramics, ancient manuscripts and curios such as a carved wooden mouse run.

So many people now visit that to spread the burden on the ancient timbers, the compound offers more attractions in two sympathetically styled annexes. Flanking the canal, **Thompson Restaurant** serves excellent modern Thai and Western dishes in several spaces: an airy white indoors, a covered terrace facing the house across a lotus pond, and a sumptuous teak bar-cum function room upstairs.

Above a **Jim Thompson Thai Silk Company** shop (*see p147*), the James HW Foundation runs the impressive **Jim Thompson Center for the Arts**. Subtly designed by Christian Duc, its galleries host exhibitions interpreting textiles and Thai culture with imagination, scholarship and finesse. Now with artistic director Grithiya Gaweewong (*see p171* **Curate expectations**), the Foundation also sponsors cultural events, international symposiums, publications, educational workshops and artists such as Pinnaree Sanpitak, Montri Toemsombat and Navin Rawanchaikul. A nearby building houses restorers, artists-in-residence and the **William Warren Library**, named after Jim's friend and biographer. Though these activities seem diverse, they all relate to the eclectic interests of their visionary founder.

Jim Thompson's House Museum

6 Kasemsan Soi 2, Thanon Rama I (0 2216 7368/www.jimthompsonhouse.com). National Stadium BTS. **Open** 9am-5pm daily. **Admission** B100; B10-B50 concessions. **Main courses** B100-B300. **Credit** AmEx, DC, MC, V. **Map** p250 F4.

Sun. *Butterfly Garden* 8.30am-4.30pm Tue-Sun. **Admission** free. **No credit cards**.
This respite from market mayhem is branded a 'Learning Park' and displays sculptures by Southeast Asian artists. The small Rail Hall of Fame houses old locomotives and various vehicles, including London taxis and World War II Japanese patrol cars. Adjacent Suan Rotfai (Railway Park, 0 2537 9221), the old railway golf course, offers bike hire, a good pool, the Butterfly Garden and Insectorium (0 2272 4359-60), scale models of Bangkok landmarks and a Traffic Town where kids can test for a Junior Driving Licence. In more contiguous green space, Queen Sirikit Park hosts the Children's Discovery Museum (*see p164*) and a botanical garden with themes such as herbs and flowers in literature.

Phyathai Palace

King Mongkutklao Hospital, 315 Thanon Ratchawithi (0 2354 7732/www.phyathaipalace.org). Victory Monument BTS. **Open** 9am-4pm Sat; by appointment Mon-Fri. **Admission** free. **Map** p252 F1/F2.
This European-style royal getaway of King Rama V became a luxury hotel, then Thailand's first radio station, then a hospital, and finally a museum. Some halls, turrets and filigree pavilions have been restored, but the fading frescoed corridors lend poignancy to the place where King Rama VI experimented with democracy at a miniature town called Dusit Thani, which had its own economy and newspaper. It houses the Army Medical Corps Museum and hosts concerts in the neo-classical grounds. There are guided tours in English by appointment with a letter a week ahead (B500 per 10-15 persons).

Siam Niramit (Magical Siam)

Ratchada Grand Theatre, 19 Thanon Tiam Ruammit, North (0 2649 9222/www.siamniramit.com). Thai Cultural Centre MRT then taxi. **Shows** 8pm daily. **Admission** B1,500. **Credit** AmEx (20% off), V.
On the pseudo-historical model of Phuket FantaSea (*see p217*), this B1.5-billion, 2,000-seat theatre has one of the world's widest and tallest sets. It presents an 80-minute cultural spectacular with special effects, 150 performers, 500 costumes – and no soul. The outdoor crafts village is much more authentic.

Suan Pakkard Palace & Marsi Gallery

352 Thanon Si Ayutthaya (0 2245 4934/www.suan pakkad.com). Phaya Thai BTS. **Open** 9am-4pm daily. **Admission** B50 Thais; B100 foreigners. **No credit cards**. **Map** p251 G3.
Named 'Cabbage Patch Palace' after the site where these five teak houses were assembled in 1952, this delightful museum was preserved after the death of its owners, Prince and Princess Chumbhot. Among their art and antiquities are Khmer Buddha statues, monks' fans, betel nut sets, shells and prehistoric

Shop and pray

Far from declining with modern lifestyles, Thai belief in spirits takes on fresh guises. The **Erawan Shrine** receives a *wai* from almost all passing shoppers, drivers and SkyTrain riders. Pilgrims whose wishes get fulfilled return with offerings and may pay for costumed dancers kept on standby to perform. By contrast, a crazed man smashed its statue in 2006 and received his karma instantly: bystanders beat him to death. Thousands scrambled to see the restored image reinstalled.

This projection of fix-all faith far exceeds the shrine's origins as a spirit house. Erected in 1956, it appeased displaced spirits who were blamed for fatal misfortunes during construction of the old Erawan Hotel. Tiled in mirror and decked in garlands and wooden elephant offerings, the shrine isn't to a spirit, nor even to Erawan (the elephant mount of Indra), but to another Hindu god, Brahma, the four-faced god of creation.

Around him are rival shrines. Indra, recently painted green, sits outside his namesake Amarin Plaza next door, opposite which the InterContinental Hotel erected a statue of Vishnu the Preserver upon his man-bird mount Garuda. Vishnu's wife Lakshmi promotes prosperity on the top of **Gaysorn Plaza** (*see p153*), facing across Ratchaprasong junction to the Police Hospital's Garuda. On the remaining corner, Ganesha (the obstacle-removing, elephant-headed son of Vishnu and Lakshmi) sits at **Central World Plaza** (*see p154*). Beside him stands the only god who could calm this competitive cosmic energy: Trimuthi, who combines Brahma, Vishnu and Shiva the destroyer. Again, the original meaning has morphed. Young worshippers interpret Trimuthi as the 'god of love'. Especially on Thursdays, they wish for a partner by offerings red incense, candles and flowers – the deity's favoured colour. Witnessing the globalised generation create a cult reinforces the endurance, depth and sheer fluidity of Thai belief.

Erawan Shrine

At Erawan mall, Thanon Ratchadamri (0 2252 8754). Chidlom BTS. **Open** 6am-10.30pm daily. **Admission** free. **Map** p251 G5.

Baan Chiang pottery. Most exquisite is the pond-side Lacquer Pavilion. A birthday gift from the prince to his wife, this 17th- to 18th-century Ayutthayan library features astonishing gold and black lacquer scenes from the life of Buddha, the *Ramakien* and Thai life. The grounds also contain the Marsi Gallery for art shows, and the multimedia Khon Museum on classical Thai drama.

Siam Society. *See p96.*

South

A physical barrier divides Thanon Sathorn Tai (north) in Bangrak from Thanon Sathorn Tai in South: a canal dug by Chinese labourers in the late 19th century. Rich locals and foreigners then built European-style tropical wooden mansions on either side; a few have survived, mainly by conversion to other uses. The splendid century-old Thai-Chinese Chamber of Commerce (built as the Bombay Department Store) got saved as the **Blue Elephant** Thai restaurant (*see p128*). Heritage gets little protection round here.

Amid outrage, at press time **Wat Yannawa** (*see below*) was trying to demolish the historic Soi Wanglee community at Charoen Krung Soi 52, where the shophouses, like the *wat's chedi* plinth, were styled to resemble the junks on which Chinese immigrants arrived at the International Pier that was once located here.

Among modern landmarks you'll see as you make the tiring walk up Sathorn Tai are the robot-themed **Bank of Asia**, designed by Sumet Jumsai, and the precariously narrow **Thai Wah II Tower**. It has a hole at the 50th floor, where you'll find the spa pool of the **Banyan Tree Bangkok** hotel (*see p51*), which is also famed for its open-air rooftop bar-restaurant, **Moon Bar at Vertigo** (*see p135*). It overlooks the suave **Sukhothai** and **Metropolitan** hotels (for both, *see p51*), and **MR Kukrit Pramoj's Heritage Home** (*see below*). Nearby, the **Goethe Institut** and **Alliance Française** (for both, *see p168*) continue a tradition of foreign promotion of Thai arts.

Tucked behind them, Soi Ngam Duphlee was the original backpackers' flop zone before Banglamphu, but became a tad sleazy. At the corner of Thanon Rama IV, a gold-crested tower contains the holistic **Life Centre**. Heading east past **Plainern Palace** (open only on Naris Day, *see p161*) you reach Khlong Toei, a port known for markets (*see p140*) and slums, and, eventually, **Bangkok University Gallery** (*see below*). The loop in the Chao Phraya river, traced by Thanons Rama III and Charoen Krung, is semi-industrialised, with only **Central Rama III Shopping Centre** and **Tawandaeng German Brewhouse** (*see p135*) to divert visitors.

Bangkok University Gallery
3rd floor, Building 9, Kluaynam Thai campus, Thanon Rama IV, Sukhumvit (0 2350 3626). Bus 22, 46, 149, 507. **Open** 8.30am-5pm Tue-Sat. **Admission** free.
Ark Fonsmut curates the faculty's lofty new spaces, which host shows by staff, students and foreign artists-in-residence. Its Brand New exhibition (annually January-March) has launched many a star.

MR Kukrit Pramoj's Heritage Home
19 Soi Phra Phinij, Thanon Sathorn Tai (0 2286 8185). Bus 22, 62, 67, 76, 116, 149, 530. **Open** 10am-5pm Sat, Sun. **Admission** B50; B20 students in uniform. **No credit cards. Map** p251 F7.
These five Central Plains stilt houses were the seat of Mom Ratchawong Kukrit, a late aristocratic prime minister in the turbulent mid 1970s. A cultural colossus, he is best known for his writing, promotion of *khon* dance and acting as an Asian prime minister in 1963 film *The Ugly American*, with Marlon Brando. Set by a pond in a garden of indigenous species, the house contains antiquities, photos and memorabilia.

Wat Yannawa
1648 Thanon Charoen Krung (0 2672 3216/www. watyan.com). Saphan Taksin BTS. **Open** *Temple* 5am-9pm daily. *Bot* 8-9am, 5-6pm daily. **Admission** free. **Map** p250 D8.
King Rama I restored this Ayutthaya-era temple, and Rama III added a *chedi* platform in the form of a Chinese junk, complete with eyes on the prow, four cannons and a shrine in the stern.

Suburbs

Devotees of arts, gods and fun find solace amid the urban sprawl.

Within two to five years new SkyTrain and subway lines will finally reach in all directions to suburbs that have appeared since the SkyTrain was envisaged in the 1970s to serve them (the lines currently only delineate Downtown). Until recently land development hadn't followed stations, so transport infrastructure has played catch-up as fertile farmland gets eaten up by underplanned *moo baan* (housing estates), golf courses, universities and some of the world's biggest shopping centres.

The growing middle classes – plus workers migrating from Downtown slums and upcountry farms – are adopting a suburban lifestyle but endure traumatic commutes. You'll need a taxi or hired car to explore these areas, although expressways have drastically cut journey times. Snippets of canal life persist on the peripheries.

East

The BTS currently ends at Onnut (Sukhumvit Soi 77), which features the ghost-story location **Wat Maha But** (*see p101*) and is also one of three routes east to the new Suvarnabhumi Airport (*see p224*). One of those routes, Thanon Bangna-Trad (and the Chonburi expressway overhead), branches off Sukhumvit and thunders through Bangna, past golf courses, factories and housing estates to the Eastern Seaboard, passing the high-tech **Bangkok International Exhibition Centre** (BITEC), **Central City Bangna** mall, the **Nation Multimedia** tower (a Cubist homage to Braque by Sumet Jumsai) and the bombastic campus that belongs to **ABAC University**.

Sukhumvit continues, hugging the estuary, into suburban Samut Prakarn province, skirting the **Erawan Museum** (*see below*), **Samut Prakarn Crocodile Farm** (*see p101*) and **Muang Boran** (*see below*).

North from Bangna, Thanon Srinakharin gives access to **Rama IX Royal Park** (*see p101*), the mega malls of **Seri Centre** and **Seacon Square**, and the **Prasart Museum** (*see p101*). It ends at Thanon Ramkhamhaeng, an artery packed with malls, shops, bars (many gay) and 1.5-kilometre-long (one mile) **Na Ram Market** (between Sois 43-53, 4pm-midnight daily) – all frequented by students of **Ramkhamhaeng University**. Beside it undulates the stands of **Ratchamangala National Stadium** (*see p203*).

Erawan Museum

99/9 Moo 1, Bang Muang Mai, Samut Prakan (0 2371 3135-6/www.ancientcity.com). **Open** 8am-6pm (5pm last entry) daily. **Admission** B150; B50 concessions. **No credit cards**.
A monument to religious harmony by the founder of Muang Boran (*see below*), this humungous 150-tonne metal statue depicts Erawan, the three-headed elephant mount of Hindu god Indra. From a kitschy museum in the base, steps and a lift up the rear legs take you to a multi-faith chapel in the body. Oddly deep and deeply odd.

Muang Boran (Ancient City)

Sukhumvit Sai Kao km33, Bangpu Mai, Samut Prakarn (0 2323 9253/www.ancientcity.com). **Open** 8am-5pm daily. **Admission** *Thais* B100; B50 concessions. *Foreigners* B300; B200 concessions. **No credit cards**.
One visionary created this under-visited, open-air architectural museum, reconstructing salvaged masterpieces and scaled-down versions of landmarks in a park shaped like Thailand. It's a sublime, relaxing half-day jaunt, but vast and without public transport, so it's best to go by car or tour. Bicycles are for hire.

Prasart Museum

9 Krung Thep Kreetha Soi 4A (0 2379 3601). **Open** by appointment 1 day ahead 9am-3pm (last entry) Tue-Sun. **Admission** B1,000; B500 per person groups of 2 or more. **No credit cards**.
It's worth the hassle (but perhaps not the price) to luxuriate in this private collection. The replicas of historic buildings here include a European-style mansion, Khmer shrine and Northern and Central Thai teak houses, plus Thai- and Chinese-style temples. Collector Prasart Vongsakul's shop in Peninsula Plaza (*see p154*) sells antiques and reproductions of the exhibits.

Rama IX Royal Park

Sukhumvit Soi 103 (Soi Udomsuk) (0 2328 1385). **Open** 6am-7pm daily. **Admission** B10; B5 concessions. **No credit cards.**
Bangkok's notoriously minimal green space is increasing. This 200-acre park honoured the King's 60th birthday in 1987. It has a small museum about him, plus botanical and water gardens.

Samut Prakarn Crocodile Farm

555 Thai Baan, Samut Prakarn (0 2703 5144-8/www.crocodilefarm.com). **Open** 7am-6pm daily. **Admission** Thais B60; B30 concesssions. *Foreigners B300; B200 concesssions.* **Credit** MC, V.
This is the world's biggest croc farm, with 100,000 occupants, including the near-extinct Siamese species and the longest crocodile at six metres (20 ft). Hourly shows feature wrestling, head-in-jaws and similar touristy stunts, as well as elephant shows and rides.

Wat Maha But

749 Onnut Soi 7, Sukhumvit Soi 77 (0 2311 2183). Onnut BTS. **Open** 7am-6pm daily. **Admission** free.
This nondescript temple by Khlong Prakhanong holds a shrine to Mae Nak, who died in childbirth over 150 years ago while her husband was at war. In a much-filmed legend, he returned to live with his wife and child, unaware they were both ghosts. Conscripts and mothers come here to donate offerings such as dresses, wigs, make-up and toys to appease the vengeful spirits. It opens 24 hours every 14th-15th and last two days of every month for *kor huai* (seeking lucky numbers) for the bi-monthly lottery.

New bronze age

Public collections of modern Thai art are rare, but there are four significant private ones located on Bangkok's fringes. The **Bangkok Sculpture Centre**, near Ramindra expressway exit, houses 120 major works displayed on lawns, ledges, warehouse gantries and the fountain terrace of this airy, dramatic edifice. Owner Sermkhun Khunawong is aiming to complete a 300-exhibit timeline of modern Thai sculpture,

from Silpa Bhirasri and Khien Yimsiri, whose fluid figurative bronzes form the centrepiece, to the surrealist hinged bodies by Manop Suwanpinta and phantasmagorical wood carvings by Kham-ai Dejdoungtae.

Jean-Michel Beurdeley shows masterpieces (by appointment, 0 2314 6645/0 2718 5520) at his home gallery on Ramkhamhaeng Soi 24, including works by luminaries such as Montien Boonma, Chatchai Pui-pia, Niti Wattuya, Natee Utarit, Wasan Sitthiket and Pinnaree Sanpitak. More accessibly, Boonchai Bencharongkul's 300-strong hoard at **UCOM** includes many primal pieces by Tawan Duchanee, as well as Chalermchai Kositphipat, Prateung Emjaroen and Kamol Tassananchalee.

To the west, **Misiem's Sculpture Garden** offers a rest from the monuments of Phuttha Monthon. Balletic modernist bronzes by the late self-taught National Artist Misiem Yipintsoi appear like sprites amid rustic landscaping here, as well as at Benjasiri Park (*see p96*) and, with her paintings, at Misiem's (*see below*), the gallery run by her granddaughter, Klaomard, in what used to be About Café. The sculpture garden includes installations by ceramicist Surojana Settabutr. Admission to each collection is free.

Bangkok Sculpture Centre

4/18-19 Nuanchan Soi 56, Thanon Ramindra, North-east (0 2559 0505 ext 119, 232/ www.thaiartproject.org). **Open** 10am-4pm every 2nd & 4th Sat of mth; also by appointment 10am-4pm Mon-Fri.

Misiem's Sculpture Garden

38/9 Thanon Phuttha Monthon Sai 7, Nakhon Pathom (office 0 2639 8056-7/www.yipintsoi.com/~aara/index.html). **Open** 9am-5pm Fri-Sun.

UCOM

Benchachinda Building, 499 Thanon Wiphawadee-Rangsit, facing Kasetsart University, Outer North (0 2953 1111 ext 23567). **Open** 8.30am-5.30pm Mon-Fri.

North-east

Outside Thanon Ratchadaphisek ring road, conurbations continue to devour marshland. Dramatic architecture surrounds Ratchayothin junction, with the pachyderm-shaped **Elephant Building**, and the gold-pointed towers of **SCB Park Plaza**, which hosts the **Museum of Thai Banking** (9 Thanon Ratchadaphisek, 0 2544 4504/4462-3, 10am-5pm Tue-Sat).

In suburban Lad Prao stands the **Kwan Im Shrine** (see below), beyond which Ramindra offers the **Bangkok Sculpture Centre** (see p101 **New bronze age**). Further north lie **Safari World**, **Siam Park** (for both, see below), **Dream World** and the museums at **Technopolis**. The latter two lie off Thanon Rangsit-Nakorn Nayok, beside which **Khlong Rangsit** offers beef noodles on floating restaurants.

Kwan Im Shrine

Chokchai Soi 39, Lad Phrao Soi 53 (Chokchai 4) (0 2514 0715). **Open** 6.30am-8pm Mon-Fri, Sun; 6.30am-11pm Sat; 6.30am-2am Chinese religious holidays. **Admission** free.
The middle-class cult of Kuan Im (aka Kuan Yin, the Chinese *bodhisattva* of mercy) prompted this massive, gaudy sculpture garden, embellished with wagon wheels, barrels and a modern pagoda. Eye-popping offerings crowd the basement museum.

Safari World

99 Thanon Ramindra km9, Klong Samwa (0 2518 1000-5/2914 4100-5/www.safariworld.com). **Open** *Safari Park* 9am-5pm daily. *Marine Park* 9am-4.30pm daily. **Admission** *Safari Park* B200; B160 children under 140cm/55in. *Marine Park* B330; B230 children under 140cm/55in. *Both* B390; B290 children under 140cm/55in. *All zones* free children under 100cm/39in. **Credit** AmEx, MC, V.
This animal park is a 150-acre enclosure containing African beasts and Marine Park. You'll need a car or tour bus to explore. Arrive by 10am for the big cats' 'breakfast show'; or there are sea lions (11am); cowboys (noon); dolphins and whales (1.40pm), war games (2.30pm) and a bird show (3.30pm).

Siam Park

99 Thanon Seri Thai, Kanna Yaow (0 2919 7200-5/www.siamparkcity.com). **Open** 10am-6pm daily. **Admission** B200; B100 children under 150cm/59in; free children under 90çm/35in. **Credit** AmEx, MC, V, DC.
The fun here comes in all guises, including fairground rides, water slides and waves lapping a faux beach.

Outer North

A century ago expatriate hunters stalked birds around **Don Muang** (literally 'city heights'). From the 1930s it became Thailand's flying hub and birds of the metallic variety still use its airport – despite the opening of Suvarnabhumi Airport (see p224) – or rest in the **Royal Thai Air Force Museum** (see below). A little south lie the **UCOM** art collection (see p101 **New bronze age**) and, heading east towards **Nonthaburi** ministry-dotted Thanon Chaengwattana Road hosts trade shows, sports and concerts at **IMPACT Exhibition Centre**. Further north at Rangsit, a monorail encircles **Future Park** mall and the underrated **South-east Asia Antique Ceramics Museum** (see below).

Royal Thai Air Force Museum

Royal Thai Air Force Base, Thanon Phahon Yothin, behind airport (0 2534 1575/1764). **Open** 8am-4pm daily. **Admission** free.
Rare exhibits include the only extant Model I Corsaire, one of just two Japanese Tachikawas, a Spitfire and Thailand's first completely home-grown aircraft, the Model II Bomber Boripatr.

South-east Asia Antique Ceramics Museum

Bangkok University Rangsit campus, Thanon Phaholyothin, Rangsit (0 2902 0299 ext 2894/ www.museum.bu.ac.th). **Open** 9am-4pm Tue-Sat. **Admission** free.
A world-class collection of prehistoric Ban Chiang and Lopburi earthenware, Sukhothai celadons and other Lanna, Khmer and Burmese masterpieces. Displaying 500 of the 2,000 items, the elegant galleries are semi-underground to evoke the Sukhothai kilns, one of which has been reconstructed. You can handle samples to learn about the restoration process.

Outer West

The margins beyond Thonburi provide distractions en route to or from **Kanchanaburi** (see p105), the canalscape around **Nakhon Pathom** (see p105) and **Hua Hin** (see p211). Within an hour of Downtown is a vast Buddhist-themed park, **Phuttha Monthon**, noted for its 40-metre (131-foot) Buddha and Utthayan Avenue, which shimmers with ornate bridges, fountains, flora and lampposts topped by a gilded phoenix. Make it a day trip, encompassing the diverse **Lord Buddha Images Museum** (5/9 Thanon Phuttha Monthon Sai 2, 0 2448 1795/08 9155 7806), the **House of Museums** (see below) and the serene **Misiem's Sculpture Garden** (see p101 **New bronze age**).

House of Museums

Baan Phipitaphan, Khlong Pho Soi 2, Sala Thammasop Road (08 9200 2803). **Open** 10am-5pm Sat, Sun. **Admission** B30; B10 concessions. **No credit cards.**
Historian Anake Nawigamune's popular culture collection has three floors of interactive retro reconstructions, including a schoolroom and pharmacy.

Further Afield

Escape the city for ancient towns, canalscape idylls and virgin jungle.

The Chao Phraya delta, one of the world's grain baskets, offers diverse sights within just a two-hour drive of the city. Beyond the river stops nearer central Bangkok (*see p74* **Quays to the city**), boat tours head north to **Bang Sai**, the 19th-century **Bang Pa-In** summer palace and the ruined Siamese capital of **Ayutthaya**. Westwards, around ancient sacred **Nakhon Pathom** are intact canal tracts, while rainforest is accessible both in **Kanchanaburi**, where the 'Death Railway' was carved along the River Kwai, and north-east at **Khao Yai National Park**. Day or overnight trips from Bangkok are easiest with a tour or hired van and driver.

Bang Pa-In & Ayutthaya

Under Queen Sirikit's patronage, resuscitated crafts now help diversify the incomes of farmers trained at **Bang Sai Folk Arts & Crafts Centre** (0 35366 252-4, www.bangsai arts.com), located 55 kilometres (34 miles) north of Bangkok in tranquil riverbank worshops. Some 17 kilometres (11 miles) upstream, the island of **Bang Pa-In** (0 3526 1673-82, www.palaces.thai.net) has since 1632 been a summer royal retreat. In 1872 Rama V turned it into an eclectic palace named after a drowned princess. Set amid animal topiary, baroque pavilions contrast with dazzling Chinese **Wehat Chamrun Palace** and gothic **Wat Nivet Dhammaparvat**. It is at its busiest in the morning.

From Bang Pa-In, longtail boats ply the scenic 45-minute trip to **Ayutthaya**, 21 kilometres (11 miles) to the north. Focused on an artificial island, this World Heritage Site is an essential visit; the former capital's destruction by the Burmese still reverberates, as in recent anti-Burmese movies. With its 400 temples razed and 90 per cent of its people gone, it was abandoned and looted until the 1950s dictator Phibunsongkhram tidied it into a showpiece. During excavations, royal regalia was stolen from the frescoed crypt of **Wat Ratchaburana** and the old ritual centre, **Wat Mahathat**. Remnants of the gilded cache – plus marvellous statuary – fill **Chao Sam Phraya Museum** (108/16 Thanon Rotchana, 0 3524 1587, closed Mon &Tue). Other treasures occupy the fretworked **Chandra Kasem**

Palace Museum (Thanon U-Thong, 0 3525 1586, closed Mon, Tue).

Dioramas at the **Historical Study Centre** (Thanon Rotchana, 0 3524 5123-4, B100) offer more perspective than the **TAT** tourist office (108/22 Thanon Si Sanphet, 0 3524 6076-7, 8.30am-4.30pm daily). Visiting the ruins requires entry to **Phra Nakhon Si Ayutthaya Historical Park** (0 3524 2284, B30 per site). By staying overnight, you can enjoy quiet, cool sightseeing before the daytrippers descend.

Bang Pa-In.

Samphran Elephant Ground & Crocodile Farm. *See p105.*

Only foundations – and the **Trimuk Pavilion**, built by Rama V for ceremonies – indicate the presence of the old Grand Palace, though the iconic triple *chedi* (built in 1492) of its temple, **Wat Si Sanphet**, remain. Thais flock next door to the heavily restored Buddha image of **Vihaan Phra Mongkhon Bophit**. Beyond a market and the exquisite teak 1894 **Khun Phaen's House**, you can get elephant rides (08 1869 9520, B200 10mins, B400 20mins, B500 30mins). Opposite is **Beung Phra Ram**, a park of lily ponds and a lone *prang*. Behind it, **Wat Mahathat** draws photographers to its root-encased Buddha head.

Outer-bank remains, seen clockwise, include **Wat Yai Chaimongkhon** to the south-east. Built by a Ceylonese sect, it boasts a 60-metre (197-foot) bell *chedi*, a reclining Buddha and a shrine to toys. East on Highway 3058, **Wat Maheyong** retains stucco elephants around a Sri Lankan-style *chedi*. To the north, the restored **Kraal** was where elephants were trained, and stunning **Wat Phramane** (Thanon U-Thong, 0 3525 1992, admission B20) is the only surviving original temple. Dominating the west is the immaculate five-*prang* **Wat Chaiwattanaram**.

To the south, King U-Thong stayed at the cloistered **Wat Phuttaisawan** before developing Ayutthaya. En route you pass **St Joseph's Church** in the old French settlement, one of many foreign quarters then housing, among others, Portuguese, Japanese, Dutch and Malays. Crafts fans can visit *khon* (*see p195*) mask-maker **ML Punsawat Sooksawasdi** (5/1 Thanon U-thong, 0 3524 1574/08 6510 2195) and the teak house carpenters at **Baan Pahan**, 13 kilometres (eight miles) north on Highway 32.

Where to stay & eat

Baan Khun Phra (48 Thanon U-Thong, 0 3524 1978, double B400-B800) is a wooden garden enclave near Chao Phrom Market's food stalls, while **Baan Suan Guest House** (23/1 Thanon Chakrapat, 0 3524 2394, double B300-B600) has the bonus of tasty home cooking. Riverside dining at **Ruen Rub Rong** (13/1-2 Thanon U-Thong, 0 3524 3090, main courses B160) includes a dinner cruise option. Just to the north, the wooden **Ayothaya Riverside House** (0 2585 6001, rates B300-B1,200) also has rooms on a boat.

Beyond it, on via Wat Kasatrathirat, are two good Thai restaurants offering river views: **Baan Watcharachai** (0 3532 1333, main courses B75-B200) has plush, Thai-style buildings set in a garden, and a dining boat; next door is the subtly rustic **Baan Mae Choi Nang Ram** (0 3525 5268, main courses B80-B300).

Getting there & around

Most tours of Ayutthaya combine 90min minibus rides with train or boat (*see p56* **Boat trips**) and call at Bang Pa-In. Otherwise, buses leave Bangkok's Northern Bus Terminal every 20mins 5.40am-8.40pm daily (B65), taking 90mins. Trains leave 4.20am-11.40pm daily from Bangkok's Hualumphong station (B12-B54, 90mins), calling at Bang Pa-In.

In Bang Pa-In, pedal rickshaws and *tuk-tuks* ply the short walk between station and palace. In Ayutthaya, *tuk-tuks* can be hired by the day (B200 per hour), as can boats at piers by Chandra Kasem Museum or Wat Phanan Choeng (B400-B600 per day), and bicycles from the tourist police (B50 per day) or near the train station (B40 per day). Or commission the Benjarong rice barge (0 3521 1036).

For special-interest itineraries, try **Classic Tour** (0 3524 4978).

Canals near Nakhon Pathom

The canal communities west of Bangkok retain some bygone lifestyles and markets, all best viewed in the early morning. Deluged by coachloads from 9pm, the orchards, stilt houses and paddling traders of **Damnoen Saduak Floating Market** in the Ratchaburi province (0 3224 1204, 6am-noon daily) are losing their atmosphere due to souvenir touting and pricey boat tours (B300-B600 per hour). Fewer tourists reach Samut Songkhram province, with its scenic **Tha Kha Floating Market** (0 3476 6208, 8am-noon on every 2nd, 7th & 12th days of waxing and waning moons), part of itineraries from **Baan Tai Had Resort** (Thanon Wat Phuang Malai-Wat Tai Had, 0 3476 7220-4), which also hires out kayaks.

Longtails (from B300 per hr) from **Samut Songkhram**'s charming riverside market serve Tha Kha and the floating market at **Amphawa** (Wat Amphawan, 6am-6pm daily), a watery orchard district with stilt-house homestays at **Baan Tha Kha** (0 3476 6170, double B350) or **Baan Hua Had** (0 3473 5073, double B350).

In Nakhon Pathom province, there's still charm at **Lam Phya Floating Market** (Wat Lam Phya, Bang Lane, 0 3439 1985, Sat &Sun only) and touristed yet untacky **Don Wai Floating Market** (near Wat Rai King, Tha Nakhon Chaisri, 6am-noon daily). Don Wai is best reached via a one-hour cruise on the Tha Chin from **Rose Garden Aprime Resort** (km32 Thanon Phetkasem, 0 3432 2544-7, www.rose-garden.com, double B3,108-B31,800), which also boasts elephant rides, golf, restaurants, a cultural show and other tours. Nearby, **Samphran Elephant Ground**

& Crocodile Farm (km Samphran, 0 2429 0361-2 com, admission B500; B2: elephant rides, croc wrest

Jaya Sri Lodge (Ngev 08 1809 4041, anuchathira a pleasant retreat in old te ceramics, mask-making, dance and agrotourism, plus trips to Lam Phya, **Wat Suwan Floating Market** and Nakhon Chaisri's two large markets, one thriving at the town's riverside, one decaying on the nearby canal dug for pilgrims to **Nakhon Pathom** town.

Siam's oldest city and entry point of Buddhism, Nakhon Pathom was a Mon centre two millennia ago. You can't miss **Phra Pathom Chedi** (0 3424 2143), reputedly the world's tallest *stupa* at 120 metres (414 feet). Since 1853 its bell shape has clad a Khmer *prang* that encased a Mon *stupa*. There's also a reclining Buddha, a circular cloister, and **Dvaravati treasures in Phra Pathom Chedi National Museum** (0 3427 0300, closed Mon, Tue, admission B30). Artefacts in the free **Phra Pathom Museum** (closed Mon, Tue) are less organised. Across town, the leafy grounds of **Sanam Chan Palace** (6 Thanon Rajamankha Nai, 0 3424 4236-7, 9am-4pm daily, admission B50) contain museums in the divine timber residences of King Rama VI of Thai, tropical European and chateau style, plus a *wat*-like theatre. For sights en route, *see pp72-78.*

Getting there

Buses leave daily from the Southern Bus Terminal to Samut Songkram (every 20mins, 4.45am-5.30pm, B52) and Nakhon Pathom (every 15mins, 5.30am-8.30pm, B38). To Nakhon Pathom, 13 trains leave 8.05am-10.50pm daily from Hualumphong station (B14-B60), while five 3rd-class trains run daily from Thonburi station (B10). To Samut Songkram, 12 3rd-class trains leave hourly 5.30am-8.10pm daily from Wongwian Yai station (B10).

Kanchanaburi

The base for exploring jungled 'Kan'buri', Thailand's fourth-largest province, is pleasant **Kanchanaburi** town, 129 kilometres (81 miles) west of Bangkok. Its infamous **Bridge on the River Kwai** (4 kilometres/2.5 miles north of today's bridge) was part of the World War II 'Death Railway' built by the Japanese to supply its army in Burma. An estimated 18,000 POWs and 90,000 Asian slave labourers perished in its construction, many interred in nearby **Chung Kai Cemetery** or the downtown **Don Rak Kanchanaburi War Cemetery**. Beside the

_ interactive **Death Railway**
.um (0 3451 2721, www.tbrconline.com,
..y 9am-5pm, B80 8-14s B30) offers much
.etter exhibits and interpretation than the
tacky tourist trap **War Museum** by the rail
bridge, or the basic but worthy **JEATH War
Museum** (Wat Chai Chumpon, Thanon Pak
Praek, 0 3451 5203, admission B30) where the
Kwae Yai (larger tributary) joins the Kwae Noi
(smaller tributary) to form the Maeklong River.
Each November, the ten-day **River Kwai
Bridge Week** has a sound and light show.

The tourist office (TAT, 310/2 Thanon Saeng
Chuto, 0 3451 1200, open 8.30am-4.30pm daily)
has information on sights and in the nearby
national parks and fertile valleys dotted with
Mon, Karen and ethnic Burmese villages. Some
65 kilometres (35 km) up Route 3199, the nine-
tier waterfalls in **Erawan National Park**
(0 3457 4234) get crowded at weekends, while
nearby **Srinakharin National Park** (0 3451
6667-8) has a reservoir. Both charge B400 entry.

Though mostly dismantled after the war, the
'Death Railway' still runs from Kanchanaburi
over rickety viaducts along the Kwae Noi to
Nam Tok (90mins, every 20mins, 8am-6pm
daily, B20 one way), where _songtaews_ (B200-
B300) shuttle to **Sai Yok Noi** falls (km46
Highway 323). It's busy with picnickers, but
inferior to the distant cascade at **Sai Yok
Yai National Park** (km82, 0 3451 6163-4,
admission B400; B200 children). Australia
has funded the impressive **Hellfire Pass
Memorial & Museum** (km75, 0 81308 2300,
www.hellfirepass.com) on the 4.5-kilometre
(three-mile) jungle trail to the hand-chiselled
rail cutting of **Hellfire Pass**. At km105-6,
Hin Dat Hot Springs feature Japanese-built
sulphurous hot baths next to a cooling stream.
From here, a poor dirt road leads to the
marvellous, multi-tiered **Phra That Waterfall**.

Highway 323 winds 260 kilometres (150
miles) to the Myanmar border, passing karst
mountains and floating guesthouses along
Khao Laem reservoir near **Thong Pha Phum**.
Heading the flooded valley, the quaint Mon
town of **Sangkhlaburi** boasts an awesomely
tall wooden bridge. At the frontier, **Three
Pagodas Pass** marks an old Burmese
invasion route with a trio of tiny _chedi_
and lots of Burmese teak furniture.

Where to stay & eat

In Kanchanaburi Town, many of the hotels
and guesthouses on Thanons Song Kwae and
Maenam Kwae have bamboo raft rooms, such
as **Sam's Place** (7/3 Thanon Song Kwae, 0
3451 3971, www.samsguesthouse.com, double
B150-B300) and its two branches. Near the wire-

operated ferry here, disco rafts moor before
night-time party trips. Bars and floating
restaurants moored along Thanon Song
Kwae usually boast good food and sunset
views. Upstream and considerably upmarket
is the **Felix River Kwai** (Tha Makham,
0 3451 5033, www.felixriverkwai.co.th,
double B2,700-B3,200).

Most remote and enchanting is **Jungle
Rafts** (0 2642 5497, www.riverkwaifloatel.com,
full-board double B2,000), an eco pioneer in a
gorge below Sai Yok Yai, where unelectrified,
oil-lamp-lit rafts offer great food, massages,
elephants, a cave temple and dancers from the
adjacent Mon village. It can be reached by boat
from its sister **River Kwai Resotel** (0 2642
5497, www.riverkwaifloatel.com, double B2,200-
B3,400), with garden cottages and a pool.

Getting there

Buses to Kanchanaburi leave from Bangkok's
Southern Bus Terminal every 20mins (5am-
10pm daily, B99). Provincial buses are scarce.
Trains leave daily to Kanchanaburi from
Thonburi and Hualumphong stations. Rail
tours (0 2621 8701 ext 5217, 6.30am Sat, Sun)
include side trips by bus.

Khao Yai National Park

Thailand's first national park (1962) and, after
Kaeng Krachan, its second largest (2,168 square
kilometres/837 square miles), is also the most
visited, marking the Khorat Plateau just 200
kilometres (124 miles) north-east of Bangkok.
Waterfalls (fullest and busiest in 'winter', when
warm clothing is essential) feature on most
of the 12 trails from **Khao Yai Visitor
Centre** (Thanon Thanarat km37, Nakorn
Nayok province, 08 1877 3127/08 6092 6531,
admission B400). You can get hiking permits
here or at park gates. Though still poached,
wildlife is abundant in this old-growth forest
and gathers more at water sources in the
hot season. Rangers run truck-borne **Night
Safaris** (B40/1 hour per trip), with variable
results, and join all independent tours.

Where to stay & eat

The Visitor Centre has basic lodging and
food, but Khao Yai is ringed by golf courses
and resorts offering restaurants and tours.
Kirimaya by ALiLa (1/3 Moo 6, Thanon
Thanarat, Pak Chong, 0 4442 6000, www.
kirimaya.com, main courses B80-B500, double
B7,200-B31,779) is a serene designer resort, with
mountain views, Maya Spa and a Jack Nicklaus
golf course. **Khao Yai Garden Lodge** (135/1

Barge your way through **Damnoen Saduak Floating Market**. *See p105.*

Thanon Thanarat km7, Pakchong, 0 4436 5178, www.khaoyai-garden-lodge.com, main courses B180-B200, double B2,500) has diverse rooms and tours. The not-for-profit **Cabbages & Condoms Resort** (Phaya Yen, Pak Chong, 0 3622 7065, www.pda.or.th/saptai, main courses B150, double B1,880-B2,500) has more eco-aware trips. Cheaper is the **Jungle House** (21/5 Thanon Thanarat km19.5, Pakchong, 0 4429 7307, www.junglehousehotel.com, double B600-B1,200 Mon-Fri, Sun; B900-B1,400 Sat).

Thai wine is vastly improving and Khao Yai's charming vineyards offer Siamese Sideways-style tastings, especially while they're fruiting (Aug-Feb) and producing (Feb-Mar). Small, picturesque **GranMonte** (52 Thanon Phausak-Kudla, 0 3622 7334, www.granmonte. com, main courses B290-B400) has a restaurant and sells other Thai wineries' output as well. Nearby **PB Valley Khao Yai Winery** (102 Thanon Mitrphap, Payayen, 0 3622 6393/0 3622 6415-7, www.khaoyaiwinery.com) ships 500,000 bottles a year. Its substantial tour includes lunch (11am & 4pm Sat & Sun & by appointment, B350). Meander further to **Village Farm** (Tambon Thasamakee, Wan Nam Khieo, Khorat, 0 4422 8407-9, www. villagefarm.co.th double B2,000-B9,000, main courses B500), a boutique winery growing Thailand's top vintage in bucolic environs, offering chalet rooms and gourmet food.

Chachoengsao

Pilgrims progress an hour east of Bangkok by train or road to the revered Buddha image at **Wat Sothorn** (0 3851 1048). It's now housed under the soaring modern spire of the royal temple's multi-billion-baht new marble *vihaan*. On weekends boats from Wat Sothorn's pier take 30 placid minutes to chug past **Chachoengsao** town's quaint Bangpakong River frontage (which faces lush plantations) to **Talad Ban Mai** (Thanon Supakit, near rail bridge, 0 3881 7336). The enchanting ancient teak shops and stalls of this much-filmed 'New Village Market' sell food worthy of culinary pilgrims. Two Chinese shrines nearby complete this memorable day trip. Contact **Bangpakong River Tour** (0 3851 4333/0 3851 888, www.bpkcharter.com).

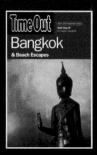

Eat, Drink, Shop

Siam Paragon. *See p154*.

Restaurants

Ahaan chao, ahaan thiang, ahaan yen and maybe even a spot of *ahaan wang* – it's always a good time to eat in Bangkok.

Great dining in Bangkok can, perhaps, be too easy. Gourmet magazines in the West rave about the city's foreign haute cuisine (*see p113* **Gold plated**). But people come here mostly to eat Thai. Too many visitors, however, settle for bilingual picture menus and air-conditioning when many a shophouse wok-slinger can conjure something superior to remember for ever. While meals can be found in almost every *soi*, market or hotel, it's quite normal to cross town for a legendary speciality (*see p117* **Streetfood shrines**). That's because food is both the staff of life and life itself in Thailand. It plays leading and supporting roles in events social and civil, royal and religious, festive and familial. What's more, the dishes, crockery and restaurant layouts are all designed for sharing.

Good Thai food and good decor rarely coincide, especially as hotels and tourist restaurants typically bland out authentic flavours and wrongly structure communal, complementary dishes in the individual starter-soup-main order of the West. Rare exceptions include **Ruen Mallika** (*see p127*), **Taling Pling** (*see p118*) and, in hotels, **Celadon** (*see p128*) at the Sukhothai and **Basil** at the Sheraton Grande (*see p48*). Look out for places where crowds of Thais choose to dine. Even if all you can do is point at what's on other tables, you'll eat well.

EATING ACROSS THE MAP
Thai food has four main variants: Central, Southern, Northern and Isaan (North-eastern). Yet this much exported cuisine is the original fusion fare, being influenced by merchants, migrants, soldiers and missionaries across historically elastic borders. Chinese, Khmers, Burmese, Indians, Indonesians, Mons, Malays and countless tribes have all stirred the pot. Meanwhile, Thais adopted the habits and ingredients of distant lands, from Portuguese bread to staple ingredients like chilli, papaya, tomato, corn and aubergine.

Bangkok continues to assimilate cuisines from across the globe. There are so many Italian restaurants – over 300 – that an Italian Chefs Association maintains standards in the face of pasta's adoption as a new staple to go with Thai concoctions involving chilli, curry, *tom yum* or holy basil. Recent years have also seen standards rise in accompanying wines, breads, cheeses, salads and health drinks.

Ethnic cuisines abound. Little India is peppered with pots of masala and cases of Punjabi sweets. Ditto Chinatown for dim sum and Cantonese. Expat enclaves include the Korea Town of Sukhumvit Plaza on Soi 12, the Arab quarter of Sukhumvit Soi 3/1 and African trader fuelstops in Pratunam; Anglo-Irish pub grub clogs the arteries of Silom and Sukhumvit. Bangkok is one of the world's best cities to eat

The best Restaurants

For cafés with class
Kuppa (*see p123*), **Café LeNôtre** (*see p119*) and **La Boulange** (*see p148*).

For tweaking Thai classics
Ruen Mallika (*see p127*), **Taling Pling** (*see p118*) and **Hemlock** (*see p112*).

For fusions that work
Greyhound Café (*see p125*), **Jester's** (*see p112*) and **Bed Supperclub** (*see p191*).

For seafood by the water
Kaloang Home Kitchen and **River Bar Café** (for both, *see p113*).

For eating with art
Eat Me! (*see p115*), **Tamarind Café** (*see p127*) and the **Thanon Phra Arthit** bars (*see p129*).

For healthy spa nibbling
Rasayana Retreat (*see p177*), **Baan Thai Wellness Retreat** (*see p47*), and Glow at the **Metropolitan** (*see p51*).

For alfresco eating in the clouds
Sirocco (*see p116*) and **Vertigo** (*see p127*).

❶ Purple numbers given in this chapter correspond to the location of each restaurant and café as marked on the street maps. *See pp248-54.*

Hemlock: a pioneer of diversity. *See p112.*

Japanese, and sushi bars and saké dens fill Soi Thaniya and Sukhumvit between Sois 23 and 55, while quality chains like **Zen** and **Fuji** prompt queues in malls.

TIME AND PLACE

While Thais eat pretty much everywhere and at any time, the types of foods available vary by the clock: *ahaan chao* (breakfast), *ahaan thiang* (daytime), *ahaan yen* (dinner and beyond). Snacks in between are *ahaan waang* (empty food). *Raan ahaan* (food shops) open early and close after lunch or early evening, specialising in one dish, such as *raan khao kaeng* (curry and rice shops), signposted by a table of silver trays or pots. At *raan ahaan tam sang* (food-to-order shops), you choose from hundreds of dishes cooked in their house style, while *raan khao thom* serves food with boiled rice soup. *Rot khen* (vendor carts) ply the streets (*see p137* **Peddle power**) and markets, selling food appropriate to the time of day. More formal restaurants in *baan* (houses) and *suan* (gardens) open for lunch (noon sharp in Thailand) and dinner (6pm to 9pm for local kitchens, but later at more international places). Some restaurants close on Sunday or Monday. Reservations are wise, sometimes a must, at hotspots from Thursdays to Saturdays and at hotels for Sunday brunch.

Nearly all drinking and music venues serve (usually Thai) food until midnight (*see pp129-135 and pp182-189*), plus *klub klaem* (drinking nibbles). Turfed out at 1am, clubbers head for street stalls or grab a hangover-clearing *khao tom* (boiled rice soup) at dawn markets. Alternatively, take to the river for a **dinner cruise**; *see p56*. Many places do take-out, and some deliver locally or city-wide, such as **Kai Thord Soi Polo** (*see p120*) and **Pizzanotti** (*see p116* **Zanotti**), while **Food by Phone** (www.foodbyphonebkk.com) bikes diverse cuisines to your door.

SERVICE AND TIPPING

The Western culture of tipping is spreading from tourist zones. Modern and hotel restaurants usually add ten per cent service plus tax to your bill; local places will not. Thais customarily leave the small change from paying the bill up to 20-50 baht. This is less of a tip than a polite gesture that you're not haggling over the price. Expats often give ten per cent.

Thai service tends to excel in helpfulness, rather than speed. Dishes may arrive together or trickle in three or 30 minutes apart. Be patient – in Thailand dishes come when they're ready (for Western food, specify the dish sequence).

urant we've given the average urse, or equivalent, since many tarter/main concept. For more .... food culture and key dishes, *see p118* **Menu and etiquette**. Note that all air-conditioned restaurants are non-smoking.

Phra Nakorn & Banglamphu

Other Asian

Chabad
96 Soi Rambuttri, Thanon Chakkraphong, Banglamphu (0 2629 2770-1/www.chabad thailand.com). **Open** 10am-10pm Mon-Thur, Sun; 10am-3pm Fri; 8.30am-10.30pm Sat. **Main courses** B150. **Credit** AmEx, MC, V. **Map** p248 B3 ❶
Banglamphu boasts a few Israeli cafés and a good falafel stall opposite Gulliver's bar, but Rabbi Nechemya Wilhelm's Chabad offers comfy, upmarket surroundings without charging much extra for the usual chips and dips and occasional North African specials, such as Moroccan-style fish.

Roti Mataba
136 Thanon Phra Arthit, nr Santichaiprakarn Park, Banglamphu (0 2282 2119). Tha Phra Arthit. **Open** 8am-10pm Tue-Sun. **Main courses** B60. **No credit cards. Map** p248 B2 ❷
The women who run Roti Mataba are experts at patting, flipping, filling and plaiting roti. The eponymous flatbread comes stuffed (with chicken, egg, veggies) and drizzled (with sweet milk or honey) or put to work as a dipping implement (alongside curries).

Thai
Thai food is mostly horrible around **Thanon Khao San**, but authentic on **Thanon Phra Arthit**. Late-night **Pak Khlong Talad** flower market (*see p140*) has stalls serving the traders, which offer fine midnight nibbling. Nearby, **Arun Residence** (*see p40*) serves superb Thai and Euro-bistro riverside dining at the Deck.

Hemlock
56 Thanon Phra Arthit, Banglamphu (0 2282 7507). **Open** 4pm-midnight Mon-Fri; 5pm-midnight Sat. **No credit cards. Map** p248 B3 ❸
A pioneer of this hip bar/restaurant strip, Hemlock maintains a near-Mediterranean breeziness (whitewashed walls and a rock-strewn interior). Exhibitions and performances upstairs add to the diversity of the wines, teas and Thai food. **Photo** *p111.*

Sky High
14 Thanon Ratchadamnoen Klang (0 2224 1947). Phra Nakorn. **Open** 8am-1am daily. **Main courses** B150. **Credit** MC, V. **Map** p248 B3 ❹
Sky High's hushed tones could be coming from politicians, journalists, poets or gossiping friends.

This is a seriously Thai place, with lasting popularity and spot-on cooking of Thai-Chinese staples. The steamed Chinese carp fish head is memorable.

Thip Samai
313 Thanon Mahachai, behind the Golden Mount (0 2221 6280 ext 0). Tha Saphan Phan Fah. **Open** 5pm-3am daily. **Main courses** B60. **No credit cards. Map** p248 C3 ❺
Pad Thai is the dish that all visitors know before getting their visa. Nicknamed Pad Thai Pratu Pi ('Ghost's Gate Noodles'), Thip Samai is a legend for serving nothing but, in a neon-lit setting. Try out the egg-wrapped version and the nutty-sweet coconut juice.

Vegetarian
Many guesthouse cafés on **Thanon Khao San** also cater to vegetarians.

Mai Kaidee
111 Thanon Tanao, down soi beside Burger King, then take first left (0 2281 7137/08 9137 3173/ www.maykaidee.com). **Open** 9am-11pm daily. **Main courses** B50. **No credit cards. Map** p248 C3 ❻
Khun May cooks up veggie versions of Thai and Chinese standards. We recommend the spring rolls. She also gives cooking classes (9am-1pm daily, B1,200 per ten dishes; private B2,000 per ten dishes). **Other locations**: 33 Thanon Samsen, Phra Nakorn (0 2281 7699).

Thonburi

International
Few Sunday hotel brunches beat **Trader Vic's** at the Marriott (*see p40*), given the jazz, river views and boat transfer (from B1,000 per head).

Jester's
Peninsula Hotel, 333 Thanon Charoen Nakorn (0 2861 2888/http://bangkok.peninsula.com). Saphan Taksin BTS then shuttle boat. **Open** 6pm-midnight Mon-Thur, Sun; 6pm-1am Fri, Sat. **Main courses** B700. **Credit** DC, MC, V. **Map** p250 D7 ❼
Facing the river through a wall of glass, Jester's offers inventive and restrained Pacific Rim fusion, including such delicacies as kaffir lime with lobster, and pork loin with chilli crab and black bean broth. Under the curving steel ceiling, giant bamboo canes and coloured ball lighting are signature touches, along with metal, breast-shaped goblets held in stands beside brushed metal placemats. One of Bangkok's best, and most individual, restaurants.

Other Asian

Mei Jiang
Peninsula Hotel, 333 Thanon Charoen Nakorn (0 2861 2888/http://bangkok.peninsula.com). Saphan Taksin BTS then shuttle boat. **Open**

11.30am-2.30pm, 6-10pm daily. **Main courses**
Lunch B1,000. *Dinner* B2,000. **Credit** AmEx, V.
Map p250 D7 🟠
Mei Jiang combines the dual traditions of haute
Cantonese cooking and the striking modernity of its
host: the Peninsula Hotel. Tableside service, jewel-
like presentation, blockbuster wines and pan-global
accents are the result. Like the clean-lined decor,
done up with local silks and smoked glass, the
results can be astonishing.

Thai

Also try **Supatra River House** or **Sala
Rim Nam** and (for these and other dinner
theatres, *see p199*). For **Yok Yor Marina
& Restaurant**, *see p56*. **Thip Thara** at
the Peninsula (*see p41*) features healthy
specialities at a stunning riverside 'teak village'.

River Bar Café
*405/1 Soi Chao Phraya Siam, Thanon Ratchawithi
(0 2879 1748-9). Tha Saphan Krung Thon (Sang
Hee).* **Open** 5pm-1am daily. **Main courses** B200.
Credit MC, V.

The glass-encased River Bar Café, tucked away near
Sang Hee Bridge, is one of the few places in the city
where you can eat sea-fresh fish in style. The simple preparations (steamed, deep-fried, spicy salads,
flamed prawns) are pleasingly unfussy and delicious. Riverbank terraces and a lofty, industrial-chic
interior provide the party setting for an attractive
crowd of foreigners and locals, although the live
music can be loud.

Dusit

There are plenty of ethnic eats in the
Vietnamese enclave around **St Francis
Xavier Church**, and Northern Thai cafés
on **Thanon Sukhothai**.

Thai

Kaloang Home Kitchen
*2 Thanon Sri Ayutthaya, at end of soi beside
National Library (0 2281 9228/0 2282 7581).*
Open 11am-10pm daily. **Main courses** B140.
Credit V. **Map** p248 C1 🟠

Eat, Drink, Shop

Gold plated

By importing top chefs from around the
world, Bangkok is adding to the global
repute of its haute cuisine. Barely three
decades old, its dining scene had been
transformed in recent years by stunning
interior themes, A-list imported products
and a zest for razor-sharp kitchen craft.

Every February the hotel LeBua at State
Tower hosts several three-star Michelin chefs
for the Epicurean Masters of the World
festival (*see p160*). During the week-long
event high-flyers jet in from abroad for
special meals in the top-class restaurants
atop this domed skyscraper – including the
alfresco **Sirocco** (*see p116*) – culminating
in a multi-chef Gala Charity Dinner, where
tickets cost a staggering $25,000.

The **Four Seasons Hotel** (*see p46*) started
this trend in 1999 with a host of international
chefs brought in for its World Gourmet Festival
(September; *see p162*), to cook signature
meals in the hotel's superlative restaurants.

In another Michelin link, the Pourcel
brothers opened **D'Sens** (*see p115*) in
2004, a Bangkok branch of their award-
winning restaurant in France. They have since
raided Pierre Gagnaire's Sketch in London,
appointing maestro Philippe Keller to oversee
their modern French cuisine. Another of
Bangkok's top-rated French restaurants,

Le Normandie (*see p115*), employs Guy
Martin, of the Michelin-acclaimed Le Grand
Véfour in Paris, as its consultant.

At the Metropolitan, **Cy'an** (*see p128*) also
put the kitchens first in appointing Amanda
Gale, once of Neil Perry's Rockpool restaurant
in Sydney. She now directs all of owner
Christina Ong's Asia restaurants. A periodic
guest chef at Cy'an is Australian David
Thompson, author of the seminal
history/recipe book, *Thai Food*, and the
first person to earn a Michelin star for Thai
cooking, at Nahm in London's Metropolitan.

In addition, several top-name resident
expats have built major reputations as *chefs-
patron* of Bangkok restaurants. The latest
such master is Hervé Frerard at **Le Beaulieu**
(*see p121*). That trail was blazed by so many
impressive Italians – especially Gianni Favro
(**Gianni**; *see p119*), Gian-Maria Zanotti
(**Zanotti**; *see p116*) and Fabio Colautti
(**Giusto**; *see p123*) – that Thailand even
has an Italian Chefs Association.

Bangkok's history of home-grown celebrity
chefs, meanwhile, dates from fiercely
contested cooking competitions that were
held until the early 20th century between
palaces. Among the city's Thai restaurants
built upon the chefs' fame are **Kalapapruek**
(*see p126*) and **Ruen Mallika** (*see p127*).

Breeze. *See p116.*

This is the kind of rough-and-tumble fish house that can be found dotting the coasts. Wooden planking, Formica, wind-beaten chairs – every cliché is in place. But the food transcends the setting with sure-handed spicing, and faultless freshness informs *tom yum*, steamed, fried and grilled. Don't forget to order a *yum*, and take your time on the way down the teak-and-temple-lined *soi* from Thanon Samsen.

Chinatown

Other Asian

Showy Chinese restaurants proliferate along **Thanon Yaowarat**, amid pricey yet unpretentious stalls serving top food, especially in **Soi Texas**; note that Chinatown shuts down around 9pm. Hindi eateries are scattered around **Pahurat Market**.

Hua Seng Hong

371-373 Thanon Yaowarat (0 2222 0635). **Open** 8.30am-1am daily. **Main courses** B100-B300. **No credit cards**. **Map** p249/p250 D5 ❿
Obscured by glass cases of sharks' fins, steamed buns and hanging roast ducks, Hua Seng Hong sits in the heartland of Yaowarat's early-evening madness. *Ba mee* noodles stir-fried with crab, plates of greens with salted fish, roast duck and oyster omelettes can be procured elsewhere – but they won't be handmade on site and served up by no-nonsense yet grinning staff as they are here.

Other locations: Charoen Krung Soi 14, Chinatown (0 2627 5030); Hong Min MBK, Pathumwan (1st floor 0 2620 9492; 3rd floor 0 2611 5643).

Royal India
392/1 Thanon Chakraphet (0 2221 6565). **Open** 10am-10pm daily. **Main courses** B70. **No credit cards. Map** p248 C5 ⑪
Pahurat teems with small curry operations, most famously Royal India. Photos of Thai politicians adorn the walls, although as Thais tend to dislike Indian food, they may not have actually sampled the dishes. A pity, as they're good and cheap.

Shangri-La Restaurant
306 Thanon Yaowarat (0 2224 5807/0 2622 7870). **Open** 10am-10pm daily. **Main courses** B300. **Credit** MC, V. **Map** p248 C5 ⑫
This Yaowarat institution is the kind of full-throttle Chinese place that belongs in the movies. It's big, always busy with families, has round tables and serves dependable (and fun) dim sum daily, as well as all the sweet and sour this and that in existence.
Other locations: 58/4-9 Soi Thaniya, Bangrak (0 2234 0861-4); 154/4-7 Silom Soi 12, Bangrak (0 2234 9147-9); Shangri-La Kitchen, 2nd floor, Silom Complex, Bangrak (0 2632 1238-9); Shangri-La Kitchen, 188-188/1 Naratiwat Soi 3, between Pipat Soi 3 & Soi Lalaisup, Bangrak (0 2636 6840-1).

Thai

Pet Tun Jao Tha
941-7 Wanit Soi 2 (0 2233 2541). Tha River City. **Open** 10am-5pm Mon-Sat. **Main courses** B50. **No credit cards. Map** p250 D6 ⑬
Nicknamed for its 'Harbour Department' locale, this is *the* place to tuck into duck and goose, roasted or stewed, served straight up with rice noodles and condiments.

Bangrak

International

For French bistro meals, head to the superior bakery **La Boulange** (*see p148*). For Anglo-Irish food, try the **Barbican** (*see p132*) and **Irish X-change** bars (*see p133*).

Angelini
2nd floor, Shangri-La Hotel, 89 Soi Wat Suan Plu, Thanon Charoen Krung (0 2236 7777). Saphan Taksin BTS. **Open** 11.30am-2.30pm, 6-11pm daily. *Bar closes* 1.15am Mon-Sat; 12.30am Sun. **Main courses** B1,200. **Credit** AmEx, DC, MC, V. **Map** p250 D7 ⑭
Reminiscent of a cathedral with its floor-to-ceiling windows and sweeping balconies, this was Bangkok's first high-class modern restaurant. The food is exceedingly good classic Italian, with the added benefit of romantic river views. There's an open kitchen and a bar on the mezzanine, where you

find the only blemish – a(8.15pm-midnight Mondit's also open for snacks

Le Bouchon
37/17 Patpong Soi 2 (0 2 BTS/Silom MRT. **Open** 7-11pm Sun. **Main courses** B600. Credit MC, V. **Map** p250 F6 ⑮
Perhaps the most authentic French bistro in town, and the top regular dining spot for local Gauls. The very small bar buzzes with *joie de vivre* as diners wait to be seated at one of only seven tables. Expect simple but good country cooking.

D'Sens
Dusit Thani Hotel, 946 Thanon Rama IV (0 2236 9999). Saladaeng BTS/Silom MRT. **Open** 11.30am-2pm, 6.30-10pm Mon-Sat. **Main courses** *Lunch* B1,000. *Dinner* B1,600. **Credit** AmEx, DC, MC, V. **Map** p251 G6 ⑯
The angular 1960s architecture of the Dusit Thani hotel penthouse (*see p44*) makes a distinctive setting for this branch of the three Michelin-starred Le Jardin des Sens in Montpellier. Owners Jacques and Laurent Pourcel are in town every few months to tweak the menu, alongside resident chef Philippe Keller, who was previously at Sketch in London. Masterful dishes like roasted turbot fillet on a bed of parsley-stuffed pig's trotter with citrus flavoured meat *jus*, and wonderful desserts, justify the prices.

Eat Me!
1/6 Phiphat Soi 2, Thanon Convent (0 2238 0931). Saladaeng BTS/Silom MRT. **Open** 3pm-1am daily. **Main courses** B300. **Credit** AmEx, MC, V. **Map** p250 F7 ⑰
Ever full, the city's premier art restaurant attracts a cool clientele for its artworks and an interesting East-West fusion menu that includes dishes such as tuna tartare with soba noodles and cabbage salad. People tend to linger for post-prandial drinks over the well-selected music.

Le Normandie
5th floor, Oriental Hotel, Charoen Krung Soi 38 (0 2236 0400/www.mandarinoriental.com). Saphan Taksin BTS. **Open** noon-2pm, 7-10pm daily. **Main courses** B1,800. **Set menus** *Lunch* B1,000 3 courses. *Dinner* B4,200 6 courses, B7,200 6 courses incl wines. **Credit** AmEx, DC, MC, V. **Map** p250 D7 ⑱
The grand dame of Bangkok dining stages high-class French cuisine, gorgeously presented, at a fraction of Paris prices. The marmalade interior, dazzling under crystal chandeliers, overlooks the river through a window wall. While the wine list is monumental in range, it has bottles from around B2,000. Feast like a film star on the six-course tasting menu (with five different wines), at around $250 a head. Hot season promotions offer incredible value. A jacket and tie are compulsory for men, and are available at the door for those who've turned up in too-casual gear.

For the best Japanese in the area, head for **Aoi**.

Sirocco, Mezzaluna & Breeze

63rd floor, LeBua at State Tower, 1055 Thanon Silom (0 2624 9555). Saphan Taksin BTS. **Open** 6pm-1am daily. **Main courses** B1,000. **Credit** AmEx, DC, MC, V. **Map** p250 D7 ⑲

An astonishing 200m-high (656-foot) rooftop restaurant, Sirocco boasts unrestrained Greco-Roman architecture and giddying views over Bangkok and the river. Sweep down the large stone staircase past the jazz quartet to the garden terrace tables and some increasingly impressive Mediterranean cuisine – this is one of Asia's best dining experiences. Sirocco's Sky Bar (seemingly on the edge of space) mixes the stiff drinks needed to look down (*see p116*), as does the Distil bar indoors (*see p132*), which shares the dome's interior with Mezzaluna, a half-moon-shaped fine-dining Italian restaurant of impeccable quality with string quartet. A few floors lower, the newer Breeze serves a Pan-Asian menu emphasising seafood on a terrace with similar vistas, accessed via a bridge lit like a galactic fantasy. Booking is essential. **Photo** *p114*.

Zanotti

1st floor, Saladaeng Colonnade, 21/2 Soi Saladaeng (0 2636 0002). Saladaeng BTS/Silom MRT. **Open** 11.30am-2pm, 6-11pm daily. **Main courses** *Lunch* B370. *Dinner* B500. **Credit** AmEx, DC, MC, V. **Map** p251 G7 ⑳

'Exuberance' sums up this restaurant – the jazz music is cranked up high, as is the conversation (the tables are so close you could spoon-feed your high-flying neighbours). Not surprisingly, it took Bangkok by storm on opening in 1998. The frenetic pace – waiters become a blur in front of the metaphysical paintings by Rincicotti – means quality can suffer on the mainly excellent, varied menu, where orange wood charcoaling is a speciality. Ebullient chef-patron Gian-Maria Zanotti – who suggests you tread on the testicles of the brass bull in the lobby floor (as they do at the Turin original) – also serves wood-fired pizzas at Limoncello and by delivery. Opposite is a classy wine bar with more Rincicotti evident in the ceramic tiling, a full food menu and live jazz too.

Other locations: Pizzeria Limoncello, 17 Sukhumvit Soi 11, Sukhumvit (0 2651 0707); Vino di Zanotti, 41 Soi Yommarat, Thanon Saladaeng (0 2636 0855); Pizzanotti delivery (0 2800 8089).

Other Asian

The Little Tokyo of **Soi Thaniya** (including the malls of **Thaniya Plaza** and **Charn Issara Tower**) acts as one huge bento box of Japanese restaurants, many with bargain prices. Indian and Muslim restaurants are concentrated around Silom's Hindu temple and along **Thanon Charoen Krung**.

Aoi

132/10-11 Silom Soi 6 (0 2235 2321-2). Saladaeng BTS/Silom MRT. **Open** noon-2.30pm, 6-10pm daily. **Main courses** *Lunch* B250. *Dinner* B450. **Credit** MC, V. **Map** p250 F6 ㉑

This traditional slate-walled tavern a few blocks south of Thaniya's Little Tokyo is the area's best Japanese restaurant. Prices are slightly higher, but reflect the quality, service and Kyoto-esque interior, all pebbles, lanterns and paper screens. **Photo** *p116.* **Other locations**: 4th floor, Emporium, Sukhumvit Soi 24, Sukhumvit (0 2664 8590-2); Ground floor, Siam Paragon, Pathumwan (0 2129 4348-50).

China House

Oriental Hotel, Charoen Krung Soi 38 (0 2236 0400 ext 3378/www.mandarinoriental.com). Saphan Taksin BTS. **Open** 11.30am-2.30pm, 7-10.30pm daily. **Main courses** *Lunch* B300. *Dinner* B700. **Credit** AmEx, DC, MC, V. **Map** p250 D7 ㉒
Just outside the Oriental Hotel, this quiet, timeless dining space occupies a Fabergé-delicate heritage house, recently redone in sumptuous 1930s Shanghai style with red silk, 'opium bed' booths, dark wood screens and a frontage-spoiling new lobby. The long menu is firmly rooted in the haunting flavours of Cantonese tradition, but its sense of fun results in some innovative creations. Top-shelf dim sum lunches too.

Indian Hut

311/2-5 Thanon Surawong (0 2237 8812). Saladaeng BTS/Silom MRT. **Open** 11am-11pm daily. **Main courses** B375-B475. **Credit** AmEx, DC, MC, V. **Map** p250 E7 ㉓
Don't be misled by the ill-advised Pizza Hut-style logo – this is one of Bangkok's best north Indian restaurants. All the dishes on the menu have a deep, robust flavour, but the creamy Kashmiri options are particularly enjoyable. The second floor area has the nicer decor.

Nam Kang

5/3-4 Soi Phiphat, Silom Soi 3 (0 2233 1480-3). Saladaeng BTS/Silom MRT. **Open** 11am-2.30pm, 5.30-10pm daily. **Main courses** B170. **Credit** AmEx, MC, V. **Map** p250 F7 ㉔
Serving high-end Seoul cuisine, this is the pick of myriad Korean restaurants. Ginseng chicken is the most popular dish – and deservedly so.

River City BBQ

2nd & 5th floors, River City Complex, Yotha (0 2237 0077-8). Tha Siphraya floor 11am-10pm daily. *5th floor* 5-11.30pm daily. **Main courses** B400. **Credit** AmEx, MC, V. **Map** p250 D6 ㉕
The Mongolian fire pot is a fun, communal style of DIY dining that has spawned Asian variants, from Japan's *sukiyaki* to Thailand's own *suki.* Grill and boil your own meat and vegetables at your rooftop table, while gawping at the stupendous riverscape.

Silom Restaurant

793 Silom Soi 15 (0 2236 4443/4268). Chong Nonsri BTS. **Open** 10am-9pm daily. **Main courses** B200. **No credit cards**. **Map** p250 E7 ㉖
Hainanese-influenced cooking was an early fusion fad throughout Asia. In Thailand – and at this seminal restaurant – pork chops, noodles and the like bear the imprint of palates colonial, Thai and Chinese all at once. Translation: protein enough to satisfy a big foreigner, with bold and slightly salty overtones of soy, garlic and spice that have had Thais smiling their way to this dining hall for several decades.

Tamil Nadu

5/1 Silom Soi 11 (0 2235 6336/6325). Chong Nonsri BTS. **Open** 10.30am-9.30pm daily. **Main courses** B120. **No credit cards**. **Map** p250 E7 ㉗
The large local Indian population around the Hindu temple has resulted in a plethora of cheap, no-frills Indian cafés. This one is clean, has air-con and offers good south Indian food, especially the *masala dosa.*

Thai

Competition keeps streetfood standards high around Patpong on **Thanon Silom**, **Thanon Surawong** and **Soi Convent**, especially at seafood stalls.

Eat, Drink, Shop

Streetfood shrines

In Bangkok, the concept of eating out only became common in recent decades. Before that, cooking and eating were very much confined to the home. Some claim that the restaurant scene has brought with it a certain homogenisation of dishes and flavours, especially ones aimed at foreigners.

In an interview with the *Nation*, Thai food scholar and Michelin-starred chef David Thompson said: 'In Bangkok it is becoming increasingly difficult to find... that complexity of flavour.' Difficult indeed, but not impossible. Thai food aficionados make pilgrimages to street stalls and single-dish shophouse specialists, whose reputation still

rings around the city. Holes-in-the-wall worth a detour include: **Kai Thord Soi Polo** (Isaan fired chicken and fixings, *see p120*); **Khrua Aroi Aroi** (curry and *khanom jeen*, *see p118*); **Mid Night Kai Ton** (late-night *khao man kai*, *see p127*); **Pet Tun Jao Tha** (duck and goose, *see p115*); **Roti Mataba** (Indian stuffed flatbread, *see p112*); and **Thip Samai** (*Pad Thai*, *see p112*). We have also noted knots of top-end stalls under area headings.

And don't let hygiene worries daunt you – millions of people eat this food every day. Just be sure to look for busy vendors, whose high turnover seems to suggest fresh food and healthy patrons.

Menu and etiquette

Like the culture itself, Thai cooking blends influences from India, China, Burma, Europe and beyond. While it can be as simple or as complex as you like, some basic norms apply. Aside from some noodle preparations, Thais eat rice with almost every meal or dish. Everywhere offers staple *khao plao* (plain white rice), aka *khao suay* (beautiful rice). With northern and Isaan cuisine come bamboo baskets of *khao niao* (sticky glutinous rice), eaten with the right hand, often to wrap mouthfuls of food. Sweetened with coconut milk, plain or sticky rice also forms the basis of many *khanom* (desserts).

Each dish explodes in the mouth with a bewildering medley of ingredients: incendiary chillies, tart tamarind, pungent fish sauces. Cooks balance most Thai food between hot, sour, salty and sweet, and diners sample an array of dishes with a similar mix of flavours. Two bedrocks of dining – used for balance – are *yum* (spicy complex salads, often with an acid-sweet-spicy harmony) and *nam prik* (chilli dips that can be pungent, spicy or smoky).

TABLE TIPS

All dishes, however, get customised using condiments: *khreung prung* (seasonings of dried chillis, vinegar with chillis, sugar and fish sauce with chillis) and *nam jim* (dipping sauces for specific food types). It's a hugely social exercise that involves giving and sharing food from communal dishes. The pre-cut morsel format makes knives redundant; with a fork in the left hand you push food on to the spoon in your right. Chopsticks are used only for noodles and Chinese dishes. In all cases there is one principal goal to Thai cooking: maximum flavour.

General terms

Styles: neung steamed; **thord** deep-fried; **phat** stir-fried; **ping** grilled (small or skewered pieces); **phao** grilled (chillis or seafood); **yaang** roasted or grilled (meats and large pieces); **op** baked; **tom** boiled; **tam** pounded; **phet** spicy; **khem** salty; **waan** sweet; **priao** sour; **jeud** bland; **sub** minced; **sod** fresh and uncooked.

Vocabulary: ah-roi delicious; **iik neung** one more; **mai phet** non-spicy; **phet nit noi** a bit spicy; **chawp phet phet** very spicy; **kin jeh** vegetarian (no dairy or spices); **mung sa virat** meat-free (includes spices).

Rice dishes (*khao*)

khao plao plain rice; **khao niao** sticky rice; **khao phat phak** vegetable fried rice; **khao**

Coca Suki

8 Soi Anuman Ratchadhon (0 2236 0107).
Saladaeng BTS/Silom MRT. **Open** 11am-2pm, 5-10pm Mon-Sat; 11am-10pm Sun. **Main courses** B250. **Credit** AmEx, DC, MC, V. **Map** p250 F6 ㉘
Sociability and *sanuk* converge in *suki*, a favourite Thai variant of Japanese *sukiyaki*, where you order trays of ingredients to cook in a table-top pot. **Other locations:** throughout the city.

Khrua Aroi Aroi

Thanon Pan, opposite Wat Khaek (0 2635 2365).
Surasak BTS. **Open** 8am-7pm daily. **Main courses** B40. **No credit cards. Map** p250 E7 ㉙
Khanom jeen is a quick-fix fave of various curries spooned over rice noodles and eaten with cooling, crunchy herbs and vegetables. This two-level shop – whose name means 'delicious delicious' – offers up tastes from jungle curries and chilli dips to coconut milk-rich Muslim varieties and an archetypal green curry.

Taling Pling

60 Thanon Pan, Silom (0 2234 4872). Surasak BTS.
Open 11am-10pm daily. **Main courses** B90. **Credit** AmEx, MC, V. **Map** p250 E7 ㉚

Buzzing with *farang* and Thai alike, this homely restaurant combines handsome old photos with modern decor in orange, pink and black. The tasty country-style cooking excels at favourites such as green curry with roti, spicy sour soup with prawn and vegetables, and pomelo salad, along with Thai desserts and Western cakes and pastries. It's named after the tree in the garden, whose fruit ends up in Thai recipes.

Pathumwan

International

The **Four Seasons Hotel** (*see p46*) offers free-flowing booze at its upmarket Sunday brunch (B2,350 plus service and VAT, including alcohol), held in various outlets. **Food Loft** atop Central Chidlom (*see p144*) started the gourmet food court fad (main courses B180), involving many top city restaurants. Its rival at **Siam Paragon** (*see p154*) isn't as good, but the mall has many fine restaurants, especially on the busy ground floor.

phat fried rice; **khao phat man koong** shrimp paste fried rice; **khao yum** southern-style rice salad; **khao kaeng** curry over rice; **khao mun kai** Hainanese-style chicken rice; **khao na ped** roast duck rice; **khao muu daeng** red-roasted pork on rice; **khao mok kai** Muslim chicken biryani.

Noodles (*kuaytiao* & *ba mee*)

Types: ba mee egg noodles; **kuaytiao** rice noodles; **sen-lek** narrow; **sen-yai** wide; **sen-mee** fine; **haeng** dry; **nam** wet, in soup.

Noodles in a bowl: ba mee muu daeng egg noodles with red-roasted pork; **kuaytiao look chin pla** rice noodles with fish balls; **kuaytiao look chin muu** rice noodles with pork balls; **khao soi** Chiang Mai egg noodles with chicken curry broth.

Noodles on a plate: kuaytiao pad thai stir-fry with prawns, ground peanuts, tofu, bean sprouts, spring onion and egg; **kuaytiao pad khee mao** fried rice noodles with chilli, holy basil and garlic; **pad si-ew kai sen-yai** fried in black soy sauce with vegetables and chicken; **kuaytiao rad na sen-yai** in gravy with vegetables and meat; **kuaytiao reua** (boat noodles) rice noodles with dark herbal broth.

Meat (*neua*) & vegetables (*phak*)

Meats: bpoo crab; **hoey** shellfish; **kai** chicken; **koong** shrimp; **moo** pork; **neua** meat/beef; **ped** duck; **pla** fish.

Vegetables: pad phak nam phrik pao stir-fried vegetables with roasted chilli paste; **phak boong fai daeng** stir-fried morning glory with garlic and chilli; **phak kha-na pla khem** Chinese kale with Thai salted fish; **pad phak nam man hoy** stir-fried vegetables in oyster sauce; **pad ka-na muu krob** Chinese kale with crispy pork; **pad tau-fak-yao nam phrik pao** long beans stir-fried with roast chilli paste; **pad phak ruam-mit** stir-fried mixed vegetables; **pad hed hom** stir-fried mushrooms; **tao-hoo trong kreung** tofu in soy gravy with vegetables; **pad phak khee mao** stir-fried vegetables with chilli, holy basil and garlic.

Spicy salads (*yum*)

yum tua plu winged bean; **yum woon sen** glass noodles with pork and shellfish; **yum hua plee** banana blossom; **yum pla dook foo** fluffy fried catfish; **yum moo yang** grilled pork; **yum som-o** pomelo; **yum pla meuk** squid; **yum maa-kheua yao** grilled long aubergine with minced pork; **som tam** shredded papaya; **larb** Isaan or northern-   ▶

Biscotti

1st floor, Four Seasons Hotel, 155 Thanon Ratchadamri (0 2254 9999). Ratchadamri BTS. **Open** noon-2.30pm, 6-10.30pm daily. **Set menus** Lunch B640 2 courses, B690 3 courses. *Dinner* B800. **Credit** AmEx, DC, MC, V. **Map** p251 G5 ❺
Politicians, film stars and tycoons choose this Tony Chi-designed, thrillingly modern restaurant where people *need* to be seen. And they're easily spotted in the huge square room of terracotta and white, dominated by a large open kitchen. Jammed at lunch and dinner with devotees of its superb Italian food.

Café LeNôtre

Ground floor, Natural Ville Executive Residences, 61 Soi Lang Suan (0 2250 7050-1). Chidlom BTS. **Open** 7am-10pm daily. **Main courses** B350. **Credit** AmEx, DC, MC, V. **Map** p251 H5 ❷
This chic outlet of a Parisian chain exudes Gallic savoir faire. The owners brought over chefs from Paris to create a short menu of decent appetisers, salads and mains such as duck confit with zucchini and tomato Bayaldi, named after Imam Bayaldi, who reportedly fainted at the richness of it. Fantastic desserts: don't miss the chocolate mousse wrapped around green tea crème brûlée.

Other locations: 1st floor, Sofitel Silom, 188 Thanon Silom, Bangrak (0 2267 5292); 5th floor, Emporium, Sukhumvit (0 2664 8289); Basement, Siam Paragon, Pathumwan (0 2129 4361-5).

Gianni

51/5 Soi Tonson (0 2252 1619). Chidlom BTS. **Open** noon-2.30pm, 6-10.30pm daily. **Main courses** B500. **Set menus** Lunch B340. Dinner B1,190. **Credit** AmEx, MC, V. **Map** p251 H5 ❸
A Bangkok institution, run by Gianni Favro, arguably the city's first foreign 'celebrity' chef. The airy interior, with bright abstract paintings and lots of natural light, sets a cheery tone for very impressive traditional cuisine and specials. Fine choices include rabbit-filled ravioli and risotto with fresh artichokes and lobster. You leave talking about the food, not the price.

Other Asian

Bali

15/3 Soi Ruam Rudi (0 2250 0711/0 2254 3581). Ploenchit BTS. **Open** 11am-2pm, 6-10pm Mon-Sat. **Main courses** B70-B180. **Credit** AmEx, MC, V. **Map** p251 H5 ❹

Menu and etiquette (continued)

style with chilli, mint, lime, roasted rice powder, fish sauce and minced meat; **muu nam tok** Isaan-style with grilled pork and roasted rice powder.

Stir-fried & fried (*phat & thord*)

Stir-fried: phat hoey lai nam phrik pao clams with roast chilli paste and holy basil; **kai phat med ma-muang** chicken with cashew nuts and dried chillis; **kai phat khing** chicken with ginger; **kai phat bai kaphrao** chicken with holy basil; **kai phat priao-waan** sweet-and-sour chicken; **neua phat nam-man hoey** beef with oyster sauce; **puu phat pong karii** crab stir-fried with curry powder and egg.

Fried: kai thord deep-fried chicken; **muu thord kratiam phrik** Thai pork marinated and fried with garlic and black pepper.

Curries & soups (*kaeng & tom*)

kaeng khiao-waan sweet green curry; **kaeng phet** red curry; **kaeng luang** southern yellow curry (no coconut); **kaeng karii** mild yellow; **kaeng Matsaman** mild Muslim curry with peanuts; **kaeng pa** jungle curry with herbs and ginger (no coconut); **kaeng panaeng** thick red curry with peanuts; **kaeng tai pla** southern curry with fish stomach; **kaeng**

som sour tamarind soup (no coconut); **kaeng jeud tauhoo/moo sub** bland soup with vegetables and tofu/minced pork; **kaeng liang** aromatic vegetable soup; **tom yum** hot-and-sour soup with kaffir lime and lemon-grass; **tom kha** coconut-milk soup with galangal and kaffir lime; **khao tom** boiled rice soup.

Chilli dips (*nam phrik*)

nam phrik kapi shrimp paste dip; **nam phrik long reua** shrimp paste and spicy fried fish dip; **nam phrik ong** roast tomato dip with minced pork and lemongrass; **nam phrik nuum** young green chilli dip with roast aubergine; **nam phrik pao** sweet roasted chilli dip with fish sauce.

Seafood dishes (*ahaan talay*)

pla meuk neung manao steamed squid in lime sauce; **puu op woon sen** crab baked with glass noodles; **hoey nanng rom** raw oysters with lime, shallots, garlic and cassia; **koong pao** grilled shrimp; **plaa jian** whole fish with ginger, onion and soy; **pla thord kratiam phrik** deep-fried fish with garlic and black pepper; **pla meuk phat phet** squid stir-fried with chilli; **po thaek** seafood hotpot.

Sumatra-born Elly Sookdhis has restored one of Bangkok's oldest restaurants to its authentic origins with superlative rendang, jackfruit curry and leaf-wrapped marinated fish (*ikan pepes*) – and the laboriously multi-baked layer cake, all served in this homely lounge and garden. Indo and Dutch expats often order *rijstafel* sets.

Thang Long

82/5 Soi Lang Suan (0 2251 3504/4491). Chidlom BTS. **Open** 11.30am-2pm, 4.30-11pm daily. **Main courses** *Lunch* B185. *Dinner* B230. **Credit** AmEx, MC, V. **Map** p251 G5 **35**
There's a clean, minimalist cool feel to this Vietnamese eaterie – with boxy rattan chairs, loungey music and strategic placing of plants (both live and painted) – which makes it a regular hangout for arty types. It gets busy, so book ahead.

Thai

Curries & More

63/3 Soi Ruam Rudee, at Soi 3 (02 253 5405-7/ www.baan-khanitha.com). Ploenchit BTS. **Open** 11.30am-2pm, 6-11pm daily. **Main courses** B460. **Credit** AmEx, DC, MC, V. **Map** p251 H5 **36**

It could be called Curries & Everything, so varied is the menu. Besides Thai soups, *som tams*, *larbs* and, yes, curries, sit own-made Western pies, pastas, steaks, lamb chops and even trout in Louisiana sauce. Fine cakes and Brittany crêpes follow. Unusually well-trained waiters whisk around this converted house with art-laden rooms on two floors, and a water-cooled, all-weather patio.
Other locations: Baan Khanitha, 67-69 Thanon Sathorn Tai, at Soi Suan Plu, South (0 2675 4200-1); Baan Khanitha, 36/1 Sukhumvit Soi 23, Sukhumvit (0 2258 4181).

Kai Thord Soi Polo

137/1-2 Soi Polo, Thanon Witthayu (0 2252 2252). **Open** 7am-10pm daily. **Main courses** B40. **No credit cards**. **Map** p251 H6 **37**
There's fried chicken and there's fried chicken from Soi Polo. Its oily, aromatic, crispy, fleshy balance has won devotion among Thai locals. Owner J-Kee, though a southerner, has four decades of experience cooking the deeply flavoured foods of Isaan.

Khrua Nai Baan

94 Soi Lang Suan (0 2252 0069). Chidlom BTS. **Open** 9am-midnight daily. **Main courses** B300. **Credit** AmEx, MC, V. **Map** p251 G5 **38**

Sauces & seasoning (*nam jim & kreung prung*)

sord phrik si racha sweet chilli sauce; **nam pla** fish sauce; **nam pla phrik** chilli fish sauce; **phrik haeng** dried chilli; **nam tan** sugar; **nam som sai chuu** clear vinegar with chilli; **phak dong** pickled vegetables; **bai horapa** sweet basil; **bai kra prao** holy basil; **ta krai** lemongrass; **phak chee** coriander; **si-ew dum** black soy sauce; **phrik Thai** white pepper; **phrik Thai dum** black pepper; **kratiam** garlic.

Desserts (*khanom*)

nam kang sai jellies, fruit, taro, water chestnuts over ice with **nam choem** jasmine sugar-syrup, and **nam krati** coconut milk or caramel; **khanom waan** flour, sugar and coconut cream wrapped in banana leaf with sticky rice and banana (**khanom kluay**) or muffin-like and deep yellow (**khanom tan**); **khanom nam kati** warm reduced coconut milk with banana (**kluay buat chii**), pumpkin (**fak thong kaeng buat**), sago and black beans (**saku tou tam**) or black sticky rice (**khao niao dam**); **sangkhayaa** custard of duck eggs, coconut cream and palm sugar, often with pandan leaves (**sangkhayaa bai toey**); **khanom boeng** cigar-shaped pancake with pastes of shredded coconut, squash, taro, dried prune or sweet wax gourd; **foy thong** (golden threads) duck egg yolks spun with sugar; **man/poek/khluay ping** grilled sweet potato/taro/banana.

Seasonal: khao niao ma-muang/thurian coconut milk sticky rice with mango/durian; **khao chae** rice in jasmine water; **krathong loy khwae** santol fruit in sweet-sour syrup.

Fruit: ap-peun apple; **cantaloup** melon; **farang** guava; **kluay** banana; **lamyai** longan (Jul-Oct); **linchee** lychee (Apr-May); **malakor** papaya; **ma-muang** mango (Feb-May); **mangkut** mangosteen (Apr-Sept); **maphrao** coconut; **ngo** rambutan (May-Sept); **noina** custard apple (July-Sept); **sapparot** pineapple; **som** orange; **som-o** pomelo; **taeng mo** watermelon; **thurian** durian (Apr-Jun).

Drinks (*deum*)

nam plao plain water; **nam soda** soda water; **nam manao** lime juice; **nam ma phrao** coconut juice; **nam krajeab** roselle flower juice; **nam ta krai** lemongrass juice; **nam ponlamai bun** iced fruit shake; **oh-liang** Chinese iced black coffee; **kafae yen** Thai iced coffee with condensed milk; **cha dum yen** Thai iced black tea; **cha Thai yen** Thai iced tea with condensed milk; **nam tao hoo** hot soya milk.

This simple white wooden house on bopping Lang Suan is a nightly dinner party of sorts, with throngs of regulars. The cooking focuses on seafood – all taken still breathing from the tanks out front. Whether you opt for Chinese veggies or steamed squid in lemon sauce, it's hard to go wrong.

Sukhumvit

International

Bed Supperclub serves inventive fusion in chic, arty environs (*see p191*). The **Bull's Head** (*see p134*) offers British staples. Excellent jazz accompanies the multi-restaurant Sunday brunch (from B1,648 per person) at the **Sheraton Grande Sukhumvit** (*see p48*). **Emporium** (*see p153*) has many popular eating places on offer.

Baan Rai Café
Thanon Sukhumvit, at Soi 63 (0 2391 9783-5/ www.banriecoffee.com). Ekamai BTS. **Open** 24hrs daily. **Main courses** B80. **No credit cards.** **Map** p252 M7 ❸

This rustic wooden 'coffee garden' serves tea and coffee in modern and local styles, plus cakes. There are also nine iMacs with internet, CDs for sale, and myriad books, some chained to outdoor tables, where you can eat Isaan food from nearby stalls. Performances sometimes grace the shady courtyard.

Le Banyan
59 Sukhumvit Soi 8 (0 2253 5556/www.le-banyan. com). Nana BTS. **Open** 6.30pm-midnight (last orders 9.30pm) Mon-Sat. **Main courses** B850. **Credit** AmEx, DC, MC, V. **Map** p251 J5 ❹

A silver salver French institution that understands the theatricality required of fine dining. Many of the dishes are prepared at the table by the formal but amiable maître d', Bruno Bischoff, or the eccentric chef, Michel Binaux – a charming double act. The speciality is pressed duck, within a menu of superb classics. The old Thai house decor has faded, but few Bangkok restaurants are better, or better value.

Le Beaulieu
Sofitel Residence, 50 Sukhumvit Soi 19 (0 2204 2004/www.le-beaulieu.com). Asoke BTS/Sukhumvit MRT. **Open** 11.30am-3pm, 6-11pm daily. **Main courses** B500. **Set lunch** B450-B650. **Credit** AmEx, DC, MC, V. **Map** p252 K5 ❹

A compact private dining room means that tables are much sought after at the first chef-patron venture by Hervé Frerard, who has enthused local Francophile foodies for years with his deft take on Gallic classics at the Heritage Club and Aldo's. Over *amuse-gueules* at the communal wine table, let Hervé tailor sensational signature courses with top-notch ingredients, from braised cheek of veal to sea urchin emulsion to the tenderest tenderloin conceivable. His three-course set lunches are fantastic value.

Giusto

16 Sukhumvit Soi 23, Sukhumvit (0 2258 4321/ www.giustobangkok.com). **Open** 11am-2.30pm, 6-10.30pm daily. **Main courses** B500. **Set lunch** B450 2 courses, B530 3 courses Mon-Fri. **Credit** AmEx, DC, MC, V. **Map** p252 K5 ㊷

The latest star in Bangkok's Italian infatuation, chef-patron Fabio Colautti has reworked a house with Gucci-esque flair to create this power restaurant and its wine bar, Glass. The glazed octagon is the zone to book. A decent selection of wines by the glass are matched individually with dishes such as fish and spicy sausage soup, and spaghetti with sea urchin and sliced *bottarga*.

Kuppa

39 Sukhumvit Soi 16 (0 2663 0450). Asoke BTS/Sukhumvit MRT. **Open** 10am-10pm Tue-Sun. **Main courses** B380. **Credit** AmEx, DC, MC, V. **Map** p252 K6 ㊸

This hangar of blond wood and metal, dominated by a working coffee roaster, is Bangkok's premier modern café. It has the scale and feel of a major international restaurant, and the menu is consistently good, from duck pizza with hoi sin sauce to mighty desserts. Cultured urbanites relish the sofas, magazines and art gallery all day till late.
Other locations: Kuppa Restaurant & Cooking School, Playground!, 818 Soi Thonglor, Sukhumvit (0 2714 9517-8).

Maha Naga

2 Sukhumvit Soi 29 (0 2662 3060). Phrom Phong BTS. **Open** 11.30am-2pm, 6-11pm daily. **Main courses** B420. **Credit** AmEx, MC, V. **Map** p252 K6 ㊤

Exquisite decor qualifies this as a destination restaurant, despite the so-so food. While Thai-Western fusions like pork chop with green curry struggle for balance, the decor is what stands out. Indian glass mosaics, Moroccan Ramadan lanterns and waiters' Moorish costumes blend seamlessly under high-ceilinged halls that flank a fountain courtyard facing an art nouveau house containing the bar.

Nasir Al-Masri

4/6 Sukhumvit Soi 3/1 (0 2253 5582). Nana BTS. **Open** 9am-4pm daily. **Main courses** B300. **No credit cards. Map** p251 J5 ㊺

The pick of Soi Arab's eateries transports you to Cairo, complete with the requisite sounds. On the

Sensational tailored meals at Hervé Frerard's **Le Beaulieu**. *See p121.*

mirror-metal terrace, men banter over Arabic music videos as they puff on shisha pipes. Inside, Islamic motifs and Ramadan lanterns dot yet more mirror-metal walls and the ceiling. All the food is good, from kebabs to dips and the Egyptian national dish, *molokaya*. No alcohol.

New York Steakhouse

JW Marriott Bangkok Hotel, 4 Sukhumvit Soi 2 (0 2656 7700). Ploenchit/Nana BTS. **Open** 6-11pm daily. **Main courses** B1,200-B5,000. **Credit** AmEx, DC, MC, V. **Map** p251 H5 ㊻
A sensation since its 2001 debut, this restaurant led the Siamese steakhouse boom, and remains unsurpassed for its club-like sophistication. It holds superb seafood in live tanks and flies in grain-fed US Angus beef (chilled not frozen); the prime cut, served from a silver trolley, is melt-in-the-mouth. The vegetables disappoint, but then this is carnivore territory. Many wines come by the glass, and there are around 20 Martinis. Booking is essential.

Pizzeria Bella Napoli

3/3 Sukhumvit Soi 31 (0 2259 0405). Phrom Phong BTS. **Open** 11.30am-2pm; 5-11.30pm daily. **Main courses** B240. **Credit** AmEx, MC, V. **Map** p252 K6 ㊼
Owner Claudio Conversi, who also makes *gelato* for many top hotels and restaurants, opened the city's first stand-alone pizza parlour in 2002. Bella Napoli was packed from day one. This small trattoria has classic Neapolitan pizzas, plus pastas and a few standard mains. The atmosphere is fun too.

Other Asian

Indian/Pakistani/Persian curry houses spread from **Soi 3 (Nana)** to **Soi 11** and especially **Soi 11/1**, with an Arabian/African enclave at **Soi 3/1** ('Soi Arab'). A dizzying variety of Japanese restaurants cram **Sois 23-55**.

Akbar

1/4 Sukhumvit Soi 3 (0 2253 3479/0 2255 6935). Nana BTS. **Open** 10.30am-midnight daily. **Main courses** B350. **Credit** AmEx, MC, V. **Map** p251 J4 ㊽
Of all the Indian restaurants around Soi 3, this mishmash of wooden ornaments, lanterns, coloured glass and Indian fabrics is the oldest. Unusually, it has a few good wines, plus Persian dishes.

Le Dalat Indochine

14 Sukhumvit Soi 23 (0 2661 7967-8). Asoke BTS/Sukhumvit MRT. **Open** 11.30am-2.30pm, 5.30-10pm daily. **Set menus** *Lunch* B500. *Dinner* B1,000. **Credit** AmEx, DC, MC, V. **Map** p252 K5 ㊾
Oozing class, this adapted house is owned by the family of the 1930s Saigon socialite Madame Hoa Ly, daughter of a French governor to Indochina. Photographs of that time line the lobby bar, while dining rooms upstairs and down brim with Asian antiques. Even ladies peek in the gents, to view the collection of phallic objects. Consistently good specialities such as prawn on sugar cane come with a bouquet of herb-strewn leaves.

Hazara

The Face, 29 Sukhumvit Soi 38 (0 2713 6048-9/ www.facebars.com). Thonglor BTS. **Open** 6.30-11pm daily. **Main courses** B200. **Credit** AmEx, DC, MC, V. **Map** p252 M7 ㊿
Here, a giant Balinese *garuda* dominates a stunning interior of pan-Asian statuary, puppet heads and carved doors. Hazara's rich North Indian curries and creamy dals has enticing vegetarian options, such as tandoor-roasted peppers stuffed with vegetables and nuts. It's far better than the Lanna Thai restaurant sharing this new Thai-style complex of quite magical grace. Try its spa before dining.

Joke Club

155/20-25 Sukhumvit Soi 11 (0 2651 2888-9). Nana BTS. **Open** 10am-2am daily. **Main courses** B120. **Credit** AmEx, MC, V. **Map** p251 J5 ⑤

Sizzling woks and high-rise bustle à la Hong Kong. Joke Club is quite a scenester, thanks to a swanky mix of thoughtful Chinese cookery and modern design: murals, dark woods, silver detailing. While an in-house singer Bacharachs away, diners feast upon staples like rice noodles, seafood and the namesake rice porridge with all the hot-sour-salty-sweet fixings.

Kaborae

1st floor, Sukhumvit Plaza, Sukhumvit Soi 12 (0 2252 5375/5486). Asoke BTS/Sukhumvit MRT. **Open** 11am-10pm daily. **Main courses** B350. **Credit** MC, V. **Map** p251 J5 ⑤

Family-style Kaborae is the pick of the café-diners in the Little Seoul of Sukhumvit Plaza, where practically every shop, restaurant and bar caters to Hermit Kingdom expatriates, with more located in the nearby *soi*. Its wonderfully diverse dishes include hot and sour soups, and the peppery noodle speciality *naingmyon*. Toast the table with the Korean rice whisky *soju*.

Koi

26 Sukhumvit Soi 20 (0 2663 4990-1/http://koi restaurantbkk.com). Asoke BTS/Sukhumvit MRT. **Open** 4pm-midnight Mon-Sat; 12.30pm-midnight Sun. **Main courses** B800. **Credit** AmEx, DC, MC, V. **Map** p252 K6 ⑤

The LA celebrity hangout Koi opened this über-chic restaurant and bar in an artfully lit garden in 2005. Its modern Japanese food, served amidst atmospheric candles, dark woods and glowing red lamps, presents options such as fried oysters with a fiery ponzu sauce in a Martini glass, and Wagyu rib-eye marinated with soy sauce, apple and saké. An Italian restaurant was set to open here too in the latter part of 2007. On Tuesdays, Thursdays, Fridays and Saturdays a flock of models on free drinks end pheromones into overdrive at the elegant teak and glass bar building, which transforms into a Fashion TV lounge.

Rang Mahal

26th floor, Rembrandt Hotel, 19 Sukhumvit Soi 18 (0 2261 7100/www.rembrandtbkk.com). Asoke BTS/Sukhumvit MRT. **Open** 11.30am-2.20pm, 6.30-10.20pm daily. **Main courses** B675. **Credit** AmEx, DC, MC, V. **Map** p252 K6 ㉞

The superb city views and the excellent, rich, north Indian dishes make Rang Mahal worth a splurge for a romantic date, but be sure to reserve a window table. The Moghul-style decor spreads from silk sofas and ornate woodwork to the die-cut menu, while a loud and entertaining Indian band plays near the long central banquet tables. There are good thalis and a terrific-value Sunday brunch buffet (B650, B325 6-12s, free under-6s). Wrap up warm as the air-con is Himalayan.

Shin Daikoku

32/8 Sukhumvit Soi 19 (0 2254 9981-3/www. shindaikoku.com). Asoke BTS/Sukhumvit MRT. **Open** 11.30am-2pm, 6-10.30pm daily. **Main courses** *Lunch* B190. *Dinner* B500. **Credit** AmEx, MC, V. **Map** p252 K5 ㊺

To reach this elegant restaurant in an old house you cross a Japanese-style wooden bridge. Owned by the popular Fuji chain found in malls, this flagship is a favourite for embassy entertaining. Shin Daikoku offers all the usual sushi and sashimi options, plus *teppanyaki* and *matsuzaka* beef. **Other locations:** 3rd floor, InterContinental Hotel, Thanon Ploenchit, Sukhumvit (0 2656 0096-8).

Xian Dumpling Restaurant

10/3 Sukhumvhit Soi 40 (0 2713 5288). Ekkamai BTS. **Open** noon-11pm daily. **Main courses** B120. **No credit cards. Map** p252 M7 ㊶

In the sea of Chinese restaurants the world over, this pocket-sized dumpling outlet in a shadowy yet neon-strewn parking lot off Soi 40 comes across as unique. The hearty Xian food seems to owe as much to Mongolian, Muslim and Silk Road influences as it does to Sino classicism. Think shredded tripe and

Nasir Al-Masri. See p123.

tofu with chilli oil, stewed aubergine, mutton soup
and doughy steamed dumplings in dozens of forms.
Pink cloths on the chairs and white-tile wallpaper
make for a setting of good-bad taste.

Thai

Flanking Thonglor BTS, stalls at the mouths
of **Soi 38** and **Soi 55** are renowned for their
eclectic foods, from *joke* (rice porridge) and
noodles to crispy pork and desserts such as the
ginger tofu soup on Soi 55. For great barbecue
and drinking food at **Ana Garden**, *see p134.*
Baan Thai Wellness Retreat (*see p47*)
serves health-conscious Thai dishes.

Greyhound Café

*2nd floor, Emporium, Sukhumvit Soi 24 (0 2664
8663/0 2260 7149). Phrom Phong BTS.* **Open**
11am-10pm daily. **Main courses** B150. **Credit**
AmEx, DC, MC, V. **Map** p252 K6 ⑤⑦
Run by, and adjacent to, the hip Thai fashion store
of the same name, Greyhound retains its quirky
minimalist style in the form of metal-strewn, whitewashed concrete, handwritten menus and tailor-
made crockery. The tried-and-tested menu features
faultless Thai staples and local fusion dishes, such
as spaghetti *pla kem* (stir-fried pasta with Thai
anchovies, chilli and garlic). The Another Hound
branch (1st floor, Siam Paragon, Pathumwan, 0 2129
4409-10) applies that inventiveness to finer dining
in grander surrounds: *miang* with Italian sausage,
lobster ravioli tom yum, or grilled marinated lamb
chop with beer and Thai spices. No surprise, then,
to find all manner of film, media and society types
nibbling here.
Other locations: throughout the city.

Kalapapruek on First

*1st floor, Emporium, Sukhumvit Soi 24 (0 2664
8410-2). Phrom Phong BTS.* **Open** 11am-10pm
daily. **Main courses** B180. **Credit** AmEx, DC,
MC, V. **Map** p252 K6 ⑤⑧
Friendly, trendy and spacious, Kalapapruek has
cushioned banquettes and lawn benches overlooking Benjasiri Park. The menu is particularly strong
on regional specialities, such as roti with curry,
Chiang Mai's beloved *khao soi* and *koong foo* (crispy
prawn with green mango salad). It's owned by the
son of aristocrat Mom Chao Bhisadhet Rachanee,
who set up the original Kalapapruek in Bangrak.
Half the menu is Western, featuring (separately)
trout and blueberry cheese pie.
Other locations: 27 Thanon Pramuan, Bangrak
(0 2236 4335); 5th floor, Emporium, Sukhumvit
(0 2614 8149); All Seasons Retail Centre, Thanon
Witthayu, Pathumwan (0 2685 3860); Ground floor,
Siam Paragon, Pathumwan (0 2129 4409-10).

Khrua Vientiane

8 Sukhumvit Soi 36 (0 2258 6171). Thonglor BTS.
Open noon-midnight daily. **Main courses** B100.
Credit MC, V. **Map** p252 L7 ⑤⑨

Ruen Mallika. *See p127.*

It's only a block from noisy Sukhumvit, but you feel like you're practically upcountry in this *soi* that's a trove of Isaan and Lao food. This sprawling wooden compound offers seating on a balcony, in cushion-seating *salas* or centrally under a roof – an inferior cover to the wonderful Banyan tree they felled to make way for it. Dancers and musicians play Pong lang nightly (7.30-10pm). It may fill with *farang*, but the food's authentic.

Ruen Mallika

189 Sukhumvit Soi 22, in sub-soi to Soi 16, Sukhumvit (0 2663 3211-2/www.ruenmallika.com). **Open** 11am-11pm daily. **Main courses** B350. **Credit** AmEx, DC, MC, V. **Map** p252 K7 ⑥

This branch of the famous ML Terb restaurant in north-east Bangkok is likewise based on the recipes of mid 20th-century celebrity chef ML Terb Chomsai. Servings are as huge as the wooden menu, which features unusual dishes such as tempura-style deep-fried flowers and the Ayutthaya-period coconut milk dessert *kanom tuay*. Opt for relaxed garden seating amid the small fountains and triangular cushions at low tables inside this Rama I-period wooden house. **Photo** *p126*.
Other locations: ML Terb Royal Thai Cuisine, 13/10 Moo 9, Thanon Kaset-Nawamin, Khlong Kum, Bung Khum, North-east (0 2946 1180-1); Yentafo Khreuang Song, 7th floor, Mah Boon Krong, 444 Thanon Phayathai, Pathumwan (0 2686 3509); Yentafo Khreuang Song, Srivikorn Building, 42/1 Sukhumvit Soi 21, Sukhumvit (0 2713 5599).

Spring Summer Winter

199 Soi Promsri 2, off Sukhumvit Soi 39 (0 2392 2747-8). **Open** 11am-2.30pm, 5.30-11pm daily. **Main courses** B250. **Credit** AmEx, MC, V. **Map** p252 L5 ⑤

Two stunning 1960s houses dominate this spacious compound. The invitingly lit Spring serves good seafood with Thai, Chinese and Japanese influences. Reliable picks include rice noodle rolls with fried sea bass, and prawns on stir-fried pepper noodles. Summer, the smaller house, specialises in chocolatey desserts, while Winter is a dry-season bar on the lawn where you can drink or dine on beanbags. Sublime.

Vegetarian

Rasayana Retreat spa has a raw food restaurant (*see p177*). **Baan Thai Wellness Retreat** (*see p47*) makes a speciality of meat-free Thai dishes.

Govinda

6/5-6 Sukhumvit Soi 22 (0 2663 4970). Phrom Phong BTS. **Open** 11.30am-3pm, 6-11.30pm Mon, Wed-Sun. **Main courses** B200. **Credit** AmEx, MC, V. **Map** p252 K6 ⑥

Despite the restaurant's name, this excellent food is all Italian: thin-base pizzas, pastas and risottos, plus own-made bread. The two-level interior has plenty of character, with a winding staircase and upstairs balcony. German beer too.

Tamarind Café & Gal

27 Sukhumvit Soi 20 (0 2663 ... cafe.com). **Open** 11am-11pm M... Sat, Sun. **Main courses** B290. ... MC, V. **Map** p252 K6 ⑥

Ultra-tasteful dining, from t... dishes on the Asian-European .... to the bright white interior, where Gallery F-Stop exhibits photos. The French-Taiwanese owners, importing their Hanoi outlet's concept, use organic produce whenever possible in dishes like burrito with sautéed veg, paneer cheese, own-made pickles, and honey and grenadine jam.
Other locations: 5th floor, MBK, Pathumwan (0 2620 9000).

North

Thai

For Thai specialities visit **Chatuchak Weekend Market** (*see p138* **Market forces**) and the farmer's **Or Tor Kor Market** opposite (*see p140*). **Reflections** (*see p50*) offers fabulously kitsch seafood dining. Victory Monument's surrounds are also famed for *kwetiao reua* (boat noodles), and a block south, Isaan restaurants along **Thanon Rangnam**.

Mid Night Kai Ton

Thanon Petchaburi Tut Mai (no phone). **Open** 7pm-4am daily. **Main courses** B40. **No credit cards**. **Map** p251 G4 ⑥

Legendary late-night food in the form of *khao man kai*, a Hainanese trader dish of chicken-flavoured rice, steamed chicken and broth offset by hits of ginger and chilli sauce. The post-party customers can't get enough, and we can see why.

Pla Dib

1/1 Areesamphan Soi 7, at Thanon Rama 6 (0 2279 8185). Aree BTS. **Open** 5pm-midnight Tue-Sun. **Main courses** B90. **Credit** MC, V.

Thai for 'raw fish', Pla Dib weds Thai, Japanese and European in dishes such as 'larb sashimi' and 'raw seafood ceviche'. Young, professional and alternative Thais huddle around minimalist, candlelit tables inside the restored house and in the rocky front yard that's also home to a wood-fired pizza oven. The warehouse aesthetic suits the small parties, gigs and exhibitions it regularly hosts.

South

International

One of the great experiences of Bangkok is to eat and drink atop a skyscraper. **Vertigo**, at the Banyan Tree Bangkok, is a full-service, premium-priced grill where the **Moon Bar** (*see p135*) overlooks the city on all sides.

Siam

Loi Si Aksorn, Thanon Chue Ploeng (0 2671 0030-1). **Open** 6pm-midnight daily. **Main courses** B350. **Credit** AmEx, MC, V. **Map** p251 J7 🚇

This 1922 home of an early Thai railway boss has antique and repro furniture for sale (the French management has a workshop opposite), such as the brass pestle-and-mortar ashtrays. The half-French, half-Thai menu does a decent job and the setting is luscious. A *digestif* upstairs after the meal is so beguiling that you'll need to be evicted.

Cy'an

Metropolitan Hotel, 27 Thanon Sathorn Tai (02 625 3333/http://metropolitan.como.bz/bangkok). **Open** 6am-10.30am, noon-2pm, 6.30-10.30pm daily. **Set menus** *Lunch* B580 2 courses, B680 3 courses. *Dinner* B2,800 7 courses, B4,530 7 courses incl wines. **Credit** AmEx, DC, MC, V. **Map** p251 G7 🚇

Chef Amanda Gale (*see p113* **Gold plated**) runs one of Bangkok's most creative kitchens at the stylish Metropolitan. Gale's Asian-Mediterranean menu features zesty tapas starters and mains such as seared tiger prawns with taleggio tortellini, parmesan, pine nuts and raisins. Attention to detail resounds in both flavour and aesthetics. Views of the pool, an icy blue bar and hand-blown Murano glass lampshades dominate an otherwise minimalist room. Amanda's innovative spa cuisine in Glow upstairs makes for a breezy lunch.

La Scala

Pool wing, Sukhothai Hotel, 13/3 Thanon Sathorn Tai (0 2344 8888). **Open** 11.30am-2.30pm, 6.30-10.30pm daily. **Main courses** B500. **Credit** AmEx, DC, MC, V. **Map** p251 G7 🚇

An open kitchen has never been less intrusive than at this fine restaurant. Long lamps and legless solid teak tables miraculously protrude from walls clad in terracotta and hand-cast bronze strips. The food is equally fine, with novel reinterpretations of classic components. Good music and swish staff uniforms add to this minimalist, yet sociable showpiece.

Thai

For **Baan Khanitha**, *see p120* **Curries & More**. The streetfood in Soi Prasat Court, opposite Suan Plu Market in Soi Suan Plu, includes **Santi Asoke** vegetarian Thai café.

Blue Elephant

233 Thanon Sathorn Tai (0 2673 9353-4/ www.blueelephant.com). Surasak BTS. **Open** 11.30am-2.30pm, 6.30-10pm daily. **Main courses** B300. **Credit** AmEx, DC, MC, V. **Map** p250 E8 🚇

This Belgium-based Thai chain converted the century-old Thai-Chinese Chamber of Commerce building into a restaurant with cooking school upstairs (*see p128* **Pan handling**). Innovation infuses the menu (think foie gras in tamarind sauce).

Celadon

Sukhothai Hotel, 13/3 Thanon Sathorn Tai (0 2344 8888). **Open** 11am-2.30pm, 6.30-10.30pm daily. **Main courses** B500. **Set menu** B1,200 4 courses. **Credit** AmEx, DC, MC, V. **Map** p251 G7 🚇

A rare hotel restaurant that serves the kind of fifth-gear cooking that attracts even discerning locals. Lotus ponds, bronze vases and Sakul Intakul's floral fantasies give the feeling of floating. The *penang* curry, banana flower salad, lotus dumplings and betel leaf starter are must-orders. Pricing is moderate considering the pedigree kitchen.

Le Lys

104 Narathiwat Ratchanakarin Soi 7 (0 2287 1898-9/0 2675 4474-5/www.lelys.info). **Open** 11.30am-10.30pm daily. **Main courses** B200. **Credit** AmEx, DC, MC, V. **Map** p250 F7 🚇

Le Lys' French-Thai owners set themselves apart with Gallic sensibilities and an oh-so-Thai menu. Vintage French wine posters hang amid Lanna textiles in a *hacienda*-style compound boasting a pétanque court. Pickled bamboo shoot soup, red curry with duck and lychee, salmon in the Thai yum, and squid with tamarind sauce lure young and old.

Pan handling

Many hotels and restaurants offer courses in Thai cuisine, but before you sign up, ensure you'll get utensils and some time on the range, not just a talking head. The **Oriental Thai Cooking School**, set in wooden buildings across the river from the Oriental (*see p45*), has top-notch hands-on classes of each style (9am-noon Mon-Sat, $120 per class). The well-equipped **Blue Elephant** (*see p128*) teaches four dishes per day (1 day B2,800, 5 days B10,000, 7 days for professionals B68,000), while **Mai Kaidee** teaches vegetarian Thai cookery (*see p112*). **Cuisine of the Sun** (0 1894 3551, cuisinebkk@hotmail.com) holds classes in Thai and foreign cooking six days a week, and chic **Pai Kin Khao** (www.pai-kin-khao.com) teaches mostly on Saturdays. **Kuppa** (*see p123*, classes every 1-2 months, from B2,500) also has a cooking school exploring themes like fusion, healthy cuisine and entertaining.

Amid the waterways of nearby Nonthaburi province, **Thai House** (32/4 Moo 8, Bangmuang, Bangyai, 0 2903 9611, www. thaihouse.co.th) runs day or residential courses in classic Thai dishes (8.30am-3.30pm Mon-Sat). Choose from one-day (B3,500), two-day (B8,950 shared room) or three-day (B16,650 shared). It's remote, but not far from the expressway and a rare chance to stay in a teak stilt house.

Bars & Pubs

Bangkok's boozers come in all forms – quirky, trendy and downright freaky.

The more do-gooders try to limit ways to drink in Bangkok, the more Thais find new ways to sup their beer, cocktails and whisky-Cokes. The clampdown on alcohol in licensed bars (*see p132* **Drink up!**) has produced ingenious new pavement bars based around stalls or open-top *tuk-tuks*. Bangkok never really stops partying – what else can be expected from the place that invented Red Bull? Few countries consume more alcohol per head than Thailand, and bars cater to all tastes and budgets, from local pubs and theme bars to dens full of vodka snobs and cocktail nests atop skyscrapers. You can find bars anywhere: off dank alleys; hidden among market stalls; teetering over canals on wooden floorboards; even occupying '70s-style homes in suburbia. In the cooler season, seemingly every other forecourt becomes a beer garden.

Despite attempts to zone nightlife (*see p190* **Zoning out**), the habit of bar owners to hop to newly in-vogue streets continues. Shareholders (often Thai celebrities) invest in emerging locations, invite their friends, get bored and move on to the next area.

Bars and clubs in zones are open until 2am; those outside zones are open until between 1am and 2am, depending on official whim. Picture ID (passport, ID card, no photocopies) is often demanded on entry, however old you are.

DRINKS & ETIQUETTE

Thai drinking habits often follow a pattern, involving live bands or karaoke, and always food. Most bars, from tiny shophouse venues to gargantuan *rong beer* (microbreweries), offer food. Listings in this chapter that note main courses indicate excellent dining. The rest have reasonably priced Thai food or a repertoire of *kub klaem* (drinking snacks), including cashew nuts fried and tossed with chilli and kaffir lime, spicy salads, deep-fried chicken cartilage and grilled meats with chilli dips.

> ▶ Places serving drinks are also listed in the chapters **Restaurants** (*see pp110-128*), **Gay & lesbian** (*see pp173-176*), **Music** (*see pp182-189*)and **Nightlife** (*see pp190-194*)as well as some malls (*see also* **Shops & Services** *pp141-156*) and **Markets** (*see pp136-149*).

When Thais go out, it's a party from the start. Groups of six or more tend to settle into one venue, their friends flitting back and forth throughout the night. Given the culture of hosting, bars can have multiple zones (lounge, disco, karaoke, restaurant, band, garden) in what Thais confusingly call a 'pub'. (The Anglo-Irish definition of pub also applies to the city's plentiful expat watering holes.) Although dividing bills is creeping in, the host (the most senior, or a birthday celebrant) often picks up the tab, usually buying a bottle of whisky to share. Chivas Regal and Johnny Walker Red or Black (B800-B2,500) are favoured, along with cheaper blends such as Spey Royal (B200-B600) and local rums like the fiery Mekong (B250). In villages and backstreets you may get plied with moonshine, an unregulated – and strong – white liquor fermented from rice.

The deployment of whisky bottle, ice bucket, mixing sodas and lime slices has evolved into a ritual. It's hard to monitor how much you're drinking, as toasts are legion and glasses are constantly topped up, usually by the youngest person present, out of respect touching left hand to right elbow. Individual bottled beers hold less appeal, hence the large shared bottles of local brews such as Singha, Chang, Kloster and licensed Heineken and the draught pitchers at the beer gardens covering every mall forecourt in 'winter'. Beer is often drunk on the rocks.

Drinks lists are more diversified in international bars, in particular with cocktails, shots and pre-mixed bottled drinks. Lychee Martinis are also big, as are boozy iced teas and wine, although knowledge of labels and how to mix and serve them is rare.

Cocktails, too, get shared, with the staple Kamikaze coming in a jug. You may even see Saeng Som whisky and Red Bull mixed in a small bucket and supped through several straws. Rival energy drinks include Shark, M-150 and Carabao Daeng.

Phra Nakorn & Banglamphu

On **Thanon Khao San**, rowdy backpacker video dens vie with a parallel scene of brash Thai pubs. Lined with trees and tiny, characterful bars displaying art, most of them run by ex-students, **Thanon Phra Arthit** has a more bohemian vibe.

Bangkok Bar

149 Thanon Rambuttri, Banglamphu (0 2629 4443).
Open 8pm-1am daily. **Credit** MC, V. **Map** p248 B2 ❶
This cramped shophouse bar prompts a 'dance-anywhere' vibe among indie types and intrepid *farang*.
Dark wood and giant candles dominate the two levels, with DJs shaping the mood with hip-hop. Don't confuse it with Bangkok Bar in Ekkamai Soi 21, although that's great too.

Bar Bali

58 Thanon Phra Arthit, Banglamphu (0 2629 0318).
Open 6pm-midnight daily. **No credit cards.**
Map p248 B2 ❷
Typical of the arty single-room bars on riverside Phra Arthit, softly lit Bali consists of four walls of pictures, as well as the requisite food and cocktails.

Boh

230 Tha Tien (Expressboat Pier), Thanon Maharaj, Phra Nakorn (0 2622 3081). **Open** 6pm-midnight daily. **No credit cards. Map** p248 B4 ❸
Like Boh's drinks list of local whisky and mixers, its outdoor setting (fluorescent lamps, set on the actual timbered pier) is hardly classy. But the views are free and the sunsets worth staying late for.

The best Bars

For indie cachet
Phranakorn Bar (*see right*) or bars along
Thanon Phra Arthit (*see p129*).

For deal-making credibility
Distil (*see p132*) and Diplomat Bar
(*see p133*).

For chilling out Thai-style
Tak Sura (*see p135*) and Lullabar
(*see p185*).

For cocktail aficionados
Zuk (*see p135*), Hu'u (*see p135*) and
Q Bar (*see p194*).

For the finest beer
Tawandaeng German Brewhouse (*see p135*) and Roadhouse BBQ (*see p133*).

For expats
The Barbican (*see p132*) and The Bull's
Head (*see p134*).

For Thai trendies
To Die For (*see p134*) and Bed Supperclub
(*see p191*).

For wines to savour
V9 (*see p133*) and Bacchus Wine Bar
(*see p133*).

Café Democ

78 Thanon Ratchadamnoen, Phra Nakorn (0 2622 2571). **Open** 11.30am-1am Tue-Sun. **No credit cards. Map** p248 C3 ❹
Named after the Democracy Monument it faces, this jazzy chillout café (by day) turns into a clubbers' bar by 10pm, when a lineup of leading Thai DJs keep the tech house, breakbeats and drum 'n' bass fresh and the dancefloor dirty.

Hippie de Bar

46 Thanon Khao San, Banglamphu (0 2629 3508/08 1820 2762). **Open** *Outside* 3pm-1am.
Inside 6pm-1am daily. *Hippie Hi* 9am-1am daily.
Credit V. **Map** p248 B3 ❺
Tucked behind an alley lined with used book shops, the retro-kitsch Hippie attracts not hippies but young, alternative Thais. Mismatched furniture, quirky wall hangings and other psychedelic paraphernalia cram into two floors and funky chairs litter the garden. A lively soundtrack veers from oldie hits to indie favourites.

Phranakorn Bar

58/2 Soi Damnoen Klang Tai, Phra Nakorn (0 2622 0282). **Open** 6pm-1am daily. **No credit cards.**
Map p248 B3 ❻
Young creatives and Khao San escapees gather on the chilled-out roof terrace for spicy Thai food and views of the floodlit Golden Mount and antics outside the *soi*'s gay bars. Others linger near the third-floor pool table listening to indie, house or '80s retro, browse art displayed by the photographer-owner on the second level, or drink whisky to live music at ground level. Supremely relaxed, with a holiday feel.

Suzie Pub

1085-9 Soi Rambuttri, Banglamphu (0 2282 4459). **Open** 6pm-1am daily. **No credit cards.**
Map p248 B3 ❼
Down an alley dubbed Soi Suzie, this US college bar-cum-dance club brought Thai nightlife to Khao San.
On weekends travellers and students cram in for the rock standards, while the laid-back weeknights leave elbow room for pool and pub dinners.

Thonburi

Dry-throated in Fang Thon? Admire views from the Three Sixty bar of the Millennium Hilton, where the jazz and cocktails format reigns. Or, head to restaurants like **Supatra River House** (*see p199*), **Patravadi Theatre & Studio 9** (*see p198*) or **River Bar Café** (*see p113*).

Three Sixty & Zeta

32nd floor, Millennium Hilton Bangkok Hotel, 123 Thanon Charoen Nakorn, Thonburi (0 2442 2000/ www.hilton.com). Hilton ferry from Tha Saphan Thaksin or Tha River City. **Open** 5pm-2am daily.
Credit AmEx, DC, MC, V. **Map** p250 D6 ❽
Taking the glazed elevator, you enter the Hilton's flying saucer-shaped penthouse bar, Three Sixty, for the full-circle panorama of both old town and new,

Three Sixty & Zeta. *See p130.*

through glare-free tilted windows overhanging the river. Aside from that, it's merely pleasant: cocktails, plush seating and live soft jazz. **Photos** *p131*.

Bangrak

Bar/restaurants and Anglo-Irish pubs dot Soi Saladaeng and Soi Convent. Cacophonous cul-de-sac **Silom Soi 4** has been trend central since the 1970s, but is now mostly gay, aside from **Tapas** (*see p194*) and newbies that are still too fresh to judge: **Luminous** and the progressive house bar **Zygosis**. **Silom Soi 2** is purely gay. Otherwise, there are the steamier go-go and neon lights of **Patpong Sois 1** and **2** (*see p191* **Adult nightlife**).

The Barbican

9/4-5 Soi Thaniya (0 2234 3590/www.greatbritish pub.com). Saladaeng BTS/Silom subway. **Open** 11am-1am daily. **Main courses** B200-B350. **Credit** AmEx, DC, MC, V. **Map** p250 F6 ❾

From the owners of the Bull's Head (*see p134*), this split-level pub goes against the Japanese-only grain of Soi Thaniya. Modishly styled in wood and smooth metal, it draws trendy expats and westernised Thais with regular DJs, lucrative prize games and Premiership screenings upstairs.

Coyote

Sivadon Building, 1/2 Thanon Convent (0 2631 2325/www.coyoteonconvent.com). Saladaeng BTS/Silom subway. **Open** 11am-midnight daily. **Main courses** B350. **Credit** AmEx, MC, V. **Map** p250 F7 ❿

This fun Mexican restaurant bar boasts the country's largest selection of tequilas and Margaritas. Among the after-work crowd, neckties loosen over two buzzing terracotta floors. Chilled jugs and gargantuan spicy platters fuel the down-to-earth mood.

Distil

63rd floor, LeBua at State Tower Hotel, 1055 Thanon Silom (0 2624 9555/www.thedomebkk.com). Saphan Taksin BTS/Pier. **Open** 6pm-1am daily. **Credit** AmEx, DC, MC, V. **Map** p250 E7 ⓫

Drink up!

Those wanting a refreshing drink in Bangkok should be aware that the city is in the grip of moral crusaders. Thaksin's 'Social Order Campaign' – purportedly designed to combat drugs and underaged drinking, but actually reducing a million incomes and impacting far beyond – peaked in 2001-4. But while the party mood has revived, the carefree old ways are over, perhaps for ever.

Police raids and urine tests recur periodically and the unrepealed early closing directives (1am for bars, 2am for clubs in nightlife zones) land later-opening venues in a pernicious, exploitable grey area as enforcement relents. Picture ID checks remain draconian, with some venues irresponsibly demanding that foreigners show actual passports, not photocopies. Following the New Year's Eve 2006-7 bombings, metal detectors, searches and CCTV now greet clubbers.

Penalties remain high for serving anyone underage, while anti-alcohol campaigners push further. After their protests drove the biggest ever Thai stock IPO (by the brewer of Beer Chang) to list in Singapore not Bangkok, the coup regime's health minister tried to ban all liquor promotion, and sales of alcohol to under-25s. Winter beer gardens advertised identical water brand logos instead, while Thai vineyards faced ruin just as wines like Monsoon Valley became

drinkable. A huge backlash thwarted the prohibitionists, though they are trying again.

Many commentators questioned restraints that would favour market-leading monopolists, and called for public education and duty based on proof, rather than the imposition of paternalistic bans to deal with the increase in drinking. The new policy also avoids the fact that moonshine – which accounts for 40 per cent of all alcohol drunk and most intoxification-related crimes – isn't advertised or available for purchase in shops. In the same vein, shops must limit alcohol sale hours and not display cigarettes, while smoking is prohibited in all public places except some bars and nightclubs.

Sanitised socialising is hardly *sanuk* (fun), so partying slips underground. Unlicensed venues and pavement bar stalls operate with a freedom denied to legitimate venues. As occasional crackdowns on go-go bars persist, streetwalkers become more visible and predatory, instead of being managed more healthily by *mamasans*. Youthful drinking, flirting and whatever else continues at house parties, only without the restraining context of licensed public places. While the crackdown claimed to undermine gangsterism in nightlife, its prohibitions have inevitably provided new opportunities for extortion. And, given the pressures, the city's fast turnover of bars and clubs is no surprise.

Bars & Pubs

Inside State Tower's celebrated golden 'Dome', sophisticated Thais, expats and tourists purr to an outstanding array of imported wines, champagnes and spirits. Expect London prices for imported oysters, fat Cuban cigars and cocktails mixed to perfection amid a glamorous decor of stone, leather armchairs and illuminated glass. Beds line the outdoor terrace – or you can skip to Sirocco's spectacular bar (see p116). Magnificent.

Irish X-Change

1/5-6 Siwadol Building, Soi Convent (0 2266 7160-1/www.irishxchange.com). Saladaeng BTS/Silom subway. **Open** 8.30am-1am daily. **Credit** AmEx, MC, V. **Map** p250 F7 ⑫
This brass and mahogany pub acts as a social embassy for British Isles expats, with Irish stew and ales aplenty on tap (including Malaysian-brewed Guinness), footie on the TV and the occasional live gig. You might just forget that you're in Thailand – presumably that's the point.

Roadhouse BBQ

942/1-4 Thanon Rama IV, at Surawong (0 2236 8010). Saladaeng BTS/Silom MRT/Samyan MRT. **Open** 11am-1am daily. **Main courses** B300-B400. **Credit** AmEx, MC, V. **Map** p250 F6 ⑬
A monster three-storey venue, distinct from the city's other pubs for its US character, barbecue food and smokery. Check out the excellent buffalo wings from the menu of ribs, burgers and steaks. The top-floor games room boasts a quality pool table and shuffleboard. Good-value wines and choice of microbrewed beers complete the picture.

V9

37th floor, Sofitel Silom Hotel, 188 Thanon Silom (0 2238 1991/www.sofitel.com). Chong Nonsi BTS. **Open** 5pm-1.30am daily. **Main courses** B800-B950. **Credit** AmEx, DC, MC, V. **Map** p250 F7 ⑭
In a land where wine is overtaxed as standard, this slick wine bar – overlooking Downtown through window walls – is the best value for sampling premium vintages (supplied by Wine Connection). International labels by the glass or bottle are paired by the sommelier to specific dishes on the global menu. V9's ingenious 'wine buffet' offers combinations of three mini-tasting glasses for the price of one glass. DJs (10pm-1.30am Mon-Sat) play sophisticated funk and chillout to facilitate that seamless drift across to the dance area.

Pathumwan

One of Bangkok's oldest bar strips, western Soi Sarasin is famed for jazzy **Brown Sugar** (see p186), but has suddenly gone mostly gay, notably at **70s Bar** (see p175). Siam Square falls quiet at night (excepting **Hard Rock Café**; see p189), but 'winter' beer gardens front Central World Plaza (Nov-Jan) with thousands of merry revellers thronging around three brewers' rival stages.

Bacchus Wine Bar

20/6-7 Soi Ruam Rudi (0 2650 8986/www.bacchus.tv). Ploenchit BTS. **Open** 5.30pm-1am daily. **Main courses** B300. **Credit** AmEx, DC, MC, V. **Map** p251 H5 ⑮
Ruam Rudi Village venues either stay for ever or last a wink. This four-floor, Japanese-run wine bar has enduring credentials: cellar (sommelier-selected), cuisine (Franco-Italian), cocktails (herbal and classic), humidor (Cubans) and decor (rusticated sandstone, water features, woodwork, subtle lighting). It makes for intimate lounging, whether at the bar, sunk in the armchairs or reclining on a 'floating' bed (both floor and ceiling are see-through). Patrons often slip into dance mode, especially at parties presided over by top local DJs.

Big Echo

1st floor, Kian Gwan Building, 140 Thanon Witthayu (0 2627 3071-4). Phloenchit BTS. **Open** 11am-1am daily. **Credit** AmEx, DC, MC, V. **Map** p251 H6 ⑯
Die-hard karaoke fans warble from over 30,000 songs (40% in English, the rest in Japanese, Chinese and Thai) at this Japanese-brand parlour. The 39 rooms (holding three to 50) offer the same nationalities' cuisines to fuel the crooning.

Diplomat Bar

Conrad Bangkok Hotel, All Seasons Place, 87 Thanon Witthayu (0 2690 9999/www.conrad bangkok.com). Ploenchit BTS. **Open** 10am-1am Mon-Thur, Sun; 10am-2am Fri, Sat. *Bands* 6.45-8.30pm, 9.45pm-12.15am Mon-Thur; 9.45pm-12.15am Fri, Sat. **Credit** AmEx, DC, MC, V. **Map** p251 H5 ⑰
Bangkok's A-list joins the genteel hubbub at this live jazz lounge. Floral installations by Sakul Intakul offset dark wood and backlit silk in this lofty hub for deal-making and pre- or post-dinner gatherings. The drinks list is extensive, and graceful service accompanies the smooth tones of the chanteuses.

Sukhumvit

Lanes off this entertainment highway harbour distinct scenes. Foreign lotharios follow microskirted legs around **Sois 3-9**, where UV-lit pool dens and techno-pumping 'bar-beers' blare non-stop. Designer bar/restaurants dot **Soi 11** and the zigzagging 'Green Route' linking the backsoi north of Sukhumvit.

A posher swathe from **Soi 53** via **Soi 55 (Thonglor)** to **Soi 55 (Ekamai)** has several nightlife mini-malls, among them **J-Avenue** (Ekamai Soi 15), **Ekamai Shopping Mall** (Ekamai Soi 10; look for the classy sign 'Get Drunk Here') and hyper-modish **H1**, opposite which Ekamai Soi 22 (**Chamchan**), a strip of bars with arty themes.

Another kind of art bar (hostess jazz joints dubbed Dali, Renoir, Van Gogh and Monet) clogs **Soi 33**, which rivals **Sois 22**, **24** and **33/1** in tourist haunts and expat pubs.

Eat, Drink, Shop

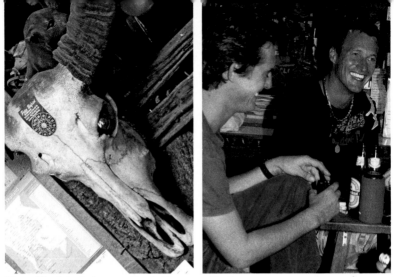

Cheap Charlie's: it does exactly what it says on the tin.

For a classier drink, nestle in the Chinese 'box-bed' at **Face Bar** (*see p125* Hazara), or compare thyself to the models preening in **Q Bar** (*see p194*), **Bed Supperclub** (*see p191*) or the bar at **Koi** (*see p125*), which glows red at night.

Ana Garden & Groove Kitchen

67 Sukhumvit Soi 55 (0 2391 1762/www.ana garden.com). Thonglor BTS. **Open** Ana Garden 5pm-midnight daily. Groove Kitchen 7pm-midnight daily. **Main courses** B500. **Credit** DC, MC, V. **Map** p252 M6 ⑬

Thais love to dine and drink in garden settings, but they're getting considerably rarer in urban Krung Thep. This fine example with wooden decks in a lush green setting provides a welcome refuge from bustling Thonglor beyond the (intentionally) broken front wall. Dinner here can turn into an all-night affair, drinking to DJ selections and laughing the night away. Partiers bop amid the trees inside the lofty air-con bar Groove Kitchen, behind a castle-like door hidden behind foliage.

Bourbon Street

Washington Square, Sukhumvit Soi 22 (0 2259 0328-9/www.bourbonstbkk.com). Phrom Phong BTS. **Open** 7am-1am daily. **Main courses** B350. **Credit** AmEx, DC, MC, V. **Map** p252 K6 ⑲

Amid the plaid-and-stetson bars of Washington Square, this New Orleans-themed bar/restaurant stands out for its long bar and Cajun-Creole food. The jambalaya, pecan pie and crawfish (fresh from the owner's farm) are highlights.

The Bull's Head

Sukhumvit Soi 33/1 (0 2259 4444/www.greatbritish pub.com). Phrom Phong BTS. **Open** 11am-1am daily. **Main courses** B300. **Credit** AmEx, DC, MC, V. **Map** p252 K6 ⑳

Despite rivals within staggering distance, this wood-and-horse-brass tavern remains the city's most authentic British pub. It draws an international (mostly UK) crowd, with old hits on the jukebox, pub grub, draught ale, games like 'toss the boss', and the Punchline Comedy Club (*see p199*).

Cheap Charlie's

1 Sukhumvit Soi 11 (08 7096 8444). Nana BTS. **Open** 5pm-1am daily. **No credit cards**. **Map** p251 J5 ㉑

Microscopic yet infinitely expandable, this outdoor bar consists of just a few stools around a counter obscured by a thicket of eccentric ephemera. Post-work expats sup beers with Thai pals here. And, yes, it's very cheap indeed.

To Die For

H1, 998 Sukhumvit Soi 55, Sukhumvit (02 381 4714). **Open** 5pm-midnight Mon-Thur, Sun; 5pm-1am Fri; 3pm-1am Sat. **Main courses** B350. **Credit** AmEx, DC, MC, V. **Map** p252 M5 ㉒

The gem of Thonglor's chic H1 complex, To Die For has Greyhound-clad waiters serving cocktails and inventive European dishes with an Oriental zest to hip young things. Lounge sofas in the courtyard add to the relaxed, intimate and classy environment. Inside, warmly lit brickwork prevents the glass and marble from feeling stark.

Tuba

34 Ekamai Soi 21 (02 711 5500). **Open** 10am-2am daily. **Credit** MC, V.

An ever-changing eclectic mish-mash of funky furniture, neon signs, robots, film memorabilia and nude oil paintings, Tuba is a kooky hangout where Thai and Japanese regulars play pool, use the free Wi-Fi, listen to jazz, watch TV or snack on the cheap, tasty Italian and Thai food. Rather like visiting a cool friend's home.

Eat, Drink, Shop

North

Located in a nightlife zone, Ratchada Soi 4 is a raucous maze of uneven *sois* with a music-festival feel from the rival sound systems. Bars like **Gig**, **Raed**, **Baku**, **China Bar** and **Snop** vary in theme but not character: tanked-up young Thais nod en masse to Thai rock bands interspersed with DJ-spun hip hop. The nearby Ratchada Soi 8 discos are more downmarket (*see p187* **Hollywood**).

Chatuchak Weekend Market-goers frequent **Viva** (*see p138* **Market forces**) and bars (many now gay) along Thanon Kamphaengphet and the *sois* behind.

Snop

58/5 Ratchada Soi 4 (0 2612 2459). Rama IX subway. **Open** 6.30pm-1.30am daily. **No credit cards.**
Beyond a white clapboarded courtyard with an open stage, inflatables floating in a pond hint at Snop's wacky interior themes, which change every three months, including staff costumes. Recently it has been a mock-school, a cartoon fantasia then a geisha/samurai incarnation of Japan. Ranks of low-table seating surround pop bands, who play nightly. The surreal is normal at this temple to kitsch.

Tak Sura

499/2 Ratchawithi Soi 12 (Soi Bot Xavier) (0 2354 9286). Rathathewi BTS. **Open** 5pm-1am daily. **Main courses** B100. **No credit cards.**
There's a blurred, smoky quality to this bar, intriguingly decked out in old train benches and Chinese tea-house chairs. Its wooden premises is an oasis of charm in a sea of concrete behind a bus stop. The yuppie-student-artist regulars sup whisky or beer and chow on chilli-laced bar snacks such as *larb gai* and Thai sausages.
Other locations: Soi Thansarot, 334/1 Thanon Phyathai, U-turn at north-west foot of canal bridge then turn right, North (0 2215 8879); 156/1 Thanon Tanao, Phra Nakorn (0 2622 0708).

North-east

Royal City Avenue (RCA) dwindled from a long crescent of 120-plus bars to a few barns of screaming teen techno. It subsequently evolved into today's sleek mega-club hub, although its edgiest venues recently closed (for reviews of the remaining ones, *see pp190-194*).

Old Leng

29/78-81 Royal City Avenue (0 2203 0972-3). **Open** 6pm-1am daily. **Credit** AmEx, MC, V. **Map** p252 L4 **㉓**
This survivor of the original RCA explosion looks like a cowboy saloon stranded in ancient China. 'Songs for Life' (Thai blues) fans flock here for live bands; smoochers gather on the quieter front deck. The clientele are mostly older, and hard-drinking.

Prop

23/51 Zone F, Royal City Avenue (0 2203 0669). **Open** 6pm-1.30am daily. **Credit** MC, V. **Map** p252 M4 **㉔**
Nestle yourself amid three floors delightfully cluttered with retro wallpaper, 'thrift shop' knick-knacks and furniture of patchwork, plastic or cracked leather (all for sale or rent). If you fancy something a bit more energetic, there's pool to be played. The soundtrack varies: Sundays is chillout lounge music; otherwise, it's rock, hip hop and Britpop.

South

Thanon Narathiwat Ratchanakharin spawned a string of bars that has declined from its heyday. Further south, **Tawandaeng German Brewhouse** is the city's best microbrewery, and home of the avant-garde show band **Fong Nam** (*see p183*). Or try your best to blag your way into the Metropolitan hotel's member-only **Met Bar** (*see p51*).

Hu'u

Ascott Sathorn Hotel, 187 Thanon Sathorn Tai (0 2676 6868/www.the-ascott.com). Chong Nonsi BTS. **Open** 5pm-midnight daily. **Credit** AmEx, DC, MC, V. **Map** p250 F7 **㉕**
A dark, laid-back Singaporean lounge that's ideal for suits to deal, date, dance or dine (with DJs on Fridays and Saturdays). Barmen have to scale a two-storey glass matrix shelving prime wines and spirits (the cocktail list stretches to 150-plus varieties). Hu'u Epicure on the glazed mezzanine serves holistic Pacific Rim fusions and exhibits photography.

Moon Bar at Vertigo

61st floor, Banyan Tree Bangkok Hotel, 21/100 Thanon Sathorn Tai (0 2679 1200/www.banyan treebangkok.com). Lumphini subway. **Open** 5.30pm-1am daily. **Main courses** B2,000-B3,000. **Credit** AmEx, DC, MC, V. **Map** p251 G7 **㉖**
One of the highest open-air bar/restaurants in the world, Vertigo boasts jaw-dropping views, so booking is essential. Its Moon Bar appears to hover at one raised end, lending the roof the feel of a Baron Munchausen flying galleon. As you sip cocktails, lounge and jazz tunes waft in the considerable breeze (beware of flapping ties and hair getting stuck in lipgloss). If it rains, the hotel has three restaurants in which to shelter.

Zuk

Sukhothai Hotel, 13/3 Thanon Sathorn Tai (0 2344 8888/www.sukhothai.com). Lumphini subway. **Open** 4pm-1am daily. **Credit** AmEx, DC, MC, V. **Map** p251 G7 **㉗**
Dark, moody and striking, this earth- and slate-toned bar lives up to its sophisticated setting with an elegant clientele. Top-line DJs ensure it's not subdued by creating an agreeably subversive vibe, with global star DJs sometimes guesting. The Martinis are among the best in town.

Eat, Drink, Shop

Markets

Carts and stalls garnish Bangkok with food, fashion and flowers – the purest expression of the sensual Thai culture.

Informal stalls may be the bedrock of Thai streetlife, but development and neat-freak officialdom threaten the continuation of the city's bountiful if messy *talad* (markets) and *rot khen* (itinerant vendors). Hired thugs razed long-standing stalls at Sukhumvit Soi 10 in 2003 and at Chatuchak's Sunday Market in 2006, as the land owners attempted to forcibly remove the traders. Vendors resist eviction at Bo Bae. Fly-pitchers are banned from BTS skybridges. Indoor markets have displaced some stalls at Pratunam and Chatuchak. Now Suan Lum Night Bazaar, equally liked and despised, appears to have been just a short-term ploy to mask the re-zoning of parkland to allow a 55 billion baht complex with a mall, hotel, condo, offices and an exhibition centre.

Still, just like the floating markets from which they derive, vendors remain fluid. No amount of campaigns to restrain their trading or encroachment of public space ever lasts long (*see p137* **Peddle power**). Nor do efforts to remedy piracy, food hygiene or extortion of vendors by officials.

On the positive side, street traders do have new paths to prosperity, prominence and even international outlets thanks to designers and bulk buyers browsing for creative entrepreneurs. City governor Apirak Kosayothin reinstated a vendor rest day (Monday) and recognises the social, tourist and cultural value of keeping Bangkok's bazaars.

Whether you're eating, shopping or sightseeing, markets are the purest expression of the sensual Thai culture, with their kaleidoscope of scents (jasmine garlands, musty puddles, durian), sounds (yelping hawkers, booming techno), sights (sleeping children, slithering eels), touch (antique silk, fake fur) and tastes (food you'll find nowhere else on Earth). Specialist *talad* cater to niches, temporary markets endow festivals with local or seasonal treats, and **Chatuchak Weekend Market** (*see p138* **Market forces**) offers just about everything else. All the while, roving hawkers are looking for you.

Bargaining is normal for goods (but never for cooked food), though only tourist traps should be pushed down more than ten to 20 per cent. Pre-armed with shop prices, you must remain polite and honour any bid they accept. Asking

in Thai can lower the starting price, and walking away from an impasse may reveal the 'best price'. Streetfood hotspots are noted under area headings in **Restaurants** (*see p110*, and *p117* **Streetfood shrines**).

Clothes

Na Ram Market (Thanon Ramkhamhaeng, between Sois 43-53, 4pm-midnight daily), in the eastern suburbs, also sells clothes.

Bo Bae

Soi Rong Muang, Thanon Krung Kasem, near Yotse Bridge, Chinatown (0 2628 1888/1999). **Open** 8am-5pm daily. **Map** p249/p250 E4.

This funky canalside *talad* specialises in wholesale clothes, from rough assembly-line wear to catwalk-worthy glamour. Bo Bae Tower has separate floors for men, women, children and babies. The outdoor area sells all manner of outdoor kit; army surplus, camping gear and the like. A ban on vendors' encroachment on the road turned violent in 2007. **Other locations:** 1st-6th Bo Bae Tower, 488 Thanon Damrongrak, Chinatown (0 2628 1888/1999).

Pratunam

Phetchaburi Road, west of Thanon Ratchaprarop, North. Tha Pratunam (0 2309 9700-3). **Open** *Day market* 10am-9pm daily. *Night market* 6pm-midnight daily. **Map** p251 G4/H4

The stalls at Pratunam ('Water Gate') burrow around the Indra and Bayoke hotels. This is come-one, come-all shopping (and at all times) for textiles, lingerie, ceramics, bags, T-shirts and street fashion. The seamstresses will stitch anything, and the market's popularity with African and Middle Eastern traders is reflected in the food available. Pratunam Centre and Platinum Mall, across roads to the east and south respectively, have displaced stalls with cheap indoor clothing shops.

Saphan Phut

Thanon Triphet, Chinatown. **Open** 8pm-midnight Tue-Sun. **Map** p248 B5.

Officials have tried to contain this plastic-covered night market, targetting it as an unwanted hotbed of potentially dangerous youth culture. Evicted from a prettified Khlong Lord over a decade ago, it is now strung like costume jewellery around Memorial Bridge. Have fun spotting the Thai designers on the prowl, amid absurdly cheap vintage clothing, T-shirts, handbags, hats and fake perfume. Street food is sold on the periphery.

Peddle power

Rot khen (vendor carts) remain integral to Thai life. Colonising any spare space by pedal or paddle, motor or manpower, they congregate at already congested places, such as *soi* mouths, shopping strips and tourist haunts. Impromptu groundsheet hawkers maximise intrusion so browsers literally stumble over 20-baht plastic fantastics they never knew they needed. *Rot khen* get piled high with brooms, ladders or furniture; other trolleys burgeon with stickers, posters or cute ceramics. In student areas, notebooks, clothes and knick-knacks catch the eye.

Food comprises half of what is peddled. Specific dishes are sold at different times of the day (doughnuts at breakfast, noodles at lunch, rolled dried squid after dark), with tell-tale bells, whistles or cries announcing what's coming round the corner. A tinkling bell heralds coconut ice-cream scooped from a drum into a bun, then slathered with peanuts. Clacks of chopstick on wood precede wheeled cauldrons of noodle soup. Hoots on a horn mean fruit. Other delicacies find fewer takers: steamed bird foetuses, anyone? Or crunchy fried insects?

Preparing fruit from iced carts resembles performance art. Within seconds, the vendor can peel a pineapple into a perfect spiral, deseed a watermelon or whittle an unripe mango. As you stroll away with your ten-baht bagful, dip each cleaved segment into a sachet of *prik kap kleua* (a pink condiment of sugar, salt and chilli).

Carts often feature specialist equipment. Popsicles emerge from iced drums; *roti* pancakes get ladled with sweet fillings upon oiled griddles; eggy *khanom krok* pop from dimpled irons carried on a bamboo yoke; liquidisers receive ladles of syrup from glass jars and condensed milk from tins to make *bun* (fruit shakes). Most amusingly, strong dark *kafae* (coffee) and brick-red *cha* (tea) get strained through blackened socks to be served hot or poured over ice in a bag and drizzled with cloying evaporated milk.

When the government offered kitsch, flimsy carts to beautify a 2003 international summit, vendors stuck with their trusty *rot khen*. Cart design has been honed for pure function, with handy slots for knives, boards, cloths, elastic bands, bags and anything else. This ingenuity originates in merchants trading from the cramped confines of boats, as they still do at remnant floating markets (*see pp103-107* **Further Afield**).

Crafts & accessories

Amulet Alley
Trok Wat Mahathat, Thanon Maharat, Phra Nakhon. **Open** 9am-6pm daily. **Map** p248 B3.
Spilling out of a riverside lane, this speciality market is the epitome of old Bangkok, with its constant flow of human traffic browsing an array of Buddhist imagery, amulets and medals. Bargaining is a must, and there are old-school food stalls aplenty. Find more amulets at Wat Ratchanadda (*see p70*), and between Saphan Khwai Station and Chatuchak Weekend Market (*see p138* **Market forces**), where occult ephemera makes for a sometimes startling browse. (*See also p26* **High spirits**).

Pahurat
Thanon Chakkaphet & Thanon Pahurat, Chinatown. **Open** 9am-6pm daily. **Map** p248 C5.
The heart of Little India, Pahurat is awash with fabrics and textiles, from rainbows of saris to Thai and Chinese silks, synthetics and cottons. Winding alleys are filled with incense sellers, tea houses stocking fine *chai* tea and *lassis*, plus food markets, collectives of sewing women and a Sikh temple. Bollywood movies and sitars blare, and the onslaught of scents and colours is truly memorable.

Eat, Drink, Shop

Market forces

Success is transforming **Chatuchak Weekend Market**, a kaleidoscopic labyrinth of 8,000-plus stalls where a quarter of a million people a week find everything under the sun (it's like a sauna). Long famed for its sheer scope of products from Thailand and hinterland Asia, JJ (from another spelling, Jatujak) has transcended ethnic knick-knack status to become a hive of young Thai talent, scoured by buyers (and copyists) from international stores. Redevelopment threats have subsided, but a seven-storey air-conditioned extension, **JJ Mall** (corner Thanons Kamphaengphet 2 & 4, 0 2618 333, www.jjmall.co.th, open 9am-9pm daily) now looms next door. It may absorb stalls evicted from Suan Lum Night Bazaar, though as rents continue to soar, JJ's demographic shifts ever upwards.

To 'do' JJ properly would take several weekends. It looks bewildering, but themed sections are numbered, colour-coded and divided by *soi* and stall numbers. These are well signed and charted, especially on *Nancy Chandler's Map*. Meeting points include the clock tower, the in-market subway station or tourist office/bank building (open weekends, with ATMs). Benches, trees, pedestrianisation and trolleybuses provide rest-stops, while cafés and toilets dot the edges. Visit early to pre-empt the heaving throngs. The following sections tackle the basics. You may well need its shipping agents (Sections 6 and 7, **TNT** 08 9202 2244, **DHL** 08 9924 9624, **Bangkok Parcel Service** 08 1457 7000).

ANTIQUES, CRAFTS & FURNITURE

Thai crafts are strewn everywhere, especially in Sections 1, 24 and 26, with some pricey antiques. Seek out hill tribe rattanware and loom parts to hang textiles from, plus musical instruments, bamboo boxes and *takraw* balls. In Section 1, you'll also find puppets, lacquerware, carvings, bronzes, amulets and Buddhas sourced from Chiang Mai and Myanmar. **Silpa Thai** arrays *khon* masks and puppets (Section 24, Soi 2, 08 9926 6530) from its Thonburi workshop (*see p77* **Walk 3: Old Thonburi**). Bargain hunters might peruse the Thai silk brought by Isaan women. You may see artisans making pottery. **JJ OTOP Centre** (Section 27, Thanon Kamphaengphet, 0 2618 2620) sells village crafts.

Wooden furniture can be bought ready to ship or crafted to spec, most cheaply from the sheds across Thanon Kamphangphet 2, which heave with reconditioned teak furniture and panelling, and even stock entire Thai houses for reassembly.

CLOTHES & ACCESSORIES

Young designers flog their outfits and fabrics in Sections 5-6, amid second-hand items,

Midway you'll find the miscellaneous category, with ceramics, monks' bowls, Chinese lanterns, kids' shoes and wrapping paper. Across from Thanon Ratchawong is the clothing area, where you can purchase fabrics, jeans and fatigues, including denim and camouflage. Towards the Mahachai end are blankets, sarongs, buttons and laces. The honking motorbikes, smoky quarters and shouting hawkers are all there purely to provide background ambience.

Sampeng

Soi Wanit 1, Chinatown. **Open** 9am-6pm daily. **Map** p248 C5.

When is an alleyway more than an alleyway? When it's an epic, bustling alleyway crammed with bric-a-brac and costume accoutrements. Sampeng is intimidating to the unwary, and so is best tackled in sections. Out east you'll discover accessories-ville, featuring hairclips, earrings, sandals and key rings.

ethnic and bohemian clobber, hats, handbags and uniforms (from Russian army to Korean boy scout). Bargain hard, as T-shirts or jeans can come as cheap as B50. New clothes fill Sections 10, 12, 14, 16, 18, and 20-26. Everything goes: beaded handbags, batik sarongs, fishermen's trousers, leather belts, denim and T-shirts in wild Japanese colours or bearing 'Thainglish' phrases, as at **Shit On Shirt** (Section 2, Soi 41/2, No 300, 08 3785 5552). **Siam Ruay** pioneered retro Thai typography on its witty, collectable T-shirts (Section 4, Soi 3, 08 5907 4954). **Props Room** crowds two branches (Section 3, Soi 3, 0 1567 9025) with theatrical jewellery. An oasis of calm, **Common Tribe** (Section 24, Soi 2, office Mon-Fri 0 2642 5382, www. commontribe.com) maintains its Eurasian casualwear in black and natural white, plus much-imitated handmade leather sandals.

DECOR & PLANTS
The boutiques in tree-shaded Sections 2-4 showcase Thai designers, who rise so quickly that their creations can often be found in Europe within months. Amid inspirational things made from zinc, *saa* (mulberry) paper, wood and lucite, look for 1970s-esque curtains and clocks at **70s Up** (Section 4, soi 1, 08 1438 2446), pop assemblage at **Anything Air** (Section 3, room 223, 08 6320 1196) or kitsch chandeliers at **Power of Color** (Section 3 Soi 4, Room 222, 08 1444 1265). A stunning black stall lit by cloth lanterns stocks both **Cha**'s aromatic teas and **Karmakamet**'s aromatic oils and candles (Section 3, Soi 3, 0 1564 0505). **Hot April** (Section 2, Soi 3, 0 9888 4276) assembles wood, weathered just-so, while **Only Sugar** epitomises the taste for cute (beside Kamphaengphet MRT, 08 9202 8949). Pick of the jewellers, **Xistnz** (Section 3, Soi 2, 08 9891 4338) makes mounts for exotic beads and stones. This area bristles with cafés, plants, herbs, seeds and flowers, plus the pots and charms that go with them. Bushes and trees take over the whole market mid week (7am-6pm Wed, Thur). More design goodies draw glances in Sections 7-8 and 24-27, including sleek room sets at **Aviv** (Section 8, Sois 16-17, 08 1906 3645) and leather innovations at **Nattha** (Section 8, Soi 17, 08 1682 5990). Art and decor lines Sections 1 and 7, notably **Ego Clay**'s ceramics (Section 7, 0 2888 7546).

PETS, BOOKS & UTENSILS
Cages of kittens and puppies sit alongside containers of reptiles, rare birds and tanks of fish in Sections 8, 9, 11, 13, 15 and 17. You may even catch a cockfight or fighting fish duel. There remains a small risk of trade in endangered species, though a fad for hissing cockroaches from Madagascar got banned. More appealing are the ceramics and kitchenware that are sold along with culinary ingredients in Sections 17 and 19; stalls selling books and magazines are here (Wed-Sun), with additional discounted titles on weekends at Sections 1 and 27.

EATING & DRINKING
JJ has also evolved a social scene. Cafés and food stalls crop up throughout, touting authentic samples of regional cuisines and snacks, with more at **Or Tor Kor** market (*see p140*) opposite. Isaan food fans scoff from pottery at **Foon Talob** (Section 26, Soi 1, 08 1838 1146). What's more, a new design awareness is sprucing up lean-to spaces, coffee houses and bars such as **Viva** (Section 26, Sois 1-2 & Section 8, 0 2272 4783, open 7am-6pm Fri, 7am-9pm Sat, Sun). Viva starts slinging juices in the morning and continues – with roadhouse fervour, good-time tunes, beer and whisky – often past 9pm. The bar strip mingling with fish shops along Thanon Kamphaengphet and the lane behind include a wide variety of gay pubs (*see p173*).

Electronics

Baan Mor (Lang Krasuang)
Thanon Baan Mor & Thanon Atsadang, Phra Nakorn. **Open** 9am-6pm daily. **Map** p248 B4.
This spare-parts paradise harbours just about any-thing for TV and audio – plus vintage LPs and army surplus (it is behind the Defence Ministry, after all).

Khlong Thom
Thanon Mahachak, between Thanon Yaowarat & Thanon Charoen Krung, Chinatown. **Open** 9am-6pm daily. **Map** p248 C4.
Foreigners rub chest-to-shoulder with Thais amid a wide assortment of engines, wheels, tractor parts and other heavy machinery in an area that's also rife with electrical repairers and a wide range of home-wares, from tools to hoses.

around Grande Ville Hotel,
9am-6pm daily. **Map** p248 C4.
old iron bridge over Khlong Ong
ring alley market dips below street
level. Shelves heave with cameras, toy guns, sunglasses and shoes, while shops stock appliances.

Woeng Nakhon Kasem

Thanon Chakrawat, at Thanon Charoen Krung, Chinatown. **Open** 9am-6pm Mon-Sat. **Map** p248 C4.
Once dubbed 'Thieves Market', this charming, hectic area hosts all things audio, as well as culinary contraptions such as ice-cream makers, mincers, coffee grinders and coconut shredders. Home cooks, DJs, producers and the curious mingle here.

Pak Khlong Talad

Thanon Chakphet, from Memorial Bridge to Khlong Lord, Phra Nakorn. **Open** 24hrs daily. **Map** p248 B5.
To grasp the Thai love of flowers properly, visit this remnant of Bangkok's original fresh market. It is most spectacular from 10pm until dawn, when night owls descend after bars close. The scent of jasmine fills the air, orchids in forms rarely seen by most non-Asians are stacked taller than people and vendors string devotional offerings with Fabergé delicacy. Not to be missed.

Thewet

Thanon Krung Kasem, west of Thanon Samsen, Dusit. **Open** 9am-6pm daily. **Map** p248 C1.
More neighbourly and less exhaustive than Pak Khlong Talad or Chatuchak Weekend Market, Thewet is pleasant with its potted plants and canal views. It is liveliest by day and picturesque at dusk.

Pak Khlong Talad
See p140.

Khlong Toei

Thanon Rama IV, at Thanon Na Ranong, South. Queen Sirikit Centre subway. **Open** 6am-dusk daily. **Map** p252 K8.
This portside *talad* offers archetypal regional Thai food, with stallholders shifting vegetables, chickens and rare herbs. The big Lao Market stocks specialities from the north-east, while off-the-back-of-a-boat items at nearby Penang Market are more rare.

Or Tor Kor (OTK)

Thanon Kamphaengphet, opposite Chatuchak Weekend Market, North (0 2279 2080-2). Saphan Kwai BTS/Kamphaengphet MRT. **Open** 6am-10pm daily.
Across the road from Chatuchak (*see* p138 **Market forces**), the Agricultural Market Organisation (OTK) sells some of Thailand's best fruit and veg, as well as prepared foods and sweets.

Sam Yan

Thanon Phayathai, at Thanon Rama IV, Pathumwan. Sam Yan subway. **Open** *Food market* noon-midnight daily. *Market* 6am-6pm daily. **Map** p250 F6.
This night-and-day happening encompasses a multi-storey building (the food is on the first floor), a wet market and a spread of street vendors. The products reflect the area's Chinese character, hence the top-grade seafood, unusual stir-fries and other more subtle (sweet and savoury) specialities. Well worth investigating.

For **Chatuchak Weekend Market**, *see* p138 **Market forces**. For **Patpong**, *see* p92.

Banglamphu

Thanon Chakkraphong, Banglamphu. **Open** 9am-6pm daily. **Map** p248 B3.
This traditional, sprawling *talad* stocks fabrics, satay, wooden crafts, fruits, clothes, uniforms – the range is enormous.

Chatuchak Weekend Market

Thanon Phahon Yothin, at Thanon Kamphaengphet, North (0 2272 4440-1). Morchit or Saphan Khwai BTS/Kamphaengphet subway. **Open** 5am-6pm Sat, Sun. *Plants only* daytime Wed, Thur.
See p138 **Market forces**.

Suan Lum Night Bazaar

Thanon Witthayu, at Thanon Rama IV, Pathumwan (022524776/www.thainightbazaar.com). Lumphini subway. **Open** 4pm-midnight daily. **Map** p251 H6/H7.
Bangkok's 'first official night bazaar', this gaudy covered maze holds several thousand stalls of souvenirs and decor items, plus beer gardens, restaurants and BEC-Tero Hall. Slated for eviction, it may still be clinging on.

Shops & Services

'Original' displaces 'copy' as Bangkok's retail mantra.

Once famed for its exotic crafts, silk and copy goods, Bangkok's diverse retail scene reflects increasingly sophisticated local tastes and the buying power of a risen economic tiger. Superlative malls sell most international brands and a revolution in clothing and decor style has brought new fashion cachet. Ethnic souvenirs have been reconceived as neo-oriental lifestyle products in which workmanship is reaping greater rewards. Yes, prices have gone up, but they still reflect great value. In Thai retail slang for this credit card cornucopia, the city stocks everything 'from pestles to warships'.

RETAIL OF TWO CITIES

In this hot, humid city, shopping is increasingly being divided between outdoor and indoor. Markets (see pp136-140) and stand-alone shops appeal for their character and craft, but as branding power spreads, so do all-in-one

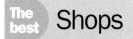

Shops

For Bangkok couture
Fashion Society (see p146), Fly Now (see p146) and Sretsis (see p147).

For repro artefacts
Triphum (see p143).

For contemporary Thai design
Panta (see p152), Sakul Intakul (see p153), Thann Native (see p151) and at the top of Gaysorn (see p153) or Siam Discovery (see 154).

For Siamese kitsch
Reflections Rooms in Bangkok (see p50) and Kit-ti's Gallery (see p150).

For Thai delicacies
Old Siam Plaza (see p154) and Or Tor Kor (OTK) market (see p140).

For expat comfort food
Villa Market (see p149) and Siam Paragon food hall (see p154).

For one-stop shopping
Chatuchak Weekend Market (see p138) and Central Chidlom (see p144).

complexes, which come to resemble artificial towns. The principal malls (see p153) line a three-kilometre (two-mile) retail corridor along Thanons Rama I, Ploenchit and Sukhumvit; most are linked by BTS elevated walkways.

At the western end, **Siam Square** – a warren of micro-boutiques supplying *dek naew* (young trendies) – is flanked by air-conditioned malls. To the west stands the maze of faddish shoplets in **Mah Boon Krong (MBK)** centre. Lined up north of Siam Square are the upper-middle clothing and decor showrooms of **Siam Discovery**, the emergent Thai fashion chains of **Siam Center**, and **Siam Paragon**, a B6-billion behemoth by the Mall Group that rattles with luxury icons. Along Thanon Rama I, Central (South-east Asia's biggest retailer) enlarged the already vast World Trade Centre into **Central World Plaza** and its **Zen** signature department store, which cater to a much broader market.

Across Ratchaprasong intersection, malls branch in three directions. South down Thanon Ratchadamri, **Peninsula Plaza** attracts high-society patrons of haute couture. North up Ratchadamri, the impressively sized crafts hangar **Narayanaphand** and discount warehouse **Big C** lead to **Pratunam Market** (see p136), which is flanked by new low-end clothing malls and electronics bazaar **Pantip Plaza**. Where Ploenchit Road starts at Ratchaprasong, swanky design plaza **Gaysorn** faces **Erawan**, another temple to import labels, and the lower-brow Amarin Plaza.

A block east stands the superior department store **Central Chidlom**. Further east in Sukhumvit's Nana district, specialist shops and souvenir stalls spread amid lesser malls such as Ploenchit Centre, Landmark Plaza, Nana Square, Times Square and Robinson, a mid-range department store chain. Finally, **Emporium** complex and upper-end shops satiate the needs of Sukhumvit's multi-cultural elite.

Bangrak district complements its nightlife with late-night shopping. Although **Silom Complex** and golf-oriented **Thaniya Plaza** close by 9pm, many shops and stalls open till at least midnight, including the notorious fake vendors of **Patpong Night Market** (see p92). Crackdowns and changing trends are consigning counterfeit goods to street stalls (though pirated CDs and DVDs still proliferate).

Baskets from **Tamnan Mingmuang**. *See p143.*

Eat, Drink, Shop

MODUS SHOPERANDI

With stores open from 10am to 8pm or even 10pm (plus periodic 'midnight sales'), shopping is flexible. Generally fixed, shop prices are low by world standards, and discounted in frequent sales, end-of-month promotions, and during each **Thailand Grand Sale** (June-July and December-January). Several stores also give instant five per cent discounts for tourists (show your passport) or for certain credit cards. However, some services, like travel agents and technical outlets, add on credit card fees. *Baht* is the only currency needed, although some antiques are priced in US dollars. Outside the airports, you can buy duty free at **King Power** (Thanon Rangnam, North, 0 2205 8888, www.kingpower.com, 10am-9pm daily).

Many retailers rely on tourists, and assistants often follow you. Don't be offended; they're keen to serve and are on commission. They'll take your selection with cash (or card) and return from the till with bagged goods, change and a receipt. Otherwise, say: '*Khor doo dai maii?*' ('Can I just look?')

Antiques & crafts

Antiques shops spread around Thanon Charoen Krung into Silom and Surawong Roads, while **Chatuchak Weekend Market** (*see p138*) has the best range of crafts. **Khao San Road** and Sukhumvit's **Nana** areas brim with souvenir crafts. Items bearing the OTOP logo are state-marketed village goods.

Narayanaphand

127 Thanon Ratchadamri, Pathumwan (0 2252 4670-9/www.narayanaphand.com). Chidlom BTS. **Open** 10am-8pm daily. **Credit** AmEx, DC, MC, V. **Map** p251 G5.
This dowdy hangar holds the country's largest inventory of Thai handicrafts – from lacquerware and ceramics to woodcarving, fabrics and gems.

NV Aranyik

3rd floor, Gaysorn, 999 Thanon Ploenchit, Pathumwan (0 2656 1081/www.niwataranyik.com). Chidlom BTS. **Open** 10am-7pm daily. **Credit** AmEx, DC, MC, V. **Map** p251 H5.
Derived from swordmaking traditions, Aranyik's much-imitated spoons, forks and knives – with twisted, textured or dimpled handles – feature on top restaurant tables around the world. Simple, elegant cutlery worth forking out for.

Old Maps & Prints

4th floor, River City Complex, Thanon Yotha, Bangrak (0 2237 0077-8/www.classicmaps.com). Tha Siphraya. **Open** 11am-7pm daily. **Credit** AmEx, MC, V. **Map** p250 D6.
Old Maps & Prints is the city's finest source of historical charts and hand-coloured engravings, mainly of Asia.

Oriental Place (OP)

301/1 Charoen Krung Soi 38, Bangrak (0 2266 0186-90). Saphan Taksin BTS/Tha Oriental. **Open** 10am-7.30pm daily. **Map** p250 D7.
This ritzy mall next to the Oriental Hotel delights the connoisseur. The galleries include Garuda (religious artefacts and rare objects) and Objects (*lingams* and antique artists' tools).

Rare Stone Museum

1048-1054 Charoen Krung Soi 26, Bangrak (0 2236 5666/5655). Tha Siphraya. **Open** 10am-5.30pm daily. **Credit** AmEx, MC, V. **Map** p250 D7.
Truly fantastic rock formations, from fossils to tektite from outer space (from B300). Owner/collector Banyong quotes a ballpark million-*baht* figure to part with a Buddha-shaped pebble.

Rasi Sayam

82 Sukhumvit Soi 33, Sukhumvit (0 2262 0729/ 0 2260 0950/www.rasisayam.com). Phrom Phong BTS. **Open** 9am-5.30pm Mon-Sat. **Credit** AmEx, DC, MC, V. **Map** p252 K5.
Among the pioneering outlets that have ensured Thai crafts retain their associated customs, Rasi Sayam, set in a converted house, stocks handiwork designs adapted for modern use.

River City

River City Complex, 23 Thanon Yotha, Bangrak (0 2237 0077-8/www.rivercity.co.th). Tha Siphraya. **Open** 10am-9pm daily. **Map** p250 D6.

A specialist mall with a fabulous range of period pieces, reproductions and antiquities that would upgrade many a museum. Auction lots get displayed in the week before gavel time.

Silom Galleria

919/1 Thanon Silom, Bangrak (0 2630 0944-50/www.thesilomgalleria.com). Surasak BTS. **Open** 10am-8pm daily. **Map** p250 E7.
Chinese antiques are the big draw at this vast atrium. Lower floors house dealers in furniture and pottery, with art outlets higher up, including Tang Gallery, Thavibu Gallery (for both *see p172*) and Panorama Museum (*see p91*). Weekdays are best for browsing.

Tamnan Mingmuang

3rd floor, Thaniya Plaza, Thanon Silom, Bangrak (0 2231 2120). Saladaeng BTS/Silom MRT. **Open** 11am-8pm daily. **Credit** AmEx, V. **Map** p250 F6.
Pornroj Angsanakul applies weaving expertise in fresh ways and exhibits astonishingly lifelike figurines. His baskets, boxes and handbags also come in wild grass, water hyacinth and ultra-fine *yan lipao* vine. On the same floor, the Legend branch (0 2231 2170) sells more mainstream souvenirs. **Photo** *p142*.

Triphum

4th floor, Siam Paragon, Thanon Rama I, Pathumwan (0 2610 9458). Siam BTS. **Open** 10am-8pm daily. **Credit** AmEx, DC, MC, V. **Map** p251 G4.
Reproduction mural paintings on tapestries and planks (plus frames and Siamese knick-knacks). All are reasonably priced, considering they're as meticulously crafted as a temple restoration.
Other locations: 3rd floor, Gaysorn, Pathumwan (0 2656 1795).

Books & magazines

After years of limited book choice in Bangkok, the new branches of **Kinokuniya** in Siam Paragon (*see p154*) and **B2S** in Central World Plaza (*see p153*) are huge and diverse. B2S boasts 200,000 books, 4,000 magazine titles and 130,000 film and music discs, plus a café and post office. For design books, try **Playground!** (*see p144*). **Thanon Khao San** stalls and shops stock quality second-hand literature (*see p71*), while **Chatuchak Weekend Market** (*see p138* **Market forces**) is unbeatable for back issues, out-of-print finds and discounted illustrated books (Sections 1 and 27). For top-notch stationery, browse the eminently monogrammed, leather-bound world that is **Libreria** (0 2661 6480), a study-like shop in the Siam Society (*see p96*), which also sells learned books on the region.

Asia Books

221 Thanon Sukhumvit, between Soi 15 & 17, Sukhumvit (0 2252 7277/www.asiabooks.com). Asoke BTS/Sukhumvit MRT. **Open** 10am-7pm daily. **Credit** AmEx, DC, MC, V. **Map** p251 J5.

An extensive selection of English-language tomes on Asian design, cooking and heritage, plus UK and US bestsellers, guidebooks, business advisories and lifestyle manuals.
Other locations: throughout the city.

Basheer Graphic Books

H1, 998 Sukhumvit Soi 55 (Thonglor), Thanon Sukhumvit, Sukhumvit (0 2391 9815-6/www.basheergraphic.com). Thonglor BTS. **Open** 11am-8pm daily. **Credit** MC, V. **Map** p252 M6.
The focus on graphic arts, design and photography titles unavailable elsewhere in town suits the swish H1 location. Browsing is positively encouraged.

Bookazine

1st floor, CP Tower, Thanon Silom, Bangrak (0 2231 0016/www.bookazine.co.th). Saladaeng BTS/Silom MRT. **Open** 10am-11pm daily. **Credit** AmEx, MC, V. **Map** p250 F7.
A broad stock of newspapers and periodicals in English, plus some popular novels, coffee-table books and a gay section.
Other locations: throughout the city.

Dasa

710/4 Thanon Sukhumvit (between Soi 26 & 28), Khlong Toei (0 2661 2993/www.dasabookcafe.com). Phrom Phong BTS. **Open** 10am-8pm daily. **No credit cards. Map** p252 L6.
Over 10,000 second-hand titles fill two floors of well organised shelves. There's a coffee corner too.

B2S at **Central World Plaza.** *See p153.*

Siamese catwalk

Angel City has designs on becoming a fashion hub, not least because Thailand's 1.2 million garment workers need brand identity fast to prevent obliteration by Chinese rivals with their lower unit costs. While young Thai designers show irrepressible creativity – and originality – few have proven to be as marketing- and logistical-savvy as **Fly Now** (*see p146*), which has twice opened London Fashion Week.

The Thaksin government hyped its B1.8-billion Bangkok Fashion City (BFC) project of 2003-6, promising to make it the 'Milan of Asia'. Although it was cancelled by the coup regime, it nonetheless had heightened exposure considerably. The labels **Greyhound** (*see p146*), **Issue**, **Kloset**, **Senada** and **Sretsis** (for all four, *see p147*) were showcased at Milan's annual White Milano fair in 2004, while the Institut Français de la Mode and the French Textile Machinery Manufacturers' Association helped to train young couturiers in Bangkok.

Still, you can't stop Thais putting on a show, especially if it involves beautiful people parading around in costume. Long predating BFC, **Elle Fashion Week** is now held twice a year (February and September), while rival Siam Paragon puts together **Bangkok International Fashion Week** (March) for brands that want to go '*inter*'.

Thailand's readiness for such moves depends on more than glamour and commercial nous, however. Following Thai supermodel Methinee Kingphayom's 'un-Thai' wardrobe 'malfunction' (her nipple sticker peeped out) at Elle Fashion Week, the Culture Ministry announced a 'dress code' for models. The conclusion, therefore, is that Bangkok's fashion quotient may ultimately depend on how socially liberal the state is willing to be.

Eat, Drink, Shop

Kinokuniya

3rd floor, Emporium, Sukhumvit Soi 24, Sukhumvit (0 2664 8554/www.kinokuniya.com). Phrom Phong BTS. **Open** 10am-9pm daily. **Credit** AmEx, DC, MC, V. **Map** p252 K6.
This Japanese chain has the biggest, best and best-organised stock of books in English, plus great ranges of magazines, maps, art, poetry and children's literature. Staff are courteous and informed. **Other locations**: Isetan, Central World Plaza, Pathumwan (0 2255 9834-6); Siam Paragon, Pathumwan (0 2610 9500).

Rim Khob Fah

78/1 Thanon Ratchadamnoen Klang, at Democracy Monument, Phra Nakorn (0 2622 3510). Tha Saphan Phan Fah. **Open** 10am-7pm daily. **Credit** MC, V. **Map** p248 C3.
Frequent workshops on Thai culture and history attract scholars, writers and students to this specialist in publications about Thailand, although titles in English are limited.

Department stores

Emporium (*see p153*) and **Siam Paragon** (*see p154*) malls feature large eponymous department stores, while **Zen** anchors **Central World Plaza** (*see p153*).

Central Chidlom

1027 Thanon Ploenchit, Pathumwan (0 2793 7777/www.central.co.th). Chidlom BTS. **Open** 10am-10pm daily. **Credit** AmEx, DC, MC, V. **Map** p251 H5.

Central's seven-storey flagship has the best selection and layout in town. It holds extensive ranges of cosmetics, international and local fashion labels, leatherware, decor, children's and sporting goods. Its B2S (*see p154*) section meets most book, magazine and stationery needs. Micro-stores include Muji, Jim Thompson Thai Silk (*see p147*), Oriental Shop and Tops supermarket. **Other locations**: throughout the city.

Isetan

4/1-2 Thanon Ratchadamri, Pathumwan (0 2255 9898-9). Chidlom BTS. **Open** 10am-9pm daily. **Credit** AmEx, DC, MC, V. **Map** p251 G5.
This Japanese store delights corporate *samurai* and home-makers. Expect imported, conservative attire for men, some colour and style in womenswear, plus superior kitchen gear and outlets by Greyhound (*see p146*), Jim Thompson Thai Silk and Books Kinokuniya. Its Oriental Shop pâtisserie is first-rate, but wraps wastefully (buy ten buns, get 11 bags).

Playground!

818 Soi Thonglor, Sukhumvit (0 2714 7888/ www.playgroundstore.co.th). Thonglor BTS. **Open** 10.30am-midnight daily. **Credit** AmEx, DC, MC, V. **Map** p252 M6.
Part of the boutique mall boom (*see p150* **Mini mall-ism**), this swish black edifice has sections on art books, stationery, homewares, music, magazines, fashion and accessories. Products are mainly fun, funky, mid-range items from home and abroad, and many things are arranged by taste rather than genres. Events in the atrium and exhibitions in the gallery add creative dynamics. The Manga! branch

at Central World Plaza focuses more on Japanese oriented cartoon character products.
Other locations: Manga!, 1st floor, Central World Plaza (0 2613 1177).

Dry-cleaning & repairs

Most malls host dry-cleaning, mending and shoe repair services, typically near the car park access. Or risk the cobblers and sewing-machine stalls on the street for a fraction of the fee.

Electronics

PowerBuy sections in **Central** department stores (*see p144 & p154*) offer personal sound systems, film and digital cameras, PDAs and all the other high-tech gadgets you might want.

Mac Studio by Copperwired

3rd floor, Siam Paragon, Thanon Rama I, Pathumwan (0 2610 9315-8/www.copperwired. co.th). Siam BTS. **Open** 10am-8pm Mon-Fri; 10am-8.30pm Sat, Sun. **Credit** AmEx, DC, MC, V. **Map** p249/p250 F4.
Adept staff demonstrate Apple models and applications at Copperwired's new (bigger, better-stocked) showroom. Great after-sales service too.
Other locations: Copperwired, 1st floor, J Avenue, Sukhumvit Soi 55, Sukhumvit (0 2712 7620).

Pantip Plaza

604/3 Thanon Petchaburi, nr Indonesian Embassy, North (0 2251 9008). **Open** 10am-9pm daily. **Map** p251 G4.
A geek's paradise, Pantip is crammed with vendors hawking hardware, applications, games, accessories, entertainment (CDs, DVDs, VCDs) and anything (new or used) that you can plug into your PC. Computers can be bought turnkey, assembled to your spec or upgraded in shops that resemble techno junkyards. Knowledgeable staff offer servicing, parts and software for Mac or PC, while competition slims the margins on new models. Warranties normally accompany big-name products, but most shops pride themselves on free post-purchase service. Pirate and unlicensed software keeps reappearing after raids, seemingly without protest from licensed outlets.

Fashion

For **Chatuchak Weekend Market**, *see p138*.

Almeta

20/3 Sukhumvit Soi 23, Sukhumvit (0 2258 4227/www.almeta.com). Asoke BTS/Sukhumvit MRT. **Open** 10am-6pm daily. **Credit** AmEx, DC, MC, V. **Map** p252 K5.
The first store to offer Thai silk 'à la carte': in other words, the lustrous cloth can be tailor-woven to cater to individual requests. It's top quality, and impressively they haven't imposed a minimum order, so order that silk hanky today.

Fun at **Playground!** *See p144.*

Atelier Pichitra

43/27-28 Sukhumvit Soi 31, Sukhumvit (0 2261 7553-5). Open 9am-6pm Mon-Sat. **Credit** AmEx, MC, V. **Map** p252 K6.

Long before she took part in Milan Fashion Week in spring 2005, Pichitra Boonyarataphan Ruksajit was the leading lady of Thai couture. Society debs and doyennes snap up her cosmopolitan creations by the rack and she has also styled the new Thai Airways uniforms. Pricey, and with good reason.

Baking Soda

3rd floor, Siam Center, Thanon Rama I, Pathumwan (0 2251 4995). Siam BTS. Open 10.30am-8.30pm daily. **Credit** AmEx, MC, V. **Map** p249/p250 F4.

Creating bold, sexy and diverse styles for the impossibly slim (male and female), Soda embellishes core items such as jeans and Ts with innovative sequinned, printed and see-through fabrics.
Other locations: No.7 by Soda, 2nd floor, Emporium, Sukhumvit (0 2664 8464).

Doi Tung by Mae Fah Luang

4th floor, Siam Discovery, Thanon Rama I, Pathumwan (0 2658 0424/www.doitung.org). Siam BTS. **Open** 11am-8pm daily. **Credit** MC, V. **Map** p249/p250 F4.

This worthy craft-preservation foundation has wowed catwalks by deviating from the conservatism typical of weaving traditions into a stylishly cosmopolitan form. Innovative hand-loomed cottons and linens provide the key materials. Rugs too beautiful to step on adorn the walls.

Fashion Society

2nd floor, Gaysorn, 999 Thanon Ploenchit, Pathumwan (0 2656 1358/www.gaysornbkk.com). Chidlom BTS. **Open** 10am-8pm daily. **Credit** AmEx, MC, V. **Map** p251 H5.

This one-stop clearing house of play and work clothes for men and women mixes leading Thai labels and up-and-coming names, such as Muse, Muung-doo and Sarit. Metal racks and raw decor produce a factory feel. Staff are friendly, not fawning.

Fly Now

2nd floor, Gaysorn, 999 Thanon Ploenchit, Pathumwan (0 2656 1359). Chidlom BTS. **Open** 10am-8pm daily. **Credit** AmEx, DC, MC, V. **Map** p251 H5.

Established over a decade ago, Fly Now entered jet-set realms through principal designer Chamnam Pakdisuk, whose voguish, feminine tailoring has twice opened London Fashion Week.
Other locations: 2nd floor, Siam Center, Pathumwan (0 2658 1735); 1st floor, Central World Plaza, Pathumwan (0 2646 1037); 2nd floor, Siam Paragon, Pathumwan (0 2610 9410/7883).

Greyhound

2nd floor, Emporium, Sukhumvit Soi 24, Sukhumvit (0 2664 8664). Phrom Phong BTS. **Open** 10am-9pm Mon-Fri; 9.30am-10pm Sat, Sun. **Credit** AmEx, DC, MC, V. **Map** p252 K6.

This legend among Thai labels offers understated essentials that work both in and out of the office. Ex-ad guru Bhanu Inkawat vamps up formal suit fabrics with bold styling. Bhanu recently entered couture territory with Grey (2nd floor, Siam Paragon, Pathumwan, 0 2129 4358), while designer/artist Jitsing Somboon styles the street-cred offshoot Playhound (found in shops and department stores). For Greyhound's hit restaurants, *see p126.*
Other locations: throughout the city.

Headquarter

3rd floor, Siam Center, Thanon Rama I, Pathumwan (0 2658 1048). Siam BTS. **Open** 11am-9pm daily. **Credit** AmEx, MC, V. **Map** p249/p250 F4.

Inspirational wear for both sexes from a trio of Thai designers (*see also pp33-35* **Bangkok by Design**), with an emphasis on details, unusual cuts and wit.

Issue

266/10 Siam Square Soi 3, Thanon Rama I, Pathumwan (0 2658 4416). Siam BTS. **Open** noon-9pm daily. **Credit** MC, V. **Map** p250 F4.
Designer Roj Singhakul incorporates ethnic hieroglyphs, primitive forms and religious symbols into his creations. Casual tops and Issue-branded T-shirts are the mainstays among this casual clubwear for young, urban Thai individualists.
Other locations: 1st floor, Siam Paragon, Pathumwan (0 2610 7862); 2nd floor, Gaysorn, Pathumwan (0 2656 1358).

Jaspal

2nd floor, Siam Center, Thanon Rama I, Pathumwan (0 2251 5918/www.jaspal.com). Siam BTS. **Open** 10am-9pm daily. **Credit** AmEx, DC, MC, V. **Map** p249/p250 F4.
Local fashion giant Jaspal takes its cue from Europe, hiring Kate Moss and other supermodels for its ads. The menswear can be a tad glitzy, but you can't argue with the quality of the high-tech stretch fabrics. The decor spin-off purveys sumptuous bedding.
Other locations: throughout the city.

Jim Thompson Thai Silk

9 Thanon Surawong, Bangrak (0 2632 8100-4/www.jimthompson.com). Saladaeng BTS/Silom MRT. **Open** 9am-9pm daily. **Credit** AmEx, DC, MC, V. **Map** p250 F6.
The Thai silk pioneer has ventured beyond pillowcases, scarves and clubby neck ties into high fashion, palatial interior design and experimental silk art projects. Witness its revival of block printing and the lustrous furnishings by trend leaders like Ed Tuttle, Christian Duc and Ou Baholyodhin.

Fly Now. *See p146.*

Branches are found at Jim Th[ompson] Museum (*see p97* **The silk root**) and five-star hotels.
Other locations: throughout the city

Kai Boutique

187/1 Bangkok Cable Building, Thanon Ratchadamri, Pathumwan (0 2251 0728/ www.kaiboutique.com). Ratchadamri BTS. **Open** 9am-7.30pm Mon-Fri. **Credit** AmEx, MC, V. **Map** p251 G5.
Pioneer of Bangkok's *dek bou* (boutique kids), Somchai 'Kai' Kaewtong has begowned local fashionistas for three decades. A breeding ground for new talent, this spacious flagship focuses on wedding dresses, evening wear and accessories.

Kloset Red Carpet

2nd floor, Gaysorn, 999 Thanon Phloenchit, Pathumwan (0 2656 1144/www.klosetdesign.com). Chidlom BTS. **Open** 10am-8pm daily. **Credit** AmEx, DC, MC, V. **Map** p251 H5.
This branch of the inventive Kloset fashion house highlights glamorous prêt-à-porter styles with bold colours and frilly accents such as lace and ribbons.
Other locations: 3rd floor, Central Chidlom, Pathumwan (0 2655 7777 ext 2907); 3rd floor, Emporium, Sukhumvit (0 2664 8748); 1st floor, Siam Center, Pathumwan (0 2658 1729); 1st floor, Siam Paragon, Pathumwan (0 2610 9000 ext 1735).

Senada Theory

2nd floor, Gaysorn, 999 Thanon Ploenchit, Pathumwan (0 2656 1350). Chidlom BTS. **Open** 10am-8pm daily. **Credit** AmEx, DC, MC, V. **Map** p251 H5.
Ethnic influences drive this fashion house. Lead designer Chanita Preechawitayakul is renowned for reconstructing Indian embroidery, Chinese silks and even grandma's tablecloths into hip streetwear.
Other locations: 3rd floor, Siam Center, Pathumwan (0 2252 2757).

Sretsis

2nd floor, Gaysorn, 999 Thanon Ploenchit, Pathumwan (0 2656 1125/www.sretsis.com). Chidlom BTS/Ratchadamri BTS. **Open** 10am-8pm daily. **Credit** AmEx, MC, V. **Map** p251 H5.
With a sensational and ultra-feminine 2003 debut collection, former Marc Jacobs intern Pimdao Sukhahuta became the darling of Thailand's fashion frontline. The quirky, retro style, with floaty chiffons and frilly laces, has made this label a continuing hit for girly baby dolls. After so much trendy monochrome, the pastels are refreshing.
Other locations: 3rd floor, Central Chidlom, Pathumwan (0 2655 7777 ext 2907); 2nd floor, Emporium, Sukhumvit (0 2664 8000 ext 1567); 1st floor, Siam Paragon, Pathumwan (0 2610 9000 ext 1734).

Theatre

2nd floor, Central World Plaza, Thanon Ratchadamri, Pathumwan (0 2255 9545). Chidlom BTS. **Open** 11am-8.30pm daily. **Credit** AmEx, MC, V. **Map** p251 G4.

Eat, Drink, Shop

.ward-winning designer Taned Boonprasarn combines hardy fabrics with lace and chiffon. His glamorous gowns and mix-and-matches with accompanying frilly details serve to evoke an extraordinary neo-romanticism.
Other locations: 3rd floor, Siam Center, Pathumwan (0 2251 3599).

Outsize

Browns

1st floor, U-Chu-Liang Building, Thanon Rama IV, Bangrak (0 2632 4442). Silom MRT. **Open** 10am-7pm daily. **Credit** AmEx, MC, V. **Map** p251 G7.
The outsized skirts, trousers and blouses here – all in light fabrics, with clean prints and patterns – are a godsend to women who find local ranges too small.
Other locations: 1st floor, Emporium, Sukhumvit (0 2664 8319); 275 Thonglor Soi 13, Sukhumvit (0 2712 7820); 2nd floor, Central Chidlom, Pathumwan (0 2655 7777 ext 3201); 1st floor, Siam Paragon, Pathumwan (0 2610 7869).

Tailors

Haberdasheries crowd tourist areas, especially **Sukhumvit Sois 3-11**, **Thanon Khao San**, **Thanon Charoen Krung** (between Silom and River City), and Downtown malls. They are typically run by Thai-Indians and stitched by

Quality tailoring at **Chang Torn.**

Thai-Chinese, who can tailor bespoke suits and dresses for bargain prices. For optimum quality and service, dismiss the '24-hour with free kimono' packages. Most tailors are well versed in formalwear and respond professionally to customers who are thorough about cut, cloth and detailing. Give them a pattern or choose from their catalogues and magazine cuttings. Insist on at least two fittings over several days.
Nothing to wear for Mardi Gras? Prize-winning designer Tu of **Sequin Queen** (www.sequinqueen.com) can run up a spangled little number in chiffon or Lycra, complete with feathered headdresses. All online orders are hand-sewn, fairly priced and custom-made (for men, women and those in between).

Art's Tailors

62/15-16 Soi Thaniya, Bangrak (0 2234 0874). Saladaeng BTS/Silom MRT. **Open** 9am-4.30pm Mon-Sat. **No credit cards. Map** p250 F6.
Master tailors hunch over long workbenches to churn out high-quality suits at this decades-old institution – a favourite with powerful pols and corporate fat cats. Quality comes at a price: a typical two-piece suit starts from B40,000, a fortune by local standards. Allow for two fittings over two weeks.

Chang Torn

95 Thanon Tanao, Banglamphu (0 2282 9390). **Open** 9.30am-6pm Mon-Sat. **Credit** V. **Map** p248 C3.
In a district full of tailors, veteran Chang Torn's comes recommended by fabric sellers. His small, unassuming version of Savile Row makes suits from B6,000, shirts from B900. Allow ten days.

River Mark

Room 238, River City Complex, 23 Thanon Yotha, Bangrak (0 2237 0077-8 ext 238). Tha Siphraya. **Open** 10am-8pm Mon-Sat. **Credit** AmEx, MC, V. **Map** p250 D6.
For those with a Milanese taste but a Mile End budget, River Mark stitches agreeable suits from B7,000. The shop also does dresses and robes.

Food & drink

Tops supermarkets are found at **Central** department stores (*see p144 & p154*), while British **Tesco Lotus** and French **Carrefour** hypermarkets face off where Thanon Rama IV meets Sukhumvit Soi 26; these supermarkets have swamped so many suburbs that they have provoked protests and even physical attacks.

La Boulange

2-2/1 Soi Convent, Thanon Silom, Bangrak (0 2631 0354). Saladaeng BTS/Silom MRT. **Open** 7am-10pm daily. **Credit** AmEx, MC, V. **Map** p250 F7.
An authentic French pavement café with pastries, sandwiches, freshly baked loaves and classic snack meals: croques-monsieurs, salads and quiches.

Cutting edge

Bangkok shines as a global gems centre, thanks to cutting expertise, professional traders and imaginatively designed settings. Aside from the brand-name and old-school local jewellers at upmarket malls and hotel arcades, young Thai designers have carved new stylistic niches, with the bold neo-tribal designs by the likes of **Lotus Arts de Vivre**, **Dinakara** and **Kit-ti's Gallery** (for all three, *see p150*). (To gauge prices, check the giant online trader **Thaigem.com**.)

The epicentre for loose gems and uncut stones is where Thanons Surasak and Mahesak cross Thanons Silom and Surwaong. Some of the world's best lapidaries hide down alleys and behind undistinguished gates (for security). Some 245 kilometres (152 miles) away, the east coast town of Chanthaburi remains a global marketplace for serious buyers, despite depletion of the area's ruby and sapphire quarries. Stones now come from Myanmar, Cambodia, Sri Lanka and Africa.

Gem dealing can, however, be treacherous for beginners, who should wise up to the infamous scams of people being duped into buying stones in the false hope of reselling them abroad at an unrealistic profit. The commonest ruse involves strangers telling tourists that the sight they're about to visit is closed for a holiday. He then entices the prey to take a tour by *tuk-tuk* that takes them for a ride in more ways than one, ending at a shop where the 'gems to resell' offers are, quite literally, too good to be true. It's hard to prosecute since the gems are real – albeit near-worthless. Heating or 'cooking' to alter a stone's appearance is an accepted practice, although that's not always disclosed. TAT (*see p235*) can advise on reputable dealers who provide honest documentation.

If your interest in gems reaches further, you can learn to identify the genuine article on short courses at the **Asian Institute of Gemological Sciences** (33rd floor, Jewellery Trade Centre, 919/1 Thanon Silom, 0 2267 4315-9, www.aigsthailand.com) or the **Gemological Institute America Thailand** (12th floor, Bisco Tower, 56/12 Thanon Sap, 0 2237 9575-7, www.giathailand.com). These also teach degree-level classes in such arcane topics as crystal structure, geology, design and synthetics. A full diploma takes six to nine months.

Ong's Tea

4th floor, Siam Discovery, Thanon Rama I, Pathumwan (0 2658 0445). Siam BTS. **Open** 11am-9pm daily. **Credit** MC, V. **Map** p249/p250 F4.
A table setting allows you to sample the leaves, mostly from China, Japan and Taiwan, amid tea ceremony calligraphy, pots and chai-sipping music. **Other locations**: Ground floor, Siam Paragon, Pathumwan (0 2610 7516).

Thaniya Spirit

62/7 Thanon Thaniya, Bangrak (0 2234 5224). Saladaeng BTS/Silom MRT. **Open** 10am-10.30pm Mon-Sat. **No credit cards. Map** p250 F6.
Bars and clubs favour this specialist drinks merchant stocking hard-to-find international tipples. **Other locations**: VAT Spirit, Thanon Ratchadaphisek, North (0 2683 9360-4).

Villa Market

595 Sukhumvit 33/1, Sukhumvit (0 2662 1000/www.villamarket.com). Phrom Phong BTS. **Open** 24hrs daily. **Credit** AmEx, DC, MC, V. **Map** p252 K6.
This *farang* haunt is *the* grocer for homesick expat comfort foods, from cheeses and tortillas to herrings and Marmite. There's also a good wine choice (often discounted) and a community noticeboard. **Other locations**: throughout the city.

Wine Connection

1 Sivadon Building, Soi Convent, Thanon Silom, Bangrak (0 2234 0388/www.wineconnection.co.th). Saladaeng BTS/Silom MRT. **Open** 9am-9pm daily. **Credit** AmEx, MC, V. **Map** p250 F6.
Service that is at once knowledgeable and professional adds to the fine selection of global labels at this mini chain. As if that were not enough, the prices are happily within the 'no-middleman' range too, adding a further reason to visit and find a few choice selections for the cellar back home. **Other locations**: 1st floor, Nana Square, Sukhumvit (0 2655 7166); 39/13-14 Sukhumvit Soi 31, Sukhumvit (0 2662 2490); 137/1 Sukhumvit Soi 63, Sukhumvit (0 2714 7548); V9, Sofitel Silom, 188 Thanon Silom, Bangrak (0 2235 7766).

Gems, gold & jewellery

Thaigem.com has earned its reputation as the leading online catalogue of precious stones, beads, crystals, jewellery and even meteorites. Gold shops proliferate in **Chinatown** (*see p88* **Proven gilt**) and the **MBK** mall (*see p154*). To avoid unfortunate rip-offs that do much to discredit the industry, *see above* **Cutting edge**. For exciting, innovative designs by **Sakul Intakul** and **T Positif**, *see p153*.

Astral Gemstone Talismans

1875 Zone C, Joe Louis Theatre, Suan Lum Night Bazaar, Pathumwan (0 2252 1230-1/www.agt-gems.com/rsb.html). Lumphini MRT. **Open** noon-8pm daily. **Credit** AmEx, DC, MC, V. **Map** p251 H5.
Vedic (or sidereal) planetary astrology is the inspiration behind the rings and pendants custom-designed by begowned ex-rock singer Richard Shaw Brown, lead singer of the Misunderstood, a cult rock band championed by John Peel in 1966 – how about that for an obscure pub quiz question? Your lucky gems (unflawed) are mounted in plenty of gold. Will stay even after the Night Bazaar shuts.

Crystal Lounge

28 Sukhumvit Soi 20, Sukhumvit (0 2258 1599/www.crystalevolution.com). Phrom Phong BTS. **Open** 11am-midnight Tue-Sun. **Credit** AmEx, MC, V. **Map** p252 K6.
Paris Hilton bought six Crystal Evolution navel rings designed by owner Bella. After founding the world's first body jewellery brand Bodysteel & Silver with husband Robert, they opened this jeweller-cum-lounge bar, where bling vies with *objets d'art* and a perfect wedding gift: Swarovski hand-cuffs.
Other locations: Bodysteel & Silver, D&D Inn, 68/3 Thanon Khao San, Banglumphu (0 2281 2884).

Dinakara

1st floor, Siam Paragon, Thanon Rama I, Pathumwan (0 2129 4399). Siam BTS. **Open** 10am-7pm daily. **Credit** AmEx, MC, V. **Map** p252 M6.
Bold statements in precious stones and metals ensure that Yukala Iamla-or's distinctively Asian creations earn devotion among artistic types.

Kit-ti's Gallery

Baan Silom, Thanon Silom nr Soi 19, Bangrak (08 1821 1275/www.kittijewelry.com). Surasak BTS. **Open** 10am-6pm daily. **Credit** MC, V. **Map** p250 E7.
Disco balls, feathers and Lego blocks are juxtaposed with expressionistic beading in Itthipon's celebrated neo-tribal accessories, which turn your décolletage into a gallery. **Photo** *p151.*
Other locations: 2nd floor, Playground!, Sukhumvit (0 2714 7888 ext 201).

Lotus Arts de Vivre

Four Seasons Hotel, 155 Thanon Ratchadamri, Pathumwan (0 2250 0732/www.lotusarts devivre.com). Saphan Taksin BTS/Pier. **Open** 8.30am-8pm daily. **Credit** AmEx, DC, MC, V. **Map** p250 D7.
Something of an Asian Fabergé, Lotus's diverse jewellery, decorations and trinkets are as mysteriously oriental as they come. One-off pieces employ exotic

Mini mall-ism

For every gargantuan mall that swallows entire city blocks, a mini-mall sprouts. What may to Westerners look like a ho-hum suburban facility has become a new badge of sophistication for upmarket urbanites who formerly drove past grungy neighbourhood shophouses on their way to glitzy goliaths like **Emporium** (*see p153*), **Siam Paragon** (*see p154*) or **Central World Plaza** (*see p153*). The Thonglor/Ekamai area of Sukhumvit in particular burgeons with new retail piazzas that residents might actually walk to.

Mini-malls come in two kinds: high-society or handy – the shopaholic's equivalent to a destination cocktail bar or the local pub. And a bar or pub is invariably part of the mix to keep their customers longer, along with an obligatory Starbucks. Leading the high-society wave, **H1** filled architect Duangrit Bunnag's glazed blocks at the north end of Thonglor with **Basheer Graphic Books** (*see p143*), decor shops and swish bar-restaurants like **To Die For** (*see p134*). A few blocks south came **Playground!**'s departmentalised zones of design, fashion, art books, stationery, music, mags (*see p144*) and restaurants such as **Kuppa**, with

its attached cooking school (*see p128* **Pan handling**). Ever faddish, Bangkokians soon flocked to J Avenue on Thonglor, with its branch of **Greyhound** (*see p146*) and a more prosaic attraction: a supermarket.

In the long run, quaint wannabes like **Penny's Balcony** on Thonglor may lack the magnetism of mini-malls anchored to practical supply outlets. Still, as the concept spreads – especially as a draw for flash new housing estates – variations emerge. **Baan Silom**, on Silom near Soi 19, surrounds a modernist core with repro-colonial arcades. Ranging from everyday services to an Italian restaurant and the jeweller **Kit-ti's Gallery** (*see above*), it livens up a low-key area.

The jury's still out on whether mini-malls muscle out or support local independents. In a parallel development, surburban superstores such as European-run Carrefour and Tesco Lotus faced state obstruction after starting to colonise corner shop territory, although Thai-owned convenience chains are arguably more responsible for displacing cobwebbed mom 'n' pop stores. In reality, there are three basic factors that determine all Thai shopping trends: ease, aspiration and air-conditioning.

materials from oyster shells and stingray leather to fine-grained roots and tyre rubber.
Other locations: 3rd floor, Oriental Place, Charoen Krung Soi 38, Bangrak (0 2235 1875).

Gifts

Chitrlada Shops (*see p81* **Chitrlada Palace**) sell products from the Royal Projects. **Reflections Shop** stocks wondrous kitsch items in plastic, resin, wire and fake fur at Reflections Rooms (*see p50*). Proceeds help village projects. For **Playground!**, *see p144*. For **Propaganda**, *see p152*.

Loft
3rd floor, Siam Discovery, Thanon Rama I, Pathumwan (0 2658 0328-30/www.loft bangkok.com). Siam BTS. **Open** 10am-9pm daily. **Credit** AmEx, DC, MC, V. **Map** p249/p250 F4.
There's something for every budget at this expansive Japanese shop jumbled with gifts ranging from odd clocks and twee frames to techie gadgets and designer pens. Myriad wrappings and cards make it a one-stop present solution.
Other locations: 4th floor, Siam Paragon, Pathumwan (0 2610 9710).

Q Concept Store
3rd floor, Siam Paragon, Thanon Rama I, Pathumwan (0 2610 9540-5/www.qconcept store.com). Siam BTS. **Open** 10am-10pm daily. **Credit** AmEx, MC, V. **Map** p249/p250 F4.
Q Concept sells quirky products, books, decor and knick-knacks from slick international brands and witty Thai designers.
Other locations: Ground floor, Central World Plaza, Pathumwan (0 2613 1388).

Roominteriorproducts
4th floor, Siam Discovery, Thanon Rama I, Pathumwan (0 2658 0411). Siam BTS. **Open** 11am-8pm Mon-Thur; 11am-9pm Fri-Sun. **Credit** AmEx, DC, MC, V. **Map** p249/p250 F4.
Got a penchant for inflatable plastic stuff? Of course you have. Roominteriorproducts, headed by an Australian designer duo, sells a rainbow of kitschy props for the modern room, such as folding chairs and beanbags in funky patterns.

Health & beauty

Chalachol
205/13-14 Sukhumvit Soi 55, Sukhumvit (0 2712 6481/www.chalachol.com). Thonglor BTS. **Open** 10.30am-7.30pm daily. **Credit** MC, V. **Map** p251 G6.
Somsak Chalachol revolutionised local hairdressing with this mini chain of unisex designer salons. While your hair is washed, your body gets a massage from a vibrating chair. Cut and blow dry from B350.
Other locations: 2nd floor, Amarin Plaza, Ploenchit Road (0 2251 1941); 2nd floor, Siam Paragon, Pathumwan (0 2610 9853-4).

Kit-ti's Gallery. See p150.

Hanako
Siam Square Soi 11, Pathumwan (0 2255 8630-2). Siam BTS. **Open** 9.30am-9pm daily. **Credit** MC, V. **Map** p250 F4.
In a city full of beauty parlours dispensing make-up, skin whitening and elective plastic surgery, this Japanese institute is perhaps the most reliable centre in which to get made over.

Thann Native
3rd floor, Gaysorn, 999 Thanon Ploenchit, Pathumwan (0 6622 2014/www.thann.info). Chidlom BTS. **Open** 10am-8pm daily. **Credit** MC, V. **Map** p251 H5.
Among efforts to turn Thai herbal remedies into modern toiletries and grooming products, the Harnn & Thann company achieves not just superior packaging, diversity and global distribution, but high performance from eco-friendly ingredients. Think rice bran scrubs, lemongrass aromatherapy oil and strings of multi-spice soaps. In products and in-store spas, Harnn embodies an old apothecary approach, while the Thann range features high-tech products. At Gayson, Thann Native also sells decor and furnishings by top Thai designers. The main branches are listed below, but there are others in malls around town. **Photo** *p152*.
Other locations: Thann Sanctuary, 5th floor, Siam Discovery, Pathumwan (0 2658 0549); Harnn, 4th floor, Siam Paragon, Pathumwan (2610 9715).

Homewares

For a wealth of Thai decor shops head to **Siam Discovery** (*see p154*), **Gaysorn** (*see p153*) and **Siam Paragon** (*see p155*); department stores in the latter and **Emporium** (*see p153*) both feature **Exotique Thai** halls of indigenous-

Thann Native. See p151.

inspired objects. On Gaysorn's third floor, **Thann Native** (*see p152*) selects premier Thai designers' work, and **D & O** showcases items by the Design & Objects Group of ten companies (www.designandobjects.com), including Hygge, Oopstuff and, from the listings below, **Sakul Intakul** and **T Positif**. For retro, try **Chatuchak Weekend Market** (*see p138*).

Ayodhya
3rd floor, Gaysorn, 999 Thanon Ploenchit, Pathumwan (0 2656 1089). Chidlom BTS. **Open** 10am-8pm daily. **Credit** AmEx, DC, MC, V. **Map** p251 H5.
A pioneer of updating trad Thai products to today's aesthetics, Ayodhya turns out understated and useful items such as seats made from tree vines and home-made soaps scented with local flowers. **Other locations**: 4th floor, Emporium, Sukhumvit (0 2664 8000 ext 1313); Panta, 4th floor, Siam Discovery, Pathumwan (0 2658 0415); 4th floor, Siam Paragon, Pathumwan (0 2129 4432).

Budji
7 Soi Sangngern Thonglor 25, Sukhumvit 55, Sukhumvit, Watthana (0 2712 9832/www.budji bangkok.com). Thonglor BTS. **Open** 9.30am-6pm Mon-Sat. **Credit** AmEx, MC, V. **Map** p252 M6.
Acclaimed Filipino designer Antonio 'Budji' Layug's airy showroom holds furniture and decorative items from his Movement 8 design group. Ergonomic seating made from indigenous materials is the trademark of Budji's tropical contemporary style.

Gilles Caffier
4th floor, Siam Discovery, Thanon Rama I, Pathumwan (0 2658 0487/www.gillescaffier.com). Siam BTS. **Open** 10am-8pm Mon-Thur, Sun; 10am-9pm Fri, Sat. **Credit** MC, V. **Map** p249/p250 F4.
French designer Gilles scored a hit with his translucent Hurricane Vase, a wooden skeleton covered with Lycra. His suave modernism also takes in leather pillows, vibrant glassware and subdued earthenware.

Lamont Contemporary
3rd floor, Gaysorn, 999 Thanon Ploenchit, Pathumwan (0 2656 1392/1048/www.lamont-design.com). Chidlom BTS. **Open** 10am-8pm daily. **Credit** AmEx, DC, MC, V. **Map** p251 H5.
Across the concourse from Lamont Antiques' East Asian collectibles you find Lamont's self-designed works of equal elan, which utilise unusual materials in fresh treatments, such as shells microsliced in lacquer trays, picture frames made of carved bone, and boxes upholstered in stingray.
Other locations: Oriental Hotel, 48 Charoen Krung Soi 38, Bangrak (0 2630 5931).

Panta
4th floor, Siam Discovery, Thanon Rama I, Pathumwan (0 2658 0415). Siam BTS. **Open** 10am-9pm daily. **Credit** AmEx, DC, MC, V. **Map** p249/p250 F4.
A showroom of Thailand's top furniture designers, including Ayodhya, Yothaka, Ango World and Planet 2001, focusing on seductively experimental furniture made from natural materials such as wood, tree vines and rattan. **Photo** *p153*.
Other locations: 4th floor, Siam Paragon, Pathumwan (0 2129 4430)

Promenade Decor
In front of Nai Lert Park Hotel, Thanon Witthayu, Pathumwan (0 2252 0160). Ploenchit BTS. **Open** 10am-7pm daily. **Map** p251 H5.
A high-end mall of interiors shops, from imports such as über-suave Christian Liaigre to Thai polymath Sakul Intakul (*see p153*). Several outlets and cafés feature the whimsical illustration of aristo stylist ML Chirathorn Chirapravati and the kitsch expressionism of celebrity artist Kongpat Sakdapitak.

Propaganda
4th floor, Siam Discovery, Thanon Rama I, Pathumwan (0 2658 0430/www.propaganda online.com). Siam BTS. **Open** 10.30am-9pm daily. **Credit** AmEx, DC, MC, V. **Map** p249/p250 F4.

A cross between Philippe Starck and Damien Hirst, Chaiyuth Plypetch has won awards for his playful innovations since 1994. Museum-standard pieces like the Match Lamp and Shark-Fin Bottle Opener have garnered international rave reviews, while the Mr P range finds cute new functions for male accessories, from light switch and key fob to bottle stop.
Other locations: 4th floor, Emporium, Sukhumvit (0 2664 8574).

Sakul Intakul

2nd floor, Promenade Decor, Thanon Witthayu, Pathumwan (0 2655 4230/0408/www.sakul flowers.com). Ploenchit BTS. **Open** 10am-6pm Mon-Sat. **Credit** MC, V. **Map** p251 H5.
Engineer-turned-florist Sakul conjures architecturally impressive flower arrangements, which are featured in his books and widely copied abroad. Inspired by Thai seeds, his flower vessels in bronze and ceramic have earned plaudits in *Wallpaper**.

T Positif

Silver Trunk Studio, Baan Silom, Thanon Silom, Bangrak (0 2266 9033/www.tpositif.com). Surasak BTS. **Open** 11am-9pm daily. **Credit** AmEx, MC, V. **Map** p251 G5.
Tam Devakul's crystal wine glasses with silver stems are finding their way to the tables of the world's top hotels. She also conceives distinctive rings, pendants, bracelets and cufflinks.
Other locations: 5th floor, Central Chidlom, Pathumwan (0 2793 7777 ext 3510).

Y50/Café 50

24-26 Ekamai Soi 21 (Thonglor 20), Sukhumvit Soi 63, Sukhumvit (0 2711 5629). Ekkamai BTS. **Open** *Y50* 10am-midnight daily. *Café 50* 6pm-midnight Mon-Sat. **Credit** AmEx, MC, V. **Map** p252 M7.
Resembling the store room of a design museum, this funky shop-bar shifts mostly Skandic chairs, lamps and table clocks from the 1950s to the '70s. A couple of shops nearby offer similar finds.

Malls

Top-floor cinemas/bowling alleys close later than shopping zones, often past midnight.

Central World Plaza

4/1-2 Thanon Ratchadamri, Pathumwan (0 2255 9500/www.centralworld.co.th). Chidlom BTS. **Open** 10am-9pm daily. **Map** p251 G4.
Central has transmogrified the dim, cavernous hulk of the old World Trade Centre into a gleaming, sun-lit 'multi-use complex' that's hugely enlarged, yet easier to navigate and far friendlier than Paragon to a wider social spectrum. Aside from new-to-Bangkok shops like Manga!, Camper and Toys'R'Us, it harbours three department stores: unchanged Isetan (*see p144*); the massive Zen (0 2100 9999, www.zen.co.th), which introduces rarer brands to hip young professionals; and Central, which exists as separate vast SuperSports, PowerBuy and B2S

stores. Connected to both Siam and Chidlom BTS by walkways, CWP features two huge cineplexes, a bowling alley, a TK Park kids' centre, and a balcony in the glazed frontage. **Photo** *p154*.

Emporium

622 Sukhumvit Soi 24, Sukhumvit (0 2269 1000/ www.emporiumthailand.com). Phrom Phong BTS. **Open** 10.30am-10pm Mon-Fri; 10am-10pm Sat, Sun. **Map** p252 K6.
Supremely successful, Emporium lures the well-off with Euro-couture (Prada, Gucci, Chanel, Hermès, Fendi) and long-established Thai jewellers. Lesser mortals come for the local and imported fashion outlets, opticians, booksellers, hairstylists, travel agents and furnishing shops. The complex hosts catwalks, exhibitions, promotions and even concerts, and also boasts a fine namesake department store and a vast (yet still crowded) gourmet food hall.

Gaysorn

999 Thanon Ploenchit, Pathumwan (0 2656 1516-9/www.gaysorn.com). Chidlom BTS. **Open** 10am-8pm daily. **Map** p251 H5.
This swanky corner landmark has posh brands (Louis Vuitton, Prada, Hermès), regional fashion houses and contemporary Thai design outlets.

Life Center

1 Thanon Sathorn Tai, South (0 2677 7177 ext 249/250). Lumphini MRT. **Open** 10am-10pm daily. **Map** p251 H7.

Frightening furniture: **Panta**. *See p152.*

Eat, Drink, Shop

Bangkok's first health-oriented mall applies sleek, branded retail therapy to the body (teeth, hearing, skin, spine, allergies, hair, skin, nutrients, slimming), alongside the all-white Lullaby Spa, all-sweaty Fitness First Plus gym and dietary outlets, from juices at Fruit and salads and more at Yum & Tum to, er… Starbucks and Auntie Annie's pretzels.

Mah Boon Krong (MBK)

444 Thanon Phayathai, Pathumwan (0 2620 9000/ www.mbk-center.com). National Stadium BTS. **Open** 10am-10pm daily. **Map** p249/p250 F4.

Don't even try to make sense of the overcrowded, boisterous, chaotic frenzy in this marketplace linked to the Pathumwan Princess hotel (*see p47*). More than 1,000 shops and stalls flog everything and anything: gold, footwear, sausages, furniture, suitcases, youth fashion and, famously, mobile phones and portable electronics. Specialists in cameras and custom portraits offer great bargains and informed service – if you can find them. On top sit a food court, SF cinema (*see p168*) and bowling rink (*see p204*).

Old Siam Plaza

12 Thanon Tripetch, Phra Nakorn (0 2226 0156-8). **Open** 9am-9pm daily. **Map** p248 C4.

Styled with touches of Thai yesteryear, this three-storey indoor bazaar holds traditional jewellers and silk retailers. Stalls selling clothes, household goods and delicacies (notably desserts) fill the atrium, with a computer repair shop on the top floor.

Central World Plaza. See p153.

Peninsula Plaza

153 Thanon Ratchadamri, Pathumwan (0 2253 9791). Ratchadamri BTS. **Open** 10am-8pm daily. **Map** p251 G5.

Flanked by posh hotels, this quiet, faux-Parisian low-rise is a yellowing throwback to the pre-1997 boom. Still, it attracts those who own at least one two-tonne, diamond-encrusted Rolex and can differentiate pre-Donatella from post-Gianni, since the city's Versace flagship shares here, alongside Bangkok's only Loewe. Staff can be patronising to non-millionaires.

Siam Center & Siam Discovery

989 Thanon Rama I, Pathumwan (0 2658 1000 Siam Centre ext 500, Siam Discovery ext 400/0 2687 5000/www.siamcenter.co.th, www.siamdiscovery. co.th). Siam BTS. **Open** 10am-9pm daily. **Map** p249/p250 F4.

Since 1973 several Thai designers have launched their careers at the Siam Center. Although global chains have muscled in, indie boutiques still cater to the trendiest of tastes (and slimmest of frames), amid sportswear and Gen-X shops for urban skate dudes and surf chicks. Manga imagery enlivens the recent white-on-white revamp, which installed a 'food-for-fun' dining court on top, a live on-air radio station (which alternates between 94.0 EFM and 91.5 HotWave), and Cheeze modelling studio.

Siam Center is like the precocious teen connected on each side to its imperious mother Siam Paragon (*see below*) and yuppie sibling Siam Discovery. DKNY, Armani Exchange and Guess provide Discovery's designer threads, while hairdressing salon Toni & Guy, Shu Uemura cosmetics and salon-spa Leonard Drake remove every last blemish. The mall's USP is interior design by anyroom, Habitat, Panta (*see p153*), Roominteriorproducts (*see p151*) and other home furnishers, now expanding into the kids' floor. **Photo** p155.

Siam Paragon

Thanon Rama I, Pathumwan (0 2610 9000/ www.siamparagon.co.th). Siam BTS. **Open** usually 10am-10pm daily. **Map** p251 G4.

Behind a six-storey atrium lobby of vertical gardens, and water cascades, this bombastic, town-sized mall likens itself to a multi-faceted gem. Forming an enormous L-shape around the cavernous Paragon department store, swish shops flaunt jewellery, decor, digital gadgets, labels (Dolce & Gabbana, Jimmy Choo, Paul Smith) and – on road-width concourses – supercar showrooms (Lamborghini, Ferrari and Maserati, no less). However, you find the customers mostly in Zara, a vast Kinokuniya bookstore and a culinary basement happily packed with gourmet restaurants, basic stalls and even a speciality food hall. Don't visit on a full stomach.

Paragon's impressively vast hulk also holds True Urban Park tech lounge, a 16-screen cinema with IMAX (*see p167*), a 50-lane Major Bowl bowling alley, a family 'edutainment' Explorium, California WOW gym, a conference hall and Siam Ocean World aquarium (*see p95*). Next up are the Siam

Opera theatre and a five-star Kempinski Hotel amid remnants of the site's mature canalside gardens. **Photo** *p156*.

Music

CD Warehouse
3rd floor, Emporium, Sukhumvit Soi 24, Sukhumvit (0 2664 8520-2/www.cdwarehouse-asia.com). Phrom Phong BTS. **Open** 10am-9pm daily. **Credit** AmEx, DC, MC, V. **Map** p252 K6.

Sample the freshest tunes from around the globe at the listening stations of Bangkok's largest and most organised music shop. Shelves packed with international new releases and seasoned favourites run alongside Thai pop, classical, Canto-pop, J-pop and world music, plus blockbuster movies.
Other locations: 5th floor, Siam Discovery, Pathumwan (0 2255 2086-8).

Do Re Me
Siam Square Soi 11, Thanon Rama I, Pathumwan (0 2251 4351). Siam BTS. **Open** 1-10pm daily. **No credit cards.** **Map** p249/p250 F4.

This treasured little shop discounts new releases on labels major and minor. The complete absence of any recogniseable organisation tests the owner's incredible memory to its limits.

Music One
3rd floor, Major Cineplex Ekkamai, Sukhumvit Soi 61, Sukhumvit (0 2714 2891/www.musicone.co.th). **Open** 10.45am-9pm Mon-Thur, Sun; 10.45am-10pm Fri, Sat. **Credit** AmEx, DC, MC, V. **Map** p251 G7.

Who says people are ungrateful? Member discounts (plus inspired alternative tastes) have fostered loyalty to this tiny but well-stocked outlet with an emphasis on chillout, mood music, indie (Thai and Brit), Japanese imports, soundtracks, death metal and 12-inchers for DJs, enabling it to compete with the chains. It also has music magazines, world charts and listening stations.
Other locations: 7th floor, Central World Plaza, Pathumwan (0 2255 6579).

Opticians

Lauderdale
1st floor, Siam Discovery, Thanon Rama I, Pathumwan (0 2658 0102-3). Siam BTS. **Open** 10am-8pm daily. **Credit** AmEx, DC, MC, V. **Map** p249/p250 F4.

Only the most stylish frames such as Lindberg make it to this classy but fairly priced boutique.

Rajdamri Optical
2nd floor, Silom Complex, Thanon Silom, Bangrak (0 2231 3165). Saladaeng BTS/Silom MRT. **Open** 10.30am-8.30pm daily. **Credit** AmEx, DC, MC, V. **Map** p250 F7.

Run by optometrists, Rajdamri's emphasis is on eye care – so expect frames that are designed for seeing through rather than being looked at.

Boutique chic at **Siam Center**. *See p154.*

Pharmacies

Boots
292/20-23 Siam Square Soi 4, Thanon Rama I, Pathumwan (0 2658 4186/www.boots.co.uk). Siam BTS. **Open** 10am-10pm Mon-Thur, Sun; 10am-10.30pm Fri, Sat. **Credit** AmEx, MC, V. **Map** p249/p250 F4.

Famous labels and good own-brand pharmaceuticals, cosmetics, perfume and beauty care products vie for shelf space at branches of this UK chemist, each of which has a pharmacist.
Other locations: throughout the city.

Photography

Photo developers found everywhere supply snaps in free flip books at low rates, often with digital processing or scanning. Professionals choose **IQ Lab** or, for artful black-and-white printing, Surat Suvanich's **Technilab** (0 1917 8057/0 2636 4989).

Foto File
1st floor, MBK Centre, Thanon Phayathai, Pathumwan (0 2611 9410/9426/www.fotofile.net). National Stadium BTS. **Open** 10.30am-8.30pm daily. **Credit** MC, V. **Map** p249/p250 F5.

A large stock of popular SLRs and lenses, new and used, makes this a favourite among enthusiasts. It also stocks high-end and monochrome films.
Other locations: FotoThailand, 3rd floor, MBK, Pathumwan (0 2611 8062).

IQ Lab
ITF Building, 160/5 Thanon Silom, entrance off Thanon Narathiwat Ratchanakharin, Bangrak (0 2266 4080/www.iqlab.co.th). Chong Nonsi BTS.

Open 8.30am-6pm Mon-Fri; 8.30am-1pm Sat. **Credit**
AmEx, MC, V. **Map** p250 F7.
The only Thai lab trusted by professionals for pro-
cessing, retouching and outputting in all formats.
Other locations: 9/32-34 Sukhumvit Soi 63,
Sukhumvit (0 2714 0644).

Shipping

Although widely on sale, antique treasures
(and even reproduction Buddha images) are
prohibited from export without a licence from
the Fine Arts Department's **Office of
Archaeology** (81/1 Thanon Si Ayutthaya,
Dusit, 0 2628 5033/5021 ext 306). Most shops
and antiques dealers offer to arrange shipping.

Bangkok Shipping Agency
*3rd floor, TSC Building, Ocean Tower 1, 170/7
Thanon New Rajadapisek, Sukhumvit (0 2261 3154-
63). Queen Sirikit Centre MRT.* **Open** 8.30am-5pm
Mon-Fri. **No credit cards. Map** p251 J6.
With its network of shippers and four decades of
service, BSA has the resources for both customs
clearing and freight forwarding, covering both air
and sea cargo.

Shoes

Footwork
*2nd floor, Emporium, Sukhumvit Soi 24, Sukhumvit
(0 2664 8375). Phrom Phong BTS.* **Open** 10.30am-
9pm Mon-Fri; 10am-9pm Sat, Sun. **Credit** AmEx,
DC, MC, V. **Map** p252 K6.
Ensuring that their European and South American
imports are consistently stylish mean Footwork's
new shoe deliveries are highly and impatiently
anticipated by both women and men.

Siam Paragon. *See p154.*

Other locations: 2nd floor, Central World Plaza,
Pathumwan (0 2255 9547); 1st floor, Siam Paragon,
Pathumwan (0 2610 9416).

Ragazze
*2nd floor, Silom Complex, Thanon Silom, Bangrak
(0 2231 3190/www.ragazze.co.th). Saladaeng
BTS/Silom MRT.* **Open** 11am-8pm daily. **Credit**
AmEx, DC, MC, V. **Map** p250 E7.
Employing both leather and lighter materials, this
Italian-influenced Thai company's bags, footwear
and wallets remain up-to-the-minute stylish.
Other locations: 2nd floor, Zen, Central World
Plaza, Pathumwan (0 2613 1028).

Sport & outdoor

No-frills sport shops flank the National Stadium
Pathumwan (*see p203*), while **SuperSports**
has branches in malls, including **Central
World Plaza**. For bling trainers, try **MBK**
and **Siam Center** (for both, *see p154*).

Pro Cam-Fis
*3rd floor, Emporium, Sukhumvit Soi 24, Sukhumvit
(0 2664 8811-2/www.procam-fis.com.hk). Phrom
Phong BTS.* **Open** 10am-9.30pm daily. **Credit**
AmEx, MC, V. **Map** p252 K6.
In case you were wondering, 'Cam-Fis' stands for
camping and fishing; you're supposed to provide the
'Pro' bit yourself. And shopping here just might
enable you to do that. The store attracts outdoors
types on the hunt for a Maglite torch, a Swiss army
knife or camouflage.
Other locations: 4th floor, Central Chidlom,
Pathumwan (0 2655 7777); 2nd floor, Siam Paragon,
Pathumwan (0 2610 9000 ext 1784); Tank, 3rd floor,
Central World Plaza, Pathumwan (0 2613 1052).

Star Soccer
*3rd floor, Siam Discovery, Thanon Rama I,
Pathumwan (0 2658 0375-6). Siam BTS.*
Open 10am-9pm daily. **Credit** AmEx, MC, V.
Map p249/p250 F4.
Thai football addicts get their balls, kits and mem-
orabilia of global and local clubs at this chain.
Other locations: 2nd floor, Pantip Plaza, Thanon
Phetburi, North (0 2251 9670).

Thaniya Plaza
*52 Thanon Thaniya, Bangrak (0 2231 2244/
www.thaniyagroup.com). Saladaeng BTS/Silom
MRT.* **Open** 10am-10pm daily. **Map** p250 F7.
A veritable world of golf: more than 30 golf shops
make this mall a must for Tiger wannabes. They
cater mainly to Japanese, hence the many Nipponese
brands, often at discounts.

Toys

Most malls have activity areas and children's
shops with international brands, local Learning
Curve educational toys for 0-12s and Plan Toys'
imaginative wooden games.

Arts & Entertainment

Features

Festivals & Events

Thais make life festive every day, but these are the biggest parties by season.

Bangkok increasingly fills its calendar with modern events, whether cultural, commercial or simply *sanuk* (fun). Thais even embrace imports like Valentine's Day, Halloween and Christmas with typical glee. Yet eclecticism has always been the hallmark of the many traditional festivals at which the nation excels. Thais mark New Year five times, officially on the Western and Thai reckonings (*see p161* **Songkran**), but also among Chinese, Indian and Mon communities.

Religious and royal holidays remain occasions for reverence. At the most important Buddhist anniversaries – **Makha Bucha**, **Visakha Bucha** and **Asanha Bucha** – devotees circle a temple *bot* three times clockwise at night, while bearing a lotus, incense and a lit candle, to symbolise the cycle of life. This is most impressive at Wat Benchamabophit, Wat Sakhet, Wat Suthat and Wat Bovornivet. No alcohol is sold on those days, and bars tend to close.

Constant events include monks' alms rounds every sunrise, and residents' daily offerings to spirit houses. Devotional rituals, including dances, happen all day at **Erawan Shrine** (*see p98*), **Lak Muang** (*see p63*) and **King Chulalongkorn Statue**, as well as in the temple festivals that take place every so often (*see p163* **Fair game**).

Advance information for events is often incomplete or changes suddenly, so check listings nearer the time in magazines, newspapers, tourist offices (*see p235*) and on the internet, as well as with venue staff. For dates of public holidays and explanations of the seasons, *see p236*.

Cool season

Loy Krathong

Waterways nationwide (Bangkok Tourism Authority 0 2225 7612-6/www.bangkoktourist.com). **Date** full moon of the 12th lunar month (Nov).
In this picturesque rite, Thais make offerings to water spirits while cleansing sins and bad luck. The Brahman-inspired offering is a *krathong*, a delicate, candlelit float made from a section of banana tree trunk (avoid the styrofoam ones), decorated with leaves, incense, flowers and other tributes. The Siamese love of finery emerges in contests for the most beautiful *krathongs* and a Miss Nopamas contest, named after the *krathong*'s ancient

Sukhothai inventor. The event is most splendid in Sukhothai (northern Thailand), but crowds flock to waterways in Bangkok too.

Fat Festival

104.5 FM Fat radio station (0 2641 5234 /www.thisisclick.com). **Date** 1st or 2nd weekend of Nov.
Run by Fat Radio, this indie gathering has grown into a mass movement embracing punks and J-Pop chicks, hip hop dudes and speed metal freaks. Thousands of such *dek naew* (trend kids) flock to a different venue each year to cheer 200 bands and DJs, and browse stalls of alternative music, film, art and handmade books.

Bangkok Theatre Festival

Santichaiprakarn Park, Thanon Phra Arthit, Banglamphu (www.lakorn.org). **Map** p248 B2. **Date** early-mid Nov.
At this charming festival, myriad kinds of modern and traditional performance overlap around the park and art bars along Phra Arthit. It's held over three weekends, and fairly accessible to non-Thais.

Ploenchit Fair

BEC-TERO Hall, Suan Lum Night Bazaar (Carolyn Tarrant 0 2204 1587/www.ploenchitfair.com). *Lumphini MRT.* **Tickets** B100; B20 concessions. **No credit cards.** **Map** p249 D1. **Date** 1 Dec 2007, but usually 3rd Sat of Nov.
Expat charity events don't get any bigger than this day of funfair rides, boozing and entertainment. An institution since the 1950s, when it all kicked off at the British Embassy.

Bangkok Marathon

National Jogging Association (0 2628 8361/ www.bkkmarathon.com). **Date** last Sun of Nov.
Launched in 1987, the annual full, half and mini-marathons through the old town start and finish at the Ministry of Defence, opposite the Grand Palace.

Trooping of the Colour

Royal Plaza, Dusit (Foundation of King Rama IX the Great 0 2356 0050-2/www.belovedking.com). **Map** p249 D1. **Date** 2 Dec.
At this grand, colourful ceremony, the Royal Guards swear loyalty to His Majesty and march past the royal family in magnificent plumed dress uniforms of brilliant hues.

Miss AC/DC Pageant

BEC-TERO Hall, Suan Lum Night Bazaar (0 2662 0164/www.missacdc.com). Lumphini MRT. **Tickets** B500-B1,000. **Map** p251 H6. **Date** 1st or 2nd weekend of Dec.

In an uproarious spoof of Miss Universe, drag queens 'represent' some 70 countries in 'national costumes', gowns, talents (from opera to fire-juggling) and even philosophising. Winners of the more mainstream ladyboy pageant Miss Tiffany, crowned in Pattaya in March, enter America's Miss Queen of the Universe (and won in 1999, 2000 and 2002). Every year the media ponders who's the prettier: Miss Tiffany or the official Miss Thailand (a real woman crowned earlier in March, who goes on to contest Miss Universe).

King's Birthday Celebrations

Nationwide. **Date** 5 Dec.

The Thais' deep reverence for their king is displayed everywhere on what is also Father's Day (and a national holiday). Decorations stretch from the Grand Palace via Ratchadamnoen Avenue to the Royal Plaza and Chitrlada Palace. In the morning His Majesty addresses massed representatives of the nation from the Ananta Samakhom Throne Hall, then thousands of people assemble on Sanam Luang at dusk to light candles and sing the 'Praise the King' song, joined across the country by millions of Thais, who also celebrate with community fairs and in rites at grandly illuminated buildings. After a magnificent fireworks display, huge stages at Sanam Luang erupt with star performers in *luuk thuung*, *morlam* and T-Pop music, *lakhon* and *likay*. Crowds filter down fairylit Ratchadamnoen to take photos.

Concert in the Park

Sala Bhirombhakdi, Suan Lum Park & other parks (Bangkok Symphony Orchestra 0 2255 66178/www.bangkoksymphony.org). **Date** 5.30-7.30pm every Sun mid Dec-mid Feb.

Free open-air concerts in city greenswards, from nostalgic Thai melodies and folk songs to country, pop, light classics and showtunes. Picnicking listeners can forage at various stalls.

New Year Celebrations

Nationwide. **Date** 31 Dec.

Thai events to mark the international New Year vary from the serenely sacred to the exuberantly secular. There is a whole host of activities on offer, including merit-making rites at temples, gala dinners at hotels, parties in nightclubs and bars, and firework displays at Sanam Luang and the river hotels. Traffic is closed around Central World Plaza for a communal countdown, but mass transit runs all night. Expect tight security all round after the 2006/7 bombings.

Indy (Book/Film/Music/Art) Festival

Santichaiprakarn Park, Thanon Phra Arthit (Ruangkrit Rakkanchanant 08 7519 9150/0 2308 0410-1/www.thaiwriternetwork.com). **Map** p248 B2. **Date** Jan/Feb.

Making a splash at **Songkran.** *See p161.*

Arts & Entertainment

This casual, open-air 'free space' enables 'independent' people (mostly young) to present their publications, music, artistry and short films. Since 2006 its Thailand Independent Awards honour writers and short film makers.

National Children's Day
Across Bangkok. **Date** 8.30am-4.30pm 2nd Sat of Jan.
Doors usually closed to the public are opened today, including the inner Grand Palace, Defence Ministry and Government House. Zoos, theme parks and many other sights are free – as are tank rides, as the Thai military forces allow civilian inspections.

Bangkok Fringe Festival
Patravadi Theatre, Thanon Arun Amarin, Thonburi (0 2412 7287-8/www.patravaditheatre. com). **Tickets** B200-B800. **Map** p248 A3. **Date** mid Jan-early Feb.
A performing arts event showcasing dance, drama, music and multimedia of East and West, in traditional, modern and fusion forms. The weekend evening shows are mostly intelligible to non-Thai speakers.

Bangkok International Film Festival
Downtown cinemas (0 2250 5500 ext 4550-3/0 2250 0814/www.bangkokfilm.org). **Date** late Jan-Feb.
Run by the Tourist Authority of Thailand, this feast of film spans diverse countries and tastes, with a major regional contingent. A movie mart, seminars and appearances by major stars lent credibility...

until BKIFF was postponed in 2007; its future timing is uncertain, although as this guide went to press the festival was slated for 19-29 July. For more on film festivals, *see p168.*

Elle Bangkok Fashion Week
Central World Plaza, Pathumwan (Elle magazine 0 2240 3700 ext 1703). Chidlom BTS. **Map** p251 G4. **Date** Feb & Sept.
Since 1999 *Elle* has showcased Thai designers in Bangkok's original fashion week. Now twice yearly and sponsored by Central, it offers some runway seats to the public, but it's easier to obtain them at runway shows on the final two public days at the Bangkok International Fashion Fair (mid Jan, 0 2511 6020-30 ext 317, www.thaitradefair.com).

Chinese New Year Festival
Chinatown (Samphanthawong District Office 0 2234 3460). **Map** p249/p250. **Date** 7 Feb 2008 (Rat), 26 Jan 2009 (Ox).
Thai-Chinese roots spring out around lunar New Year, when lion and dragon dances, firecrackers, Chinese opera and redoubled convoys of interesting food carts take over Chinatown's Yaowarat and Charoen Krung roads.

Epicurean Masters of the World
LeBua at State Tower, 1055 Thanon Silom, Bangrak (0 2624 9555/www.thedomebkk.com/ www.epicureanmasters.com). **Map** p250 D7. **Date** early Feb.

Spell bound

At the shamanistic **Tattoo Festival**, more than a thousand entranced men impersonate the creatures depicted on their skin. Devotees gather to get more tattoos and honour past tattoo masters such as the late abbot of Wat Bang Phra in Nakhon Chaisri, on Bangkok's western outskirts.

Around dawn on the day of the festival, men snap into character (whether tiger, snake, bird, hermit, monkey or other talismanic beings) and storm an altar at the temple. The culminating stampede (which occurs around 8.30am) stops when sprayed by holy water.

Western-style tattoos are hip, but traditional ones (*sak yantra*) can unnerve the bourgeoisie because they are considered a magic amulet. Activated by a *mantra* (spell), amulets may induce protection, popularity, love or prosperity, but apparently only 'work' if the bearer behaves morally.

The festival-goers wear every kind of amulet. They are typically slung around the neck (or covering car dashboards) and usually consist of miniature images of the Buddha,

Hindu gods, venerable monks or great kings like Rama V. Others range from herb roots and natural oddities to cabalistic diagrams that resemble tattoos but are on cloth or rolled foil that can be tiny enough to embed under the skin. Often hung from a belt, the phallic *palad khik* is also thought lucky by shopkeepers, as are fish traps and dolls of a beckoning woman or a golden 'ghost boy'.

Thailand has the world's largest amulet trade, with aficionados poring at collectibles on stalls in Thanon Phra Chan's **Amulet Alley** (*see p57* **Phra Nakorn** *and p137* **Markets**), **Wat Ratchanadda** (*see p69*) and **Chatuchak Weekend Market** (*see p138*). Amulets can theoretically only be 'rented', yet prices can reach millions of *baht*, depending on quality, rarity, antiquity, the status of the monk who made them – or simply fashion.

Tattoo Festival
Wat Bang Phra, Nakhon Chaisri-Bang Phra, Nakhon Chaisri (0 3438 9333-96). **Date** late Feb/early Mar.

For its second festival in 2007, this hifalutin' hotel's spectacular restaurants charged B1million for its closing seven-course dinner by eight three-Michelin-star chefs, in an effort to put Bangkok on the millionnaires' map (*see p113* **Gold plated**).

Hot season

Makha Bucha
Nationwide. **Date** full moon of 3rd lunar month (late Feb/early Mar).
On this national holiday Thais head for temples at dusk to mark the occasion when the star Makha burned at its brightest, and 1,250 disciples gathered to hear Buddha's last major sermon before he attained nirvana.

Traditional Thai Games & Sports Festival
Sanam Luang, Phra Nakorn (Thai Sports Association 0 2640 6572). **Map** p248 B3. **Date** Mar-early Apr.
There's more to Siamese sports than *Muay Thai* (kick boxing): fighting kites, *krabi-krabong* swordsmanship, Thai chess (with martial artists enacting moves on a huge board) and *takraw lod buang*, an ancestor of *sepak takraw* in which players punt a rattan ball through a suspended hoop. The Thailand International Kite Festival is now held every two years (next in March 2008), in Hua Hin.

Bangkok International Fashion Week
Siam Paragon, Pathumwan (0 2610 8110/8333/ www.bangkokinternationalfashionweek.com). Siam BTS. **Map** p251 G4. **Date** mid Mar.
The Thaksin government's Bangkok Fashion City project was cancelled, but this mall will inherit four days of catwalk shows in tents and an indoor trade fair to showcase Thai designers with global potential. Some seats will be available to members of the public, and in-the-know fashionistas may be able to crash the parties.

Chakri Day
Public holiday. **Date** 6 Apr.
Three royal ceremonies on this public holiday mark the 1782 founding of Thailand's current Chakri dynasty. The king first pays his respects to the Emerald Buddha in Wat Phra Kaew, followed by rites in the neighouring royal pantheon honouring all nine Chakri kings and finally at the Rama I statue by Memorial Bridge.

Songkran
Public holiday. **Date** 13-15 Apr.
The infamous water throwing at the Thai New Year evolved from Indian powder-tossing into gentle rituals of reverence and purification, such as sprinkling monks and Buddha images with lustral water. Thais also honour elders, clean the house, make sand *chedi* in temples, crown Miss Songkran and revere the Phra Buddha Sihing image at Sanam Luang. By contrast, in a mass catharsis of breakneck modernisation, youngsters grab water pistols, buckets and hoses for giddy attacks on everyone, day and night, at this hottest time of year. Often the water's iced, dyed or mixed with talc. Officials try (and fail) to limit excesses to peak areas like Patpong (*see p91*) and Thanon Khao San (*see p71*), where shows are staged. Wear nothing precious and pack electronics and wallets in plastic. Most Bangkokians head out of the city for up to a week, so traffic is light. However the jams in and out are awful, with typically 500 dead and 34,000 injured from accidents. The Mon people celebrate Songkran on 20-22 April in Phra Padaeng, just south of Bangkok, with parades and courting rites (details on 0 2463 7800).

Naris Day
Baan Plainoen, Thanon Rama IV, 1st soi east of the expressway, South (Naris Foundation 0 2249 4280). Khlong Toei MRT. **Tickets** Show B300-B500. *Open day* free. **No credit cards. Map** p251 J7. **Date** *Show & exhibition* 4.30-8pm 28 Apr. *Open day* 9am-5pm 29 Apr.
Descendants of King Rama V's brother Prince Naris, a revered arts polymath, commemorate his birth in 1863 by opening his traditional house. Browse the exhibitions in between the classical Thai dance show on 28 April, or all day on 29 April.

Demonic
Thailand Cultural Centre amphitheatre, Thanon Ratchadaphisek, North-east (0 2247 0028/Lakfah Sarsakul 08 1750 0591). Thailand Cultural Centre MRT. **Date** 3 May 2008.
A biennial mosh pit of local death metal, hardcore and other underground bands. The venue may alter.

Royal Ploughing Ceremony
Sanam Luang, Phra Nakorn (Department of Agricultural Extension 0 2579 0121-7 ext 130/www.doae.go.th). **Map** p249/p250 D4. **Date** early May.
These Brahmin rites to forecast the year's rainfall and harvest officially launch the rice-planting season. After a day of Buddhist chanting and the king's blessing of rice seeds, a costumed procession ends with this ritual field being ploughed by sacred white oxen, and sown with the blessed rice. Farmers from all over Thailand then rush in to gather the lucky seeds for planting.

Rainy season

Visakha Bucha
Nationwide. **Date** full moon of 6th lunar month (late May/early June).
Buddhism's holiest date, when Lord Buddha was born, enlightened and died. Devotees make merit by bringing food to monks in the morning. In the evening, temples hold sermons and candlelit processions. It's also a public holiday, and most bars and businesses are closed.

Arts & Entertainment

Rice is blessed at the **Royal Ploughing Ceremony**. *See p161.*

La Fête

Alliance Française (0 2670 4231/www.alliance-francaise.or.th). **Map** p251 G7. **Date** 3rd Sat of June.
Run simultaneously around the globe, this Franco-backed festival encompasses all kinds of music and arts, including (but not limited to) Thai collaborations, at various venues.

Asanha Bucha & Khao Phansa

Nationwide. **Date** full moon of 8th lunar month (late July/early Aug) & following day.
The anniversary of the Buddha's first sermon after attaining enlightenment is observed with temple rituals. Next day is Khao Phansa (the start of the rainy season), when monks begin 'Buddhist Lent': three months of meditation and prayer while confined within boundaries of their temples. Some Thai youths still become a novice for the duration of this period, a step to Thai manhood that earns their parents karmic merit.

HM The Queen's Birthday

Nationwide. **Date** 12 Aug.
Heralding this royal anniversary, which is also Mother's Day, many thousand points of light decorate Thanon Ratchadamnoen and other venues. A glittering spectacle.

Short Film & Video Festival

Khun Chalida Uabumrungjit 08 1615 5137/Thai Film Foundation 0 2800 2716-7/www.thaifilm.com. **Date** mid Aug.
Indie films are given the opportunity to shine in various venues at this free festival, which is becoming incresingly international in scope.

World Gourmet Festival

Four Seasons Hotel, 155 Thanon Ratchadamri, Pathumwan (0 2251 6127). Ratchadamri BTS. **Map** p251 G5. **Date** mid Sept.
Since 1999 this premium event has raised Bangkok's reputation as a hub for global fine dining, though once-bargain prices now approach Western levels. For ten days, leading foreign chefs prepare to-die-for meals, along with cookery classes, demonstrations and wine tastings.

International Festival of Music & Dance

Thailand Cultural Centre, Thanon Ratchadaphisek, North-east (0 2661 6830-4/www.bangkokfestivals .com. **Date** mid Sept-early Oct.
Bangkok's biggest annual arts festival stages world-class performances at Thai middle-class prices. The focus is on opera, ballet and orchestral music, often by Eastern European companies, with leading jazz, world music and dance from elsewhere.

Chinese Mid-Autumn Festival

Nationwide. **Date** full moon of 8th Chinese lunar month (late Sept).
Tiers of mooncakes in eateries herald this ethnic Chinese festival. In 14th-century China, mooncakes conveyed messages among Han Chinese plotting to overthrow the Mongols. Traditionally eaten only after being offered on an altar to the goddess of mercy Guan Im, the cakes – some filled with pungent durian fruit paste – are now scoffed down with tea. Held at the same time, the Chinatown Food Festival fills Thanon Yaowarat with stalls.

Fair game

The blueprint for many Thai festivals is the *ngan wat*, the temple fair. Temple compounds historically held secular activities, from education and medicine to martial arts, but they also hosted village merriment, touring performers and, since their mid 20th-century boom, roving film projections. Festivals served as an important pressure valve for relaxing social strictures, and *ngan wat* unabashedly came to witness much irreverence, flirting and larking about.

As more modern pursuits encroach on traditional ones, *ngan wat* have evolved into huge, elaborate attractions in an attempt to bring people back into the *wat*. Although festivals or rites are the pretext, and parades the showpiece event, raising funds is imperative, so many *ngan wat* have gone commercial, earning income from myriad stalls, rides and sideshows, plus singing contests and speciality foods.

Temple fairs are also the best places to experience Thai popular culture. Rival stages blare *likay* (*see p188*) or *talok* (comedy; *see p199*), *luuk thung* folk tunes (*see p187*) or the latest T-Pop diva. On the margins, punters place illegal bets on cockfights, boxing, lotteries or gaming. Drink – often moonshine – plays lubricant, not least for the spirit mediums dispensing fortunes.

Many fairs stage beauty pageants, a serious pursuit in image-conscious Thailand, where a runner-up once snatched the winner's crown live on TV. Some national contestants honed their perma-smiles and perma-hair at provincial fruit fairs, such as Miss Lychee or Miss Rambutan.

As *ngan wat* are informal and free, they're open to all. Held on each *wat*'s annual day – and at one or two temples in any given area at festive times – *ngan wat* rarely feature in media listings, so keep an eye out for the trademark festive lights and signs. Alternatively, you could try any of these three famed Bangkok fairs.

Golden Mount Temple Fair
Wat Saket, 344 Thanon Chakkraphatdiphong, Phra Nakorn (0 2621 0576). Tha Saphan Phan Fah. **Map** p248 C3. **Date** Nov; either side of Loy Krathong (*see p158*).

Wat Hualumphong Temple Fair
728 Thanon Rama IV, Pathumwan (0 2233 8109). Samyan MRT. **Map** p250 F6. **Date** during Chinese New Year.

Wat Phlubphlachai Temple Fair
5 Thanon Mitreechit, Chinatown (0 2222 5396). **Map** p250 D4. **Date** during Chinese New Year.

Navaratree Hindu Festival
Maha Uma Devi (Wat Khaek), 2 Thanon Pan, Bangrak (0 2238 4007). Surasak BTS. **Map** p250 E7. **Date** Oct.
For the temple's annual festival, Thanon Silom, between Khlong Chong Nonsi and Soi 19, is pedestrianised for devotees to worship Hindu shrines set up in the road. Fevered rites, blessings, spirit-channelling and parades of men pierced in acts of self-mortification culminate in the massed smashing of coconuts on petal-patterned sidewalks. Wear white.

Ok Phansa
Nationwide. **Date** full moon of 11th lunar month (Oct).
The rainy season officially ends on this public holiday, and with it the three months of Buddhist Lent, with *wat* rituals and the traditional shaving of monks' scalps and eyebrows.

Vegetarian Festival
Across Bangkok. **Date** early/mid Oct.
Food stalls and restaurants go veggie (look out for yellow pennants) for this ten-day Chinese Buddhist-Taoist period of purging meat and heating foods by white-clad devotees (those in Phuket practice self-mortification; *see p219*). Chinatown explodes with colour, incense, temple offerings and the strains of Chinese opera, notably in Charoen Krung Soi 20.

World Film Festival of Bangkok
Downtown cinemas (Kriengsak Silakong 08 9026 3232/0 2325 5555 ext 3447/8/www.world filmbkk.com). **Date** mid-late Oct.
Run by the *Nation* newspaper, this cinefest of around 150 movies focuses on independent auteurship, Asian films and specific themes. For more on film festivals, *see p168*.

Bangkok Pride Festival
Thanon Silom, Bangrak (www.bangkokpride.org). Saladaeng BTS/Silom MRT. **Map** p250 F6.
Date late Oct-early Nov.
Bangkok's gay days number 365 a year, but that hasn't stopped this week of cabarets, parties, costume shows, plays, sporting contests and the Utopia Awards for Asia's gay lib pioneers (www.utopia-asia.com). It opens with the 'Pink in the Park' fair in Lumphini Park and closes with a late-afternoon parade, before a night of parties.

Children

Angel city for your little angel.

Family matters above all else to Thais, who coddle children at every opportunity. They react with delight at infant visitors, which can bewilder those with novelty blonde hair. However, surveys show that many elders disapprove of youth behaviour, which increasingly values materialism, gratification and appearance, at the expense of study, morality and diligence. Ironically, that critique equally applies to the society those elders have bequeathed to their offspring. Official remedies tend to favour force and face over reform of education away from rote learning, seniors fearing where critical thinking may lead. So the state institutes bans against under-age drinking and internet gaming, test for drugs in schools and even proposed a 10pm teen curfew.

Meanwhile, insufficient attention is paid to what a child needs, and not just of poor pre-teens selling garlands so that their family can eat. Rich kids suffer too. Overindulged by nannies and doting parents, many can't tie their shoelaces at ten, or cross a road safely at 14, because they've been driven everywhere. Child obesity has increased alarmingly. While adults give up seats on buses for kids, it's common to see infants perched on the tank of a mother's motorbike with a toddler clung to her back or, indeed, a juvenile driving a motorbike with no protection at all.

Thais remain cheery fatalists, but Westerners indulge in much hand-wringing, especially about child labour. Though exploitative or dangerous employment is far rarer than in neighbouring countries, children helping the family business are integral to farming, crafts and shophouse trades. Despite the drawbacks, many claim that life lessons in discipline, perseverance, apprenticeship, sharing and social obligation make for an unselfish, respectful person.

These dichotomies stem from technological development having sped ahead of welfare and education, and a disregard for safety reinforced by faith in karma. So exercise caution with cheap toys or electrical appliances and when walking hazardous streets, especially with a buggy (use baby slings instead). Still, there are many fun family activities in Bangkok. Support group BAMBI is a useful resource.

Attractions

Sure-fire hits with kids include boat tours (see p56) and **Dusit Zoo** (see p81). Distant attractions aimed at families may be paired into day trips, like **Rose Garden** with **Samphran Elephant Ground** (for both, see p105); **Safari World** with **Siam Park** (for both, see p102); or **National Science Museum** with **Dream World** (both see below). Hotels can book such excursions. Family events focus on **Children's Day** (second Sat in Jan; see p160), when restricted landmarks are open, and Thai Mother's Day, the **Queen's Birthday** (Aug; see p162).

For active kids, aside from sports venues (see pp201-04), parks, malls and department stores contain play areas. At **Central Chidlom** (see p144), Build-a-Bear tailors teddies, while in Jamboree at **Emporium** (see p153) you can design a toy character in the Imaginarium. **Siam Paragon** (see p154) has myriad attractions in its fourth floor Explorium, plus **Siam Ocean World** aquarium (see p93). **Central World Plaza** (see p153) holds a kids' zone and TK Park learning centre for Thais. **MBK** mall (see p154) and Siam Square cater to teens.

Bangkok Dolls
85 Soi Mor Leng, Thanon Ratchaprarop, North (0 2245 3008). **Open** 8am-5pm Mon-Sat. **Admission** free. **Credit** V.
This small doll museum and cottage industry has occupied its modest location since the 1950s. Its bright displays of ornate costumes and traditional scenes (the Ramayana, monks, ethnic groups, stilt houses) have a homespun charm. Most of the dolls were made here in an intriguing process you can watch, with some on sale for B290-1,300.

Children's Discovery Museum
Thanon Kamphaengphet 4, Chatuchak, North (0 2615 7333/www.bkkchildrenmuseum.com). Morchit BTS/Chatuchak Park MRT. **Open** 9am-5pm Tue-Fri; 10am-6pm Sat, Sun. **Admission** Thais B70, B50 under-15s. Foreigners B150, B120 under-15s; may differ for special events. **No credit cards.**
A house of fun with hands-on exhibits galore, including a percussion music room and a TV/music studio where the young can star in their own movie or newsroom. Or they can visit the animal section, domain of tropical fish, parrots, snakes, reptiles and small fluffy mammals. Bring ear plugs on weekdays,

when school parties raise the decibels. Nearby Chatuchak Park has a playground, jungle gym and railway museum (*see p96*).

Dream World

62 Moo 1, Thanon Rangsit-Ongkarak, Pathum Thani (0 2533 1152/www.dreamworld.com). **Open** 10am-5pm Mon-Fri; 10am-7pm Sat, Sun. **Admission** B120; B95 children under 145cm/57in (excl rides); pass B360 (25 rides, excl some rides). **No credit cards.**

All the usual theme-park rides, including roller-coasters, the Big Splash, Snow Land, a petting zoo and Disneyesque characters. It concedes a few Thai touches like elephant rides and massage.

National Science Museum

Techno Thani, Thanon Rangsit-Nakhon Nayok, Klong 5, Klong Luang, Pathum Thani, North-east (0 2577 9999/www.nsm.or.th). **Open** 9.30am-4pm Tue-Fri, 9.30am-5pm Sat-Sun. **Admission** B50, B60 (with Natural History Museum); free children & students. **No credit cards.**

An undervisited high-tech museum housed in astonishing steel, glass and fibreglass cubes balanced on their points. It'll take half a day to explore its six floors, the first three of which are best for kids. English-speaking assistants explain the interactive exhibits.

Babysitting & childcare

Because many homes have maids or extended families, there are few babysitting agencies, and playgroups are members-only, so for childminding consult **BAMBI**. Most major hotels offer childminders for B200-B300/hour, plus B100-B200 per hour per extra child, as noted in Where to Stay (*see pp38-52*).

BAMBI (Bangkok Mothers & Babies International)

www.bambiweb.org.

A non-profit group offering help and information to pregnant women and parents of young children, from education to entertainment and healthcare. The website lists weekly playgroups and monthly meetings.

Where to stay & eat

While many hotels focus on business or designer service, the more spacious ones score family points, such as the **Sukhothai, Pathumwan Princess**, group tour hotels and river hotels, especially the **Marriott Bangkok Resort** and **Shangri-la**. Many families prefer short-stay serviced apartments for their kitchenettes, mini-suites and residential informality. For reviews, *see p38-52* **Where to Stay**).

Nearly all restaurants welcome kids and the staff are invariably doting. Thai dining can be great fun, with shared dishes and hands-on grub such as wrap-in-a-leaf *miang* or cook-at-your-table *suki* (try the **Coca** and **MK** suki chains in any mall). Why not try eating on cushions at a dance show or aboard a boat? Vendors sell Thai popsicles from metal tubes, scoop ice-cream into bread rolls and slather crushed ice desserts with multicoloured jellies, though some distrust ice at streetstalls. Or watch Thai desserts being made at **Old Siam Plaza** (*see p154*). Many hotels' Sunday brunches offer kids' clubs with clowns, magic and playrooms, including the **Marriott Bangkok Resort** (11.30am-2.30pm Sun, from B1,499; B750 3-12s; free under-3s; *see p40*) and **Shangri-la** (11.30am-2.30pm Sun; from B1,350; B675 6-12s; free under-6s; *see p45*).

Jamboree at Emporium. See p164.

Arts & Entertainment

Film

With its VIP cinemas, celebrated auteurs and prized locations, Siam has star presence.

Thailand's film scene has gone from arthouse curio to global player, with Cannes lauding Thai directors, Hollywood remaking local thrillers (*Shutter, 6ixtynin9, Bangkok Dangerous*) and distributors clamouring for the next action kickfest (*see p167* **The big leap**). Filmgoing is a treat, with festivals and superlative cinemas proliferating. Still, current output is only a fraction of the 1950s-'70s boom, when Thai superheroes battled Japanese monsters and Mitr Chaibancha/Petchara Chaowarat romances featured a Burton/Taylor-esque frisson.

Meanwhile, Thailand has become a major location for Hollywood blockbusters. Sometimes it plays itself (*The Beach, Air America*, Stallone's 2008 comeback *Rambo IV*), or stands in for elsewhere (*Good Morning Vietnam, The Killing Fields, Alexander*) or plays a fictional land (Bond's *The Man with the Golden Gun* and *Tomorrow Never Dies*). The resulting crew expertise ensures that directors like Oliver Stone keep returning.

NEW THAI CINEMA

While socially conscious film briefly flourished in the 1970s, Nonzee Nimibutr started today's new breed of creative directors with his 1950s-set hoodlum hit *Dang Bireley's and the Young Gangsters* (1997) and broke his own box office record in 1999 with a sumptuous remake of the perennial Thai ghost story *Nang Nak*. Along with *Iron Ladies* – Yongyuth Thongkongtun's biopic of ladyboys in Thailand's volleyball team – these were given international releases. Previously, few Thai movies had English subtitles because a foreign market hadn't been imagined. Since Wisit Sasanatieng's hand-tinted Siamese cowboy fantasy *Tears of the Black Tiger* (2001), the better Thai movies make more money abroad than at home.

Wisit caused more swoons with his wistful tribute to the underclass in *Citizen Dog* (2005) and homage to ghost story conventions in *The Unseeable* (2006). In 2006 he won the third Silpathorn Award for mid career achievement, following fellow indie icons Pen-ek Rattanruang and Apichartpong Weerasethakul.

Pen-ek leveraged his reputation from imaginative social commentaries (*Fun Bar Karaoke, 6ixtynin9, Mon Rak Transistor*) to work with Asian stars and celebrated cinematographer Christopher Doyle on both the meditative *Last Life in the Universe* and the offbeat thriller *Invisible Waves*. Funded by the French, and influenced by their poetic style, Apichartpong was the first Thai to be invited to Cannes, winning the Un Certain Regard award for *Blissfully Yours* (2002), an experimental love story involving an illegal Burmese immigrant, and the Special Jury Prize for *Tropical Malady* (2004), a gay tiger-spirit-possession parable. Initially, his achievements gained minimal recognition from Thai officialdom, distributors and festivals, which also ignored his co-direction of artist Michael Shaowanasai's *The Adventures of Iron Pussy*, a spoof about a transsexual ex-barboy secret agent.

Thai tastes generally prefer teen melodramas, ghost schlockfests and patriotic costume dramas, such as Thanit Jitnukul's rousing *Bangrajan*. These typically become marketing vehicles for their singer/model/MC stars whose mannered acting and slapstick humour limit outsider appeal. However, new standards in art direction and logistics distinguish two nationalistic, fancifully 'historical' epics by aristocrat MR Chatri Chalerm Yukol (aka Than Mui). *Suriyothai* (2002) and the even longer *Naresuan* trilogy (2007; *see p13*) successively smashed budget and audience records through dutiful filmgoing.

Critic Anchalee Chaiworaporn reviews Thai releases in English at **www.thaicinema.org**.

First-run & IMAX cinemas

The number of screens in Bangkok has quintupled in a decade. Many multiplexes boast velvet upholstery, waiter service, massage recliners, VIP lounges and Thailand's first cinema membership scheme. By contrast, Thai film's open-air origins continue at local fairs and the **Goethe Institut** (*see p168*). Schedules (between 11am and midnight daily) often change with no notice, so you can't plan ahead. Don't trust printed ads: on the day call the cinemas' recorded lines or surf **www.movieseer.com**. After 15 minutes of trailers, films start with the King's Anthem, for which everyone must stand.

Proposals to replace the draconian 1931 Film Act with age ratings keep faltering. Censors seem keen to preserve their arbitrary power.

Arts & Entertainment

Although Vaseline and cuts get applied less often to 'unacceptable' images (sex, nudity, smoking), the Film Board is still perfectly happy to ban movies that might offend official sensitivities (such as *Anna and the King*).

EGV

6th floor, Siam Discovery, Thanon Rama I, Pathumwan (all branches 0 2515 5555/ www.egv.com). Siam BTS. **Tickets** B120-B500. **Screens** 7. **Credit** DC, MC, V. **Map** p249/p250 F4.
Go to see a film in a branch of this chain and you're guaranteed great seating and sight-lines. More impressive still are the plush velvet recliners with tables, massage chairs and waitress service in the Gold Class theatres (also found in many of its branches). EGV runs D-Cine – on-demand digital mini-theatres – here and at Metropolis.
Other locations: Seacon Square, Thanon Srinakharin, East; Central Pinklao, Thonburi; EGV Metropolis, Big C, Thanon Ratchadamri, Pathumwan.

Major Cineplex

7th floor, Central World Plaza, Thanon Ratchadamri, Pathumwan (all branches 0 2515 5555/www.majorcineplex.com). Chidlom BTS. **Tickets** B120-B500, some seats B1,000 Mon-Thur. **Screens** 6. **Credit** DC, MC, V. **Map** p251 G4.
A multiplex with clear views and superb seats, including opera and honeymoon chairs.
Other locations: Thanon Phra Pinklao, Thonburi; Ekamai, Sukhumvit Soi 61, Sukhumvit; Ratchayothin, Outer North; Central Rama 3, South; The Esplanade, Thanon Ratchadapisek, North-east.

Paragon Cineplex, Enigma & IMAX

5th floor, Siam Paragon, Thanon Rama I, Pathumwan (0 2515 5555/www.paragon cineplex.com). Siam BTS. **Tickets** B140-B600. **Screens** 16. **Credit** DC, MC, V. **Map** p249/p250 F4.
Major's 600-seat Krungsri IMAX theatre (3-D or DMR effects) and 1,140-seat, balconied Siam Pavalai theatre headline at the country's most luxurious cinema, hosting festivals and premières. The 34-seat

The big leap

Along with horror and comedy, action films have always enjoyed immense popularity in Thailand. But action aesthetics were mostly appreciated by the masses rather than critically acclaimed, and the genre was often considered B-grade. It all changed in 2004 when Prachya Pinkaew's *Ong-Bak: Muay Thai Warrior* and its main star Tony Jaa became hits in the West through Luc Besson's distribution. Ever since, action (*muay thai* especially) has become synonymous with Thai cinema, as seen in Ekachai Uekrongtham's biopic of the transsexual boxer *Nong Toom Beautiful Boxer*, the upcoming *Muay Thai*

Chaiya and Preecha Songsakul's *Pahayut: Muay Thai Chaiya*.
With extreme acrobatics and tightly choreographed moves, former stuntman Tony Jaa has become Thailand's first global star after the groundbreaking *Ong Bak* and *Tom-Yum-Goong* (*The Protector*). In 2007 he was set to both direct and star in *Ong Bak 2*. Another ex-stuntman, Dan Chupong, is being groomed by Sahamongkol Film as Jaa's protégé. He's appeared in Panna Rittikrai's *Born to Fight* and Chalerm Wongpim's *Khon Fai Bin* (*Dynamite Warriors*), an Isaan spectacle in a cowboy and Chinese flying swordplay hybrid.
The rush is on to find more Thai action stars, of every gender, age and nationality. Children throw punches in *Power Kids*, while Prachya cast his third actioner, *Chocolate*, with a Thai female tae kwon do star, a Korean boxer, and a Dutch wrestler. Producers are innovating to enhance the fighting scenes, using tango in *The Bullet Wives* and Thai athletes from football, rugby, gymnastics, tae kwon do and cycling in *Born to Fight*.
Like the soup Tom-Yum-Goong is named after, Thai action is hot, spicy and full of a variety of surprising flavours.

Enigma private cinema has a lounge bar and suits parties (B3,000/pair, or membership: B30,000/11 pairs, B50,000/20 pairs, B100,000/50 pairs).

SFX

6th floor, The Emporium, Sukhumvit Soi 24, Sukhumvit (all branches 0 2268 8888/www.sfcinema city.com). Phrom Phong BTS. **Tickets** B120-B250, B80 after 8.30pm Mon-Wed; B140-B250 Thur-Sun. **Screens** 6. **Credit** MC, V. **Map** p252 K6.
The only rival chain to Major/EGV offers comfy seats, festival screenings and a wide choice of food.
Other locations: SF Cinema City, Mah Boon Krong Centre, Pathumwan; Central Ladprao, Thanon Phahon Yothin, North; SF World, Central World Plaza.

Art-house & festivals

Film festivals in Bangkok have gone from barely annual to monthly. Despite a passionate niche following, these lag behind regional rivals due to organisational failures and schisms. In brief, the **Bangkok Film Festival**'s original sponsor, the *Nation* newspaper, founded the **World Film Festival of Bangkok** (mid-late Oct; *see p163*) after the TAT used state muscle and money to comandeer the **Bangkok International Film Festival** (late Jan-Feb; *see p160*). Each programmes 100-150 films and awards prizes, though the latter's delay in 2007 may make the rivals merge. Foreign cultural

Modern film-going in luxury and comfort.

bodies pioneered this boom with national film festivals held by **Alliance Française** (*see below*) and Germany's **Goethe Institut** (*see below*) and the EU Film Festival (EU Delegation 0 2305 2600 ext 2646, historically May/June, but in 2006 it was held in November, so check first). **The Short Film & Video Festival** by the Thai Film Foundation, Chalida Uabumrungjit, (mid Aug, 08 1615 5137, www.thaifilm.com) showcases emerging talents for free.

Alliance Française

29 Thanon Sathorn Tai, South (0 2670 4200/ www.alliance-francaise.or.th). **Open** 9am-6pm Mon-Fri; 8.30am-5pm Sat. *Film* 5.15pm Sat. **No credit cards. Map** p251 G7.
This cultural centre includes a café, library and language school. It shows French movies with English subtitles (5.15pm Sat, free), hosts short film festivals and sponsors events, often in Thai collaborations.

Goethe Institut

18/1 Goethe Gasse, Sathorn Soi 1 (JUSMAG), South (0 2287 0942-4 ext 22/www.goethe.de/bangkok). Lumphini MRT. **Open** *Cultural office* 9am-6pm Mon-Fri. **Map** p251 H7.
This charming villa-style cultural and language centre screens German films outdoors (Wed 7.30pm, Dec-Feb, with English subtitles, free), hosts the Science Film Festival (Nov, prices vary) at other locations and sponsors outside events. The wooden balconies host exhibitions and Bangkok Poetry readings (schedule on www.bangkokpoetry.com).

House

3rd floor, UMG Cinema, Royal City Avenue, Thanon Rama IX, North-east (0 2641 5177-8/www.house rama.com). **Tickets** B100. **Screens** 2. **No credit cards. Map** p252 M4.
Comfy and modern, Bangkok's first art-house cinema offers niche and festival films (its top grosser was a Taiwanese gay movie).

Lido Multiplex

Thanon Rama I, facing Siam Center, Pathumwan (0 2252 6498/www.apexsiam-square.com). Siam BTS. **Tickets** B100, earliest screening on Sat & Sun B80 **Screens** 3. **No credit cards. Map** p249/p250 F4.
Host of the Little Big Film Festival, Lido lacks good seating or soundproofing, but shows progressive World film. Owners Apex also run two old cinemas flanking Lido: the tatty Siam and stunning art deco Scala, which still has hand-painted posters.
Other locations: Scala, Siam Square Soi 1, Pathumwan (0 2251 2861/Tickets B100-120/Screens 1). Siam, Thanon Rama I, Pathumwan (0 2251 1735).

National Film Archive of Thailand

93 Thanon Puttha Monthon Sai 5, Outer West (0 2482 2013-5/www.nfat.org). **Open** 8.30am-4.30pm Mon-Fri. **Tickets** free.
This repository hosts free informal screenings of Thai and foreign films (Fri 6pm, Sat 3pm), some subtitled.

Galleries

From spiritual to minimal, from pop to protest, Thai art goes global.

H Gallery. *See p172.*

The major news on the Bangkok arts scene is that the long needed, long delayed **Bangkok Metropolitan Art Museum** is finally due to open in late 2007. However, as this guide went to press, the BMA still hadn't appointed a curator to provide either exhibitions or a permanent collection, so don't hold your breath. Of course, no need can be met in Thailand without it being duplicated by a rival, so the Culture Ministry is building its own contemporary art gallery with an extension to the **Thailand Cultural Centre** (*see p198*).

When these new projects are completed, the calibre of Thailand's galleries will have finally caught up with that of its artists, many of whom have made international splashes, most recently at the Venice Biennale, the New York and Sydney retrospectives of Montien Boonma, and *Bangkok Bangkok* in Barcelona and Brussels. At home, the biennial **Bangkok International Art Festival** (next held in February/March 2009) provides another focus on Thailand's rapidly diversifying art.

MURALS, MORALS AND MALLS

New ideas and individualism are weaning Thai art from revered templates – whether Thai tradition or Western modernism. Historically, most Thai painting and sculpture conveyed religious messages in temples, where mostly anonymous artisans emulated their masters. Students still hail Silpa Bhirasri (born Corrado Ferroci) as the father of Thai modern art. An Italian sculptor commissioned to cast monumental bronzes, Bhirasri founded the country's first art school in 1943, which became Silpakorn University, and enabled a generation of artists to flower before the reactionary dictatorships took hold. Hierarchy persists in official titles like National Artist for revered masters, joined in 2004 by the Silpathorn Award for mid-career achievement, which was won in 2006 by Chatchai Puipia, who's known for conflicted self-portraits.

The first Silpathorn Award-winner, Chalermchai Kositphiphat, shows how Thai spiritual modernism developed out of murals. In turn he has reinvigorated temple art, including painting the murals at Wat Buddhapadipa in Wimbledon, London, with luminaries Panya Vijinthanasarn and Sompop Budtarad. National Artist Chakraphan Posyakrit also returned to murals; *see p71* **Wat Tri Thosathep**. Spiritual modernism takes other forms too:

Pratuang Emjaroen merges Buddhist cosmology into surrealist abstractions; Tawatchai Somkong's brushwork wields raw energy; and the flamboyant Thawan Dutchanee evokes a shamanistic oriental Bosch. Others like Montien Boonma have used materials such as clay, seeds, handmade paper and gold leaf to convey earthier values. Many artists portray ordinary life with a social conscience, such as Chalood Ninsamer, Damrong Wong-uparaj and Maitree Parahom. Montree Toemsombat startled the 2003 Venice Biennale by meditating with Thai calligraphy covering his body.

Conceptual art about pop culture has also gained Thais acclaim abroad. Nawin Rawanchaikul's installations in taxis and *tuktuks* have starred in Japan and Europe; Rirkrit Tiravanija wows New York and Berlin with event-like art inspired by everyday Thainess; and Surasi Kusolwong's installations of the mundane include a show about consumerism at Tate Modern.

Some Thai artists deliberately break rather than tease conventions, cultivating a bohemian appearance and voicing protests. Photographer Manit Sriwanichpoom stages 'Pink Man' compositions in traditional contexts to critique consumerism, while Chumphon Apisuk of Concrete House (57/60 Thanon Tivanon, Nonthaburi, North, 0 2526 8311) organises the radical Asian performance art festival **Asiatopia** in Chiang Mai, which takes place every other November.

Exhibition spaces

The best places to see Thai art, as with Thai antiques, are mostly private. There is a lack of arts endowments and little public art, although the new art museum projects offer hope and private collections dot the suburbs, at **UCOM**, the **Jean-Michel Beurdeley Collection**, **Misiem's Sculpture Garden** and **Bangkok Sculpture Centre** (for all, *see p101* **New bronze age**). Modern masterworks also fill the **Peninsula Hotel** (*see p41*), and **Benjasiri Park** (*see p96*) has some sculpture. Recent art is largely absent from the **National Gallery** collection (*see p63*), although the **Queen's Gallery** (*see p69*) hangs Bangkok Bank's prestigious annual contest canvases. For four decades the **Goethe Institute** (*see p168*) has supported nearly every major Thai artist, a role now championed by the **Alliance Française** (*see p168*), and perhaps soon by the state. The biggest collection is online at www.rama9art.org, which has a forum, galleries and a 50-year archive.

Dedicated to Queen Sirikit ,**Queen's Gallery** hosts world-class exhibitions. *See p69.*

Curate expectations

When Thailand's most globally celebrated artist, Rirkrit Tiravanija, opened a Bangkok base at **Gallery Ver** (*see p172*) in 2006, it was emblematic of the zeitgeist that its exhibitions should be curated by Pratchaya Pinthong, one of Thailand's young 'third generation' of curators. Also a conceptual artist, Pratchaya was himself selected for a 2006 exhibition at the **Queen's Gallery** (*see p69*) by two further young curators: Manuporn Luengaram, who had worked at the legendary hive of creativity, About Café, and Australian academic David Teh.

Another About Café alumnus, Thanavi Chotpradit, has meanwhile built credibility at **100 Tonson** (*see p172*), hosting global names here and presenting Thai artists abroad, and Goldsmiths graduate Ark Fongsamut showcases fresh talent annually in Brand New at **Bangkok University Gallery** (BUG; *see p99*) and at the French-sponsored festival **La Fête** (*see p162*).

Like Teh, two expat curators earned their spurs here as critics. British writer/artist Steven Pettifor – author of *Flavours: Thai Contemporary Art*, an essential profile of current luminaries – has managed shows for **H Gallery** (*see p172*) and **Bed Supperclub** (*see p191*). Fellow columnist Josef Ng, a censured performance artist at home in Singapore, is adding Thai talents to the Chinese roster of Beijing's Tang Contemporary Art via its Bangkok branch, **Tang Gallery** (*see p172*).

Bangkok's previous curatorial wave began in 1997, led by three women who had graduated overseas. Klaomas Yipintsoi founded About Café, which now exhibits her grandmother's art, while she conserves **Marukhathaiyawan Palace** in Hua Hin (*see p211*). Lukana Kunavichayanond managed Tadu Contemporary Art before starting the M)phosis fashion brand. Gridthiya Gaweewong established the alternative Project 304, then curated in international ventures such as the ongoing Saigon Art Festival (with Rirkrit). In 2007 she became art director of the **Jim Thompson Center for the Arts** (*see p97* **The silk root**).

The new curators are open to collaboration, although earning the trust of some artists takes time in this seniority culture. But they can be sure that it's worth persevering: pioneer curator two decades ago, Apinan Poshyananda – author of *Modern Art in Thailand* – now has the rank to persuade government to support contemporary art, and public museums where curators can exhibit it.

In a culture that fosters compliments, it takes daring to be a critic like Thanom Chaphakdee, a lecturer and member of performance art collective Ukabat, which is notorious for protest art. Curating is also a challenging new field here, but infused with new experimentation (*see above* **Curate expectations**).

Friday newspapers and *BK* (weekly), plus Bangkok 101 and the free map *Art Connection* (monthly) list openings and review shows.

Commercial galleries

The showing of art in social spaces has taken hold since the late 1990s, when it was pioneered by art bars on Thanon Phra Arthit and **H Gallery**, which hung art in hairdressers, car showrooms and restaurants like **Eat Me!** (*see p115*). Many bars, hotels, eateries and malls hang art, among them **Playground!** (*see p144*), **Pla Dib** (*see p127*) and **Dick's Café** (*see p176*). Photography gets exposure at **Hu'u** bar (*see p135*), **Phranakorn Bar** (*see p130*), **Gallery F-Stop** (*see p127* **Tamarind Café**) and, for photo-journalism, the **Foreign**

Correspondents Club of Thailand (0 2652 0580-1, www.fccthai.com). Shop-like galleries and framers with mixed stock are found along Sukhumvit, between Sois 3 and 55. Admission is free to the following spaces.

Carpediem Galleries
Ruam Rudi Building, 1-1B Soi Ruam Rudi, Pathumwan (0 2250 0408/www.carpediemgallery. com). Ploenchit BTS. **Open** 10.30am-6pm Mon-Sat. **Credit** AmEx, DC, MC, V. **Map** p251 H5.
Singaporean Delia Oakins presents South-east Asian artists, including Symon and Krijono of Indonesia, Martin Loh of Singapore and Thai Thawun Pramarn, plus Italian Luigi Rincicotti.

Gallery 55
2nd floor, Alma Link Building, 25 Soi Chidlom, Pathumwan (0 2655 2588/www.gallery55s.com). Chidlom BTS. **Open** 10am-6pm Mon-Sat. **No credit cards. Map** p251 H4.
Ferdie H Ju has moved his Bangkok gallery again after also becoming a major dealer in Shanghai. He promotes Chinese artists who sublimate traditional Chinese aesthetics into original expression, counter-ing the sensationalism of China's pop art industry.

Gallery Ver

2nd floor, 71/31-35 Khlong San Plaza, Thanon Charoen Nakorn, Thonburi (0 2861 0933/www. verver.info). **Open** noon-7pm Wed-Sun. **No credit cards**. **Map** p251 H4.

Named for the Thai slang for 'severe' (from the English 'over'), this breezy riverside space is the new home base for Rirkrit Tiravanija, a world-renowned process artist of everyday life, and one of few Asians in Tate Modern's great artists mural. His text-free magazine (with CD commentary) carries the same name. Pivotal Thai art figures attend the openings for the multimedia shows and installations, which are typically curated by artist Pratchaya Phinthong.

H Gallery

201 Sathorn Soi 12, South (08 1310 4428/www. hgallerybkk.com). **Open** noon-6pm Thur-Sat; by appointment Mon-Wed, Sun. **Credit** MC, V. **Map** p250 E7.

US dealer H Earnest Lee helped foster a young new market for emerging Thai artists through hip openings in this converted wooden house, at other venues and in New York. Look out for Thaweesak 'Lolay' Srithongdee (perverse pop characters), Top Changtrakul (cartoonesque mindscapes), Jakkai Siributr (fabric art), Jaruwat Boonwaedlom (fragmented photo-realism), Somnuek Huangtanapan (abstractions of cultural symbols), Pomm Jitpratuk (filigree figurative paintings) and minimalist abstract master Somboon Hormthienthong. Photo p169.

HOF Art

244, 108 Vibhavadi Rangsit Soi 16/32, North (0 2690 1347-8/www.hof-art.net). Access via soi between exits of Ratchadaphisek MRT. **Open** 10.30am-6pm Tue-Sat. **Credit** MC, V.

An heir to About Café's former art/clubbing combo, this four-floor, rough 'n' ready hub of 'highly optimistic and friendly modern art' offers art classes and workshops, art residency rooms and a roof terrace, where parties with DJs and live music attract *dek sur* (artsy types). Shows veer from pop and abstract painting to light and sound art.
Other locations: Third Place, Thonglor Soi 10, Sukhumvit Soi 55, Sukhumvit (0 2714 7929).

Kathmandu Photo Gallery

87 Thanon Pan, Bangrak (0 2234 6700). Surasak BTS. **Open** 11am-7pm Tue-Sun. **Credit** MC, V. **Map** p250 E7.

Photographer Manit Srivanichpoom and artist filmmaker Ing K have refurbished a shophouse facing the Hindu temple into a retro haven for artful lenswork. Above the cosy, mint-green shop-gallery, which stocks South Asian crafts and books on photography and philosophy, nestle the photography gallery and a rooftop sanctuary.

Numthong Gallery

Room 109, 1129/29 Bangkok Co-op Housing Building, opposite Samsen Station, Thanon Toeddamri, Dusit (0 2243 4326). **Open** 11am-6pm Mon-Sat. **No credit cards**.

Numthong Tang champions artistic individuality with a magnificent roster of works by modern masters like Natee Utarit, Niti Wuttuya, Chatchai Puipia, Kamin Lertchaiprasert and Montien Boonma.

100 Tonson

100 Soi Tonson, Pathumwan (0 2684 1527/ www.100tonsongallery.com). Chidlom BTS. **Open** 11am-7pm Thur-Sun. **Credit** MC, V. **Map** p251 H5.

Canny curatorship makes this converted modernist house a showcase for many leading local folk such as Thaiwijit, Chatchai Puipia and Sutee Kunavichayanont, expat Thais like New York-based Richard Tsao, and global names including Damien Hirst and Louise Bourgeois.

Surapon Gallery

1st floor, Tisco Tower, Thanon Sathorn North, Bangrak (0 2638 0033-4). **Open** 11am-6pm Tue-Sat. **Credit** AmEx, MC, V. **Map** p251 G7.

Selecting exquisite works (with prices to match) for this fine two-storey space, Surapon focuses on prominent painters of Thai subjects (notably dance and Buddhism), such as Prasong Luemuang, Itthipol Thangchalok and Surasit Saokhong.

Tang Gallery

Unit B-28, Silom Galleria, 919/1 Thanon Silom, Bangrak (0 2630 1114 ext 0/www.tang contemporary.com). Surasak BTS. **Open** 11am-7pm Mon-Sat. **Credit** AmEx, DC, MC, V. **Map** p250 E7.

This large space in a mall of arts and antiques puts the spotlight on big-ticket Chinese artists, plus Thai and other Asian artists and photographers such as Manit Srivanichpoom. Opulent opening bashes too.

Thavibu Gallery

Suite 308, 3rd floor, Silom Galleria, Thanon Silom, Bangrak (0 2266 5454/www.thavibu.com). Surasak BTS. **Open** 11am-7pm Tue-Sat; noon-6pm Sun. **Credit** AmEx, MC, V. **Map** p250 E7.

Thailand's first online gallery also hangs exhibitions by established and aspiring artists from the lands featured in its name (THAiland, VIetnam, BUrma – and Laos).

Auctions

Art auctioneering came to Thailand with the sell-offs after the 1997 crash via **Christie's** (0 2652 1097, www.christies.com), which sometimes gets out the gavel for paintings, watches, jewellery and ceramics. Specialising in Thai works, **Bangkok Art Auction** (0 2652 1393-4, www.bangkokartauction.com) started in March 2006 and will auction every November. The **Riverside Auction House** of River City mall (*see p142*) shows East Asian antique lots for a week before the monthly auctions (1.30-4pm 1st Sat). **Sotheby's** (0 2286 0788-9, www.sothebys.com) sources Thai art and jewellery for trading abroad, occasionally auctioning here.

Gay & Lesbian

The city of 'angels in disguise' is pink, proud and playful.

Although it was only in 2006 that the TAT finally started promoting Thailand as Asia's most gay-friendly hub, for a long time tolerance has been earning the country 'pink *baht*' with a natural ease that at least partly justifies its 'gay paradise' label. Foreigners enjoy the liberty, yet most Thais who fancy their own gender remain closeted. Still, despite a prudish social elite heavily schooled by Christians, many gays and *tom-dees* (tomboy and femme lesbians; *see p174* **How-dee!**) manage to rise to high rank.

SIAM WHAT I AM

Thai tolerance derives from Buddhist karma and from sexuality being seen as private. Families 'know but don't talk about it', although Sino-Thai gays hide it more and can be forced to marry. Homophobic violence is unheard of and outing someone loses face for the 'outer', not the gay. Historically, the 'third sex' was accepted for feminine *kathoey* (ladyboys) as *nang faa chamlaeng* (angels in disguise), while many so-called 'real men' got wed and discreetly paid 'money boys' or kept *kathoey*. Since the early 1990s a flexible '*gay*' identity has visibly emerged, spanning disco bunnies, muscled guppies and artsy divas. Most 'money

boys' are straights earning a living, although many masseurs are gay. Predatory 'professional boyfriends' get support from lovers abroad, but some Thais simply prefer a Western partner, usually an older man, and the freedoms that may bring. *Tom-dee* couples often pet overtly, although lesbian nightlife only went public in 2006 (*see p174* **How-dee!**).

Every year sees gay parades in Bangkok (November; *see p163*), Phuket (February, www.gaypatong.com; *see p219*) and Pattaya (November/December, www.pattayagayfestival.com; *see p208*), the latter two endorsed by politicians. Nor is the public shy about cheering them, since *kathoey* have always been fixtures in village fairs, TV soaps and movies (notably *Iron Ladies*, *Beautiful Boxer* and *Saving Private Tootsie*). Dancer/author Pakorn Pimton founded **Bangkok Gay Festival** (www.bangkokgay festival.com) in 1999 in protest at raids on bars and saunas, and a short-lived ban on gays on TV. It has since been eclipsed by a rival parade from a wider coalition of volunteer, business and academic groups, **Bangkok Pride Week** (www.bangkokpride.org; *see p163*), during which the **Utopia Awards** (www.utopia-asia.com) honour queer pioneers.

Arts & Entertainment

How-dee!

In a city where gays and ladyboys are so visible, lesbians finally went public in 2006, joining the Bangkok Pride parade (*see p163*), cheering the all-dyke band Mister Sister and opening not just one but two women-only venues, **Shela** (*see p175*) and **Zeta** (*see p176*). Previously, they'd socialised at discrete lesbian-owned pubs or the large socials still run every Saturday by **Lesla** (*see p230*), which has a centre, library and bilingual website. In fact, the advocacy group **Anjaree** (08 6677 9009, www.anjaree.net) had long championed both lesbian and gay rights before any male organisations, while **Sapaan.org** holds discussion groups in Thai – so it was about time that the city's sapphic scene was publicly acknowleged.

Around Downtown, you'll also spot many a crop-haired *tom* (butch) in masculine attire demonstratively clutching her glamorous *dee* (femme, from 'la-dy'). The slang labels reflect the defined roles of Thai lesbian identity, as documented by sociologists such as Megan Sinnott (in her book *Toms and Dees*). Echoing the bygone *kathoey*/'real man' duality, a *tom* typically drinks, dresses and joshes laddishly, often protectively out of largely unfounded concern that her *dee* might defect to a man. But now, with such a supportive scene, why would she?

TIPS AND MEMBERS

Out venues have exploded since the mid 1980s and cruising permeates malls, streets and parks. The original focus of Thanon Silom (Bangrak), where Soi 2 is all-gay and Soi 4 ever more so, has diffused. Trendy queens have recently colonised nearby Soi Sarasin (Pathumwan), while more exuberant suburbanites make the east end of Thanon Kamphaengphet's bar strip (North) a fun detour. Less affluent, less affected locals and students flock to the discos and karaokes of Trok Sake (Phra Nakorn) and distant Thanon Ramkhamhaeng (East, especially at Lamsalee area, Soi 89/2), where decor, cabarets and beauty contests have a folkier flair. Opulent saunas, massage parlours and male spas proliferate. Early bar closing sparks a late-night migration to after-hours bars (follow the drift) or uninhibited saunas around Lad Prao, Ramkhamhaeng and Sutthisarn. For clubwear, Silom night market stocks disco gear; for camp costuming, trawl **Pratunam Market** (*see p136*) and **www.sequinqueen.com**.

Host, go-go and massage venues gather around Thanon Surawong (in Bangrak), at Soi Tawan and Soi Duangthawee Plaza, while the Thai-style 'boy bars' of Saphan Kwai (North) have declined. Freelance prostitutes hang out by Saranrom Park, western Lumphini Park and Robinson's at Silom, without the health checks that host bars enforce.

The pioneering gateway **www.utopiaasia. com** gives events, insights, listings for gays and lesbians, and **www.dreadedned.com** has listings and forums. Among the free monthly bilingual listings magazines are *Gay Max* and its *Guide Line* map, or the clearer *Bangkok Variety* and its *Gay Guide Bangkok* map (downloadable at **www.gayguidebkk. com**). **Bookazine** (*see p143*) stocks international gay books and magazines, notably the savvy *The Men of Thailand* and the language book/tape *Thai for Gay Tourists*.

Among memberships, **Long Yang Club** (*see p230*) is the Thai chapter of the international group for Asian gays and their admirers, and the upscale network **www.gyent.com** holds frequent parties and trips; **www.Fridae.com** says it will stop its Phuket dance parties.

Most hotels are gay-friendly, specifically **Tarntawan Place** (*see p45*), **Babylon Barracks** (*see p176*) and **Malaysia** (*see p52*). Specialist tour firms include **Gay Booking Tour** (0 2932 5177, www.gay. bookingtour.com), **Gay Guide in Thailand** (0 5936 9409, www.gayguideinthailand.com), **Kinnara Tours** (0 2671 3863, www.kinnara tours.com/gay), **Oriental Escape** (0 2883 1219, www.orientalescape.com) and **Lesbian**

Adventures Thailand (08 9886 9317/08 9501 5306, www.lathailand.com); some offer tailored tours including shopping, food and nightlife.

Venues listed in this chapter do not charge for admission unless otherwise stated.

Bars

Balcony

86-88 Silom Soi 4, Bangrak (0 2235 5891/www. balconypub.com). Saladaeng BTS/Silom MRT. **Open** 6pm-1am daily. **Credit** AmEx, MC, V. **Map** p250 F7. People-watching terraces spread out from this popular rendezvous. It's cheap and cheerful, with happy hour prize draws and ultra-familiar staff, plus chalkboards in the loos for scrawling profundities.

The Expresso

8/6-8 Silom Soi 2, Bangrak (0 2632 7223/0 2234 6151). Saladaeng BTS/Silom MRT. **Open** 9pm-2am daily. **No credit cards. Map** p250 F7. A 'lounge' with people-watching windows and a soothing water wall, which turns into a flamboyant club, where the cabaret ladyboys migrate from DJ Station to resume their oneupwomanship banter.

JJ Park & Club Café

8/3 Silom Soi 2, Bangrak (0 2235 1227). Saladaeng BTS/Silom MRT. **Open** 10.30pm-1am daily. **Credit** AmEx, MC, V. **Map** p250 F7. A show gay bar with loyal customers, JJ is warm and chatty, with nightly singers (real and lip-sync) and comics. Upstairs it connects via nooks to Club Café, a Moorish chill-out bar with under-floor water.

70s Bar

231/16 Thanon Sarasin, Pathumwan (0 2253 4433). Ratchadamri BTS. **Open** 6pm-1am daily. **Credit** AmEx, DC, MC, V. **Map** p251 G6. Dressy young Thai gays have taken over this packed retro bar. Many spill out to other newly gay bars on this long-standing strip, such as the trendier Room or more frolicsome Kluenzak, above which At Barber, a daytime hairdresser's, has a nightly bar and roof terrace overlooking Lumphini Park.

Shela

106/12-13 Soi Lang Suan, Pathumwan (0 2254 6463). Chitlom BTS. **Open** 8pm-2am daily. **Credit** AmEx, MC, V. **Map** p251 G6. This curtained pub for *phuying rak phuying* (women who love women) attracts mainly thirtysomething professionals. Bar stools, pool tables and red booths surround a stage where female-led bands play Thai love songs, with comic relief from a ladyboy singer.

Telephone Pub

114/11-13 Silom Soi 4, Bangrak (0 2234 3279/ www.telephonepub.com). Saladaeng BTS/Silom MRT. **Open** 6pm-2am daily. **Credit** AmEx, DC, MC, V. **Map** p250 F7. Fun and flirty, this was Bangkok's first Western-style gay bar. It still fills with pretties, expats and tourists. Phones enable cross-room dialling.

Watch or be watched at **Balcony**.

Clubs

Bed Supperclub (*see p191*) runs the **Think Pink** gay night party on Sundays (show 11.45pm-midnight), while **www.gyent.com** holds roving party nights, as does the glam-indie **Rehab** (www.rehabisfab.com), run by Thai-Brit electroclash band Futon.

DJ Station

Silom Soi 2, Thanon Silom, Bangrak (0 2266 4029/www.dj-station.com). Saladaeng BTS/Silom MRT. **Open** 10pm-2am daily. **Admission** B200 incl 2 drinks. **No credit cards. Map** p250 F7. Despite extending via a bridge across Soi 2, all three floors heave with Thais and *farang* of all ages and tastes; it's more commercial the higher up you go. Costume parties mark several festivals. A less crowded option is the same owner's Disco Disco (DD) dance bar opposite.

GOD (Guys on Display)

60/18-21 Silom Soi 2/1, Bangrak (0 2632 8033). Saladaeng BTS/Silom MRT. **Open** 9pm-5am daily. *Shows* midnight-12.30am daily. **Admission** B120 before 1am (incl 1 drink); B240 after 1am (incl 2 drinks). **No credit cards. Map** p250 E7. Replacing Freeman's fab former cabaret, this three-storey club attracts post-DJ Station partiers with edgier dance tracks. Keep an eye on your valuables in the top-floor darkroom.

Arts & Entertainment

Mogue

362-363 Thanon Kamphaengphet, North (0 2618 6681). Kamphaengphet MRT. **Open** 8pm-1am daily. **Admission** free before 10pm; B100 Fri, Sat after 10pm (incl 1 drink). **No credit cards.**

The most throbbing joint of this now mostly gay bar strip – dubbed 'OrTorGor' after the nearby food market – barely contains the enthusiasm of unaffected young Thai crowds (with a few foreigners). Steps lead from the balcony on to the bartop, where cabaret artistes sashay and giggly lads jiggle.

Saké Coffee Pub

Soi Damnoen Klang Tai, Thanon Ratchadamnoen, Phra Nakorn (0 2225 6000). **Open** 8pm-1am daily. **Credit** AmEx, DC, MC, V. **Map** p248 C3.

Here, less affluent youths fuelled by Thai whisky and hormones bop to a bewildering succession of Thai and Western hits and hoot at the saucy cabaret.

Zeta

29/67-69 Royal City Avenue, North-east (0 2203 0994/www.zetabangkok.com). **Open** 7pm-1.30am daily. **Credit** MC, V. **Map** p252 L4.

Zeta reflects RCA's young weekend crowds, but only lets in women. Vast prints of female figures along the mezzanine set the tone, while cute waitresses serve *toms* and *dees* dancing around whisky tables to Thai/Western pop from the all-girl band and DJ.

Restaurants & galleries

Eateries citywide are gay-friendly, especially **Café Siam** (*see p128*), **Eat Me!** (*see p115*) and **Thang Long** (*see p120*), while decor queens adore outlets in the **Metropolitan** and **Sukhothai** hotels (for both, *see p51*).

Art at Play

114/5 Silom Soi 4, Bangrak (08 1812 0133/ www.artatplay.com). Saladaeng BTS/Silom MRT. **Open** 6pm-midnight daily. **Credit** AmEx, MC, V. **Map** p250 F7.

Artist/bodypainter Neung's gallery of abstract and homoerotic paintings provides a calm respite amid a strip of gay bars.

Coffee Society

12/3 Thanon Silom (0 2235 9784/www.coffeesociety. co.th). Saladaeng BTS/Silom MRT. **Open** 24hrs daily. **Main courses** B150. **Credit** MC, V. **Map** p250 F6.

With cosy wooden nooks, internet access and a people-watching patio, this café acts as a pre- and post-club rendezvous-cum-retreat. It was featured in the film *Love 101*, and stocks many Thai gay movies like *Silom Soi 2*. Nearby Bug & Bee serves exactly the same purpose.

Dick's Café

894/7-8 Soi Pratuchai, Thanon Silom, Bangrak (0 2637 0078/www.dickscafe.com). Saladaeng BTS/Silom MRT. **Open** 11.30am-1am daily. **Main courses** B170. **Credit** MC, V. **Map** p250 F7.

Survey the eye-popping cavalcade in this traffic-free, tout-ridden *soi* of go-go-boy bars from this courteous enclave of a bar-restaurant. Its design accents come from the movie *Casablanca* and male-inspired paintings from Art at Play.

L-Zub Zip

674 Lad Phrao Soi 101, North-east (08 1734 2759/08 1926 4624). **Open** 6pm-2am daily. **Main courses** B90. **Credit** V.

Gregarious host P'Wan welcomes all genders to L-Zub Zip ('L' for lesbian, Zub Zip for 'gossip'), a bar-restaurant favoured by *tom-dee* regulars for homely Thai fare and 'live karaoke'. The feel is convivial, despite the limited drinks list and bright lighting.

Sphinx & Pharaoh's

Silom Soi 4, Bangrak (0 2234 7249/www.sphinx pub.com). Saladaeng BTS/Silom MRT. **Open** 6pm-1am daily. **Main courses** B140-B275. **Credit** AmEx, DC, MC, V. **Map** p250 F7.

This comfy, intimate bar-restaurant serves the scene's best food (Thai and international); Pharaoh's upstairs is a cosy karaoke lounge.

Saunas & fitness

Babylon & Babylon Barracks

34 Soi Nantha, Sathorn Soi 1, South (0 2679 7984-5/www.babylonbangkok.com). Lumphini MRT. **Open** noon-midnight daily. **Admission** B230 Mon-Fri; B260 Sat, Sun. **Credit** MC, V. **Map** p251 G7.

Perhaps the world's most opulent gay sauna, with a gym, pool, garden bars, restaurants (with jazz on Sundays), mazes, cabaret, periodic foam parties and a hotel (Babylon Barracks; rooms B1,600-B4,500).

Chakran

Soi Aree 4 Tai, Phahon Yothin Soi 7, North (0 2279 1359/5310/www.aboutg.net/chakran). Aree BTS. **Open** 3pm-midnight Mon-Thur; 2pm-midnight Fri-Sun. **Admission** B230 Mon-Thur; B250 Fri-Sun. **No credit cards.**

Meaning 'unquenched warrior desire', this sauna features shadow-play showers and intimate perches around the pool, rooms and restaurant. Favoured by 'sticky rice' (Asians who love Asians), it's run by the V Club massage parlour nearby.

Muffil Sauna

Lad Phrao Soi 113, North-east (0 2734 0536). **Open** 5pm-morning daily. **Admission** B99 Mon-Thur, Sun; B140 Fri, Sat. **No credit cards.**

An expansive new sauna down a quiet suburban *soi*, with imaginative nooks, mazes and pulsating lamps.

Sauna Mania

35/2 Soi Pipat 2, Thanon Convent, Silom (0 1817 4073/www.thailandout.com). **Open** 5pm-midnight Mon-Thur; 3pm-midnight Fri, Sun; 3pm-6am Sat. **Admission** B100 Mon, Tue; B140 Wed-Sun. **No credit cards. Map** p250 F7.

A clean, minimalist, mostly Asian sauna with themed nights of varied – or no – attire.

Mind & Body

Asia's spa capital pampers, purges and massages you till you swoon.

A decade ago Siamese herbal medicine (*ya samoon prai*) faced oblivion, marginalised by pharmaceutical monopolies and the government imposition of conventional medicine. But the crash of 1997 renewed interest in all things indigenous. Thailand soon became the holistic capital of South-east Asia and the state founded the **Institute of Thai Traditional Medicine** (0 2965 9683, www.ttmdf.com). Bangkok now boasts an unrivalled breadth of high-quality spas, massage houses and healing centres, from budget to chic, urban to resort. Siam's escape from colonisation had left intact such indigenous practices as acupressure, massage, herbal steam, herbal baths, tonics, infusions and meditation. *Ya samoon prai* stems from Ayurvedic teachings brought from India by Buddhist missionary monks during the second and third centuries BC, and integrated with Chinese systems, folk remedies and shamanism. Hence the spiritual element that spas often revive (or exploit) in their design, therapies and marketing. Chinese influence includes acupuncturists and public sessions in parks of *qi gong* and t'ai chi. Many hotels, gyms and spas offer yoga, *chi kung* or Pilates.

STANDARDS AND ETIQUETTE

Companies, spas and collectives tout herbal beauty and body treatments; some, such as **Harnn & Thann** (*see p151*), have become global brands. Meanwhile, there are efforts to standardise the labelling of ingredients and efficacy of remedies sold in markets and shops in places such as Phra Chan and Chinatown.

Licences stipulate whether massage (*see p180*) is healing, pampering or something naughtier. Although spas politely deploy towels and disposable briefs, even at many 'respectable' parlours hands have been known to explore. Remember to point out any medical conditions before undergoing a treatment.

For further listings and explanations, read *Thailand's Luxury Spas* by Chamsai Jotisalikorn.

Holistic wellness

The top of **Erawan** mall (*see p141*) harbours high-tech body therapies, while the **Life Center** mall (*see p153*) focuses on health. *See also p230* **Complementary medicine** *and p225* **Health tourism**.

Bahlavi Natural Health Centre

191-193 Soi Ranong 1, Thanon Rama VI, North (0 2615 8822/www.balavi.com). **Open** *Clinic* 8.30am-8pm Mon, Wed, Fri; 8.30am-5pm Tue, Thur, Sat, Sun. *Fitness* 8.30am-8pm daily. **Credit** MC, V.

English-speaking Dr Banchob offers colonic irrigation and five-day fasts, supervised by doctors, alongside Thai massage, body treatments, *chi kong* (10.30am-noon Saturday) and hydro-aerobics (6-7pm Wednesday, Thursday, Saturday, Sunday) in a homely, inexpensive traditional compound.

Bodhi & Holistic Medical Centre

20th floor, 253 Building, 253 Sukhumvit Soi 21, Sukhumvit (0 2640 8090/www.thebodhi.com/ www.hmcthai.com). Asoke BTS/Sukhumvit MRT. **Open** 10am-9pm daily. **Credit** AmEx, MC, V. **Map** p252 K5.

High-tech diagnostics and workouts at the Bodhi emphasise body-styling using Vacumassage, Hypoxi training and flotation tanks. The HMC seeks holistic rebalancing through blood, telemetric, free radical or food intolerance testing, with treatments ranging from chelation to airnegy, plus colonics and nutri-medicine. Check-up packages are available (from B4,500). The space-age environs are soothing too.

Other locations: The Bodhi, 4th floor, Erawan, 494 Thanon Ratchadamri, Pathumwan (0 2250 7882); HMC, 8th floor, CRC Tower, All Seasons Place, Thanon Witthayu, Pathumwan (0 2654 3936).

HydroHealth

4th floor, Erawan, 494 Thanon Ratchadamri, Pathumwan (0 2250 7800/www.hydrohealth.co.th). Chidlom BTS. **Open** 10am-8pm daily. **Credit** AmEx, DC, MC, V. **Map** p251 G5.

Originally founded in Hong Kong, the region's leading colonics centre packages well-reputed, hyperclean irrigations via machine with infrared detoxifying sauna and lymphatic drainage massage, all in sleek surroundings.

Mor Parinya Ya Thai

9 Thanon Maharat, Phra Nakorn (0 2222 1555). Tha Phra Chan. **Open** 8am-7pm daily. **No credit cards.** **Map** p248 B4.

Housed in a typical old apothecary, this outlet offers Thai and Chinese herb preparations, plus Thai, herbal, acupressure and reflexology massages. The recipes for aphrodisiac, herb and alcohol *ya dong* are real knee-tremblers.

Other locations: 4 Thanon Maharat, Phra Nakorn (0 2221 8756); 655/13 Thanon Bangkok-Nonthaburi, North (0 2585 4312).

Suite retreats

From offering massage simply as a holiday add-on, Bangkok's hotels led the way in creating destination spas, where therapies are integrated into your stay – and even into your diet. The concept of the 'holistic retreat' was pioneered by **Chiva Som** on the coast at Hua Hin (*see p211*), while at its urban equivalent, **Baan Thai Wellness Retreat** (*see p47*), many of the suites (situated in old teak houses) feature a dedicated treatment room for the daily massages – which are included in your room rates.

Bigger hotel spas simulate that sense of remoteness through otherworldly layouts, ritualistic procedures, VIP-standard pampering and exotic treatments – and rarely for less than B2,000 per therapy. Beyond the exquisite packaging and breathless prose, their (often own-brand) lotions and potions are invariably made using organic ingredients. Many mix Thai components such as lemongrass, rice bran and white clay with pan-Asian herbs in scrubs and muds.

Baan Thai.

CHi Spa.

Rasayana Retreat & Restaurant

57 Soi Prommitr, Sukhumvit Soi 39, Sukhumvit (0 2662 4803-5/www.rasayanaretreat.com). Thonglor BTS then taxi. **Open** 9am-9pm daily. **Credit** AmEx, DC, MC, V. **Map** p252 L6.

This quiet detox centre is modern with Chinese touches. Having alkalised your diet, you'd typically start on the low-stress, high-modesty colonic irrigation machine, with organic replenishments. Finish at the garden café, which serves juices and raw food cuisine (the pasta, sushi and pizza are a delicious revelation). Dining only is fine, and it also does delivery. Cleansing/fasting programmes include emotional support, with hypnotherapy counselling for those purging addictions. Pilates classes are also offered.

S Art & Science MedicalSpa

Ground floor, Bhakdi Building, 2/2 Thanon Witthayu, Pathumwan (0 2253 1010/www.smedspa.com). Ploenchit BTS. **Open** 10am-10pm daily. *Clinic* 10am-8pm daily. **Credit** AmEx, DC, MC, V. **Map** p251 H4.

Holistic purifications (one hour to three days), colonics and hydrobath massage at this detox centre and clinic. Also massage, facials and body wraps, plus yoga, reiki, Pilates and Ayurvedic options.

Spas

See also *p178* **Suite retreats** *and p50* **Suk11 Guesthouse**, the best guesthouse spa.

Arima Onsen

37/10-14 Soi Surawong Plaza, Thanon Surawong, Bangrak (0 2235 2142-3). Saladaeng BTS/Silom MRT. **Open** 9am-1am daily. **No credit cards**. **Map** p250 F6.

Reflexology, *akasuri* body rubs, Thai massage and Nipponese-style communal showers, steam room and baths, plus VIP rooms and hair/nail care. **Other locations:** 62/10-14 Soi Thaniya, Thanon Silom, Bangrak (0 2234 1777-8).

The latest trend is to offer therapies from abroad – Balinese massage; shiatsu from Japan; Tibetan hot stone massage, Indian Ayurveda and myriad Chinese healing systems; these themes are often reflected in the decor. Bangkok's first purpose-built Ayurvedic refuge recently opened above the stately, house-style **Oriental Spa** (0 2659 0444, 9am-10pm daily). The city's original hotel spa, it requires a boat trip from the Oriental (*see p45*). Hotel guests get priority, so non-guests must book.

i.sawan Residential Spa

The **Banyan Tree**'s spa (*see p50*, 9am-10pm daily) affords amazing skyscraper views. A long, luxurious menu of packages combines Thai, Swedish and Balinese massages, petal-strewn baths and in-house fusion treatments.

The Shangri-La chain's name inspired its Himalayan-themed **CHI Spa** (*see p45*, 1pm-midnight daily). Spa suites feature herbal steam facilities and pulsating hydrobaths. The multi-therapy treatments ('journeys') utilise incense, colour and sound therapy, even Tibetan singing bowls.

Remarkably cosy and sensual given the Metropolitan's minimalist decor (*see p51*), the **Como Shambhala Urban Escape** (8.30am-9.30pm daily, www.comoshambhala.bz) excels at unfussy treatments and beautifications, including steam and hydrobath. The Metropolitan Bath starts with dry brushing and a salt scrub, and ends with a juice from the health restaurant, Glow. Booking essential.

Named after the Thai heaven, the Elysian villas of **i.sawan Residential Spa** at the top of the Four Seasons (*see p46*) deliver sensory rapture to honeymooners, burnt-out execs and visitors (9am-10pm daily). Despite the indulgences (iPod, tea corner), i.sawan's themed packages emphasise results.

Located in a neo-colonial annex of the Peninsula (*see p41*) and run by ESPA, the **Peninsula Spa** (9am-5pm daily) raises the bar with details such as adjustable beds with iPod access, and proper menus. Never has health improvement felt (or tasted) so good.

Divana Massage & Spa

7 Sukhumvit Soi 25, Sukhumvit (0 2661 6784-5/ www.divanaspa.com). Asoke BTS/Sukhumvit MRT. **Open** 11am-11pm Mon-Fri; 10am-11pm Sat, Sun. **Credit** AmEx, DC, MC, V. **Map** p252 M5.

A homely domain in a lush garden, Divana features ceramic jar showers and proper beds with pillows. Geared to couples and families, it emphasises pampering, with scrubs, mud wraps, massages, steams, facials and milky baths. While the ultra-modesty is a comfort to many, it can just miss out on the deep thoroughness wanted by some spa aficionados. **Other locations**: Divana Divine Spa, 103 Thonglor Soi 17, Sukhumvit (0 2712 8986); Divana Nurture Spa, 8 Sukhumvit Soi 35, Sukhumvit (0 2261 4818-9).

Palm Herbal Retreat

522/2 Thonglor Soi 16, Sukhumvit Soi 55, Sukhumvit (0 2391 3254/www.palmherbalspa.co.th). Thonglor BTS. **Open** 10am-10pm daily. **Credit** AmEx, DC, MC, V. **Map** p252 M6.

At this pleasant spa, you may be greeted by the thumping of a mortar and pestle grinding fresh herbs for the natural therapy preparations provided. Aside from traditional body treatments, it offers Thai, Swedish and aromatherapy massage.

Sareerarom Tropical Spa & Prana Yoga

117 Thonglor Soi 10, Sukhumvit Soi 55, Sukhumvit (0 2391 9919/www.sareerarom.com). Thonglor BTS. **Open** 10am-10pm daily. **Credit** AmEx, DC, MC, V. **Map** p252 M6.

Tucked quietly away in a calming water garden, Sareerarom's lounging pavilions, villa-like rooms and suites exude a pared-down Asian chic. The experienced masseuses combine Balinese, Swedish and Thai strokes, using imported essential oils. A tea house brews leaves from across Asia. Prana Yoga runs athletic classes in Baron Baptiste-style Vinyasa yoga here and at All Seasons Place.

Arts & Entertainment

Other locations: Prana Yoga, 801, 8th floor, CRC Tower, All Seasons Place, 87 Thanon Witthayu, Pathumwan (0 2685 3775).

Massage

Traditional Thai massage (*see p180* **A knead to relax**) is found in temples such as **Wat Pho** (*see p66*), which also teaches the art in English. Parlours proliferate in tourist areas, including **Surawong Plaza** on Thanon Surawong, and (cheaper) **Banglamphu**. Tip generously as most masseurs earn meagre piece rates.

Foundation for Employment of the Blind

2218/86 Thanon Chan, South (0 2678 0763-8/www. fepblind.ksc.net.th). Tha Sathorn (Saphan Taksin). **Open** 9am-8pm daily. **No credit cards.**
Furthering careers for the sightless, whose touch skills are revered, this centre offers massage (traditional and herbal) and reflexology.
Other locations: 597/152 Yudee Soi 4, Thanon Chan, South (0 2689 9699).

Health Land

Thanon Sathorn Nua Soi 12, Bangrak (0 2637 8883/ www.healthlandspa.com). Surasak BTS. **Open** 9am-11pm daily. **Credit** MC, V. **Map** p250 E7.
In a great-value centre crowded with Thais, Health Land extended an old mansion to provide effective, no-nonsense Thai massage on three floors of pleasant cubicles (or group rooms with TV). Other floors offer reflexology, aromatherapy, tourmaline sauna, facials, a juice bar and Ayurvedic therapy (at a bargain B300 per hour), all well explained. Supplements include herbal compresses and a Vichy shower.

Other locations: 96/1 Sukhumvit Soi 63, Thanon Sukhumvit, Sukhumvit (0 2392 2233); 142/6 Thanon Charansanitwong, Thonburi (0 2882 4888); 70/21 Thanon Srinakarin, East (0 2748 8135-9).

Nicolie Asian Massage Centre

Sun Square, 1041/5 Thanon Silom, Bangrak (0 2233 6957/www.nicolie-th.com) Surasak BTS. **Open** 10.30am-10pm daily. **Credit** AmEx, MC, V. **Map** p250 E7.
This impressive parlour set in a townhouse (with lots of stairs) offers two pan-Asian approaches to the body: in massages, and in its exquisite antiques collection. Massages include Thai, shiatsu, Chinese *tui na* and Ayurvedic, with Balinese elements in the signature blend. Executed with care, the treatments range from realignment to lymphatic drainage.

Pian

108/15-16 Thanon Khao San, Banglamphu (0 2629 0924). **Open** 8am-midnight daily. **No credit cards.** **Map** p248 B3.
Intense competition keeps prices low and quality high in Banglamphu's cramped open parlours, of which Pian is the best. Men and women give reflexology, traditional and herbal massage, as well as (rather public) Swedish oil massages.
Other locations: Nancy, 98 Soi Chanasongkram, Thanon Phra Arthit, Banglamphu (0 2280 7594).

Ruen Nuad

2nd floor, 42 Thanon Convent, Bangrak (0 2632 2663). Saladaeng BTS/Silom MRT. **Open** 10am-9pm daily. **Credit** MC, V. **Map** p250 F7.
This picturesque wooden house (at the rear of a restaurant complex) provides Thai, aromatherapy and herbal massages, with classy attention to detail.

A knead to relax

Nearly every visitor to Bangkok gets a massage. For a healing *nuad paen boran* – an ancient massage to relieve aches, tension or fever – look for signs saying 'massage for health' or 'traditional massage', often depicting the body's meridian lines or foot reflexology points. At parlours signed simply *nuad* (massage), nubile numbered masseuses do their job naked, save for oil and make-up. The notice 'massage by men for men' implies something similar.

Traditional practitioners tend to be female, although most parlours employ men too, sometimes blind, since they are believed to have the most intuitive touch. Unlike Swedish, shiatsu or Balinese styles, Thai massage doesn't use oils (although spas combine techniques using aromatherapy). The Central and gentler Northern Thai styles

both use yoga-like stretches and acupressure along energy meridian lines, applied using thumbs, arms, elbows, knees or feet.

Lying face up in pyjamas, you first get a foot scrub and lengthy leg work. Tell them about any pains or weaknesses. Those with heart problems should ask not to have their blood paused at the armpits and groin (the idea being to flush out stagnant veins). For diagnostic expertise, ask for an *ajahn* (teacher). Feedback helps, even if it's just *jeb* ('it hurts'), *baobao* ('softer') or *jakkajee* ('it tickles').

A session should last 90 to 120 minutes and, despite occasional pain, relax you into a snooze. Aches may temporarily appear later where tension was released. Like other therapies, it detoxifies tissues, a purge helped by the herbal tea served at the end.

Thann Sanctuary

*5th floor, Siam Discovery, Thanon Rama I,
Pathumwan (0 2658 0550/www.thann.info/
www.harrn.com). Siam BTS.* **Open** 10am-9pm daily.
Credit AmEx, DC, MC, V. **Map** p249/p250 F4.
These micro-parlours reflect the brand styles of
Thann (contemporary Asian) and Harnn (herbal
apothecary). As well as facials and body cleansers,
the massages include Ayurvedic, Swedish, Thai aromatic and a deeply concentrated Black & White
Onyx Stone Massage.
Other locations: Harnn, 4th floor, Siam Paragon,
Pathumwan (0 2610 9715).

Wat Pho

*2 Thanon Sanamchai, Phra Nakorn (0 2225 4771/
www.watpomassage.com). Tha Tian.* **Open** 8.30am-
6pm daily. **No credit cards. Map** p248 B4.
Thailand's most famous massage and reflexology
school. Massages in open-air *salas* inside the *wat's*
Sanamchai gate are in public view. Murals illustrating the Bangkok massage technique and statues
of athletic *ruessi dutton* yogis were nominated in
2007 for 'UNESCO Memory of the World' protection.
Other locations: Course registration, 392/25-28
Penphat Soi 1, Thanon Maharat, Phra Nakorn (0 2221
3686); Chetawan Thai Traditional Massage School, 3rd
floor, Sailom Building, Chaengwattana Soi 15, Outer
North (0 2962 7338-40).

Meditation

Visitors can learn *vipassana* (insight meditation)
in Bangkok, although the calm surroundings of
a rural retreat can make initial change easier
to achieve. The influential monk Buddhadasa
Bhikku founded International Dhamma
Hermitage at **Wat Suan Mokkh** (Highway 41,
Chaiya, Surat Thani, 0 7743 1596, www.suan
mokkh.org), on the mainland near Ko Samui.
Here, non-religious silent retreats (B1,500, first
ten days of month) have equal space for women.
In Ko Pha-ngan, regular Vipassana retreats at
Wat Kow Tahm Meditation Centre (www.
watkowtahm.org) can be booked via PO Box 18,
Ko Pha-ngan, Surat Thani 84280.

International Buddhist Meditation Centre (IBMC)

*Room 106, Vipassana Section,
Mahachulalongkornrajvidyalaya University,
3 Thanon Maharat, Phra Nakorn (0 2623
6326/www.mcu.ac.th/IBMC/www.vipassanadhura.
com).* **Open** 1-8.30pm Mon-Sat. **Map** p248 A4.
The IBMC's English-language classes include meditation (1-4pm, 6-8pm daily), Dhamma talks (second
and fourth Saturday of the month, 3-5pm) and country retreats over weekends or five to seven days.

Wat Mahathat

*3/5 Thanon Maharaj, Phra Nakorn (0 2222
6011/www.section-5.org).* **Open** 7am-8pm daily.
Map p248 A3.

Instruction (in English) can be arranged for meditators staying in or outside the *wat's* crowded dorms.
The routine (6.30am-9pm) includes meals and meditation (7-10am, 1-4pm, 6-8pm daily). Group walking, sitting practice and retreats are also offered.

World Fellowship of Buddhists

*616 Soi Methiniwet, Sukhumvit Soi 24, Sukhumvit
(0 2661 1284-7/www.wfb-hq.org). Phrom Phong
BTS.* **Open** 8.30am-4.30pm Mon-Fri. **Map** p252 K6.
English-speaking monks from Wat Pah Nanachart
give monthly talks on meditation here (2-6pm, first
Sunday of the month).

Yoga

Iyengar Yoga Studio

*3rd floor, Fifty-fifth Plaza, 90 Sukhumvit Soi 55,
Sukhumvit (0 2714 9924/www.iyengar-yoga-
bangkok.com). Thonglor BTS.* **Open** 9am-6pm Mon;
9am-8pm Tue-Thur; 9.30am-5.30pm Sat; 8.30am-1pm
Sun. **No credit cards. Map** p252 M7.
German instructor Justin Herrold commands a loyal
following for his Hatha yoga classes in English.

Yoga Elements Studio

*23rd floor, Vanissa Building, 29 Soi Chidlom,
Pathumwan (0 2655 5671-2/www.yogaelements.
com). Chidlom BTS.* **Open** 7am-9pm Mon-Fri; 9am-
6pm Sat, Sun. *Classes* hourly in Thai & English.
Credit DC, MC, V. **Map** p250 F6.
Thailand's first studio to teach Vinyasa (as well as
Ashtanga and Tibetan styles). Visiting *lamas* and
swamis give monthly workshops.

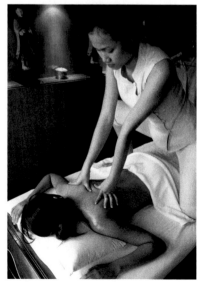

Nicolie Asian Massage Centre. *See p180.*

Arts & Entertainment

Music

Embracing folk, fusions and full-on indie modernity, the sounds of Siam beguile.

Luang Pradit Phairoh Foundation. *See p183.*

Thai music flirts with going *inter* – getting exposure abroad. The Thai Kylie, Tata Young, boasts a pan-Asian fanbase, rocker Sek Loso has strummed at New York and Glastonbury, while recording in English has helped electronica act Futon saunter from Tokyo through Paris to London. Otherwise, Thais sing in their native tongue at poorly-publicised gigs, so visitors perceive no music scene in Bangkok – as they might have concluded in the Seattle of 1990, the London of 1966 or the Soweto of 1980.

In actuality, Thailand lives for *pleng* (songs), which come in many alluring forms. So you can settle for 'Hotel California' on a loop in tourist bars, wait for *morlam* to be appropriated by Messrs Sting, Simon, Byrne and Albarn, or hail a cab: the radio is usually tuned to **Luuk Thung Mahanakorn** (95.0FM, http://radio.mcot.net/fm95). Marvel at the sideways logic of *luuk thung* and *morlam* folk (*see p187*), with its techno beats, brass blasts and worldlywise female raps. Or there is the blind busker's plaintive *khaen* (mouth organ), the hip hop b-boys busting out the breaks to rap act Thaitanium or T-Pop gigs at Centrepoint (*see p184*), or join the masses blowing their end-of-month salary at any bar, pub or beer hall.

Elusive to the uninitiated, gigs get limited listings in English in newspapers or magazines. Check online at **www.bangkokgigguide.com** or MySpace (*see p194* **One Nighter in Bangkok** for pages to link from). **Pattaya Music Festival** every March (contact the **TAT** for info; *see p235*) has mushroomed into the country's greatest music jamboree of all styles; the smaller **Bangkok Music Festival** (Nov 2006) may or may not recur. Gigs by big-name international acts are, however, generally still fairly sparse.

Admission to listed venues is free unless otherwise stated, and most serve low-priced Thai food. First, 'Bangkok's Moulin Rouge', where every form of Thai musical variety act takes the stage:

Tawandang German Brewhouse

*462/61 Thanon Narathiwat Ratchanakharin,
at Thanon Rama III, South (0 2678 1114-6/
www.tawandang1999.com).* **Open** 4.30pm-1am
daily. **Shows** *Fong Nam music* 7pm-1am, *shows*
9-10.30pm Mon-Sat. **Bands** 6pm-1am Sun.
Credit MC, V.

The melting pot of all Thai music styles – *pleng
puer cheewit, luuk thung, morlam, phiphat* and
cheesy covers – can all be caught in the mind of
only one man: Bruce Gaston. A 1970s New York
avant-gardist, this US composer joined and went
on to lead the premier *phiphat* ensemble, Fong Nam
('bubbles'). He transcribed the complete Thai canon
into both Thai and Western notation, and com-
posed fusions so good he became a household
name, with official commissions.

Since 1999, he's gigged (Mon-Sat) at this 1,600-
diner *rong beer* (microbrewery) under a barrel-
shaped dome serving Thai and German fare with
yard-tall tabletop kegs. Each night's extravaganzas
draw from a repertoire of fireworks, dancing girls,
film, shadow puppets, ladyboys, godzilla, old Thai
ballads, Elvis, jazz pieces by the King, riffs from
Herbie Hancock to Led Zep via Carabao, and blasts
of the T-Pop that comes on next. It's Sgt Hanuman's
Lonely Hearts Club *phiphat wong* and he wants you
all to sing along. On Sunday three bands play covers. At the branch, a similar format (7pm-midnight
daily) features Chinese acrobats (8-9pm).
Other locations: 51/199-200 Ramintra Soi 34,
North-east (02 944 5131-2).

Classical

Thai *phiphat*

Hearing a *phiphat wong* (Thai classical
orchestra) is a fascinating experience but
hard to find other than as tourist dance
accompaniment (*see right* **Gong show**).
Recitals of varying quality occur (rarely) at
the **Thailand Cultural Centre** (*see p195*),
National Theatre (5-7pm Sat, Sun, Dec-Apr,
B20, music emphasis on Sat, with dance on Sun;
see p198) or **Phyathai Palace** (*see p98*),
often presided over, or participated in, by
royalty. *Phiphat* also plays a part at events
like **Bangkok Theatre Festival** (*see p158*)
and **Naris Day** (*see p161*), and informally at
Santichaiprakarn Park (*see p70*). For its
silver jubilee in 2007, leading *phiphat* ensemble
Fong Nam (*see above* **Tawandang German
Brewhouse**) will mark the 120th anniversary
of Thai-Japanese relations in late Sept with a
show honouring Yukio Mishima and Thai poet
Angkarn Kalyanapong, then a folk opera on
World Aids Day (Dec 1) with AIDS orphans.

Luang Pradit Phairoh Foundation

*47 Thanon Setsiri, Dusit (0 2279 1509,
www.thaikids.com).*

Newcomers are free to hear and join in practice sessions at this *phiphat* school (9am-5pm Sat, Sun)
which holds its *wai khru* ceremony in August.

Western-style orchestral

Paradoxically, there are a lot of well-publicised
Western classical performances – by the
Bangkok Symphony Orchestra (BSO;
0 2255 6617-8, www.bangkoksymphony.org),
multiple chamber groups and visiting
ensembles. The BSO often plays free open-air
concerts in the cool season. Emerging as the
region's leading opera company, **Bangkok**

Gong show

Phiphat (Thai classical music) may
seem dense to the uninitiated, but it
has an accessible pulse, and it can
truly fascinate. The simple motifs don't
move melodically or harmonically, but
simultaneously forward and backward,
building into layers of contrast. However,
beyond the hotel ensembles' standardised
snippets to accompany dancers, there's
still no national *phiphat* orchestra, or even
regular concerts. But break apart those
hotel medleys and you'll be surprised
to find symphony-sized structures.

However, interest has revived thanks
to a hit 2004 movie about rival *ranat*
(gong-rimba) players, *Hom Rong* (*The
Overture*). Set during the mid 20th century
repression of Thai traditions by the Phibun
dictatorship, *Hom Rong* was ironically
used by the government to encourage
the learning of musical instruments like
the *ranat*, *cha-ke* (three-string banjo),
khlue (flute), *khim* (dulcimer), *ree chava*
(woodwind), *saw sam sei* and *saeng*
(string section), cymbals, gongs and
cymbal-phones. The *ranat* players who
starred in *Hom Rong* are now able to draw
keen audiences to schools like the **Luang
Pradit Phairoh Foundation** (*see left*).
There and in **Santichaiprakarn Park**
(*see p70*) you can hear – and incredibly,
even join – weekend practice sessions.

Though *Phiphat* is hard to meld with
other music, fusions have been achieved
by Boy Thai, Kangsadan and, using
northern instruments, Changsothorn.
The leading fusion act Fong Nam (*see
left* **Tawandang German Brewhouse**)
recorded the entire Thai canon in five
volumes, called *Siamese Classical Music*.

Opera (www.bangkokopera.com; *see p196*) performs European classics and new operas by founder SP Somtow. He also assembled the **Bangkok Sinfonietta** and organises recitals at which the BSO, Meefa Orchestra and Rangsit Philharmonic regularly take the pit at the **Thailand Cultural Centre** (*see p199*). Look out for Somtow's protégé composer/musician Trisdee na Phattalung. Bangkok Music Society (08 1648 7648) performs four concerts per year.

Indie & rock

Siam Square is Bangkok's crossroads of hip, alternative individualism, known as *indie*. Packs of spikey-haired *dek naew* (indie kids) rush into the Japanese CD store at Soi 5, or weave between the coin-op karaoke booths, art spaces and coffee shops to **New DJ Siam** (292/16 Siam Square Soi 4, 0 2251 9066), a hole in the wall that stocks the best CDs of the Thai and international underground. **Centrepoint Plaza** (Siam Sois 3-4, 0 2252 1754-6) even mixes indie into its T-pop gigs.

Aside from the acts recounted in **Dek naew** (see p184), look out for **Goose** (Radiohead-alike experiments), **Apartment Khunpa** (think Black Crowes), **Space Bucha** (free improv with laptop FX), and **Flure** (grunge, then modern rock). The breakout band is

Dek naew

Out of sight of responsible adults and most visitors, *dek naew* (indie kids) revel in No Wave-style noise festivals, weekly punk-a-thons, quirky electro-culture-clash party nights, and a skewed scene of sly lounge acts fronted by shy starlets singing softly below the radar. Bangkok has a wild soundscape. Something big, important and international is brewing.

The ground was laid in 1994 by Bakery, a label almost alone in discovering and developing alternative talent, from Modern Dog (a proto rap-rock quartet) to Orn Aree (a Siamese Sinead meets PJ Harvey), Rik (a black mass enchantress) to Joey Boy (the *rap Thai* pioneer). Exposed to New York as a student, co-founder Kamol 'Suki' Sukosol overcame limited airtime and distribution to deliver extravagant shows, videos and packaging never before seen here.

Then when the baht was devalued in 1997, the generation studying abroad were forced to stay at home and become disgruntled artists. International bands seldom visited or played here. So they were sufficiently resourceful to form their own. Japan fought Britain who fought the USA for influence, and they all won in their own way.

In 2000 the dam burst. Dozens of little labels – Hua Lampong Riddim (with its genius act Photo Sticker Machine), Small Room, Junkfood, Free/Airport, NYU Club, Genie, Lucky Café and Panda – recorded and pressed their artists' CDs. Next, foreign producers got involved: David Coker (ex-Futon), Sean Dinsmore, Dum Dum Project, Yuka Honda (Cibo Matto) and Tony Doogan (Belle & Sebastian) for Modern Dog, the AbbaTeens Swedish team for sultry Kylie-alike Tata Young, and Owen Morris for the English debut of axe hero Sek Loso.

It happened in Seattle, in Osaka, in Sweden. Now it's happening in Bangkok, all but unheard by the non-Thai speaking world. The next Ryuichi or Caetano or Cardigans or even Enya is on the *dek naew* iPod, as may be the next important international rock act. Or at least the next *Ketchup Song*.

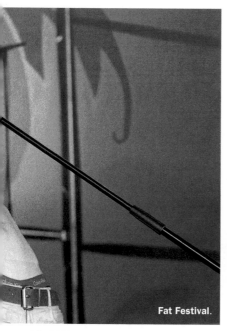

Fat Festival.

Thai/UK/Japanese fusion foursome **Futon** (electroclash meets bastard pop), whose avant-garde **Rehab** parties and album '*Never Mind the Botox*' have got them some serious gigs abroad and the drummer from the Britpop group Suede. An even wilder live act, **Paradox**, deliver Kiss-meets-kitsch showmanship.

Hear them all on **104.5 Fat Radio** (www.thisisclick.com), which runs **Fat Festival** (Nov, *see p158*), while **Demonic** (*see p161*) convenes metal-headz in biennial worship. Another trailblazer, **House of Indies** (0 2664 0399, www.houseofindies.com) still trains DJs, but now focuses on new dance and theatre. Nightclubs host *Rap Thai* MCs, but indie rock still lacks a solid home, relying on venues like **Club Culture** (*see p192*) and roving parties like Dude/Sweet and Chicks Rock (*see p194* **One-nighter in Bangkok**), whose MySpace pages offer links to gigs.

Immortal Bar

1st floor, Bayon Building, 249 Thanon Khao San, Banglamphu (08 1750 0591/www.immortalbar.com). **Open** 6pm-1.30am daily. **Bands** *Reggae* 9.30pm-1.30am Mon, Sun. *Hard rock* 9.30pm-midnight Tue-Thur; *Metal, guest bands* 8-9.30pm Fri. **No credit cards.**
A totemic space as dilapidated and charming as New York's CBGBs or the Garage in London,

Immortal embraces any underground band (send demo) especially rock/punk/speed-metal, reggae, hip hop and drum 'n' bass. The owner, who plays hard rock here (Tue-Thur), runs Demonic metal fest biennially (*see p161*).

Lullabar

Mahannop Soi 1, Phra Nakorn (08 6339 1390/ www.myspace.com/lullabar). **Open** 5pm-1am Tue-Sun. *Band* 10.30pm-midnight Tue-Thur; 9.30pm-midnight Fri-Sat; (no band on Sun). **No credit cards. Map** p248 C3.
Drums occupy a quarter of the room in this tiny venue, at a charmingly weathered wooden house down an old town lane. Sup from the limited menu of beer, spirits and drinking snacks to the rumble of emergent Brit Pop-style rock, punk and indie bands like Desktop Error.

Nang Len

217 Sukhumvit Soi 63, Sukhumvit (0 2711 6564). Ekkamai BTS then taxi. **Open** 6pm-1.30am Mon-Sat. *Bands* 9-10pm, 10.30-11.30pm, midnight-1.30am Mon-Sat. **Credit** MC, V. **Map** p252 M6.
Popular among the university set, Nang Len's dark, polished interiors, ceiling-high tinted glass windows and subdued lighting cram the nubile masses around low drinking tables (the name means 'lounge around'). Three indie/pop cover bands per night are punctuated by MTV-style hip hop DJs. Demands to see original passports.

Arts & Entertainment

Brick Bar.

Cosy regulars' pub where newcomers can jam the blues nightly (except Mondays acoustic and jazz sets). A lively local rather than destination venue.

Bamboo Bar
Oriental Hotel, 48 Charoen Krung Soi 38, Bangrak (0 2236 0400). Saphan Taksin BTS. **Open** 11am-1am Mon-Thur, Sun; 11am-2am Fri, Sat. *Piano & bass* 6-8pm. *Singer* 10pm-1am Mon-Thur; 10am-2am Fri, Sat. **Main courses** B280. **Credit** AmEx, DC, MC, V. **Map** p250 D7.
This snug, low-ceilinged institution is a cool cocktail lounge of 1940s mystique. Despite the long jazz pedigree and fine house band, the US singers have dipped in quality.

Brick Bar
1st floor, Buddy Lodge, 265 Thanon Khao San, Banglamphu (0 2629 4477/www.brickbarkhaosan .com). **Open** 7pm-1am daily. *Bands* 8pm-1am daily (3 bands) **Credit** AmEx, MC, V. **Map** p248 B3.
Resembling a cavernous Chicago speakeasy adorned with vintage blues Americana, this cracking jazz and blues bar hosts a nightly trio of bands (ska, jazz, blues) as cool as the beers, playing to a trendy young crowd who jive around the wooden stools or play pool on the mezzanine. Part of the Buddy Lodge group that dominates Khao San: Buddy Beer lounge, The Club (*see pp190-94* Nightlife), Tom Yum Goong restaurant, Sunset Street/Sanook (open-air café/restaurant) and Sidewalk Café (208 Thanon Khao San, 0 2282 5573), a garden bar at an old house opposite.

Brown Sugar
231/20 Thanon Sarasin, Pathumwan (0 2250 1826). Ratchadamri BTS/ Silom MRT. **Open** 11am-2pm, 5pm-1am Mon-Fri; 5pm-1am Sat-Sun. *Bands* 10pm-1am Mon, Thur, Sun; 8pm-1am Tue-Wed, Fri-Sat. **Credit** AmEx, MC, V. **Map** p251 G6.
An old favourite that retains an earthy, clubby ambience, but is getting shabby. Thai and expat musicians and singers reel out less commercial jazz with often inspired playing, with jams (some Sun), plus a bit of blues (Fri, Sat).

Living Room
1st floor, Sheraton Grande Hotel, 205 Thanon Sukhumvit, Sukhumvit (0 2653 0333, 0 2649 8353). Asoke BTS/Sukhumvit MRT. **Open** 8.30am-12.30am daily *Bands* 9-11.45pm Mon-Thur, Sun; 9.30pm-12.30am Fri, Sat. **Credit** AmEx, DC, MC, V. **Map** p251 J6.
Though not especially intimate, this lounge bar attracts the best jazzmen, notably residencies by genial ex-Ramsey Lewis bassist Eldee Young.

Saxophone Pub & Restaurant
3/8 Thanon Phayathai, south-east side of Victory Monument, North (0 2246 5472/www.saxophonepub .com). Victory Monument BTS. **Open** 6pm-1.30am daily. *Shows* 9pm-1.30am Mon-Wed, Fri-Sun; 7pm-1.30am Thur. **Credit** AmEx, DC, MC, V.
Any night can be fun at this knocked-through, two-storey log and beam sculpture, a kind of trompe l'oeil

Rock Pub
Hollywood Street Centre, 93/26 Thanon Phyathai, Pathumwan (0 2251 9980 daytime, 08 6977 0621/ www.therockpub-bangkok.com). Ratchatewi BTS. **Open** 7pm-2am daily. *Bands* 9.30-11.30pm, midnight-2am daily **No credit cards**.
Map p249 & p250 F3.
Entering via the mouth of an Angkor version of the talking tree from *The Wizard of Oz*, Bangkok's heavy metal devotees shake their heads to local bands expertly riffing on standards, from Scorpions to Judas Priest.

Jazz & blues

Jazz holds a special place in Thailand due to King Bhumibol being both an accomplished composer and saxophonist. He has played with legends such as Benny Goodman and Duke Ellington, and still jams with jazz luminaries visiting for concerts. Jazz festivals happen in Bangkok somewhere around the time of his 5 December birthday, and also every June near his palace in **Hua Hin** (*see p211*). Jazz also features in hotel lobby lounges, notably the **Diplomat Bar** (*see p133*).

Ad Here The 13th
13 Thanon Samsen (opposite Samsen Soi 2), Banglumphu (08 9769 4613). **Open** 6pm-midnight daily. *Acoustic* 8.30-9.30pm Wed, Sat. *Bands* 9.30pm-midnight daily. **No credit cards**. **Map** 248 C2.

hunting lodge. The regulars lay down roots, rock, reggae, jazz and blues, and are all competent-to-great. And the sound system excels – a rarity. But Friday belongs to T-Bone. All husky rasp and flapping dreads, Gop leads the band seamlessly from ska to samba over to reggae up to *tropicalista* and around to Senegal stomp. JRP Little Big Band does Latin/jazz standards (Wed 9-11pm).

Luuk grung (T-Pop)

Thai multimedia giants Grammy and RS Promotions have built a T-Pop duopoly of songwriters, musicians, producers, manufacturers, retailers and radio/TV/movie outlets. Many of their *luuk grung* ('city kids') popstars are exotically pale *luuk khrung* (half-*farang*). Grammy reluctantly accepted that, amid the cookie-cutter pop-fluff, wonderful aberrations could emerge. For every Nicole, Kathariya, Nat or Mai, there's now a Palmy, the Australian-raised Belgian-Thai hippie chick; or a Panadda, who's all poetry and pathos; or a Bua Choompoo, akin to Japan's Hikaru Utada. Amita 'Tata' Young also seized the liberty to shift from puppy-love Barbie doll to hip hop vamp emulating Kylie/Britney. Attracting

Brown Sugar. *See p186.*

Culture Ministry censure for her pan-Asian hit 'Sexy, Naughty, Bitchy', Tata polarises Thais, yet millions of people around Asia evidently love her funky hits.

Led by part-Cliff, part-Elton, part-Bowie perennial Thongchai 'Bird' McIntyre, the boys of T-Pop aren't as important or as liberated as the girls, but occasionally acts do break out. A blend of Bon Jovi and U2, Sek of Loso (as opposed to jet-setting *hi-so*) flips from edgy ballads to rocking protests.

Hollywood & Hollywood Awards

72/1 Thanon Ratchadaphisek Sois 8, North-east (0 2246 4311-3). Thailand Cultural Centre MRT. **Open** 9pm-2am daily. **Bands** 10pm-midnight; midnight-2am daily. **Credit** AmEx, DC, MC, V.
T-Pop penetrates everywhere, but for live renditions join the teenyboppers in Hollywood's two halls and their near-identical neighbour Dance Fever, all seemingly held together by neon. Each can hold 2,000 crisply dressed fans indulging in full force *sanuk*: laughing, drinking, flirting, dancing and singing in unison.

Luuk thung & morlam

You may choose to miss reggae in Bangkok, but would anyone ignore reggae in Kingston? Samba in Rio? Blues in Chicago? *Luuk thung* or *morlam* in Bangkok? A plaintive country music, *luuk thung* ('child of the rice field') conquered the capital in the late 1980s, mostly through its own Patsy Cline, **Phomphuang Duangjian** (who died, aged 31, in 1992). She blew the style wide open with her perfect pitch (emotional and musical), encyclopaedic memory of every song she'd ever heard (she was illiterate) and her showmanship. *Luuk thung* gigs took on the spectacle of Superbowl shows, with dancing girls, orchestras and a cavalcade of co-stars.

Attention grew after the crash of 1997, with a heady flow of one-hit-wonder waiters and 'real people'. At temple fairs and hard-to-find venues (like weekends at **Rama IX Plaza**, *see p199*; or **Saphaa Din**, *see p188*), hit-makers Lam Yai, Joy Apaporn, Pamela or the blond Jonas or Kristy may appear, even the divas Jintara or Siriporn. A Thai Dolly Parton, **Jintara Poonlap** is the sassy singer with a tiger's purr, a kitten's growl and a heartbreaker's shattered heart just looking for some relief. Like Aretha's soul or Loretta Lynn's country, **Siriporn Amphaipong** has a sandpaper sob that is sorrowful, desperate, and eloquent.

Siriporn sings *morlam* (literally, 'doctor dance'), an ancient folk music of Isaan that began as devotional music, the way soul began as gospel. The wildest ride is *likay*-style *morlam*, which starts with a chanted rap over church-organ chords on *khaen* (bamboo mouth

Arts & Entertainment

Grammy: legends of T-Pop. *See p187.*

organ). A flurry of guitar arpeggios announces the *phra ek* (lead actor/singer) in glittery costume and make-up, who croons sweet plaintive hits. Yours will be the only dry eye – unless you speak Lao. All *morlam* is sung in that North-east dialect, but singers flip into Central Thai, since the genre has somewhat merged with *luuk thuung*. Countering each *phra ek* with witty, catchy half-rap, half-torch tunes come the flirty ladyboys (*kathoey*) and taunting female lead (*nang ek*), dressed as if for the Miss Khorat Pageant. She seems to love the guy until unleashing the best, most accusatory use of the universal syllables of disgust 'eee-uuu'.

Khrua Yaa Jai
15/8 Lad Phrao Soi 71, North-east (0 2542 4147). **Open** 4pm-12.30am daily. *Shows* 8pm-12.30am daily. **Credit** DC, MC, V.
Folk star Mike Piromporn owns this *luuk thung* and *pleng puer cheewit* ('songs for life'), named 'Kitchen of Medicine for the Heart' after his hit album.

Isaan Tawandaeng
484 Thanon Pattanakarn, east of Khlong Tan intersection, East (0 2717 2320-3). **Open** 6pm-1.30am daily. *Shows* 8pm-1.30am daily; Concert every Thur 11.30pm-1am. **Credit** AmEx, MC, V.
There's a diverse roster of *morlam/luuk thung* (daily), from dancing girl revues to formation crooners in Day-Glo tuxedoes, at this comfortable venue. It has branches that (from 8pm nightly) offer *pleng puer cheewit* bands instead.
Other locations: Baan Mai Daeng Saad Saengduean, 24 Yasoob Soi 2, Thanon Wiphawadi Rangsit, North (0 2691 5346-7); Tawandaeng Saad Saengduean, 50/261 Thanon Kaset-Naowamin, North-east (0 2510 5027-28).

Pleng puer cheewit

Meaning 'songs for life', *pleng puer cheewit* is the bluesy, radical folk rock of the 1970s. Its 1980s second wave boasts a mega-star in Ad Carabao (*see p189* **Ad then multiply**), and the 2006 anti-Thaksin protests anointed a third wave led by aristo Hugo Chakrabongse of **Siplor** (Ten-wheel Truck). With a loyal 'October generation' following, Thailand's countless *pleng puer cheewit* clubs often resemble the set for *Rawhide*, complete with log walls, wagon wheels, apache headdresses and buffalo skulls stuffed with fairylights. Most start with acoustic balladeers around 8pm; some merge into US country and western venues. Food is fiery Isaan, beer is cheap and whisky is sold by the bottle. A bill for four may cost under B1,000. Also check the branches of **Isaan Tawandaeng** (*see above*).

Raintree Pub & Restaurant
116/64 Soi Rang Nam, Thanon Phayathai, North (0 2245 7230). Victory Monument BTS. **Open** 6pm-1am daily. *Shows* 8.30pm-1am daily. **Credit** MC, V.
Despite the country and western motifs, this stalwart feels more like a little blues bar with *pleng puer cheewit* sets nightly.

Saphaa Din
888/2 Soi Sukhalumjiak, Thanon Sukhaphiban 1, North-east (0 2943 8993). **Open** 6pm-1am daily. *Bands* 7pm-1am daily. *Shows* 11pm-1am Fri-Sat (only on special occasions). **Credit** MC, V.
This folk venue (meaning 'Earth Parliament') serves mixed bills of acoustic strumming preceding *pleng puer cheewit* and *luuk thung*.

International & covers

Most local Thai venues reprise rock, pop and country faves with fine home-grown bands. Expect repeated requests for the likes of 'Hotel California'. Tribute acts include several Elvii, Fab Four clones the Better, and a Thai Tom Jones. The last of these plays **Radio City** (*see below*), while **Dicken's Pub** (Ambassador Hotel, Sukhumvit Soi 11, 0 2254 0444) stages Elvis sightings (Tue, Thur-Sat, birthday convention 8 Aug).

Dontree nanachat (global roots music) gets little exposure, though earnest, Thai-singing, American rocker and ethno-pharmacist Todd 'Thongdee' Lavelle holds roots jamborees to bring world peace. A one-band global rhythm tour, T-Bone rule Fridays at **Saxophone Pub** (*see p186*) and frontman Gop also plays percussion elsewhere, as at **Tapas** (*see p194*).

Many hotels proffer shiny disco lounges with US bands spreading funk/pop/hip hop around Asia's expat circuit. Opening with a splash, such clubs lure the yuppies but get *farang*, then draw the freelance artists of the demi-monde, and become – tadaa! – throbbing pick-up joints.

Arabian Night

Ground floor, Grace Hotel, 12 Sukhumvit Soi 3, Sukhumvit (0 2253 0651-75/www.gracehotel.th.com). Nana BTS. **Open** (except Ramadan) midnight-2am daily. *Bands* midnight-2am daily. **Credit** DC, MC, V. **Map** p251 J5.
An awesome Arabic band blasts souk rhythms to back mesmeric singers in a vast, ornate interior. From midnight some nights, bellydancers shimmy on tables under a shower of bank notes.

Hard Rock Café

424/3-6 Siam Square Soi 11, Pathumwan (0 2254 0830/www.hardrockcafe.co.th). Siam BTS. **Open** 11am-1am daily. *Bands* 9.30pm-1am daily. **Main courses** B300. **Credit** AmEx, DC, MC, V. **Map** p249 & p250 F4.
Part of the global formula, with George Harrison dominating its memorabilia and a *tuk-tuk* on the façade. Good, solid pop-rock and American fuel food.

Radio City

76/1-3 Patpong Soi 1, Bangrak (0 2266 4567). Saladaeng BTS/Silom MRT. **Open** 6pm-2am daily. *Band* 10pm-2am. *Shows* 11pm-1am Mon-Sat. (11pm-midnight Elvis; midnight-1am Tom Jones). **Credit** MC, V. **Map** p250 E7.
A change from Patpong's gynaecological shows, Thais impersonate personalities like Elvis and Tom Jones to a high standard. Knicker-throwing is optional. Upstairs is Lucifer disco (*see p193*).

Señor Pico

1st floor, Rembrandt Hotel, 19 Sukhumvit Soi 18, Sukhumvit (0 2261 7100/www.rembrandtbkk.com). Asoke BTS/Sukhumvit MRT. **Open** 7pm-1am daily.

Shows 7.30pm-midnight Tue-Sun. **Main courses** B350. **Credit** AmEx, DC, MC, V. **Map** p252 K6.
The Latin boom has faded, but this Cal-Mex restaurant continues to host good bands from Cuba.

Spasso

1st floor (lower lobby), Grand Hyatt Erawan Hotel, 494 Thanon Ratchadamri, Pathumwan (0 2254 1234). Ratchadamri or Chidlom BTS. **Open** noon-2.30pm, 6.30pm-2am daily. *Band* 10pm-2am daily. **Credit** AmEx, DC, MC, V. **Map** p251 G5.
If you've ever wondered how to get middlebrow diners to bop to black/white US pop-soul showbands, Spasso provides the Bangkok template.

Ad then multiply

Ad Carabao is the most prolific, prodigious and, possibly, profligate musician/artist/ personality in Thailand without question. Slight, humble and fiftyish, he resembles Carlos Santana or Willie Nelson: wispy moustache, stringy hair wrapped in a bandana. Like their forebears and folkier rivals, Caravan, his *pleng puer cheewit* band formed in solidarity with 1970s anti-dictatorship protests. Exiled to the Philippines, and naming the band Carabao (Tagalog slang for 'water buffalo') they learned to rock with a new vengeance. Channelling influences like Nelson and Santana, but also Dylan, Springsteen and not least some 1,000 years of Thai folk, Carabao has cut a dozen classic albums (increasingly in solo projects) – notably *Made in Thailand*, *Welcome to Thailand* and the *Bangrajan* movie score.

But music isn't the half of it. A cultural conscience, he berates materialists, sex tourists and even generals involved in teak smuggling, who he named in a live televised concert. Lest you dismiss him as sanctimonius and puritanical, check out his original odes to toking, rocking, loving and cock fighting.

He's everywhere: acting as a taxi driver on TV; advertising Beer Chang; protesting the nightlife crackdown's damage in song lyrics; launching an energy drink, Carabao Daeng (Red Buffalo); championing Shan independence from Myanmar; and appearing at an anti-piracy rally with the prime minister. What Fela Kuti was to Nigeria, Bob Marley to Jamaica, Caetano Veloso to Brazil, Bono to the MTV nation, Ad Carabao was, and is, to Thailand. But for the language disconnect, he would be an international superstar.

Arts & Entertainment

Nightlife

From cool clubs to go-go bars to one-nighters, Thailand's famed nocturnal scene is thriving.

Almost as soon as the 2006 coup overthrew the prudish Thaksin regime, Bangkok regained some of the legendary nightlife zest he had suppressed. Clubs and authorities started treating the rigorous closing times as elastically as before Thaksin's notorious Social Order Campaign, partying like it was 1999. In short, nothing can stop Thais having a good time. That said, investment in clubs has proved risky: the resilient ones continue to bring in leading world DJs (Claude Challe, Jazzy Jeff, Danny Howells and Louis Vega among others) and maintain Bangkok's credibility as an Asian party hub.

In style, sound, music, drinks and DJs, clubs have improved hugely. DJs first surfaced in Bangkok back in the 1970s, but were soon displaced by a pub scene of seated chit chat, *kup klaem* (drinking snacks) and covers from Filipino bands or karaoke. The economic boom saw outlandish mega-discos, with some unofficial rave venues. When the crash of 1997 came, nightclubbing shifted from hangars holding 2,000 to shophouse dance bars squeezing in 200, with a few chic, mid-sized clubs in between.

The best Nightspots

For intimate vibes
Tapas (*see p194*) and Groove Kitchen at **Ana Garden** (*see p134*).

For the best DJs
Bed Supperclub (*see p191*), **Café Democ** (*see p130*) and **Club Culture** (*see p192*).

For model fabulousness
Escudo (*see p192*), **Bed Supperclub** (*see p191*) and **Koi** (*see p125*).

For partying the local way
Hollywood (*see p192*) and **Santika** (*see p194*).

For neon raving
Hollywood & Hollywood Awards (*see p192*).

At most local clubs revellers jiggle around a forest of tall tables, snacking and topping up their whisky-cokes while DJs talk over pop-dance requests. Downtown playlists are more cutting edge, but mostly hip hop. Among home-spun DJs, a few are liberal rich kids who experienced clubbing abroad; others learn from them or the pioneering expat DJs like Billy V, Christian, Emanuel or the Specialist; some study turntabling at places such as **House of Indies** (*see p185*). Listen out for DJ Spin champions Oatawa and Kolor One, Café Democ graduates Spydamonkee and Dragon, Q Bar alumnus Joeki, Arsit and veteran Seed, a pioneer of Thai indie rock who featured on a Hed Kandi album. Increasingly, clubs focus their music around periodic parties or weekly themed nights (*see p194* **One-nighter in Bangkok**).

ZONING OUT
When Thaksin imposed nightlife zones in 2001, he demarcated only three for this city of ten-plus million people in a windfall for a few landowners. These aren't fairly spread, and coincide with the main strips where businessmen buy sex. The **Patpong** zone includes the original cosmopolitan, part-gay bar strip **Silom Soi 4** and all-gay **Silom Soi 2** (*see p132*). The **Thanon Ratchadaphisek** zone harbours the raucous theme bars of **Ratchada Soi 4** and lo-tech disco barns of **Ratchada Soi 8** (notably **Hollywood**; *see p192*). The **Thanon Phetchaburi** zone is mostly massage parlours, but embraces the **Royal City Avenue** (RCA) clubs.

Other, earlier-closing districts host bar strips, while large discos stud the suburbs, especially along **Thanons Kaset-Nawamin**, **Ramindra** (both in North-east) and **Narathiwat Ratchanakharin** (South). Mysteriously, the responsible, world-class clubs of **Sukhumvit**, especially around Sois Thonglor and Ekamai, don't fall in an official zone.

Tourist resorts get some exemptions, while all-night Full Moon Parties continue at **Ko Pha-ngan** (*see p214*), with minor beach scenes at **Ko Samet** (*see p208*) and **Krabi** (*see p219*).

In the venues listed below, admission is free unless otherwise stated, and most serve food. The majority expect to see government-issued

Bed Supperclub.

picture-ID, and some demand original passports. For bars with DJs, see *pp129-135* **Bars & pubs**; for clubs featuring live bands, see *pp182-83* **Music**.

Adult nightlife

For decades visitors have been ushered – by concierges, guides, sensationalist reportage and tourist publications (including official ones) – to Bangkok's sex-orientated nightlife (*see p193* **Go-go, going… gone?**). Anecdotes, boasts and jokes pump up its 'sexotic' reputation – though the rather unerotic reality suffers from premature expectation.

Go-go bars aimed at Westerners are now being marginalised by more discerning locals and visitors, as well as real-estate pressures on **Patpong** on Silom (*see p91*) and Sukhumvit, where several 'bar-beer' (open-air hostess bar) areas have been cleared; the scene still booms on Sois 21-23 (**Soi Cowboy**), Soi 22 and Soi 3-8 (**Nana**, especially **Nana Entertainment Plaza** at Soi 4).

The Thai- and Asian-orientated sex industry is far larger, but less visible. They tend to favour karaoke bars (Soi Thaniya's are for Japanese only), jazzy cocktail lounges (Sukhumvit Sois 33, 55 and 63), 'no-hands' restaurants (where you are fed and so forth by hosts/hostesses) and massage parlours, notably along Thanons Phetchaburi and Ratchadaphisek. Some members' clubs bask in gratuitous opulence.

The moralistic crackdown initially tamed the sex shows, but many have resumed. Inflated bar bills and doped drinks are rarer now, and many bars post fixed prices. But those exploring the scene should be alert to touts, scams, their valuables and dubious scenarios.

Nightclubs

Many bar-restaurants generate clubbing cred, especially **Bangkok Bar** (*see p130*), **Café Democ** (*see p130*) and Groove Kitchen at **Ana Garden** (*see p134*), while alt scene parties recur at **Pla Dib** (*see p127*) and **At Barber** (*see p194* **One-nighter in Bangkok**).

Hotels continue to open slick nightclubs with varying coolness quotients. The sleek Met Bar opens only to members and guests of the **Metropolitan** (*see p51*), **Syn** draws a hi-so clique to the **Nai Lert Park**, and **87-Plus** nightclub at the Conrad (*see p46*) now mixes DJs with the international live cover band format typified by **Spasso** (*see p189*).

Bed Supperclub

26 Sukhumvit Soi 11, Sukhumvit (0 2651 3537/ www.bedsupperclub.com). Nana BTS. **Open** 7.30pm-1am daily. Set menus B1,350 Mon-Thur, Sun; B1,750 Fri, Sat. **Credit** AmEx, DC, MC, V. **Map** p251 J5.
Evolving far beyond the inspiration of Amsterdam's Bed bar, this brilliantly hip venue keeps on redefining itself via performance art, exhibitions and a stream of world-leading DJs. Divided into restaurant and bar-club, it's an all-white orgy of futuristic flourishes: spacey oval pod architecture, mattresses, low

Arts & Entertainment

lighting, see-through floors and look-at-me stair-cases leading to look-at-you balconies. The cocktails excel and so do the inventive fusion dishes by chef Paul Hutt. As dining winds down, the bar shifts into clubbing mode, with frequent parties and theme nights such as Think Pink for A-gays (Sundays). Strict ID checks.

The Club
123 Thanon Khao San, Banglamphu (0 2226 2910/www.theclubkhaosan.com). **Open** 7pm-1am daily. **Admission** free; concerts from B300. **Credit** MC, V. **Map** p248 B3.
Glow-stick-brandishing backpackers and Thai lovers of house music flock to the rejuvenated, laser-sprayed dancefloor of Khao San's only large night-club. Radiant walls sponsored by drinks brands and enormous visuals help light two dark floors dotted with silver sofas. On Thursday nights DJs recreate the psychedelic vibe of a Full Moon Party.

Club Culture
Thanon Sri Ayutthaya, North (08 1832 2363). Phyathai BTS. Open 9pm-2am Tue-Sun. **No credit cards. Map** p251 G3.
After transforming Bangkok's dance music scene in its former incarnation (Astra on RCA), Club Culture combines a traditional Thai ambience of teak wood carvings and gilded mirrors with a stream of inter-national DJs. Throngs of music lovers in their 20s and 30s come to see the underground house, techno, drum'n'bass and electro acts passing through town.

Escudo & Huh
4th floor, Duchess Plaza, 4/1 Sukhumvit Soi 55 (Soi Thonglor), Sukhumvit (0 2381 0865-6). Thonglor BTS. **Open** 7pm-2am Mon-Thur, Sun; 7pm-3am Fri, Sat. **Credit** AmEx, DC, MC, V. **Map** p252 M5.
On top of Swenson's ice-creamery, Escudo's heav-ing crowds of titivated hi-so Thais collectively bob to mainstream hip hop and R&B, while house music pumps upstairs in Huh. Both interiors are faux-plush, with velvety sofas, chandeliers, renaissance murals and ubiquitous LCD screens. Prices are just as luxurious – typical of the hi-so Thonglor scene – and original passports are a must for foreigners.

Glow
96/4-5 Sukhumvit Soi 23, Sukhumvit (02 261 3007/www.glowbkk.com). Asoke BTS/Sukhumvit MRT. **Open** 6pm-1am daily. **Credit** MC, V. **Map** p252 K5.
Glowing fixtures slowly change colour in this dark lounge club. Mixologists serve the largest pours in town to a mixed clientele. The vodka freezer holds more than 50 imported varieties, while signature cocktails include the Glowpirinha and the powerful Glow Iced Tea. DJs play everything except hip hop.

Hollywood & Hollywood Awards
72/1 Thanon Ratchadaphisek Sois 8, North-east (0 2246 4311-3). Thailand Cultural Centre MRT. **Open** 9pm-2am daily. Bands 10pm-midnight; midnight-2am daily. **Credit** AmEx, DC, MC, V.
These two neighbouring, near-identical disco show halls are seemingly held together by neon. Both fill with youths in street-clothes raving to live *luuk grung* T-pop amid tiny tables piled with whisky mixer sets and chicken knuckles. Oscar statues over-see Awards' cinema-like foyer.

Lava
Basement, Bayon Building, 249 Thanon Khao San, Banglamphu (0 2281 6565). **Open** 8pm-1am daily. **No credit cards. Map** p248 B3.
This basement club changes hands more often than the decor (cement, metallic stools and glass tables). Currently red and true to its name, Lava gets pretty hot, especially when the fug of young locals bobs and paws the air to nightly hip hop. It's sur-prisingly light on backpackers.

Lucifer
3rd floor, Radio City, 76/1-3 Patpong Soi 1, Bangrak (0 2266 4567). Saladaeng BTS/Silom MRT. **Open** 10pm-2am daily. **Admission** B150 (incl 1 drink). **Credit** MC, V. **Map** p250 F6.

Q Bar. *See p193.*

Arts & Entertainment

Go-go, going... gone?

Bangkok boasts an entire genre of novels by foreigners that revel in its – we quote – 'seething underbelly', in which prostitution looms large. Prurient-cum-prudish tabloids and politically correct crusaders paint a rather shrill, West-exploits-East narrative that takes this ribald reputation beyond cliché into caricature. The famously sleazy Patpong has become a parody of itself. Amid the souvenir stalls, touts brandish menus ('Ping-pong show? Throw dart show?') to coach parties of families who come to peek – and perhaps to make themselves feel more righteous.

Spectators fuel sex tourism as much as the libidinous, or the simply lonely buying drinks for 'companions' (who are numbered, as pointing is considered rude). Some pay the 'bar fine' (B200-B500) to take the bar girl/bar boy (for a tip) to a short-time hotel, a weekend in Pattaya, or maybe – many hookers hope – a new life here or abroad. The fantasy can go both ways.

While the flesh trade is too lucrative for the authorities to stop, many Thais bristle at the national loss of face and point to bigger red-light industries abroad. The government now cracks down on sexual expression generally, and to some extent trafficking, in which some girls get sold or deceived into bonded brothels. Official statistics tend to be a tenth of NGO estimates – 200,000 and two million sex workers respectively, of which many thousands are under-aged. Illegal Asian immigrants elude the counts, as do the untold bar girls lost to the tsunami in Patong, Phuket.

Some 60 per cent of Thailand's 11.65 million tourists are male. That surplus of men evidently includes substantial numbers of sex tourists, particularly apparent in Patpong, Patong, Pattaya and the Malaysians' naughty getaway, Had Yai. Yet only about five per cent of prostitutes service Westerners.

For bar-girls in tourist areas, prostitution presents a route to financial and social freedom. The same goes for the several thousand largely straight bar-boys who are 'gay for pay'. Newspapers fret about already affluent students selling themselves to buy luxuries. A procurer-turned-activist in Chiang Mai claims that half the male students he knows do this. Why, he posits, should they prefer turning tricks to flipping burgers? Also, studies suggest that Thais tend to view sex as a private recreational urge less tied to love or morality than Western culture usually asserts.

One in four Thai males admits to buying sex regularly (60 per cent in some surveys). Beliefs that deflowering virgins boosts longevity and libido – and assumptions that young girls are clean of STDs including HIV – are common among Asian men. For many, group massage parlour visits are as conventional in business as golf meetings. Research reveals that some Thai wives find this preferable to husbands taking *mia noi* (minor wives).

But having gone some way in overcoming taboos through family planning and AIDS awareness campaigns, Thailand is gingerly questioning male sexual impunity. Harassment, wife-beating and paternity duties have started to be taken more seriously. In 2002 a Thai senator was prosecuted for sex with three girls below the 'statutory rape' age of 15 (the age of consent is 18).

Society still won't extend male liberties to females, however. Hurrumphing greeted reports of women hiring gigolos, and tales of the teen trend for *gig* (minor boyfriends). Ironically, the rite of passage for males to pay to lose their virginity has declined because of something still deemed immoral: pre-marital sex between sweethearts.

Devil-uniformed attendants welcome you to this satanically decorated disco with diabolically loud trance luring young tourists and expats. Well laid-out and utterly different to the 'Pong's go-go bars, it sits above Radio City and shares owners with Muzzik Café opposite.

Narcissus
112 Sukhumvit Soi 23, Sukhumvit (0 2258 4805). Asoke BTS/Sukhumvit MRT then taxi. **Open** 9pm-2am daily. **Admission** B300 (incl 2 drinks) Mon, Tue, Thur, Sun; B500 (incl 3 drinks) Wed, Fri, Sat. **Credit** AmEx, DC, MC, V. **Map** p252 K5.

Fronted by the pseudo-classical Pegasus hostess club, this temple to kitsch attracts fewer beautiful people, but remains busy thanks to a decade of quality offerings, a tourist-friendly attitude and a fine sound system (house and trance), DJed once a year by Paul Oakenfold.

Q Bar
34 Sukhumvit Soi 11, on sub-soi to Soi 3, Sukhumvit (0 2252 3274/www.qbarbangkok.com). Nana BTS. **Open** 8pm-1am daily. **Admission** B400 (incl 2 drinks) Mon-Thur; B600 (incl 2 drinks) Fri-Sun. **Credit** AmEx, MC, V. **Map** p251 J4.

Opened at the turn of the new millennium and inheriting the worldwide repute of celebrity photographer David Jacobson's original Q Bar Saigon (and co-owner Andrew Clark's trend awareness), this slick, New York-style conversion of a house takes off nightly. Superbly trained (and cute) bartenders mix an astonishing range of imported spirits. Q Bar pioneered themed music nights here (currently reggaeton/bhangra on Mondays, Afro/Latin/percussive house on Tuesdays, hip hop on Wednesdays and Sundays; house on Thursdays to Saturdays) and launched many local DJs, while global legends guest on the decks and hip Thais, expats and visitors take to the dancefloor. Bangkok's first user of vari-colour lighting, the bar's padded walls and organic furnishings lend panache, plus there's a chill-out space, balcony and high-end sushi restaurant Wasabi. **Photo** *p192*.

Santika

235/11 Sukhumvit Soi 63 (between Ekamai Soi 9 & Soi 11), Sukhumvit (0 2711 5887/www.santika club.com). **Open** 7pm-2am daily. **Credit** AmEx, DC, MC, V. **Map** p252 M6.

Now spelled with an S not a Z, this humungous party house teems with young Thais and a sprinkling of expats, all marking their territory in groups. Spiral staircases link tiers of terraces dotted with high tables, offering diverse vantage points. Intermittent live bands cover the hits and the standard drinks are reasonably priced.

Slim & Flix

29/22-32 Block S, Royal City Avenue, Northeast (0 2203 0226-8/08 1645 1177). **Open** 6pm-1.30am daily. **Credit** AmEx, DC, MC, V. **Map** p252 L4.

Book a table in advance if you want one, as the chances of getting one upon arrival are, ahem, slim. Still, if you end up unseated it's more fun to roam the three interconnected zones catering to live Thai rock under chandeliers, hip hop and, in a white area branded Flix, local and imported pop-dance. Black leather sofas and low tables dot the interior, while the outdoor seating area is cordoned off by no-nonsense doormen.

Tapas

114/17 Silom Soi 4, Bangrak (0 2234 4737). Saladaeng BTS/Silom MRT. **Open** 7pm-1am daily. **Admission** B100. **Credit** AmEx, DC, MC, V. **Map** p250 F6.

With its origins dating back to the mid 1990s housing boom, Tapas still keeps regulars happy with its smart blend of intimate house party terrain, people-watching terrace tables and upstairs members' bar. DJs Neng, Wut and Tee spin Latin, deep, funk and house music, often featuring percussionist/MC Noom from T-Bone (11pm-1am Wednesday, Friday and Saturday). As a venue so integral to the lives of a host of media types and beautiful people (both Thai and long-stay *farang*), Tapas remains a place to be seen.

One-nighter in Bangkok

Just as important as knowing Bangkok's premier nightspots is a familiarity with its peripatetic 'one-nighter' parties. The city's clublands focus is shifting from burnt-out superstar DJs and whisky barn hip hop hegemony to special events orchestrated by homegrown talent.

MySpace networkers bring their friends to intimate, scene-building venues such as **Café Democ** (*see* p130), **Pla Dib** (*see* p127), **At Barber** (3rd floor, 297 Thanon Sarasin, Pathumwan, 0 2254 8668) and two venues that are really only vibrant on party nights: Jazzlt at RCA and Polly's Bar in Lang Suan Soi. These provide a sense of community for the creative new club nights notified on flyers, at MySpace, in websites like www.bangkokrecorder.com and via emailing shots by party hosts.

After five years building a loyal clan of young Thai hipsters, Bangkok's original indie night, **Dude/Sweet** (www.dudesweet.org), remains the most popular one-nighter. Every couple of weeks, a thousand-plus *daek naew*

bounce to Brit-pop DJs and the occasional live indie band such as Futon. Its success has inspired a crop of smaller nights, such as **Soma** (www.myspace.com/clubsomabkk), **Happy Alone** (www.myspace.com/happy aloneparty) and the punk-edged **Arcadia** (www.myspace.com/arcadia_bangkok).

Ladies run the show at **Chicks Rock** (www.myspace.com/chicksrockbangkok), where female DJs play sassy chick-only electro and rock. DJs from the **Glitch Organization** offer pure electro at **Videotape** (www.myspace.com/vdovdo), while **Homebass Communications** are a drum'n'bass collective featuring veteran member DJ Dragon.

Anything goes at Gene from Futon's **Whatever!** (www.myspace.com/whatever bangkok), where 'cheese is gold'. Meanwhile, the ironically titled **Club Professionals** (www.myspace.com/clubprofessionals) hands the turntables over to the people – proof if it were ever needed, that 'everyone's a DJ these days'.

Performing Arts

Choose carefully and be rewarded with memorable spectacles.

In a land where dance-drama embodies sacred and royal rites, performers often face dilemmas about how to develop their arts. Half a century ago the state froze the development of Thai dance, imposed a titled hierarchy of virtuoso National Artists, and began to scold innovators who didn't follow their templates (see *p198* **Dramas about drama**). As a result, many dancers and audiences alike have abandoned traditional forms in favour of foreign modes, from ashen Butoh minimalism to gowned Martha Graham histrionics. Physical theatre and mime are other imports that are being interpreted by cash-strapped local companies.

Ironically, the official template doesn't shy away from glitzy modernisation, so long as it conforms to its vision of Thainess. You see the stereotypical result at dinner theatres (see *p199*), the **Siam Niramit** tourist spectacle (see *p98*), and the higher-quality *khon* at **Sala Chalermkrung** (*see p198*). Unfortunately, amid all the special effects, the actual dancing can be lacklustre.

On the artiste's level, however, dance retains its magic. In the most classical form, *khon*, performers must undergo years of codified training, whereas pure wit may suffice for a *talok* (comedy) star. To this day Thai thespians believe they must succumb to their characters' spirit. Before every show, from grand *lakhon* to fairground *likay*, cast and crew convene for a *wai khru* rite to honour their masters. Even boxing matches begin with a balletic routine. Performance is also an everyday offering at the **Erawan Shrine** (see *p98* **Shop and pray**), **Lak Muang** (see *p63*), major funerals that stage *khon*, and processions for weddings, ordinations and festivals.

Companies & theatres

Seeing a great Thai dance performance is down to serendipity. Lack of publicity and poor scheduling, especially by national institutions, deprive Thai performance of potential audiences. Tourists have to rely on luck or insider knowledge to see an authentic performance but it's possible – at elite gatherings, festivals or temple fairs.

Plays are an import championed by King Rama VI, who acted and built theatres at palaces including **Phyathai** (*see p98*),

Mareukathayawan in Hua Hin (*see p211*) and **Sanam Chan** in Nakhon Pathom (*see p105*). Today companies like Crescent Moon, Moradok Mai and Theatre Box stage original plays and revivals of foreign works in Thai on socially challenging topics.

Thai and expat amateurs at the **Bangkok Community Theatre** (www.bct-th.org) put together creditable plays and musicals in English every quarter, and meet on the first Thursday of every month at the **British Club** (see *p91*). The mainly *farang* **Bangkok Poetry** (www.bangkokpoetry.com) draws a hip crowd to sociable poetry slams at the **Goethe Institut** (see *p168*).

The **Thailand Cultural Centre** has been the default stage for ballet, opera, musicals and the annual **International Festival of Music & Dance** (*see p162*), but faces competition

Dancers at the **Erawan Shrine**. *See p98.*

Arts & Entertainment

Dancing with gods

Thai traditional performance involves variations on a theme. That theme is sacred devotion. Before each show, participants conduct a *wai khru* – making offerings and prayers to their teachers, past masters and relevant deities.

KHON

This intricate and venerated genre, originally performed only for royalty, remains rare. Highly trained masked performers dance the *Ramakien*, the Thai take on India's *Ramayana*. In this colour-coded epic, the hero, Prince Rama of Ayodhya (green),

retrieves his abducted wife Sita from the ten-faced demon king Totsakan (red; gold when romantic). Rama enlists help from his brother Laksana (yellow), his adopted son Ongkot (blue), the monkey king Sangkhip (orange) and Hanuman (white), the prankish monkey general. A full rendition of its myriad episodes takes weeks, so today you see only abridgements or pivotal episodes.

From early childhood dancers undergo codified training, their role determined mostly by body type. Character traits include warlike 'lifts', Totsakan's jolting jumps and Hanuman's gymnastics and monkey twitch. Choreographic symbolism, elaborate costumes and live music eliminate the need for stage design, though official shows attempt to update it with sets and lasers. By contrast, top ballet and contemporary dancer Peeramon Chomthavat founded a hyper-authentic troupe. Named Aporn Ngam ('beautiful costume') after the Rama IV-era outfits he meticulously embroiders, they dance internationally and at **Bangkok Theatre Festival** (*see p158*) and **Origin Cultural Programs** (*see p56*). There's a *Khon* Museum at **Suan Pakkard Palace** (*see p98*).

LAKHON

Lakhon (drama) has two main threads. *Lakhon nok* typically features Jataka tales (Buddha's past lives), with rousing action and melodramatic plots. The more refined court recital, *lakhon nai*, belongs to the inner royal sanctum. One certain staging is at **Naris Day** (*see p161*). In meticulously tuned choreography that emphasises

from the upcoming Broadway-standard theatre, **Siam Opera**, due to open in early 2008 (*see p154* **Siam Paragon**). Almost all theatrical forms appear at the **Bangkok Theatre Festival** (see *p158*).

TICKETS

Thai TicketMaster (0 2262 3456, www.thai ticketmaster.com) sells tickets to major shows, as well as popular music and sports events.

Bangkok Opera

232/14-16, Moo Baan Ruamjit, Sukhumvit 22, Sukhumvit (0 2663 3236-7/www.bangkokopera.com). **Tickets** B500-B5,000. **Credit** MC, V.
Thailand's first Western opera company was founded by Somtow Sucharitkul, an Eton-schooled bon vivant avant-gardist who spent 15 years living

in Los Angeles as the screenwriter and science fiction novelist SP Somtow. He penned the *Mahajanaka Symphony*, based on the king's translation of this Buddhist scripture, then the first Thai opera, *Madana* (2000), adapting a Hindu folk legend and his ghost opera *Mae Nak*. Then came a new ending for Puccini's *Turandot*, the Ramayana-based *Ayodhya*, and his karmic Wagner Ring Cycle (one episode a year, 2006-9).

Chang Theatre

(08 1985 0281/www.pklifework.com). **Open** performances only. **Tickets** B500. **No credit cards**.
The LifeWork Dance Company, run by innovative choreographer Pichet Kluncheun, performs award-winning modern deconstructions of traditional forms. His theatre space was due to move location as this guide went to press.

emotion, dancers convey the romance and tragedy of such masterpieces as *Inao, Unarut* and *Ramakien*. Today *lakhon* TV signifies soaps, whose plots and exaggerated acting recall *lakhon nok*'s successor, *likay*.

LIKAY

This once ubiquitous musical theatre blends action, fantasy, tragedy and romance in diverse storylines, from folk fables to literary vignettes. High-pitched resonant singing, extravagant costumes and expressive choreography characterise this popular folk derivative of *lakhon nok* and Malay traditions. It starts with the *ohk khaek*, a solo burlesque of an Indian. From famous companies to struggling temple fair players, *likay* has declined. Many talents adapt to *luuk thuung* or *morlam* music (see *p187*); others even busk on Thanons Tha Prachan and Silom. Led by Pradit Prasartthong, the theatre-in-education group **Makham Pom** (0 2616 8473-4) cultivates appreciation of *likay* and other neglected genres through topical, satirical plots.

MANOHRA & LAKHON CHATRI

Representing a mythical bird, the rare southern art form *manohra* (aka Norah) has Malay associations. Shimmying in a beaded costume, with a buffalo horn tail, the dancer twirls brass nail extensions with speed and complexity. After duelling with a masked hunter to rhythmic percussion, the bird survives to dance another day. Its derivative *lakhon chatri* is performed daily as an offering at **Lak Muang** (*see p63*).

PUPPETRY

To Thais, dance and puppetry are indivisible. *Khon* derives its flat-stanced, masked aesthetic from *nang* (shadow puppetry); later, *hun* (marionettes) emulated the glittery stylisation of *khon*. Rooted in Southern Thai/Malay folk tradition, *nang* (named after animal hides that are die-cut and dyed) silhouettes characters in front of and behind a backlit screen (hence today *nang* means cinema). Since Ayutthayan times, *nang yai* has seen outsize puppets with no moving parts manoeuvred on sticks by dancers who step *khon*-style. The less formal, more popular *nang talung* (with hinged, moving parts) has more movement, percussive music and satirical commentary sung by the sole *talung* (narrator/puppeteer).

Hun vary in complexity. Artist Chakraband Posyakrit leads one of several troupes performing *hun krabok* – small painted glove puppets with hands moved by sticks beneath textile capes. At the **Thai Puppet Theatre** (*see p198*), uncannily lifelike *hun lakorn lek* involve a toddler-sized, *khon*-style puppet manipulated by three dancers.

Meanwhile, young master dancer Surat Jongda recreated *hun luang* (royal puppets) that move fluidly via internal strings tugged at its support-pole. For **Siam Puppet Theatre** (anuchathira@hotmail.com), cultural expert and *khon* dancer Anucha Thirakanont combined all these elements in large *hun lakorn* (drama puppets) that 'dance' with astonishing grace. Surat and Anucha's puppets can be seen at occasional events.

Company of Performing Artists

Dance Centre, Soi Klang Racquet Club, Sukhumvit Soi 49/9, Sukhumvit (0 2259 8861 Mon-Fri/studio 0 2712 8323/www.dance-centre.com). Thonglor BTS. **Open** *Office* 10am-6pm Mon-Fri; 10am-5pm Sat. *Studio* 4.30-7.30pm Mon-Fri; 8am-8pm Sat, Sun. **Tickets** B800-B2,500. **Credit** AmEx, DC, MC, V. **Map** p252 L5.
Run by Vararom Pachimsawat, CPA stages fusions of classical ballet, Thai and contemporary dance at malls, parks and theatres, and hosts the Dance Day festival each May in Benjasiri Park (*see p96*).

King Power Theater

King Power Complex, 8 Thanon Rangnam, North (0 2205 8888). Victory Monument BTS. **Open** Showtimes vary. **Tickets** vary. **Credit** AmEx, MC, V.

Artistic director Pracamkrong Pongpaiboon programmes diverse traditional and modern performances in a new theatre, with a permanent troupe of Joe Louis' puppets (*see p198* **Thai Puppet Theatre**).

Muang Thai Ratchadalai Theatre

Rear of Esplanade Mall, 99 Thanon Ratchadaphisek, near Soi 5, North (0 2669 8500/www.scenario.co.th). Thailand Cultural Centre MRT. **Tickets** vary. **Credit** phone for details.
Opening in mid 2007, Thailand's first theatre purpose-built theatre for Broadway-style shows, will host Thai and international productions.

National Theatre

Thanon Rachinee, beside National Museum, Phra Nakorn (0 2224 1342/0 2222 1092/www.finearts. go.th). Tha Chang. **Open** Shows 2-5pm 1st or 2nd

Sun of mth; call for details. Phiphat 7-9pm 2nd Fri of mth. **Tickets** B60-B100. **No credit cards**. **Map** p248 B3.

Planners want to build a replacement at the Thailand Cultural Centre for this faded venue, which has no company, no café, no shop, and almost no publicity or explanation for its rare shows of traditional dance and music.

Patravadi Theatre & Studio 9

69/1 Soi Wat Rakang, Thanon Arun Amarin, Thonburi (0 2412 7287-8/www.patravaditheatre. com). Ferry from Tha Chang to Tha Wat Rakhang. **Open** 9am-5pm daily. Shows Theatre usually 7.30-9pm Fri-Sun. Studio 9 7.30-8.30pm Sat, Sun. **Tickets** B400-B1,000. **No credit cards**. **Map** p248 A3.

Thailand's former Broadway diva Patravadi Meechudhon – actor, teacher, dancer, producer, director and writer – turned her riverside compound into the open-air Patravadi Theatre in 1992. Now with a tent-like roof, café and gallery, this space for independent theatre arts and dance offers occasional shows, while the new Studio 9 has live music or performance after dinner.

Sala Chalermkrung

66 Thanon Charoen Krung, Chinatown (0 2224 4499/0 2623 8148-9). **Open** Khon 8.30pm Fri, Sat. **Tickets** B1,000-B2,000. **No credit cards**. **Map** p249/p250 D5.

Amid art deco grandeur, condensed *khon* is staged at Sala Chalermkrung with more narrative clarity and audience explanation than is provided elsewhere. The

dancing is fair to good, and the staging spectacular, if a little impersonal. This historic theatre also hosts film premières, Bollywood films and other events.

Thai Puppet Theater

(formerly Joe Louis)
Suan Lum Night Bazaar, 1875 Thanon Rama IV, Pathumwan (0 2252 9683-4/www.thaipuppet.com). Lumphini MRT. **Open** 9.30am-9.30pm Mon-Fri; 1-9pm Sat, Sun. Shows 7.30-8.45pm daily. **Tickets** B400 Thais; B900 foreigners. **Credit** AmEx, MC, V. **Map** p251 H7.

Here, beautiful 70cm-high (28in) *hun lakhon lek* puppets come uncannily (and wittily) to life through manipulation with sticks by three dancing handlers. Despite the loss of his puppets in a fire, National Artist Sakon Yangkeawsod and his children rebuilt this last remaining troupe, calling it Joe Louis Theater after his nickname, until state subsidy required a less confusing moniker. Their well-explained shows will continue here for least a couple of years. Some puppets also perform at King Power Theatre (*see p197*).

Thailand Cultural Centre

Thanon Thiam Ruam-mit, North (0 2247 0028/ www.thaiculturalcenter.com). Thailand Cultural Centre MRT. **Tickets** vary. **No credit cards**.

Built by the Japanese, this state-run concert hall also has a small hall, an idealised Thai lifestyle exhibition and versatile outdoor spaces. It's home to the Bangkok Symphony Orchestra and most visiting dance and music performances (including September's International Festival of Music & Dance; see p162). Its uncomfortable seating, poor

Dramas about drama

Thailand is at a cultural crossroads. As masters pass away, audiences dwindle and authenticity gives way to clichéd tourist-orientated formats, opinions diverge on how best to preserve and develop indigenous dance-drama. The Culture Ministry has presented the mid career Sipathorn Awards to pioneering performers such as Pradit Prasartthong of arts-in-education troupe Makhampom, fusion choreographer Manop Meejamras of **Patravadi Theatre** (*see above*) and LifeWork's Pichet Kl+uncheun, Thailand's most internationally acclaimed modern and traditional dancer (*see p196* **Chang Theatre**), who deconstructs ancient choreography with compelling modernity. These artists have renewed the potential of classic forms by reinterpreting them.

Meanwhile, the state has tried to impose staging standards, sponsors abridged *khon* spectacles at **Sala Chalermkrung** (*see above*) and sought new powers over contemporary

performance that dares to adapt the *Ramakien*, the Thai version of India's *Ramayana* epic. In 2006 bureaucrats admonished *Ramakien: A Rak Opera* (an avant-garde musical held in New York by top Thai stars including Pichet and Manop) without having actually seen it. They then tried to remove a scene from *Ayodhya*, Somtow Sucharitkul's operatic orchestration of the Indian *Ramayana* for **Bangkok Opera** (*see p196*), likewise without having read his libretto. These productions allegedly offended conventions of *khon*, although neither performed *khon*, and both interested new audiences in the *Ramayana*.

Somtow went public with the issue in a Siam Society lecture and in an open letter to the coup government (http://web.mac.com/ somtow/iWeb/Somtow/Writings/049444E1-5E8A-4523-8201-C5E64B36CAF8.html). Expect an ongoing debate about artistic licence, and 'ownership' of Thai arts heritage.

cafeteria, ageing facilities and muddy, ankle-twisting trek from the MRT will all be trumped by Siam Opera (*see p195*), although the site will eventually gain a new national theatre, a modern art gallery and various other spaces in a state-of-the-art extension.

Comedy clubs

Punchline Comedy Club
The Bull's Head, Sukhumvit Soi 33/1, Sukhumvit (0 2233 4141-2/www.greatbritishpub.com). Phrom Phong BTS. **Open** Shows 9-11pm Fri, Sat every 2 months in 2nd or 3rd wk. **Tickets** B1,500. **Credit** AmEx, DC, MC, V. **Map** p252 K6.
Big-name international stand-ups headline every two months at this terribly English pub.

Rama IX Plaza
Soi Soonvichai, Thanon Rama IX, nr Yaek Ramkhamhaeng, North-east (0 2717 2300-2). Rama IX MRT. **Open** 6pm-1am daily. Shows 8.40pm-1am daily. **Admission** free. **Credit** AmEx, MC, V.
A bastion of irreverent variety, whether you fancy slapstick *talok* (comedy), concerts by *luuk thuung* chart-toppers, showcases of dressed-to-the-nines backing dancers, or outrageous drag burlesques.

Dinner theatres

This genre tends towards poor food, service and value, with lacklustre shows favouring regional dances over *khon* or *lakhon*. Better ones include **Yok Yor** (*see p56*) and the following.

Sala Rim Nam
Opposite Oriental Hotel, 48 Charoen Krung Soi 38, Bangrak (0 2236 0400). Saphan Taksin BTS then Oriental shuttle boat. **Open** 7-10pm daily. *Shows* 8.30-9.30pm daily. **Set menu** B2,180; B1,750 concessions. **Credit** AmEx, DC, MC, V. **Map** p250 D7.
Excerpts of *khon* are performed in the round at this opulent, *vihaan*-style restaurant – run by the Oriental – which offers a reasonable Thai menu.

Silom Village
286 Thanon Silom, between Sois 22 & 24, Bangrak (0 2234 4581). Surasak MRT. **Open** 11am-6pm daily. Shows indoor 8.20-9.10pm daily, outdoor 7.50-8.10pm, 8.50-9.10pm daily. Set menu B600. **Credit** AmEx, DC, MC, V. **Map** p250 E7.
Regional dances and martial arts draw the camera-happy to this restaurant-cum-arcade, where you can consume lobster and *lakhon* simultaneously.

Supatra River House
266 Soi Wat Rakhang, Thanon Arun Amarin, Thonburi (0 2411 0305/0874/www.supatrariver house.net). Own ferry from Tha Maharat/ferry from Tha Chang to Tha Wat Rakhang. **Open** 11am-2pm, 5.30-10pm daily. Shows 8.30-9.15pm Fri, Sat. Main courses B800. **Credit** AmEx, MC, V. **Map** p248 A4.
River views of the Grand Palace and Wat Arun make reservations essential at this gorgeous Thai

Mambo.

restaurant in an old teak house, where classic recipes get slightly de-spiced for *farang*. Weekend dances are held at a tree-shaded stage.

Kathoey cabarets

Perhaps Thailand's most globally famous performers are its lip-synching ladyboys (*kathoey*). These spectacular cabarets are commercial rather than saucy; grittier, wittier and more inventive are the drag shows put on by many gay clubs (*see pp173-76*).

Mambo
Washington Theatre, 496 Thanon Sukhumvit, by Soi 22, Sukhumvit (0 2259 5715/5128). Phrom Phong BTS. **Open** Office 10am-6pm daily. Shows 8.30-9.30pm, 10-11pm daily. **Tickets** B600-B800. **Credit** AmEx, DC, MC, V. **Map** p252 K6.
Normally based at the large Washington Theatre, Mambo has toured London and the Edinburgh Festival. An extra charge is levied according to the number of photos you take.

New Calypso Cabaret
1st floor, Asia Hotel, 296 Thanon Phayathai, North (reservations 0 2653 3960-2/after 6pm 0 2216 8937-8/www.calypsocabaret.com). Ratchathewi BTS. **Open** *Office* 9am-5pm daily. *Shows* 8.15-9.30pm, 9.45-11pm daily. **Tickets** B1,000. **Credit** AmEx, MC, V. **Map** p249/p250 F4.
Bangkok's original ladyboy cabaret has intimate, plush table seating.

Arts & Entertainment

Sport & Fitness

Where to play, exercise or spectate.

In sport, Thais punch above their weight, and not just in *muay thai* (kick boxing) and Western boxing styles for which they win WBC belts and Olympic golds. Their Asian Games and SEA Games teams finish at or near the top, with women weightlifters the current heroines. Tennis is a new pet sport thanks to Paradorn Srichaphan, Tammy Tanasugarn and Danai Udomchoke. Meanwhile, Chanya 'Cherry' Srifuengfung has a name in equestrianism. Even pop star Jetrin 'Jay' Wattanasin has been a world champion jet-skier.

Thai golf, always strong among businessmen, boomed despite Tiger Woods' seeming lack of interest in his mother's homeland. Thais instead prefer to cheer home-grown golfers like Thongchai Jaidee, Thaworn Wiratchan and Prom Meesawat.

Thailand draws headlines for its football obsession; which focuses more on foreign mega-teams than local clubs. A gilded statue of David Beckham supports the altar of Wat Pariwat, Thanon Rama III. After Thaksin's government failed to buy Liverpool FC, Beer Chang sponsored Merseyside rivals Everton, though players like Teerathep 'Leesaw' Winothai struggled while training there.

Thais are understandably languid in the fierce and humid day-time heat, but at dawn and dusk parks and *sois* fill with exercisers, much of their energy expended in local games like *takraw* (*see below* **Kick start**).

Kick start

Indigenous Thai sports face divergent fortunes. Some are withering away, while **muay thai** kick boxing has become a global sport with rankings and matches managed by the World Boxing Council (WBC) and run by the **World Muay Thai Council** (0 2369 2213-5, www.wmcmuaythai.com). Many foreigners train in *muay thai*, some going on to win titles. All fighters must wear the sacred *mongkhon* headband during the *wai khru rum muay* ritual dance to honour their teachers before every bout. They must also don the *prajiad* armlet throughout the fight, which a live band accompanies at an ever-faster fast pace. Thai boxers often wear extra amulets.

The commercialisation of this ancient hand-combat has spurred interest in older versions, such as the southern *Muay Chaiya* style taught at **Baan Chang Thai** (*see p203*) Performed with more grace and complexity, while wearing a loincloth and rope-bound wrists, ancient *muay* is often seen at festivals, including the **Traditional Thai Games & Sports Festival** (*see p161*), alongside *krabi-krabong* stick combat and Thai chess. Using slightly different pieces and rules, this variant can involve costumed martial artists enacting each move on a human-scale board. The event incorporates the **International Kite Festival** every other year, though each windy season you can see string-cutting *chula* kites in aerial fights.

Thailand dominates South-east Asia's most graceful sport, **takraw**, an acrobatic game in which players knock a woven rattan ball over a net, volleyball style, or through a high hoop. Still played in parks and open grounds in late afternoon, it's losing popularity to football.

Some perennial pastimes have been pushed semi-underground because they involve betting on animal contests. Famously, iridescent-finned male *pla kad* – **Siamese fighting fish** – contest in tall jars. You may hear of matches around the *pla kad* shops in Section 9 of **Chatuchak Weekend Market** (*see p138* **Market forces**).

Around the market's north end, bamboo coops hold prize **fighting cocks** (*kai chon*). Battling birds is legal only at two pits per province, though it actually takes place everywhere, even in backstreet Bangkok. Breeding is a serious business – witness Kamnan Vichien's **Fighting Cock Farm** (3 Moo 9, Thanon Suan Samphan, Nong Chok, East, 0 2543 1425). Fish and cock fans pursue these shadowy sports through magazines available everywhere, regardless of the letter of the law.

Active sports/fitness

Diving & water sports

Planet Scuba

666 Thanon Sukhumvit, Klongtoey (0 2261 4412-3/www.planetscuba.net). Phrom Phong BTS. **Open** 10am-8pm Mon-Sat; 11am-6pm Sun. **Rates** B4,200-B13,600. **Credit** AmEx, DC, MC, V. **Map** p252 L5.
Start your PADI certification here and complete it at sea in Pattaya; session times vary. Dive schools dot every resort, notably Phuket, Ko Tao and Pattaya (*see pp207-222* **Beach escapes**).

Football & basketball

To join in a casual football game, call the **British Club** (0 2234 0247/www.british clubbangkok.com) or pay B2,200/hr to hire the five-a-side indoor pitch at **New International School of Thailand** (NIST, Sukhumvit Soi 15, Sukhumvit, 0 2651 2065/reservations 08 1000 6997). Most parks regularly feature basketball and soccer games.

Golf

Beautiful courses surround Bangkok, Khao Yai, Pattaya, Phuket and Kanchanaburi, with pro management increasing. Their great value causes many to get swamped by North Asian tour groups; Westerners prefer those listed. All rent equipment. Cooler tee times cost more and fill up fast. For peer reviews of courses view **www.thaigolfer.com**.

Bangsai Country Club

77/7 Moo 3, Thanon Samkoksena, Thangluang (Route 3111), Ayutthaya province (0 3537 1494-7). **Open** 7am-8pm Mon-Fri; 6am-8pm Sat, Sun. **Rates** *Visitors* B550 Mon-Fri; B1,180 6.30am-8.30am, B1,080 noon-3pm Sat, Sun. *Caddy* B220. **Credit** MC, V.
A challenging 18 holes with well-tended greens. Far, but fast to reach.

No 1 Driving Range

19/7 Thanon Pracha Utitht, North-east (0 2935 6270). **Open** 10am-1am Mon-Fri; 10am-midnight Sat, Sun. **Rates** non-member B350 per 11 trays; member 280 per 10 trays **No credit cards**.

Royal Bangkok Sports Club. *See p204.*

Top-class range, with landscaped holes, bunkers and water hazards, plus a bar, Japanese restaurant and coaching. Pay by coupon.

Royal Golf & Country Club

69 Sukhumvit Soi 77 (Soi Onnut), beside Suvarnabhumi Airport, Samut Prakarn province (0 2738 1010, www.royalgolfclubs.com). **Open** 6.30am-6pm daily. Last reservation Sat, Sun 1.30pm **Rates** *Visitors* B2,400 (B1,500 with Visa card) Mon-Fri; B3,200 6.30-11.30am Sat, Sun, B 2,200 (B1,700 with Visa) after 11.30am Sat, Sun *Caddy* B250. **Credit** AmEx, DC, MC, V
A user-friendly, Japanese-designed 18-hole course with fast greens.

Vintage Club

549/1-4 Thanon Panvithee, Klongdan, Bangbor, Samut Prakarn province (0 2707 3820/www.vintage thaigolf.com). **Open** 6am-6pm daily, *last ticket (Tee Off)* around 2.48 pm. **Rates** *Visitors* B1,400 Mon-Fri; B2,500 Sat, Sun. *Caddy* B250. Golf cart B700 **Credit** AmEx, MC, V
This well-maintained 18-holer lies 10 mins from Thanon Bangna-Trad. Full-facility clubhouse.

General fitness centres

At dawn and dusk in parks like **Lumphini** (*see p93*), **Saranrom** (*see p65*), **Benjakitti** and **Benjasiri** (for both, *see p96*), people jog, dunk basketballs, tap rattan *takraw* balls, work-out at open-air gyms, practise martial arts, play Thai chess, or join aerobics classes, the last of these also at City Hall (Thanon Dinso, Phra Nakorn) and the plaza spanning Khlong Chong Nonsi at Thanon Surawong. Benjasiri also has skateboard ramps.

Runners can join **Jog & Joy** trips (0 2741 1900 ext 0, www.jogandjoy.com), or get a compulsory silly name with the expatriate 'drinking club with a running problem', **Hash House Harriers** (www.bangkokhhh.com).

Some hotel health clubs also have day rates, so you can get your endorphine fix without the need to commit to membership.

California WOW Experience

Liberty Square, Thanon Silom, at Soi Convent, Bangrak (0 2631 1122/www.californiawowx.com). Saladaeng BTS/Silom MRT. **Open** 6am-midnight Mon-Sat; 8am-10pm Sun. **Rates** B800 per day; B1,500 per week (foreigner only). **Credit** AmEx, MC, V. **Map** p250 F7.
A multi-floor, all-hours gym chain with immodest window walls, high-tech machines, loud music, huge classes and a hard-sell attitude – but no pool.
Other locations: 1st floor, Jasmine Tower, Sukhumvit Soi 23, Sukhumvit (0 2665 2999); 4th floor, Siam Paragon (0 2610 9755); 1st floor, The Esplanade Ratchadapisek (0 2660 1999); 1st floor, Major Cineplex, Pinklao (0 2433 7199); *women only* 3rd floor, Phoenix Tower, Sukhumvit Soi 31 (0 2260 7999).

Fitness First

4th floor, Landmark Plaza, Landmark Hotel, Thanon Sukhumvit, Sukhumvit (0 2653 2424/ www.fitness first.com). Nana BTS. **Open** 6am-10pm Mon-Fri; 8am-9pm Sat-Sun. **Rates** B1,000 per day; B1,700-2,300 per mth (min 3mths). **Credit** AmEx, DC, MC, V. **Map** p251 J5.
A well-equipped UK chain, but this one lacks a pool.
Other locations: Bio House Building, Sukhumvit Soi 39, Sukhumvit (0 2262 0520-2); 23rd-24th floor, Central Pinklao Tower (0 2884 7820-7); 3rd floor, Q House Lumpini (0 2677 7133)

National Stadium Hua Mark

Thanon Ramkhamhaeng, East (0 2314 4678). **Open** *Gym* 10am-7pm Tue-Sun. *Pool* 6am-8.30pm Tue-Sun. **Rates** *Gym* B20; B580 per yr (gym plus any 2 sports). *Pool* B30 6am-6pm Tue-Sun; B50 6-8.30pm Tue-Sun. **No credit cards.**
The indoor stadium, velodrome and Ratchamangala Stadium have a public gym and pool.

National Stadium Pathumwan

Thanon Rama I, Pathumwan (0 2214 0120/www. bsd.osrd.go.th). National Stadium BTS. **Open** *Pool* 3pm-8pm Tue-Fri; 8am-noon, 3pm-8pm Sat-Sun. **Admission** *Swimming* B50 adults; B30 under-25s. **Membership** *Swimming* B1,000 per yr adults; B600 per yr under-25s. **No credit cards.** Map p249 & p250 F4.
Hosts soccer matches, and has a 50m pool for members, and a gym (B1,000 per course, Sat, Sun).

Soi Klang Racquet Club

Sukhumvit Soi 49/9, Sukhumvit (0 2714 7200, 0 2712 8010/www.rqclub.com). Phrom Phong BTS. **Open** 6am-11pm daily. *Pool* 6.30am-9pm daily. **Rates** B450 per day Mon-Fri; B550 per day Sat, Sun; B15,000 per yr. **Credit** AmEx, MC, V. **Map** p252 L5.
A smart sports centre with raquet sports, basketball, snooker, swimming, gym and a branch of Dance Centre (0 2712 8323, www.dance-centre.com).

Horse riding

There are also riding options in **Hua Hin** and **Pattaya** (*see p207*).

Garden City Polo Club

37 Moo 5, Thanon Bangna-Trad km 29, Samut Prakarn province (0 2707 1534-8). **Open** *riding* 9-11am, 2.30-4.30pm Tue-Sun. **Rates** B800 per hr, B700 per hr concessions Tue-Fri; B1,200 per hr, B800 per hr concessions Sat, Sun. **No credit cards.**
This residential country club has a range of excellent facilities, with jumping, dressage and coaching all on offer.

Motor sports

PTT Speedway Karting Stadium

31/11, 2nd floor, RCA Plaza, Rama IX Road, Soi Soonvijai, Bangkapi (0 2203 1205-7/www.karting stadium.com). **Open** 4pm-mignight Mon-Thur;

4pm-1am Fri; 1pm-1am Sat; 1pm-midnight Sun. **Rates** B195 per 5mins; B390 per 10mins; member B350 per 10 mins. **Credit** AmEx, MC, V.
Set indoors (with aircon clearing the fumes), this 800m (half-mile) track has 160cc and 270cc karts reaching 60km/h (37mph). Helmet, protective clothing and briefings provided.

Muay thai & martial arts

You can join in group t'ai chi and martial arts at **Lumphini Park** (4.30-8am daily, *see p93*).

Baan Chang Thai

38 Ekamai Soi 10, Sukhumvit Soi 63, Sukhumvit (0 2391 3807). Ekamai BTS. **Open** 9am-8pm daily. **Map** p252 M6.
Preserving and teaching traditional crafts, this converted house holds courses on an ancient southern form of *muay thai*, plus puppet making and painting. Limited English is spoken, but bargain prices.

Fairtex

99/8 Soi Boonthamanusorn, Thanon Theparak km9, Bangplee Yai, Outer East (0 2757 5147/www.muay thaifairtex.com). **Open** 7am-10pm Mon-Fri; 9am-9pm Sat-Sun. *Boxing class* 7-8.30am, 2-3pm Mon-Fri; 2-3pm, 6.30-9pm Sat; 4-9pm Sun. **Admission** Nonmembers B450 per class, B650 per day (2 classes). **Membership** B1,700 per month to B12,000 per year. **Credit** MC, V.
Founded in 1975, Thailand's smartest *muay thai* camp has trained many world champions, Thai and foreign. It also has a gym and pool, and a training resort in Pattaya (packages B1,300-2,600/night). **Other locations**: Fairtex Sport Club & Resort, 179/201 Thanon North Pattaya, Pattaya (0 3848 8196).

Snooker & pool

Many snooker dens earn disrepute for ne'er-do-well gamblers, though most have decent tables, straight cues and cheap beer. Pool tables proliferate around Nana hostess bars (*see p191*) and Thanon Khao San (*see p71*).

The Ball in Hand

Rajah Hotel, 18 Sukhumvit Soi 4, Sukhumvit (08 1917 8530/08 6978 8321). Nana BTS. **Open** 11am-1am daily. **Credit** AmEx, DC, MC, V. **Map** p251 J5.
Most Nana pool dens aim to show bar girls handling cues and bending over tables. This parlour caters to those focusing on the 8-ball. The dozen superior tables boast attendants, a full bar and contests (women on Saturdays, men on Sundays, internationals in April, October or November).

Pro Q Snooker

5th floor, Charn Issara Tower I, Thanon Rama IV, Bangrak (0 2234 0011). Saladaeng BTS/Silom MRT. **Open** 9am-1am daily. **Rates** B120 per hr. **No credit cards. Map** p251 G6.
A respectable parlour with 12 tables.

Swimming

The best hotel lap pools are at the **Pathumwan Princess** (*see p47*), **Metropolitan** (*see p51*) and **Sukhothai** (*see p51*). Siam Park (*see p102*) offers a variety of aquatic environments, even waves.

Thai-Japan Centre

Thanon Maitreejit, North-east (0 2245 3360).
Open 10am-9pm Mon-Sat; 1-9pm Sun. **Rates** B15 adults; B5 concessions. **Membership** B40 per yr adults; B20 per yr 18-24s; B10 per yr under-18s. **No credit cards.**
Multi-lane Olympic pool with starting blocks.

Tennis

Redevelopment is robbing Bangkok of its courts, so try **Soi Klang Racquet Club** (*see p203*) or the **Lawn Tennis Association of Thailand** (0 2718 4788-9, www.ltat.org) for courts, most hiring racquets. Hotels with courts include the **Conrad Bangkok** (*see p46*), **Grand Hyatt Erawan** (*see p47*), **The Oriental** (*see p45*), **Nai Lert Park Hotel** (*see p47*), and **Sukhothai** (*see p51*).

Santisuk Tennis Court

26 Sukhumvit Soi 38, Sukhumvit (0 2391 1830).
Thonglor BTS. **Open** 7am-10pm daily. **Rates** B80-B100/hr; *lights* B60/hr; *racket* B50/hr.
No credits cards.
Cement courts (five outdoor, three indoor) with coaching, knocker and racquet hire.

Ten-pin bowling

Most malls have top-floor bowling alleys beside their cinemas, costing B60-B100 a game. Book on weekends, especially for **Major Bowl** in Central World Plaza (0 2255 6591, www.majorbowlhit.com, 11am-midnight daily); **Blu-O Rhythm and Bowl** in Siam Paragon (0 2129 4625, www.blu-o.com, 11am-midnight daily) and **SF Bowl** in Mah Boon Krong (0 2611 7171-4, www.sfcinemacity.com, 10am-1am Mon-Thur, Sun, 10am-2am Fri- Sat).

Spectator sports

Football

For league games, internationals and European team tours, try the **Football Association of Thailand** (0 2216 2954, www.fat.or.th).

Horse racing

Illegal gambling is rife, and there is always frisson in this rare forum where the rich and poor rub shoulders.

Royal Bangkok Sports Club (RBSC)

1 Thanon Henri Dunant, Pathumwan (0 2255 1420-9/www.rbsc.org). Siam BTS. **Races** noon-6pm every fortnight, Sun. **Admission** B50-B1,000. **No credit cards. Map** p251 G5.
A century-old club with wide-ranging facilities, whose members either own or run the country. Members only, except during races. **Photo** *p202*.

Royal Turf Club

183 Thanon Phitsanulok, Dusit (0 2628 1810-5).
Races noon-6pm every fortnight. **Admission** B50-B300. **No credit cards. Map** p249 E2.
Holds biweekly races and four annual derbies, as well as testing and registering Thai thoroughbreds

Motor sports

North of Pattaya, **Bira International Circuit** (Highway 36, km14, 0 3893 6089, office 0 2971 6450 ext 428, www.grandprixgroup.com) is Thailand's main motor sports circuit. It opens 9am-5pm daily (call for availablity), and also has a museum on royal racer Prince Bira.

Bangkok Drag Avenue

6/1 Moo 11 Klong Ha, Klong Luang, Pathum Thani (08 1348 1727, 0 2986 4040/ www.bangkokdrag.com). **Open** *Races* 5pm-1am Sat.
Motorcycles 10am-5pm Sun. *Practice* 6pm-0.30am Fri. **Admission** *races* B60, *motorcycles* B40; *practice* B40. **No credit cards.**
Seeking to turn Bangkok's notorious street racing scene legal, the B90-million new BDA strip holds mainly half-kilometre (quarter-mile) car races (plus some gymkhana events and motorcycle drag racing) every weekend, with practice rounds on Fridays.

Muay thai

Bills at the two major stadia progress from juniors to amateurs, pros and prize fights, with novelty shows and animated gambling adding to the colour (*see p200* **Kick start**). Ringside seats are far better, but it's possible that prices may be inflated for foreigners.

Lumphini Stadium

Thanon Rama IV, beside Suan Lum Night Bazaar, Pathumwan (ringside reservations 08 9764 8203/ Old Lumphini 0 2251 4303, 0 2252 8765). Lumpini MRT **Open** 6.30-10.30pm Tue, Fri; 5-8pm, 8.30pm-midnight Sat. **Tickets** B1,000-B2,000. **No credit cards. Map** p251 H7.
Likely to be relocated, this legendary venue has major title fights and equipment shops.

Ratchadamnoen Stadium

1 Thanon Ratchadamnoen Nok, Dusit (ringside reservations 0 2281 4205). **Open** 6.30-11pm Mon, Wed, Thur; 5-8pm, 8.30-midnight Sun. **Tickets** B1,000-B2,000. **No credit cards. Map** p248 B3.
This art deco stadium has both basic facilities and its own equipment shops.

Beach Escapes

Le Royal Meridien Phuket Yacht Club. *See p217.*

Getting Started

How to make the most of the Thai coast.

Thailand's Indian Ocean beaches have been mostly rebuilt after the December 2004 tsunami, though scars remain and big business took advantage over small-scale operations. Lookout posts, evacuation routes, a warning buoy and various memorials act as rare sentinels amid the majestic marinescapes and gentrifying resorts of the tourism hubs. During that recovery, the unravaged Pacific shore received helter-skelter investment. Now more visitors than ever crowd the superb strands and mouthwash-green waters of all the country's coasts.

Along the Andaman Sea, some 600-800km (400-500 miles) south of Bangkok, spread the mass and elite tourism capital of **Phuket** (*see p216*), achingly picturesque **Krabi** (*see p219*), beachnik retreat **Ko Lanta** (*see p220*), and the most wave-traumatised locales: the island idyll of **Ko Phi Phi** (*see p221*) and mid-market **Khao Lak** (*see p219*), where rainforest meets reef. Across the Kra Isthmus lie the Thai Gulf islands of unhurried **Ko Samui** (*see p212*), dive-mad **Ko Tao** (*see p215*) and rugged, full-moon partying **Ko Pha-ngan** (*see p214*). A shorter drive either side of Bangkok, regal **Hua Hin** (*see p211*) hosts sedate hideaways, while the Eastern Seaboard harbours brash **Pattaya** (*see p207*), quirky **Ko Samet** (*see p208*) and eco-wannabe **Ko Chang** (*see p210*).

Everywhere the trend is upmarket. Designer chic and spa preciousness are eclipsing the backpacker ethic. Yet budget huts remain and many luxury pool villas are a bargain. With planning negligible, national park regulations ineffective and sustainability ignored, many beauty spots have been blighted by traffic, touts and techno. The flipside is the ample amenities.

BEDS AND MEALS

Rooms often get booked out in high season, especially at weekends. During the monsoons there are good discounts, although smaller resorts may shut. For coastal seasons, *see p236* **When to go**. As accommodation often determines the character of a destination, many beach descriptions come under the relevant **Where to stay** section.

Resort food varies from designer cuisine, through bland tourist fodder, to authentic places where the locals eat. On remote beaches food quality plunges and prices inflate, so island-hoppers should take practical supplies.

Getting there

By air

New budget airlines (*see p224*) have multiplied flights to airports at **Phuket** (0 7632 7230-7) and **Krabi** (0 7563 6541-2). Bangkok Airways (www.bangkokair.com), which owns airports at **Ko Samui** (0 7742 2234) and **Trat** (0 3952 5767-8; for Ko Chang), has finally reduced its hefty fares and fees. Booking airport pickups avoids taxi touts and rip-offs. Thailand's first seaplane service, **Destination Air Shuttle** (0 7632 8638, www.destinationair.com) connects Phuket airport directly with Andaman seafront resorts between Khao Lak and Krabi.

By road & rail

Beaches near Bangkok can be reached by hired car (*see p226*), airport pick-up or bus (from Bangkok terminals, *see p225*). Add an hour for buses to: Hua Hin (3hrs), frequent buses (B160); Pattaya (2hrs 30mins to 2hrs 40 mins), half-hourly buses (B117); Ko Samet (3hrs plus 40min ferry), hourly buses to Ban Phe pier (B157); and Ko Chang (4-5hrs plus 1hr ferry), frequent buses to Trad (around B230-B241), then *songtaew* to Laem Ngop pier.

You'd lose 24 hours heading south via night buses or trains from Bangkok's Hualumphong Station (*see p225*). However, rail is a nice way to reach Hua Hin (11 daily, departing every 30mins, taking 5hrs, B154-B662). A taxi to Hua Hin/Pattaya/Ban Phe costs B2,200-plus. Most hotels will arrange airport transfers. Increasingly, minibuses replace buses linking airports, towns and resorts, where it's easy to hire motorcycles (from B200) and jeeps/cars (from B1,200).

Resources

ATMs, banks and exchange booths, plus **phone** and **internet** access, are plentiful in main resorts, but scarce and pricey on Samet and remote beaches. TAT offices for **tourist information** open 8.30am-4.30pm daily. The **tourist police** national hotline (1155) alerts your nearest station. Beaches in natural reserves charge entry fees (www.dnp.go.th/parkreserve, B400, B200 concessions).

Beach Escapes

From weekend getaways to southern island retreats.

The bar and 'Opium den' at **Mantra**. *See p208.*

Eastern Seaboard

Pattaya

Pattaya has hosted raunchy mass tourism since US troops came for R&R during the Vietnam War. Uneven clean-ups of both pollution and the sex trade have resulted in crude contrasts: eyesores scar a potentially fine corniche; few swim in waters that are no longer dirtied by sewage; watersports and attractions draw families, go-go bars remain top of many visitors' must-see lists.

As if in a counterfeit Elmore Leonard novel, guys in vests pose with bikes, babes and Ray-Bans. Menus come in English, German, Arabic and Russian – nationalities that recur in lurid reports on underground activities in the Pattaya Mail. Yet mainstream tourists face little risk and some stay to open businesses, hence pubs

called Rosie O'Grady's, Scot's Bar and Pat's Pies. Morphing into a town, Pattaya now boasts malls, 15 golf courses and a largely artificial culture. The centre is walkable, or you can flag down a *songtaew* anywhere.

The next bay south, longer, cleaner Jomtien Beach, has sparser boutique resorts, delectable seafood and fewer Pattaya-esque mistakes.

Activities

Watersports and fishing trips proliferate. **Blue Lagoon Watersports Club** (23/4 Na Jomtien Soi 14, 0 3825 5115-6) offers a private beach, jet-skis, speedboats, windsurfing and kite surfing. Island reefs, wrecks and instruction are the diving draws at **Aquanauts** (437/17 Thanon Beach Soi 6, 0 3836 1724) and **Mermaids** (75/122-5 Thanon Jomtien Beach, 0 3823 2219-20). **Gulf Charters** (Ocean Marina Yacht Club, Jomtien, 0 3823 7752) rents yachts, while **Bungee Jump & Paintball Park** (248/10

Thanon Thepprasit, 0 3830 0608, www.paint ballpark-pattaya.com), **Pattaya Kart Speedway** (248/2 Thanon Thepprasit, 0 3842 2044) and coastal **Phoenix Golf Club** (Thanon Sukhumvit km158, 0 3823 9391-8, rates B1,400 Mon-Fri, B2,000 Sat, Sun, caddy B250) are self-explanatory.

Sanctuary of Truth (206/2 Naklua Soi 12, 0 3836 7229 ext104, admission B250-B500), a fantastical, pantheistic wooden temple, also offers a dolphin show, horse riding and speed boat trips. **Tiffany's** (464 Thanon Pattaya 2, 0 3842 1700-5, B500-B800) is the best of the three ladyboy cabarets. Rather more refined, **Liam's Gallery** (352/107 Soi Pratamnak, 0 3825 1808, www.liamsgallery.com) displays a fine collection of Thai contemporary art.

Where to stay, eat & drink

The upmarket **Dusit Resort** (240/2 Thanon Pattaya Beach, 0 3842 5611-7, www.dusit.com, rates $150-$315) has a near-private beachfront, lush gardens and sporty facilities. **Sugar Hut** (391/18 Thanon Thappaya, www.sugarhut pattaya.com, rates B6,900-B11,200, main courses B200) offers gorgeous stilt bungalows and fine Thai food with optional floor seating. Music memorabilia and a climbing wall adorn the funkily designed **Hard Rock Hotel & Café** (429 Thanon Beach, 0 3842 8755-9, www.hardrockhotels.net, rates B6,700-B7,800, main courses B500). Horse riding and an oriental teahouse are the attractions at spacious **Horseshoe Point** (Thanon Siam Country Club, 0 3873 5050, www.horseshoepoint.com, rates B5,062-B8,828). Set in gardens on a near-private beach, **Cabbages & Condoms Resort & Restaurant** (366/11 Phra Tamnak Soi 4, 0 3825 0035, www.cabbagesandcondoms. co.th, rates B2,119-B11,064, main courses B230) puts a condom under your pillow. Among rare budget digs, **J House** (595/2-3 Thanon Beach, 0 3842 9446, rates B800) overlooks the sea.

Bruno's maintains fine European cuisine and service (Chateau Dale Plaza, Thanon Thappraya, 0 3836 4600-1, main courses B500). South Pattaya is full of Middle Eastern cafés, while **Shenanigans** (Marriott Pattaya Resort, 0 3871 0641-3, main courses B300) offers Irish food, Guinness and bands. **Hopf Brew House** (219 Thanon Beach, 0 3871 0650, main courses B250-B350) mixes homebrew beer, German food and, on Saturdays, live opera! The stunningly designed new showpiece bar/restaurant, **Mantra** (Amari Orchid Resort, 240 Thanon Pattaya Beach, 0 3842 9591, www.mantra-pattaya.com, main courses B200-B300) has seven open kitchens serving everything from Asian to Mediterranean food.

Hell-themed, trance temple **Lucifer's Disco** (Walking Street, 6pm-2am daily) attracts young *farang*, while others frequent the open-air beer bars, brimming with 'hostesses'. Pattayaland Sois 1, 2 and 3 have the most massage parlours and go-go bars, with short-stay rooms upstairs.

Gay & lesbian

Pattayaland Soi 3 is signed 'Boys' Town'. Amid the go-go and massage outlets are classier bars in gay hotels, such as **Café Royale** (0 3848 303, www.caferoyale-pattaya.com, rates B1,100-B3,000, main courses B220-B340) and **Ambiance Hotel** (0 3842 4099, www. ambiance-pattaya.com, rates B1,100-B3,600, main courses B140). The gay beach is situated just north of Royal Jomtien Resort; nearby **Dick's Café** (413/129 Thanon Tappraya, 0 3825 2417, www.dickscafe.com) is busy from breakfast till sundowners. Another crowd-puller is the **Pattaya Gay Festival** (www.pattaya gayfestival.com) in late November.

Resources

Hospital

Bangkok Pattaya Hospital, 301 Thanon Sukhumvit, Naklua (0 3825 9999/www.bangkokpattaya hospital.com).

Tourist information

TAT, 609 Thanon Phra Tamnak (0 3842 8750). Also try www.pattaya.com.

Ko Samet

A favoured retreat for Bangkokians, this dagger-shaped isle immortalised by poet Sunthorn Phu is actually a national park (0 3865 3034). Chic resorts are now gentrifying its shambolic fringe of resorts with minimal amenities and aesthetics, but pricing out its young regulars. Boats from Baan Phe dock at **Na Dan**, near which the squeaky white sand of **Had Sai Kaew** starts the string of pretty east coast bays. Aside from the jet skis, tours and inflatable banana rides, the calm is disturbed only by beach massages, snorkelling and a mellow party scene.

Where to stay, eat & drink

From densely packed Had Sai Kaew, resorts get sparser as the coccyx-bruising road judders to **Ao Phai, Silver Sand** (0 3864 4074, rates B1,500-B2,000), which hosts the grooviest beachside disco, and the lodges of **Samet Villa** (0 3864 4094, rates B1,800-B4,200). Just beyond, gay-friendly **Tubtim Resort** (Ao Tubtim,

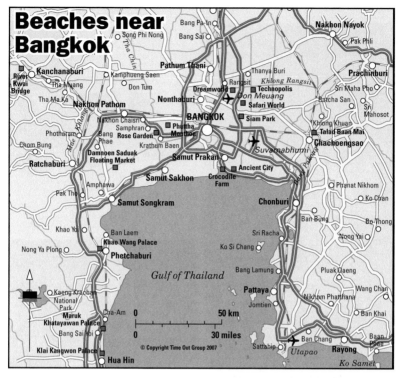

0 3864 4025-7, rates B600-B1,500, main courses
B40-B300) serves great seafood.

The busy half moon of **Ao Wong Deuan**
is best reached by boat. Guided groups pack
themselves in at the seafood restaurants,
leaving little room for anyone else. Trendier
types don their dancing shoes and kick back to
DJs at **Vongduern Villa** (formerly Taleburé,
0 3864 4260, 08 1863 9868, www.vongduern
villa.com, rates B1,200-B3,500, main courses
B60-B300), where retro-chic bungalows survey
the bay. A short hike further, **Ao Thian** has
eccentric shoreline huts at **Lung Dum** (0 3864
4331, rates B500-B1,200).

The best food is up north at sleekly
minimalist **Moo Ban Talay** (Ao Noi Na, 0
3864 4251 ,01838 8682, www.moobantalay.com,
rates B5,500-B9,000, main courses B250-B450),
which has a spa but poor sand and sea.
Remote, upmarket resorts with their own
ferries dot the humid west, home to the snazzily
romantic **Ao Phrao Resort** (0 384 4100-3,
www.samedresorts.com, rates B5,900-B16,500,
main courses B100-B400), and the southern tip,
where the same owners recently opened the
luxury **Paradee** (0 2438 9771, www.samed

resorts.com, rates B15,000-B25,000, speedboat
from pier to resort B6,000). Booking is now
essential on Samet.

Resources

Hospital
*Phe Health Centre, Thanon Phe-Klang-Klam
(0 3865 2613).*
*Rayong Hospital, Thanon Sukhumvit, Rayong
(0 3861 1104/www.rayonghospital.net).*

Tourist information
Minimal leaflets at piers. Try www.kohsamet.com.

Getting there & around

By road
Buses from Ekamai Bus Station (almost hourly,
7am-8.30pm daily, B157) reach Baan Phe port in
four hours, cars in three. Minivans to/from the
north-west corner of Victory Monument and
Baan Phe (hourly, 5am-10pm, B250-B300) are
hard to locate but it's worth asking the pier to
arrange one. On Samet, open *songtaew* ply
rutted tracks, so many visitors walk.

Saboey Resort & Villas. *See p213.*

By boat

Ferries to Na Dan (B100 return; 30mins) depart Baan Phe bus station pier (hourly, 9am-5pm daily) and Nuan Thip pier 500m into town (hourly 24hrs, return hourly 8am-6pm daily, plus waiting). A few serve Wong Deuan (45mins). Pricey speedboats (0 3865 1999) go direct to beaches. Boats rarely run after dark.

Ko Chang

Thailand's second largest island (0 3953 8100) is one of 46 national park isles bordering Cambodia. Since ex-PM Thaksin proclaimed it the 'next Phuket' in 2002, a land-grab by developers has outpaced supposedly sensitive planning. Trucks shake and rumble the road around forested mountains, which contain three waterfalls. Ko Chang is named after an elephant-shaped southern headland. Though pachyderms aren't indigenous, Thais don't miss a trick, and there's a refuge at **Ko Chang Elephant Camp** (22/4 Had Khlong Son, 08 1919 3995), and **Chang Chutiman** (0 9939 6676) runs elephant treks.

Boats dock at Tha Dan Kao, while shops, bars and restaurants centre on north-western **Had Sai Khao** beach. Dive shops access the so-so reefs (October-April/May) and offer watersports, including dinghy sailing on Klong Prao. Some head south to islands (open in dry season only) such as Ko Mak, which boasts white sand and internet, and the larger, ever more exclusive Ko Kood.

Where to stay & eat

Accommodation on Had Sai Khao veers from backpacker huts to smarter air-con bungalows like **Top Resort** (0 3955 1364-5, www.topresort-kohchang.com, rates B1,440-B2,960) and **Cookie Bungalow** (08 1861 4227, rates B2,000-B5,000, main courses B80), known for its seafood. **Baan Nuna Bungalows** (08 1821 4202, rates fan B400, air-con B800, main courses B95-B200) serves decent pizzas and Thai fare.

Heading south, resorts get sparser. On Ao Klong Prao, **Klong Prao Resort** (0 3959 7216, 08 1830 0126, www.klongpraoresort.com, rates B1,600-B3,500) is set on a lagoon with a private

Beach Escapes

beach. Across the *khlong*, **Panviman Resort** (0 3955 1290-6, www.panviman.com, rates B7,500-B8,000) has chic bungalows and a pool, while **Boutique Resort & Health Spa** (0 3955 1050, www.kohchangboutique.com, rates B1,400-B3,200) offers treatments in wooden salas. The only five-star property, **Amari Emerald Cove** (0 3955 2000, rates B7,400-B13,000, main courses B300), boasts a 50-metre pool, Sivara Spa and the Italian restaurant Sassi.

On Ao Kai Bae, **Koh Chang Cliff Beach** (0 3955 7034-5, www.kohchangcliffbeach.com, rates B4,200-B7,500) has villas and a pool overlooking its hideaway beach; in the resort-pocked south-east, **Bang Bao**, a fishing village on stilts, offers homestays and fresh seafood.

On Ko Mak, the best bungalows are at **Ko Mak Resort** (0 3950 1013, 03952 2134, www.kohmakresort.com, rates B2,000-B3,800). Ko Kood's finest is the expansive **Beach** (08 9115 2818, www.thebeachkohkood.com, rates B2,500-B6,800), boasting 24-hour electricity.

Resources

Hospital

Ko Chang International Clinic, 9/14 White Sand Beach (0 3955 1151).

Tourist information

TAT, 100 Thanon Trad-Laem Ngop, Laem Ngop (0 3959 7659-60). Also try www.kohchang.com.

Getting there & around

By road

Songtaew link bus station, pier and island bays.

By boat

Hourly ferries to Tha Dan Kao go from Laem Ngop (6am-7pm daily, 1hr, B140). Car ferries leave east of Laem Ngop (B200 per car) by Ko Chang Ferries (0 3951 8588-9) or Centre Point Pier Ferry (0 3953 8196). Ferries depart Laem Ngop for Ko Maak (3pm daily Nov-Apr, returning 8am; 3hrs). To reach Ko Kood you need a tour or hotel booking.

Gulf of Thailand

Hua Hin & Cha-am

Founded as a royal spa, Hua Hin retains palaces, a quaint railway station and traces of fishing village charm, having restrained pollution, prostitution and development. The king still lives at the art nouveau **Phra Ratchawang Klai Kangwon** ('Far from Worries Palace') in Hua Hin, but it's tourable

when he's away. Its miles-long beaches stretch north past condos, resorts and the stunning teak **Phra Ratchaniwet Marukhathaiyawan** palace to **Cha-am**, a ho-hum resort catering to raucous Thai *sanuk*. South is Pranburi, a yachtie haven with designer hotels. Sand and water quality are middling, and weekends can get crowded. Hua Hin's beaches are generally quieter south of the Sofitel towards **Had Khao Takiap**. The pace is picked up on **Khao Takiap** where a sandy beach ensemble of water sports, coconut palms and great Thai eateries has blossomed. Hua Hin has a walkable centre, but limited transport.

Diversions include golf and **Khao Sam Roi Yot National Park** (0 3261 9078), where you can kayak in wetlands amid karsts that inspired its '300 peaks' name.

Where to eat & drink

Aside from Hua Hin's no-frills seafood jetty restaurants, for Thai try the garden at homely **Baan Youyen** (29 Hua Hin Soi 51, 0 3253 1191-2, www.youyen.com, main courses B75-B500); the chic beach property **Let's Sea** (83/188 Talay Soi 12, 0 3253 6888, www.letussea.com, main courses B180-330); or the dinner-theatre **Sasi** (83/159 Nhongkae, 0 3251 2488, www.sasirestaurant.com, set menu B750); and, out of town, **Supatra by the Sea** (122/63 Thanon Takiab, Nong Gae, 0 3253 6561-2, www.supatrabythesea.com, main courses B100-B350), with fine hill/ocean vistas. The waterfront **Brasserie de Paris** (3 Thanon Naresdamri, 0 3253 0637, main courses B350-B700) excels. The mammoth **Hua Hin Brewing Company** (Hilton Hotel, 0 3251 2888, www.huahin.hilton.com), makes a change from beer bars, as does the folk music venue **Takeang Pub** (aka J Gene Pub, Soi Bintabat).

Where to stay

Hua Hin has some world-class spa resorts. **Chiva Som Health Resort** (73/4 Thanon Phet Kasem, 0 3253 6536, www.chivasom.com, rates B16,890-B55,800 incl three meals and daily massage) attracts superstars to its villas and holistic treatments, while guru therapists also check into **Evason Hua Hin** (Pranburi, 0 3263 2111-40, www.sixsenses.com, rates B6,238-B17,655), where minimalist design and clean lines define the pool, villas and spa. Visitors such as the Beckhams and hip hotel mavens gush about the remote, all-white **Aleenta** (Pranburi, 0 3261 8333, 0 2508 5333, www.aleenta.com, rates B6,650-B9,500), though cheery **Veranda Resort & Spa** (737/12 Thanon Mung Talay, 0 3270 9099, www.verandaresortandspa.com, rates B7,500-B18,500) is a fuller designer experience.

Anantara Resort & Spa (43/1 Thanon Phet Kasem, 0 3252 0250-6, www.anantara.com, rates B6,300-B13,300) feels villagey, while **Sofitel Central Hua Hin** (1 Thanon Damnoen Kasem, 0 3251 2021-38, www.centralhotelsresorts.com, rates B8,945-B16,360) maintains its 1920s 'grand hotel' nobility. Aristocrats have opened their old wooden beach mansions of **Baan Bayan** (119 Thanon Petchkasem, 0 3253 3544, www.baanbayan.com, rates B4,700-B26,875); a cheaper, antiquey option is **Ban Somboon** (13/4 Soi Kasemsamphan, 0 3251 1538, rates B900). Hidden away from the crowds on Takiap Beach, a short walk from a traditional fishing village, is the luxuriously beachy **Anantasila Villa** (33/15 Soi Mooban Huadon, www.anantasila.com, 0 3251 1879, rates B4,000-B12,000).

Resources

Hospital

San Paolo Hua Hin Hospital, 222 Thanon Petchkasem (0 3253 2576).

Tourist information

TAT, 500/51 Thanon Phetkasem, Cha-am (0 3247 1005-6).

Ko Samui

Ever-smarter hotels, restaurants, spas and villas upgrade Samui, but impair its water supply and landscape of sweeping beaches, rugged capes and forested hills. Yet somehow its laid-back roots remain: fishing, coconuts, backpacker huts, New Age pilgrims.

The commercial/official hub of **Nathon** port boasts Hainan-influenced teak shophouses, a market and great hawker food. Just south at Lipa Noi beach, **Samui Dharma Healing Centre** (Sawai Home Bungalows, 0 7723 4170, www.dharmahealingintl.com, rates B500-B700) runs Buddhist fasts at simple beach huts. The North Coast water is less clear than in the east, but calm year-round. It spans **Bophut**, Samui's most charming village, and Had Bangrak – called **Big Buddha Beach** for the 12-metre (39-foot) statue in **Wat Phra Yai** – which is tranquil despite the cutely rustic airport nearby.

On the east, **Chaweng**'s crescent of fine sand, swimmable waters and arching palms is both party central and a vaguely sleazy lesson in non-planning, boasting Samui's better shops. Over a ridge with giddying views, beautiful **Lamai** bay has crystal waters, lovely sands and boulders at the southern end. Two of these, **Hinta Hinyai** ('Grandpa and Grandma Rocks'), resemble genitals and have become a tourist trap. Lamai

town is a mess, with poor restaurants and hostess bars. Roads then fork inland to **Nam Tok Ta Nim** waterfall, with mountain views en route, or around the quieter southern beaches at Laem Set and Taling Ngam.

Activities

Samui lacks reefs, but umpteen companies serve nearby coral (best May-Oct). Try **Easy Divers** (0 7741 3373, www.easydivers-thailand.com) or the boutique scuba/eco-adventure/watersports outfit **100 Degrees East** (Big Buddha Beach, 08 6282 2983, www.100degreeseast.com). Yachties have UK charter giant **Sunsail** (0 7623 9057, www.sunsailthailand.com) and the independents **Samui Ocean Sports** (08 1940 1999, www.sailing-in-samui.com) and **Siam Commercial Boat Charter** (08 1895 1183). Explore the wildlife and sea caves-riddled karst islets of **Ang Thong Marine National Park** by kayak via **Sea Canoe** (Lamai, 0 7621 2172, www.seacanoe.net) or **Blue Stars Kayaking** (Chaweng, 0 7741 3231, www.bluestars.info).

Eco-award-winning cyclist Michael Yantis rents top-end mountain bikes at **Red Bicycle** (just south of Hinta Hinyai, Lamai, 0 7723 2136, www.redbicycle.org) for half-day tours and longer. Above Maenam, **Canopy Jungle Tours** (0 7741 4150, canopyadventures @hotmail.com) lets you slide by cable between the treetops. The prize-winning **SITCA** teaches Thai cooking (Chaweng, 0 7741 3172, www.sitca.net, B1,200-B1,600).

Where to stay & eat

Just north of Nathon, purists treasure **Bang Makham**'s southern cuisine (Ao Bang Makham, 0 7742 6181, main courses B250). In Maenam, **Napasai** (0 7742 9200, www.pansea.com, rates $290-$990) stands out, with tasteful, French-influenced villas.

Many quaint old shophouses overlooking Bophut Beach have been turned into guesthouses, restaurants or shops. The **Lodge** (Fisherman's Village, 0 7742 5337, www.apartmentsamui.com, rates B1,350-B2,100) is an immaculate beachside boutique hotel with sea views from its hardwood floored rooms. The **Shack** (Fisherman's Village, closed Sun, main courses B200-B550) barbecues marinated meat and seafood, while fans of salad and herbal tea go to **Healthy & Fun Yoga Café** (Fisherman's Village, 0 7724 5046, www.healthyandfun.net, main courses B160). **Sala Samui Resort & Spa** (Choeng Mon, 0 7724 5888, www.salasamui.com, rates $200-$925, main courses B400-B700) offers

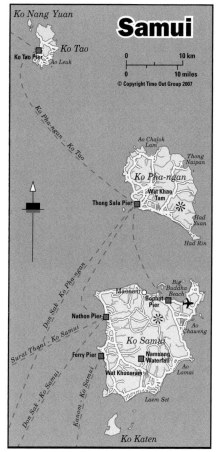

Chaweng, 08 1894 2327/08 9724 4425, www.sawadee.com/samui/jungleclub, rates B600-B3,500, main courses B150-B300) is a basic, chill-out bungalow set-up minus fan or air-con (not needed at this altitude), with fine French/Thai food and a decent pool.

On Lamai's shallow, coral-strewn north, **Spa Samui** (0 7723 0855, www.spasamui.com, rates B500-B5,500) is famed for its colonics courses. Devotees break fasts at its award-winning vegetarian café where free thinkers connect. It has a hillside branch. The 'Lanna minimalist' **Pavilion** resort and spa (124/24 Lamai beach, office 0 2223 3083-7, www.pavilionsamui.com, rates B6,000-B12,000) presides over Lamai's swimmable middle stretch.

Mind & body

Day spas and most resorts pride themselves on offering myriad healing options. The quality massages and treatments at **Baan Sabai** (Big Buddha Beach, 0 7724 5175, www.ban-sabai.com) take place in teak salas. Hot stone massage is one of many therapies amid the silk, carved stone and bubbling baths of **Four Seasons Tropical Spa** (Central Chaweng, 0 7741 4141-3). The sauna and plunge pool built around boulders distinguish **Tamarind Springs** (Lamai beach, 0 7742 4221, www.tamarindsprings.com).

Nightlife

Samui's weekly version of Glastonbury festival, the family-friendly **Secret Garden Festival** (Big Buddha Beach, 5.30-11pm Sun) mixes Thai and Western rock, plus the odd big name, as does **Fisherman's Village Festival** (Bophut, Aug). The hillside **Q Bar Samui** (Chaweng Lake, 08 1956 2742, www.qbarsamui.com) offers top global DJs, superlative drinks and sultry bar staff, just like its Bangkok parent.

The mellower **Pangaea** (Choeng Mon, 0 7724 5888) has imaginative cocktails, tropical tapas and funky music, while families and fans of TV sport flock to Irish-themed **Tropical Murphy's** (Central Chaweng, 0 7741 3614-5). Chaweng's big clubs (both free) – **Green Mango** (Beach Road, 0 7742 2148) and **Reggae Pub** (Chaweng Lagoon, 0 7742 2331) – draw large laddish crowds nightly. The style-conscious escape to Soi Colibiri's stark white **POD Bar** (0 81891 4042), boutique-cum-lounge bar **ESP** (0 8738 06153), and modern wine bar **Bellini's** (0 7741 3831, main courses B200-B400), which has fine northern Italian cuisine and the Molotov sports bar for many variations and forms of vodka.

total privacy in its 53 pool villas, as well as fine Pacific Rim cuisine.

Among Bangrak's decent budget digs, **Shambala** (0 7742 5330, www.samui-shambala.com, rates B600-B1,000, main courses B80-B200) has simple bungalows in a shoreside garden, plus superb Thai food. Nearby, the petite **Saboey Resort & Villas** features large elegant rooms and a Spanish/Moorish menu (0 7743 0456, www.saboey.com, rates B4,900-8,900, main courses B400-B700; **photo** *p210*).

On Chaweng, **Poppies** (South Chaweng, 0 7742 2419, www.poppies-samui.com, rates B6,900-B11,000, main courses B300-B500) offers luxurious cottages in a seaside garden, plus Thai/International fine dining. Commanding Samui's best panorama, **Jungle Club** (South

Resources

Hospital

Bangkok Samui Hospital, Thanon Thaweeratphakdee, Chaweng (0 7742 9500/www.samuihospital.com).

Tourist information

Thanon Thaweeratphakdee, Nathon (0 7742 0504/tatsamui@tat.or.th).
TAT, 5 Thanon Thalad Mai, Ban Don, Surat Thani (0 7742 0504/0720-2).
Also browse *Samui Guide, Samui Dining Guide, Samui Spa Guide* and *Samui Directory*, or www.kosamui.com and www.samuiguide.com.

Getting around

By road

Thailand's third largest island, 21km by 25km (13 by 15.5 miles), Samui takes 50mins to circle by car, or 90mins by motorbike, which are lethal on the narrow, hilly, often sandy roads. Hire a *songtaew* anywhere as a bus (B20-B70) or night taxi (up to B300; less if part-loaded). Motorcycle taxis are quick and negotiable, yellow 'metered' taxis a rip-off.

By boat

Ferries link Nathon with Surat Thani (2hrs) via Seatran Ferry (0 7727 5060/0 7725 1555, bus hourly 5.30am-5.30pm daily, B80; then boat hourly 6am-7pm daily, B110, B180 bus/boat package); or with Don Sak by car ferries (6am-7pm daily; to avoid 2-3hr waits, arrive by 8am) via Racha Ferry (0 7747 1152-3, boat hourly 5am-7pm, B100).

Ko Pha-ngan

An hour by ferry from Samui, Pha-ngan is ten years behind, slightly less beautiful, but friendlier. It attracts a blend of backpackers, entrepreneurs, dreamers and wasters to its smaller, craggier, often reef-laden bays, despite erratic electricity and torturous transport. Coconuts and fishing remain village mainstays.

East of the commercial centre of Thong Sala port sits **Wat Kow Tahm Meditation Centre** (*see p181*). The other ferry dock, **Had Rin West**, is rocky and shallow, and backs on to the headland's better beach, **Had Rin East**. Home of the Full Moon Parties, it would suit swimming and snorkelling were it not for the longtail traffic.

Where to stay & eat

Amid Had Rin's backpacker huts, the best of the few decent rooms are at **Drop In Club Resort & Spa** (0 7737 5444,

Sri Panwa. *See p217.*

www.dropinclub.com, rates B3,000-B19,900), which has a pool. Had Rin dining is quite cosmopolitan, with high-quality Italian, the **Shell** (Had Rin Lake, 0 7737 5149, main courses B150-B200), and Indian, **Om Ganesh** (Main Road, 0 7737 5123, main courses B150). For burgers and beers, try the quieter **Outback Bar** (Main Road, 0 7737 5126, main courses B200). On Had Yuan beach, there are stilt bungalows at **Big Blue Bungalows** (0 7742 2780, www.bigbluedivingsamui.com, rates B600-B800), some sleeping six, plus a good restaurant.

Inspiration for *The Beach*, Had Tien's **Sanctuary Spa & Wellness Centre** (08 1271 3614, www.thesanctuary-kpg.com, treatments B400-B2,500, rates B100-B4,400) is a B60 boat or 90-minute hike from Had Rin, offering sea-view suites, fine seafood/veggie cuisine and separate centres for fasters and spa treatments. The B100 dorm beds come with chores.

Flanked by Thaan Prawet and Wung Thong falls, the snorkelsome double bay of **Thong Naipan** in the north-east is better accessed by boat than the potholed track. The brick cottages with huge balconies at **Panviman Resort** (0 7744 5101, 0 2910 8660, www.panviman.com, rates B4,500-B17,000) have sea views; there's also a good international menu. Down the family-orientated beach, **Dolphin** (no phone, rates B300-B400) has decent bungalows and a great bar serving wholefood dishes.

On sleepy Had Salad, the chilled **Salad Hut** (0 7734 9246, rates B1,500-B2,500) offers renovated bungalows, some fan-cooled. Overlooking Had Yao to the west, **Tantawan Bungalows** (0 7734 9108/08 1956 0700, www.tantawanbungalow.com, rates B500-B1,200) has passable fan bungalows with shared bathrooms, great vistas, superb cuisine and a good pool.

Nightlife

Many visitors still come for one thing only: Full Moon Inc. Every month up to 10,000 committed partyheads rave to the hard trance on **Had Rin East** at the world's biggest beach party. Most stay on Ko Pha-ngan, but many speedboat in from northern Samui, filling rooms on both isles. Since Samui's party beach succumbed to villas, most months Had Rin also holds smaller Half Moon and Black Moon parties (consult www.kohphangan.com); dates shift on Buddhist lunar festivals.

Otherwise on Had Rin's bar strip, **Harmony** (behind Bamboozle restaurant), and **Backyard** (road to Had Leela, 9pm-2am) play uplifting trance and hard trance respectively.

Resources

For tourist information, *see p212* **Ko Samui**. Only Thong Sala and Had Rin have banks and ATMs.

Hospital
Koh Pha-ngan Hospital, north of Thong Sala (0 7737 7034).

Getting around

By road
Beach-hopping is pleasurable but slow. *Songtaew* run to all accessible beaches from Had Rin and Thong Sala (B50) when a ferry docks, otherwise it's once or twice a day, and at bar closing time in Had Rin. The rutted tracks are dirt-biker heaven, but even the paved roads can prove to be terrifying slaloms for the unwary. Many simply decide to don a decent pair of boots and hike.

By boat
Ferries from Don Sak (Surat Thani) to Thong Sala (2.5hrs; B200) at 7am, 10am, noon, 2pm, 4pm, 6pm; contact Racha Ferry (0 7747 1151-3). Express boat from Nathon (Samui) to Thong Sala (45 mins) at 11am (B150), 5pm (B200); contact Songserm Travel (0 7742 0157). Catamaran from Maenam (Samui) to Thong Sala (30mins; B250) 8am, noon, 5pm; contact Lomprayah Travel (0 7742 7766). Boat from Big Buddha (Phra Yai or Bangrak) to Had Rin

(1hr; B150) 10.30am, 1pm, 4pm, 6.30pm; contact Big Buddha pier (0 7742 7650). Speedboat from Big Buddha to Thong Sala (30 mins; B250) 8am, 1.30pm; contact Seatran Discovery (0 7742 0003). Several east and north coast beaches have no land access. Longtail taxis run from Had Rin East (B60 by day to Had Tien, B300 at night), demanding payment of up to B1,000 for longer rides, or B1,500-B2,000 for day charter.

Ko Tao

'Turtle Island' resembles a turtle diving south to Ko Pha-ngan and Ko Samui. Rocky and jungly, it has a long western strand facing **Ko Nang Yuan**, three islets linked by a tri-star beach. Non-divers can feel out of place, but relish 11 quiet beaches, notably **Leuk**, **Jansom** and **June Juea**. Tao is walkable, but has bike taxis and a few *songtaew*.

Boasting good coral, swim-throughs and an abundance of large fish, the 24 dive sites have good visibility (late May-early Oct). Snorkelling gear can be rented all over; **Black Tip Diving & Water Sports** (Ao Tanote, 0 7745 6488-9, www.blacktipdiving.com) also has kayaks, wakeboards and waterskis, and attractive bungalows (rates B800-B3,000).

Where to stay & eat

Over 20 resorts cater to and teach every level of diver, notably **Koh Tao Coral Grand Resort** (Had Sairee, 0 7745 6431-3, www.kohtao coral.com, rates B3,500-B9,000), **Buddha View Dive Resort** (Chalok Baan Kao, 0 7745 6074, www.buddhaview-diving.com, rates B900-B1,500; priority to diving guests) and **Planet Scuba** (Mae Had pier, 0 7745 6110, www.planet-scuba.net, rooms B300-B1,000, package B9,800 including four days' diving; diving half-day B2,000). A pioneer, **Ao Leuk Resort** (Ao Leuk beach, 0 7745 6692, rates B450) retains a real island feel. **Sensi Paradise Resort** (0 7745 6244, www. kohtaoparadise.com, rates B1,200-B17,000) is a good upmarket option close to Mae Had. **Baan Charm Churee** (Jansom Bay, 0 7745 6393-4, www.charmchureevilla.com, rates B3,200-B9,200) offers wood-and-wicker rooms on a beautiful private beach. **Nang Yuan Island Dive Resort** (0 7745 6088-93, www.nangyuan. com, rates B1,500-B7,700) is the islet's sole, beautiful venue.

The charming, cheap **New Heaven Bakery** (Sairee Village & Thian Og, 0 7745 6554) serves the best coffee. Italians swear by the home-made fare at **La Matta** (Mae Had, 08 9001 4046, main courses B115-B380. Scoff pizza and

Bailey's cheesecake at **Farango Pizzeria** (Mae Had, 0 7745 6205, main courses B150-B250).

Nightlife

Diving buddies often become drinking buddies, notably at **Safety Stop** (Mae Had, 0 7745 6209, main courses B20-B320). Beach parties vary by day: on Had Sairee at the **AC Bar** meat market (0 7745 6197, Tue, Thur, Sun), amid the *tiki* torches and sand sculptures of **In Touch** (0 7745 6514, Wed, Sat), and Dry Bar (Fri), which occupies a gnarled live tree; and on Mae Had at the **Whitening Bar** (0 7745 6199).

Resources

For tourist information, *see p212* **Ko Samui** or try www.kohtaoonline.com.

Hospital

Chumphon Hospital, 222 Thanon Pisitpayabarn, Chumphon 0 7750 3672-4). See also *p212* **Ko Samui**.

Getting around

By road

Tao is walkable. Taxi bikes and pick-ups cost B50-B100 per head, more at night. Avoid hiring bikes or 4WDs as the poor state of roads can easily incur damage.

By boat

Songserm Travel (Tao, 0 7745 6274, Bangkok 0 2280 7897) have one express boat per day per route linking Mae Had with Chumphon (Ta Yang; 3hrs; B450), Pha-ngan (1.5hrs; B150), Samui (2.5hrs; B250) and Surat Thani (6hrs; B550). Lomprayah Travel (0 7742 7765-6) runs catamaran from Mae Had to Samui (1.5hrs; B550) 9.30am, 3pm. Boats may not run in poor weather. Longtails day charter costs around B1,500.

Andaman Sea

Ko Phuket

Thailand's largest, richest island (49km by 27km/30 by 17 miles) has been a trading post for millennia. A 19th-century tin rush turned Phuket City into the province's capital, drew Chinese settlers and left the rainforested hills scarred. From the 1970s Phuket mined an even richer seam: tourism. Fishing villages became smart resorts or ramshackle shanties, offering diving, yachting and 'eco-adventures'.

Over bridges from the mainland, Route 402 skirts Phuket International Airport and threads south to Phuket City past rubber plantations, the **Heroines' Monument** (to two women who helped repel the Burmese in 1785) and Kathu, where **Ban Kathu Heritage Centre** (Ban Kathu School, 0 7632 1246, open by appointment) hosts a dusty Mining Museum. Like Singapore, Melaka and Penang, Phuket City retains Sino-Portuguese shophouses and mansions, gaily decorated in Greco-Roman and 'lucky' Chinese motifs. Some tin baron homes along Thanons Yaowarat, Krabi, Thalang and Deebuk have become bars, boutiques or galleries; **Chinpracha House** (Thanon Krabi, 08 9646 9080, 9.30am-4pm daily) preserves that lifestyle perfectly. Named from *bukit* (Malay for 'hill'), Phuket City hugs Khao Rang hill. The park at the summit offers views west to Phangnga bay and the Sea Gypsy village on Ko Siray.

Most tourists stay around the bays that scallop the western and southern coasts, and now at the long northern Mai Khao beach near **Sirinart National Park** (0 7632 7152/8226). Ao Bang Thao Mai fits hotels and golf courses of Phuket Laguna around lagoons in old mining pits, while many of the ritziest hotels, shops and villas snuggle in quieter Surin and Kamala beach. Tsunami-hit fisherfolk share Kamala beach with **Phuket FantaSea** (0 7638 5000, www.phuket-fantasea.com, show B1,000-B1,500), a gaudy theme park with a vast buffet restaurant and a 3,000-seat theatre for a pyrotechnic spectacle, including elephants.

Ringed by hills, the crescent of Ao Patong is raw tourism, with pestering touts, gem stores, stalls selling fakes and hostess bars clogging the Soi Bangla strip. The developed lower west coast has arguably the best beaches, from broad, duned Karon to prettier, family-friendly Kata, where twin bays frame the snorkel-friendly Ko Pu islet. Kata Yai hosts September's windsurfing championships.

There are stunning views from beyond here, and particularly at the southern cape Laem Phrom Thep, which gets crowded at sunset. East around the cape arcs dramatically beautiful, windswept Nai Harn beach.

Activities

Try eco tours (B1,500-B2,000 incl lunch and transfers) by **Siam Safari** (45 Thanon Chao Fa West, Chalong, 0 7628 0116, www.siamsafari.com), **Phuket Union Travel** (64/23 Thanon Chao Fa West, Chalong, 0 7622 5522-33, www.phuket-union.com) or **Asian Premier Holidays** (74/90 Poonphon Night Plaza, Phuket City, 0 7624 6260, www.asianpremier.com). Mountain bike specialists include

Bike Tours (10/195 Thanon Kwang, Phuket City, 0 7626 3575, 01797 6540, www.bike toursthailand.com). Several 4WD tours twist through the jungles and plantations. Elephant treks are mostly short bush rambles; some include mangrove kayaking.

Canoe trips explore sea caves in the jungled karst islets soaring out of Phang-nga Bay. The eco-sensitive pioneer of this now often reckless mass activity, John 'Caveman' Gray, has split from **Sea Canoe** (0 7621 2172, www.seacanoe. net) to offer similarly inspirational tours at **John Gray's Sea Canoe** (0 7625 4505-7, www.seacanoe.com). Bring water, a T-shirt and sunscreen. Most boat tours of Ao Phang-nga National Marine Park take in 'James Bond Island' (Ko Tapu, where *The Man with the Golden Gun* was shot).

Phuket is Thailand's diving HQ, with a recompression chamber in Patong and 50-plus companies, including **White & Blue Dive Club** (0 7628 1007-8, www.white-bluedive.com), **Dive Master** (0 7629 2402-3, www.divemaster.net), **Scuba Cat** (0 7634 5246, www.scubacat.com) and **South-east Asia Liveaboards** (0 7634 0406, www.seal-asia.com). Aside from day trips, liveaboard tours take in dramatic reefs and pelagic fish at the Similan, Surin or Phi Phi islands. Access and visibility drop during the monsoon, when beach rip tides also make swimming risky.

Golf flourishes at **Blue Canyon Country Club** (165 Thanon Thepkasatri, Had Nai Yang, 0 7632 7440, www.bluecanyonclub.com), **Phuket Golf & Country Club** (80/1 Thanon Wichitsongkhram, 0 7632 1038-41, www.phuketcountryclub.com) and the **Laguna** (www.lagunaphuket.com).

Phuket is Asia's yachting hub. **Boat Lagoon Marina** (20/27 Thanon Thepkrasattri) hosts charter giants **Sunsail** (0 7623 9057, www.sunsailthailand.com), yacht services, a hotel, a spa and restaurants. Day sailors may prefer the rather ramshackle **Ao Chalong Yacht Club** (Thanon Chaofa, www.acycphuket.com). Super-yachts berth at **Yacht Haven Marina** (Laem Phrao, east of Sarasin Bridge, 0 7620 6704-5, www.yacht-haven-phuket.com), while **Royal Phuket Marina** (68 Thanon Thepkrasattri, www.royalphuketmarina.com) proffers swanky spas, cafés and champagne bars.

beach, turtles coexist with the sublime **JW Marriott Phuket Resort**(0 7633 8000, rates $377-$2,968),with its chi-chi Mandara Spa, and quirky, Bill Bensley-disigned **Indigo Pearl** (0 7632 7006, www.indigo-pearl.com, rates B12,000). On private Nai Thorn beach, the palatial residences at **Trisara** (0 7631 0100, www.trisara.com, rates $575-$3,960) boast private pools, live-in maids and iPods. **Banyan Tree Phuket** (Laguna Phuket, 0 7632 4374, www.lagunaphuket.com, rates $550-$3,400) has tasteful seaside villas and a gorgeous spa.

More elite still are the hillside bungalows of **Chedi Phuket** (Ao Surin, 0 7632 4017-20, rates $160-$780) and Ed Tuttle's style-setting pared-down villas at **Amanpuri** (Ao Surin, 0 7632 4333, www.amanresorts.com, rates $675-$7,350). **Twin Palms** (0 7631 6500, www.twinpalms-phuket.com, rates $170-$590) earns plaudits for its immaculate modernism and gardens, while beside it at Surin, **Surin Bay Inn** (0 7627 1601, www.surinbayinn.com, rates B1,000-B3,000) balances impeccable rooms with value.

Patong's choicest beds are now at the handsome, artful **Burasari** (32/1 Thanon Ruamjai, 0 7629 2929, www.burasari.com, rates B2,700-B7,600). Between Karon and Kata, **Mom Tri's Boathouse** (182 Thanon Kok Tanoad, 0 7633 0 015-7, www.theboathousephuket.com, rates B4,000-B35,000) is the flagship of pioneer resort architect Tri Devakul. **Sri Panwa** (Cape Panwa, 0 7637 1000, www.sripanwa.com, rates B36,000-B48,400) ensures a cutting-edge ambience in its hillside villas.

Spread up a slope, the suave **Le Royal Meridien Phuket Yacht Club** (Ao Nai Harn, 0 7638 0200-19, www.phuket-yachtclub.com, rates $120-$610) has hosted parties by **Bed Supperclub** (*see p191*) and commands Ao Nai Harn bay, a beach where guests get shuttled downhill from the panoramic villas of fruit-hued **Mangosteen Resort & Spa** (0 7628 9399, www.mangosteen-phuket.com, rates B6,500-B11,000). Contrastingly minimalist, **Evason Phuket Resort** (100 Thanon Viset, Rawai, 0 7638 1010-7, www.six-senses.com, rates B6,500-B50,000) also lacks a direct beach, but has exclusive use of Ko Bon's velvety offshore sands. Similarly, **Maiton Island** (0 7621 4954-8, www.maitonisland.com, rates from B6,500) is the preserve of one posh villa resort.

Where to stay

Phuket has around 500 hotels (many bookable via www.phuket.com or www.hoteltravel.com), with the best beds up north and budget rooms limited to Patong, Karon and Phuket City, with no bargain bungalows. At virgin Mai Khao

Where to eat

Locals grab an *oliang* (Chinese coffee) over morning dim sum, *pa tong goh* (Chinese doughnuts) or *tao sor* (stuffed Chinese buns) in Phuket City's holes in the wall or Patong's Soi Sainamyen stalls. **Somchit** and **Ton Pho**, both by the clock tower on Thanon Phuket, serve Hokkien noodles *chek* (dry) or *sapam* (soupy) for lunch. Overlooking city and sea, **Thungka** (0 7621 1500, main courses B250) offers authentic southern fare. Nearby **Tamachart** (Soi Puton, 0 7622 4287, main courses B200) has intriguingly quirky jungle decor.

Resort restaurant quality varies hugely. **Patong Night Market** (Thanon Ratcha Uthit) is cheap, but basic. For better seafood than Patong's seafront strip, head north to **Pan Yaah** (249 Thanon Prabaramee, 0 7634 4473, main courses B250), which overlooks Patong, or the bayside **Rockfish** (Kamala Beach, 0 7627 9732, main courses B350), with superb concoctions and cool DJs.

Silk Restaurant & Bar (Plaza Surin, 0 7627 1702, www.silkphuket.com, main courses B500) serves posh southern Thai cuisine in a sophisticated setting. For Pacific Rim fusion, try the coolly minimalist **Supper Club** (20/382 Thanon Srisoonthorn, 0 7627 0936, main courses B500) or the Mediterranean-hued **Tatonka** (382/19 Thanon Srisoonthorn, 0 7632 4349, main courses B350), both near the Laguna gate.

Mind & body

Unlike Samui's New Age wellness, Phuket tends towards high-class pampering, though its many tin-roofed herbal saunas (often at an alfresco massage parlour) purge the pores for as little as B50. Worth a splurge is the world-renowned **Banyan Tree Phuket** (*see p217*), which devises its own treatments, while the holistic **Six Senses Spa** at Evason Phuket (*see p217*) is the best at non-Thai massage. Phuket's first spa, the jungly **Hideaway Spa** (157 Thanon Nanai, Patong, 0 7634 0591, Laguna Entrance, 0 7627 1549; www.phuket-hide away.com) adapts ancient recipes for its herbal steam rooms.

Nightlife

In Phuket City trendy Thais frequent the loud, stark bar **GorTorMor** (Thanon Chana Charoen). Phuket's expat hangout, the **Watermark** (Boat Lagoon Marina, Thanon Thepkasattri, Ko Kaew, 0 7623 9730, main courses B550), shakes and stirs the island's best cocktail selection, plus top-end Thai and Mediterranean/Asian fusion food. Irish beer, hearty meals, quizzes and events are legion at the **Green Man** pub (82/15 Thanon Pratak, Rawai, 0 7628 0757/1445-52, www.the-green-man.net, main courses B200). **Reggae Bar** (Soi Naya, Nai Harn Lake) has a genuine Rasta-run atmosphere.

High in the hills above Bang Tao/ Laguna, **360** (Phuket Pavilions, 0 7631 7600, www.phuketpavilions.com) offers amazing coastal and inland views. More glam than those working the Soi Bangla beer bars, ladyboys parade in **Simon Cabaret** (8 Thanon Sirirach, Patong, 0 7634 2114, www.phuket-simoncabaret.com).

Shopping

Island shopping is transforming, thanks to global brands (and multiplex screens) at **Central Festival** (Phuket City, www.central festivalphuket.com), the art and objets d'art at the refined **Plaza Surin** (Surin Beach, 0 7627 1741, www.theplazasurin.com) and at the swish shop clusters by Laguna's gate and inside the Laguna at **Canal Village** (0 7632 4453-7). **Mom Tri's Boathouse** (*see p217*) holds art exhibitions, book launches and talks by visiting authors.

Souvenir-hunting, tailor selection and braving touts are evening entertainment at Patong, although **Jungceylon** mall (182 Thanon Rat-u-thit 200 Pee, 0 7636 6022, www.jungceylon.com) revolutionised the resort's tacky market scene with a breadth of retail, dining and entertainment. Pearls are prominent in Patong and Rawai. **Mook Ko Kaew** (41/6-7 Thanon Vichitsongkram, 0 7622 2563-4) sells both natural and cultured pearls.

Festivals

Phuket Vegetarian Festival (Oct, 1st 9 days of 9th lunar month) sees self-mutilating devotees parade in and around Chinese temples, with lots of firecrackers and tofu-heavy food. The parades and entertainment of **Patong Carnival** (1 Nov) herald the week-long **Phuket International Seafood Festival**. **Phuket Laguna Triathlon** overlaps with the yachties blowing in for Asia's two biggest sailfests, the **King's Cup Regatta** (early Dec, www.kings cup.com), which parties nightly in Phuket, and the island-hopping, sleep-aboard **Phang-nga Regatta** (Chinese New Year, www.bayregatta. com). Then come architectural walks at the **Phuket Heritage Festival** (following Chinese New Year, 0 7622 2932); **Phuket Gay Festival** (Feb, www.gayphuket.com); and **Baan Kata Art Festival**, featuring art and music at Mom Tri's Boathouse (Mar). After convoying down from Bangkok, Harley fans rev up in Patong for **Phuket Bike Week** around Songkran (mid Apr).

Gay & lesbian

Thanks to Phuket's 'pink baht' income, Phuket Gay Festival (Feb/Mar, www.gaypatong.com) can parade through Patong to the bars and clubs of phallic **Paradise Complex**, notably the unmissable cabaret at **Boat Bar Disco** (125/20 Thanon Rat-u-thit, 0 7634 2206, www.boatbar.com), drinks at the quieter **James Dean Guest House** (Rat-u-thit Soi 5, 0 7634 4215, www.jamesdeanbar.com, rates B700-B1,000) or **Sphinx Restaurant & Theatre** (120 Thanon Rat-u-thit, 0 7634 1500, www.sphinxthai.com), which has a cabaret show. Patong's gay-friendly hotels include **Club Bamboo** (47 Thanon Nanai, 0 7634 5345, www.clubbamboo.com, rates B2,200-B12,000) and seafront **Thara Patong Beach Resort** (170 Thanon Thaweewong, 0 7634 0135, www.tharapatong.com, rates B4,600-B7,000).

Resources

Hospital

Bangkok Phuket Hospital, Phuket City (0 7625 4421/www.phukethospital.com).

Tourist information

TAT, 73 Thanon Phuket, Phuket City (0 7621 2213, www.phukettourism.org). Also consult *Phuket Gazette* (www.phuketgazette.com) and *Phuket Post* (www.phuketpost.com), plus www.phuket-maps.com.

Getting around

Roads are surfaced but hazardously twisting. *Songtaew* provide lackadaisical service; otherwise, it's hotel shuttles, *tuk-tuks*, motorbike taxis and a few taxis. Fares get more extortionate the later and more remote the ride.

Khao Lak

A 70-kilometre (44-mile), one-hour drive north of Phuket, Khao Lak suffered most from the tsunami, but has recovered fairly well. Its long sweeping beach and parallel lush virgin forest remain two of the South's natural highlights. Although stretches of beachside land remain barren, resorts have reclaimed the prime sites.

Where to stay & eat

On the road to Khao Lak proper, up-and-coming Natai Beach hosts the cool modern suites and spa of **Aleenta** (0 2508 5333, rates B11,775-B23,505). Working up the coast from the south, choose from **Khao Lak Resort** (0 7642 8111, www.khaolakresort.com, rates B2,000-B6,000), which has a varied selection of hillside and beachside rooms and bungalows; the ultra-opulent traditional Thai style **Mukdara Beach Villa & Spa Resort** (0 7648 6199, www.mukdarabeach.com, rates B7,500-B13,000) or **Ayara Villas** (0 7648 6478, www.ayara-villas.com, bungalow B2,400-B3,500), which has an excellent beach location and simple, charming, air-con bungalows. For dining in the main town near Nang Thong beach, **Tiffy's Café** (opposite Bank of Ayudhya, main courses B100-150) serves Thai staples, good coffee and quality sandwiches; **Ruen Mai Seafood** (beside SCB Bank, 0 7642 0156, main courses B200-300) has myriad fish dishes and **Pizzaria Spaghetteria** (0 7642 0271, main courses B250-350) does authentic pasta and pizza. Further north, the beautiful **Similana Resort** (0 7642 0166, rates B2,900-4,500), scatters down a tousled hillside to its own beach, while the rebuilt **Le Méridien Khao Lak** (0 7642 7500, www.starwoodhotels.com, rates $130-$150) brings all-mod-con family friendliness.

Resources

For a hospital, *see p216* Phuket.

Tourist information

TAT, 73 Thanon Phuket, Phuket City (0 7621 2213/www.phukettourism.org). Also try www.khaolak-info.net or www.khaolak.net.

Getting around

Ten hot and stuffy non-air-con buses per day between Takua-pa and Phuket Town (B60) ply the delta of routes permeating this elongated area, which is far better negotiated by hired car. Unless you like the idea of a mobile sauna.

Krabi

Krabi Airport brought mass tourism to **Laem Phra Nang**, a breathtaking karst cape. Roadless and cut off by towering cliffs, the cape is getting ever-denser accommodation on the back-to-back bays of sandy West Railay and mangrovey East Railay. A trail leads past caves to the paradisical Had Phra Nang beach, home of sunbathers and full-moon rites to its cave's fertility deity.

Longtail ferries leave from humdrum **Krabi Town**, passing **Susaan Hoi**, a fossil shell beach, but most people reach it by boat from nearby **Ao Nang**, a laid-back hub of resorts, restaurants and internet cafés. Agencies hawk trips to islands, reefs, lagoons and inland eco tours, including **Sea Canoe** (0 7569 5387), the scuba outfits **Aqua Vision** (0 7563 7415, www.aqua-vision.net) and **Reef Watch** (0 7563 2650), and, in Krabi Town, **Chan Phen Travel** (145 Thanon Utarakit, 0 7561 2004).

Ko Phi Phi's **Zeavola**. See p221.

Railay is a rock-climbing centre with hard après-climb partying. Climbing outfits offer training (half-day B800, up to 3-day B5,000), most reputably **King Climbers** (Ao Nang, 0 7563 7125; Railay, 0 7562 2581, www.railay. com) and **Tex Rock** (Railay East, 08 1891 1528, www.texadventurecamps.com).

Where to stay, eat & drink

Krabi Town's limited options include **Star Guest House** (72 Thanon Khong Kha, 0 7563 0234, rates B150), which has trad decor and a river view. **May & Mark** (6 Thanon Ruen Rudee, 0 7561 2562, main courses B70-B150) serves great food. At Ao Nang, try the **Cliff** (0 7563 8117, www.k-bi.com, rates B8,000-B12,000), a hilltop getaway with handsome garden villas. Reached only by boat or path from Ao Nang, **Central Krabi Bay Resort** (0 7563 7789, www.centralhotelsresorts.com, rates B6,375-B50,000) fills cliff-ringed Pai Plong bay with swish rooms, diverse restaurants and three pools, while distant **Sheraton Krabi Beach Resort** (0 7562 8000, rates $200-$588,www.sheraton.com/krabi) has brought long Nong Thale beach into contention.

Dominating Railay and Phra Nang beaches, the sublime **Rayavadee Resort** (0 7562 0740-3, www.rayavadee.com, rates B35,000-B150,000) has villas and full facilities. For bungalows, beach restaurants and pools, try **Sand Sea Resort** (0 7562 2609, www.sandsearesort, rates B1,450-B3,450), **Railay Bay Resort** (0 7562 2571/2, rates B2,000-B7,000) on gentrifying Railay West. The less salubrious east side has decent rooms at **Railay Village** (0 7562 2578, rates B800-B2,500), tasty Thai food at **Coco's** (main courses B100) and a string of chill-out party places, notably **Skunk Bar**. Climbers tend to stay at grittier Tonsai beach.

Resources

Hospital

Krabi Hospital, 325 Thanon Utrakit, Krabi Town (0 7561 1212/http://hospital.moph.go.th/krabi).

Tourist information

Krabi Tourism Centre, Thanon Utrakit, Krabi Town (0 7562 2163/4). Also try www.krabi.com and www.railay.com.

Getting around

By road

Songtaew and hotel buses ply Ao Nang, Krabi Town and Krabi Airport. Leam Phra Nang is walking only.

By boat

Longtails run between Laem Phra Nang and Krabi Town (30mins plus waiting) or Ao Nang (10mins), where a ticket booth fixes fares. PP Family (0 7561 2463, www.phiphifamily.com) runs ferries to Phuket, Phi Phi, Krabi, Railay, and from Hua Hin pier south of Krabi Town to Ko Lanta. Ao Nang's ticket booth standardises longtail taxi fares to Railay and elsewhere.

Ko Lanta

Inhabited mostly by Muslim Thais and *chao lay* (sea gypsies), fast-upgrading Ko Lanta Yai belongs to a National Marine Park blessed with dive sites and awesome karst outcrops. Down the sandy west coast from the northern pier hub, **Ban Sala Dan**, backpacker bungalows, lively bars and internet cafés crowd **Had Khlong Dao** and **Ao Phrae-Ae** ('Long Beach'). As the roads deteriorate south through **Had Khlong Khoang**, **Had Khlong Nin** and **Ao Kantieng**, designer getaways mix with ramshackle huts.

From Ban Sala Dan, land, boat and kayak trips explore the east coast's caves, mangroves, Muslim village life in **Sangka-u**, and **Lanta**, a town of old wooden shophouses. Other tours take in a bat cave and a seasonal waterfall.

Where to stay & eat

Angular **Costa Lanta** (0 7568 4630, Bangkok 0 2662 3550-1, www.costalanta.com, rates B6,050-B9,460) is the chic pick of Khlong Dao's resorts. The finest digs are at **Pimalai Resort** (0 7560 7999, Bangkok 0 2320 5500, www.pimalai.com, rates B12,000-B85,000) on superb Ba Kan Tiang beach. Nearby Zen-chic **Sri Lanta** (Klongnin Beach, 0 7566 2688, 0 2712 8858, www.srilanta.com, rates B3,500-B4,500) is similar, but more laid-back. Veggie fare is good at **Sanctuary** (Phrae-Ae beach, 08 1891 3055, closed mid May-mid Oct, rates B650-B850, main courses B100).

Resources

For tourist information, *see p219* **Krabi**.

Hospital

Ko Lanta Hospital, 118 Thanon Sanga-ou, Ban Sala Dan (0 7569 7100).

Getting around

By road

An hourly van service (0 7562 2197, B150) runs from Lanta to Krabi Town (7am-5pm) and back (6am-3pm). Dusit Van (0 7563 1994, B170, B200 incl airport) from Krabi-Lanta 11am, 1pm, 4pm; return 8am, 1pm.

By boat

PP Family (0 7561 2463) runs boats (Oct-Apr) from Ban Sala Dan to Krabi Town 8am, 1pm, returning 10.30am, 2pm; or year-round Krabi (Klong Jirad) to Lanta 8am, 1pm, returning 10.30am, 2pm; or to Ban Hua Hin pier south of Krabi Town. Boats run from Ao Nang to Lanta (Ban Sala Dan) 10.30am, returning 1.30 pm.

Ko Phi Phi

The wondrous pelagic vistas of this island duo drew so many visitors since the 1980s that Phi Phi became a byword for development, from damaged reefs and brackish water to garbage overload. Damage to Maya Bay on Phi Phi Leh while filming *The Beach* proved minor compared with how the 2004 tsunami scoured the tourist village on the sandbar of Phi Phi Don. Thaksin hampered its recovery so it could be turned into an upmarket eco-resort, but with

backpacker volunteer help the crowded mess of bars and guesthouses returned regardless. Areas unaffected by the wave have fared better.

Boat trips take in Leh's impenetrable cliffs, picturesque bays and the Viking Cave, so named for its mariner's murals, where men on bamboo scaffolds harvest swift's nests for the Chinese soup delicacy. The many scuba shops do early and late dives to avoid the daytripping hordes.

Where to stay & eat

At the northern tip of Phi Phi Don, the four-star **Holiday Inn** (Laem Thong Beach, 0 7562 1334, www.phiphi-palmbeach.com, rates B5,100-8,000) provides quiet, garden bungalows. On Loh Ba Gao bay, the secluded **Phi Phi Island Village Beach Resort & Spa** (0 7621 5014, www.ppisland.com, rates B5,700-9,800) offers luxury beachfront villas and suites. The last word in eco-friendly luxury, however, is **Zeavola** (0 7562 7000, www.zeavola.com, rates B11,000-29,000, main courses B400-B500; **photo** *p220*), which has beautifully fitted villas and some of the island's finest dining. Most independent dining is around Ton Sai. Try mellow **Hippies Bar & Restaurant** (main courses B100-B200); **Hibachi** (main courses B200) for its Japanese buffet; **Pappaya** (main courses B100-B150); or the **Reggae Bar**, which mixes music and *muay thai* boxing, and contains an expat café, **Little Britain** (main courses B200-B300).

Resources

See p216 Phuket or *p219* Krabi. The website www.phi-phi.com is a good resource.

Hospital

See p216 Phuket *or p219* Krabi.

Getting there & around

By sea

Ferries from Phuket's Rasada pier (1.30-2hrs, B600, B1,000 round trip, incl pick-up from Phuket Town, Patong, Kata or Karon; fee for other pick-ups) depart 8.30am, 1.30pm, returning 9am, 2.30pm; contact Andaman Wavemaster (0 7623 2095) and PP Cruise (0 7621 1253). From Lanta (Sala Dan, 1hr; B450) ferries depart 8am, 1pm, returning 11.30am, 3pm; contact Ao Nang Travel (0 7623 2040-1). From Ao Nang (Krabi, 2hrs; B390) ferries depart 9.30am, returning 3.30pm; contact Ao Nang Travel (0 7623 2040-1). Phi Phi Island Village and Zeavola run speedboat transfers from Phuket's Boat Lagoon Marina. Phi Phi Don is all walkable. Longtails can be chartered to Ko Phi Phi Leh and remote beaches.

Beach Escapes

113 Hua Hin 67, Petchkasem Road. Prachuab, 77110, Thailand
Tel: +66 32 533 678 Fax: +66 32 533 679
Email: huahin@verandalodge.com - www.verandalodge.com

VERANDA LODGE

Directory

Directory

Getting Around

Arriving & leaving

By air

The new Suvarnabhumi Airport, 25km (15.5 miles) east of Downtown at Nong Ngu Hao (Cobra Swamp), opened in September 2006 with such problems that non-connecting domestic flights were at press time due to be relocated back to Don Muang (Highest Ground) 27km (17 miles) north. Either is 30-45mins from downtown via expressway, but longer in rush hour.

Don Muang Airport

Thanon Wiphawadi Rangsit, Outer North (to be announced /Arrivals to be announced/Departures to be announced /www.airportthai.co.th). **Thai Airways check-in** 0 2535 2242. **Tourist police** 0 2535 1641/1155. **Don Muang police station** 0 2535 6222/5666. Facilities reopening at Don Muang for domestic routes (except international connections with Chiang Mai, Phuket and Krabi) will in all likelihood include tourist, hotel and tour information, phones and 24hr banks/currency exchanges, internet, left luggage, public taxis, limousines, airport express buses and shuttle buses to Suvarnabhumi.

Suvarnabhumi Airport

Thanon Bangna-Trad km15, East (0 2132 1888/www.airportthai.co.th). **Airport Information Counter Arrivals** 0 2132 9328-9. **Departures** 0 2132 9324-7. **Thai Airways check-in** 0 2132 0040. **Tourist police** 0 2132 1155/1155. **Police station** 0 2132 4000. **TAT counter beside entrance** 1 (0 2132 1155). **Car parks** (0 2132 9114, free for first 15mins, then B25 for 1hr up to B250 for 7-24hrs).

The new airport (*see p22* **Landing in Cobra Swamp**) occupies the world's biggest single terminal, yet still doesn't have enough space, especially with so many retail outlets by King Power

Duty Free (0 2134 8888/www.kingpower.com), which incredibly don't stock many magazines nor any newspapers. Services include 24hr currency exchanges/ATMs (banks 8am-5pm daily), left luggage (0 2134 7795-6), lost property (0 2132 1880), VAT refunds (4th floor; east 0 2134 0675-6, west 0 2134 0677-8), internet, massage parlour, restaurants and not enough toilets – one of many design oversights being remedied. Shuttlebuses from the terminal serve the nearby, comfortable Novotel Suvarnabhumi Airport Hotel (0 2131 1111, www.novotel.com, rates B9,000-B11,700). A rail link to Phyathai BTS (via a city check-in at Makkasan) will open in 2008; for taxi and bus services, *see below*.

Suvarnabhumi Airport taxis

Public Taxi-Meter *Arrivals, 2nd floor (0 2132 9112-4).* **Open** 24hrs daily.
To help prevent scams, you keep the card carrying the driver's number in case of complaints or lost property (0 2132 1880). At journey's end, you pay the meter fare (B200-B400 to city), plus a B50 airport surcharge; you pay expressway tolls.
TG Airport Limousine *1st floor (airport call centre 0 2132 1888/ drivers direct 08 4146 3658/ 08 9145 6288/www.thaiair.com).* **Open** 24hrs daily.
This luxury limousine service runs to or from the city (car B800, van B1,100), or other locations (car B500 per hr, van B600 per hr/B6,500 per day).
Airport Associate *(0 2982 4900/ www.aaclimousine.com).* **Open** 24hrs daily.
Cars with driver (Merc from B500 per hr, van B700 per hr) to city, Pattaya (B2,900), or elsewhere. Reliable, but no counter at airport.

Airport buses

Suvarnabhumi Airport Express *(08 9452 4849).*
Yellow Airport Express buses serve four city routes, departing the terminal's ground floor every 30mins 5am-midnight daily, B150 per person; city to airport B50 Thais; B100 foreigners. Express routes: AE1 (Silom), AE2 (Banglumphu), AE3 (Sukhumvit),

AE4 (Hualumpong Station). The reopened Don Muang Airport will likely have express buses to the same destinations, and a shuttle bus to Suvarnabhumi.
Suvarnabhumi Transit Centre Shuttle Bus *(0 2132 9191-3).*
Shuttles run every 15mins, 5am-11pm daily, between each terminal floor and a transit centre, for connections with orange BMTA local buses (every 5 mins 24hr, B35), faster minivan services (B40-B50) and long-distance buses.

Airlines

Air Asia *reservations 0 2515 9999/ Suvarnabhumi 0 2134 3510/www. airasia.com.*
Budget airline founded in Malaysia serving provinces and region.
Bangkok Airways *reservations 0 2265 5555/Suvarnabhumi 0 2134 3999/www.bangkokair.com.*
Boutique airline serving provinces, Asian World Heritage Sites and its own airports in Samui, Sukhothai, Trad and Cambodia.
Nok Air *reservations 1318/ Suvarnabhumi call centre 0 2132 1888/www.nokair.com.*
Thai Airways' budget offshoot, serving provinces.
One-Two-Go *reservations 0 2229 4260/Suvarnabhumi call centre 0 2132 1888/www.fly12go.com/ www.orientthai.com.*
Budget airline serving provinces and region.
PB Air *reservations 0 2261 0220-8/ Suvarnabhumi 0 2134 7924-5/ www.pbair.com.*
A private airline serving provinces and region.
Thai Airways *reservations 0 2628 2000/Suvarnabhumi 0 2130 0064/ 0016/www.thaiairways.com.*
National flag carrier with global and domestic routes.

Maps & navigation

Many signs are in English, which is widely spoken, though often faltering. Transliterations into English often vary between guides, maps and signs. As many streets look alike and building numbers can be non-contiguous, ask directions using body language and key

Health tourism

Some come to Thailand for herbal therapies, but others (including some national health services) seek high-tech medicine at up to half Western rates: surgery, gamma-scans and Caesarean sections (auspicious birth dates make Caesareans the norm in Thailand). Private Thai hospitals also offer five-star surroundings and smiley care. Bumrungrad Hospital (*see p231*) even has room service from restaurants in its atrium. Dental tourism, in particular, benefits from expertise derived from the Thais' low pain threshold. However, some specialists say you get what you pay for and cases of misdiagnosis do surface, partly driven by widespread over-prescription.

Thailand is also reputed for plastic surgery (slim noses and eyelid folds carry social cachet). An informal global network among ladyboys advises on coming here to change sex. Born in the wrong body? Avoid the plethora of dubious clinics and consult the Society of Plastic & Reconstructive Surgeons at Sirirat Hospital (*see p231*).

words rather than abstract phrasing, since Thais rarely think in a cartographic way. One-way systems are common and taxi shortcuts can seem strange, but may be following traffic radio advice. Mobile phones help people locate each other and enable you to obtain translation. Venues and hotels often write directions in Thai.

Central Bangkok street maps given at the back of this guide start on page 248. Free tourist maps are so-so; bookshops sell better ones, some marking bus routes. A unique, hand-drawn chart of the city's quirkiest shops, eats and sights is *Nancy Chandler's Map of Bangkok*; it's invaluable for Chinatown and Chatuchak Market. The *Groovy Map* also covers nightlife scenes.

Public transport

Bus services

BMTA Buses
0 2246 0973/hotline 184/ www.bmta.co.th.
The Bangkok Mass Transit Authority, with private firms, runs over 13,400 buses on 442 routes around Bangkok and adjacent provinces. It's mindbogglingly complex, with new and old buses, air-con and fan, having the same number but different colours and prices – and often varied routes, with return legs sometimes diverted through loops and one-way systems. Signs are all in Thai. Cramped standing is usual in rush hours. Licensed minibus routes serve many areas.

Air-conditioned buses are blue with a white stripe or white and articulated (5am-11pm). Fares: B11-B19. Orange buses (5am-11pm) charge B12-B24. Mauve Micro-

Buses have TV and a guaranteed seat for B20.
Non-air-conditioned buses are red/cream (5am-11pm, B7), or newer white/blue ones (5am-11pm, B8). Red/cream ones using expressways cost B5.50; running as nightbuses (11pm-5am) it's B5. Short, battered and furiously driven green buses cost B6.50 daytime, B5 after 10pm. Buses using expressways add B2; night buses add B1.50.

Bus passes: Any route pass (B1,700 1mth). Coupon booklet for specific route (25 coupons, 1 per trip), fares depend on route, 10% off normal fare. Sold at any bus terminus (like Victory Monument).

Bus Rapid Transit
0 2354 1224-7.
Brainchild of Bangkok Governor Apirak Kosayothin, the BRT will have dedicated central bus lanes with stations every 700m reached by bridges. By mid 2008, the first line will run 16.5km from Chong Nonsi BTS via Thanons Narathiwat Ratchankharin and Rama III to Rama IX Bridge. If successful, BRT lines may proliferate, though some may get replaced by BTS or MRT lines.

Long-distance buses
Rot tour (inter-provincial buses) are the mainstay of ordinary Thais and often sell out, so book ahead through travel agents, hotels or bus terminals. Buses without air-con can be gruelling and cramped; rot air (air-con buses) may be roomier, particularly the VIP buses serving food and drink, though overnighting by road is draining and drivers can be reckless. Be alert to the security of your bags and valuables. Minibuses run regular upcountry routes, often from Banglamphu or Soi Ngam Duphlee. www.transport. co.th provides information on all bus terminals (call centre 0 2576 5599).

Eastern Bus Terminal (Ekamai) *300 Thanon Sukhumvit, at Soi 42, Sukhumvit (0 2391 8097). Ekamai BTS.* **Open** 4am-midnight daily. **No credit cards. Map** p252 M7/8.
Northern & North-eastern Bus Terminal (Morchit 2) *999 Thanon Kamphaengphet 2, North (0 2936 2852-66).* **Open** 24hrs daily. **Credit** MC, V.
Also serves the central region.
Southern Bus Terminal *147 Thanon Boromratchachonnani, Thonburi (0 2435 5605).* **Open** 5am-9pm daily. **Credit** MC, V. Nicknamed Sai Tai Mai, it also serves the west. The terminal may relocate.

Songtaew
The mouths of local roads and narrow lanes often have ranks of open-sided pick-up truck buses called *songtaew* ('two rows') after the bench seating, *seelor* (four-wheelers) or *hoklor* (six-wheelers). Often painted with pastoral scenes and lucky imagery, they cost B3-B10 and have vague schedules, stopping at will. Just hail and hop on, paying the driver when you buzz (or bang loudly) to alight.

Rail services

BTS SkyTrain
BTS Information Centre (0 2617 7340-2/www.bts.co.th). **Open** 6am-midnight daily. *New Year* 24hrs.
This privately run elevated Bangkok Transit System (BTS) has two lines that intersect at Siam: the dark green Sukhumvit line (Morchit to Onnut) and in future to Samrong; and light green Silom line (National Stadium to Saphan Taksin, extending soon to Thanon Phetkasem). Saphan Taksin links to the Expressboat Central Pier (*see p227*). The BTS connects (sort of) with the MRT at Saladaeng/

Silom, Asoke/Sukhumvit and Morchit/Chatuchak Park.

Trains operate 6am-midnight daily, every 5mins (3mins in peak hrs: 7-9am, 5-8pm Mon-Fri). Clean, efficient and engineered by Siemens, the BTS has a 100% safety record. Food, drinks and smoking are banned, though the concourses host shops and stalls. More escalators and 'SkyBridges' to buildings are being built. Some stations have feeder bus routes (free with pass).

Machines issue **Single-journey** tickets (B10-B40) but don't take notes, so people queue for B5 and B10 coins from the counter. Passes are convenient but not discounted. The **Sky Card** (refillable, minimum B200 plus B30 deposit) is valid for 2yrs and depletes according to distance. The **1-Day Pass** (B120), **30-Day Adult Pass** (20 trips B440, 30 trips B600) or **30-Day Student Pass** (under-23s only; 20 trips B340, 30 trips B450) have no distance limit. From 2007, the sensor-readable 'Smart Pass' (refillable, valid 5yrs) will have the 30 Day Pass conditions.

MRT Subway

Bangkok Metro (0 2354 2000/ www.bangkokmetro.co.th).
The Mass Rapid Transit (MRT) underground blue line arcs 20km (12 miles) from Hualumphong railway station via Rama IV and Ratchadaphisek to Bang Sue railway station. See BTS (*above*) for interchange stations. It will extend through Chinatown, Pak Khlong Talad and Thonburi and loop back to Bang Sue. By 2011 it's envisaged that orange and purple lines will run above and below ground, plus an airport link and other lines running over the State Railway routes to replace the aborted Hopewell rail line project.

Trains run 6am-midnight, every 3mins peak, 7mins off-peak. The 18 stations each have escalators, lifts, toilets, shops and disabled WCs. Entrances open a metre above the highest recorded flood level. Counters or machines issue Single Journey electronic tokens (B15-B39, B8-B20 children, seniors), or Stored Value Cards (refillable, minimum B200 plus B50 deposit, B13-B33; B10-B27 students; B8-B20 children, seniors).

State Railway of Thailand

Hualumphong Station, 1 Thanon Rong Muang, Chinatown (booking 0 2225 6964/schedule hotline 1690/ www.srt.or.th). **Open** *Trains* 4.20am-11.40pm daily. *Booking (3-60 days ahead)* 8.30am-4.30pm daily. *Tour desk* 8.30am-4pm daily. **Credit** MC, V. **Map** p249 & p250 D/E5.

The State Railway of Thailand (0 2621 8701) runs all long-distance routes (to the east coast, lower Isaan, Nong Khai, Chiang Mai, Kanchanaburi and the Malaysian border). Most trains depart from this Italianate terminus, calling at Samsen, Bang Sue, Don Muang, Makkasan and Hua Mark stations, but are too slow and infrequent to act as city mass transit. Some trains for Nakhon Pathom, Kanchanaburi, Prachuab Khiri Khan and Chumphon depart from **Bangkok Noi** station, Thonburi (0 2411 3102), which has a tourist centre. A short line from **Wong Wian Yai station** in Thonburi runs to Mahachai in Samut Songkram via Samut Sakhon.

Taxi services

Taxi-meter

With radios and meters, these air-con cars are cheap, plentiful and gather at shopping, tourist, nightlife and event locations. With ranks still a vague idea, they'll stop for you instantly. A red front light means it's available. Signal by flapping your fingers, palm down (up is rude).

Taxis are coloured by company. Don't get in if the driver refuses to use the meter. Poor maintenance often indicates a dodgy driver. Front seatbelts are compulsory. It helps to give directions in Thai (especially written) rather than to show maps. Starting rate is B35, rising at B2 increments with a 'traffic jam' surcharges, but no night-time increase. Drivers often lack small change; tip up to 10%.

For safety and ease, 24hr call taxis (listed below) will pick up within 15-20mins (B20 surcharge) and offer full-day taxi hire (from B1,800).
Radio Taxi *hotline 1681.*
Siam Taxi *hotline 1661.*
Bangkok Taxi Radio Centre 0 2880 0888.
Nakornchai Transportation 0 2878 9000/www.taxithai.com.

Taxi motorcycle

Urgent trips may require a daredevil pillion ride on *rot motocy* (or *rot jakrayan yon*) from mafia-run ranks at the mouths of most *soi*. Short runs cost B10-B20 (agree the fare first), while distant trips via main roads equate to taxi rates after the necessary bargaining. Helmets are compulsory, but rarely worn in *soi*. To ask for a helmet, say *ow muak garn knock*.

Tuk-tuk

Relished by tourists as 'authentic', the various kinds of funky *samlor* (three-wheelers) are customised from Japanese motorised rickshaws.

Tuk-tuk means 'cheap-cheap' and replicates their LPG-fuelled chainsaw rasp; quieter electric *tuk-tuk* haven't caught on. The bench may fit three, reasonably slim, *farang*.

Tuk-tuks are open-air, so you get rain, fumes, soot and sweat en route, and even the compensating *sanuk* (fun) may fade if you haven't agreed the price beforehand. Less nippy than motorcycle taxis and pricier than taxis, they're getting rarer, partly due to self-defeating attempts to tout, cheat and overcharge.

Driving

Drivers need an international licence (foreign licences aren't accepted). Thais drive on the left, front seatbelts are compulsory and speed limits are 80kmh within Bangkok, 90kmh outside. Bangkok driving can be undisciplined but predictably so, though upcountry it can be reckless. Beware of lane-switching, too-close driving, high-risk overtaking and swarming motorcycles. Fines (and licence points deductions) can seem arbitrary. Expect expressway tolls, narrow *soi* and many 'one-way' and 'no right turn' detours.

Car & van hire

Rental firms (taking most major credit cards) offer cars from B850 per day (most including insurance). Along with travel agents, most also rent a car/van with driver (B1,900-B3,000 per day, overnight B3,500 per day, plus tip). All exclude petrol and tolls. For route advice, contact the **Department of Highways** (0 2354 6668-76, www.doh.go.th). For road problem assistance try the **Transportation Safety Centre** (0 2280 8000, hotline 1356, www.mot.go.th) or **Highway Police** (0 2354 6007/hotline 1193).
Avis *(0 2255 5300-4/www.avis.co.th).* **Open** 7.30am-6pm Mon-Sat; 8am-6pm Sun.
Budget *(0 2203 0250/www.budget. co.th).* **Open** 7.30am-7.30pm daily.
Japan Rent *(0 2259 8867-70/www.japanrenthailand.com).* **Open** 8am-5pm Mon-Sat.
Highway Car Rent *(0 2266 9393-8/www.highway.co.th).* **Open** 7am-10pm daily.
Lumphini Car Rent *(0 2255 1966-8).* **Open** 8am-6pm daily.

Krung Thai Car Rent *(0 2291 8888/www.krungthai.co.th).* **Open** 8am-5.30pm Mon-Sat.

Thai Prestige Rent-A-Car *(0 2941 1344-8/2231-3/www.thaiprestige. yellowpages.co.th).* **Open** 8am-5pm Mon-Sat.

Parking & services

Street parking is restricted (and banned 5am-10pm on some highways and bus lanes). Car parks in malls, hotels and offices charge from B50 per hr, often with a free initial period if you get the ticket stamped at a venue on site. Double parking is common, even in car parks, and has a procedure: park in neutral, wheels straight, handbrake off, so the car can be shunted. Pay attendants of street parking outside busy venues a B10-B20 tip.

Petrol, now unleaded, is cheap (B24-B26 per litre) at the plentiful pumps. Open 5am-midnight daily (many 24hrs) with attendants, many with shops, toilets, ATMs, car washes, air hoses and repair services. In case of breakdowns try:

B-Quik Service

16th floor, 253 Sukhumvit Soi 21, Sukhumvit (0 2664 2111/battery delivery 0 2664 2000/www.b-quik. com). Asoke BTS/Petchaburi MRT. **Open** 8am-9pm daily. **Credit** AmEx, DC, MC, V. **Map** p252 K5/4. Solves breakdown woes.

Carworld Club

2/1 Thanon Rama IV, Sukhumvit (0 2612 9999/www.cwc.co.th). Sirikit Centre MRT. **Open** 8.30am-5.30pm daily. Breakdown service 24hrs daily. **Credit** AmEx, DC, MC, V. **Map** p252 J7. Full breakdown services.

Water transport

Canal boats

Quick, exhilarating, but cramped and awkward, covered longtail boats ply **Khlong Saen Saeb,** an east–west canal from Tha Saphan Phan Fah (Golden Mount, for old town) taking 15-17mins to Tha Pratunam (change boats) and 40mins to Tha Bang Kapi. Useful stops are at Bobe Market; Phyathai (for Siam & BTS); Pratunam (for markets); Ratchadamri (malls); Chidlom (Central Dept Store); Witthayu (hotels and embassies); Nana (hotels); Asoke; Thonglor; Ekamai; and Ramkhamhaeng (stadiums and malls).

Services, run by Family Transport (0 2375 2369, 0 2374 8990), operate every 2-11mins, 5.30am-7.30pm Mon-Fri, and every 5-11mins 6am-6.30pm Sat, 6am-7pm Sun. Tickets cost B8-B18, rising every four piers. Maps may show obsolete routes on Khlong Phadung Krung Kasem or Khlong Banglamphu.

Tour touts may try to stop foreigners using local *rua hang yao* ('longtail boat') routes down Thonburi canals from Tha Chang and Tha Tien piers, but their commuter timings make return trips difficult anyway.

Expressboats

Chao Phraya Express Boat (0 2623 6001-3). **Open** 6am-7.30pm Mon-Fri; 6am-6.40pm Sat, Sun. **Map** p248 A3. The private river bus service covers 18km (11 miles). Buy tickets from boat conductors or many of the 35 piers, which are signed in English, between Tha Nonthaburi (N30) and Tha Wat Rajsingkorn (S3), via Tha Sathorn (Central Pier), which links to Saphan Taksin BTS. Roof flags identify boat speed:

Yellow flag (rush-hour express) Few stops, N30 to Sathorn only (45-50mins). Mon-Fri every 10mins 6.10-6.30am, every 4mins 6.30-8.40am, every 15mins 4.30-6.20pm. Returns start at 3.45pm, then every 10mins 4-7.30pm. Fare: B18.

Orange flag (express) Major piers, N30 to S3 (1hr). Runs Mon-Fri every 5mins 5.50-9.15am, every 15mins 3-5.50pm. Returns every 15mins 6.30-8.45am, every 20mins 2-4pm, every 10mins 4-6pm, every 15mins 6-7pm. Sat every 15mins 6.45-8.40pm, 4-6.20pm; Fare: B13.

No flag (local) All piers, N30 to S3. Returns Mon-Fri every 15mins 6-8am, every 20mins 8am-6.40pm. Sat, Sun every 20-25mins 6am-6.40pm. Fare: B9-B13.

Expressboat tours Tourist Boat (every 30mins, 9.30am-3pm) from Sathorn Pier to piers at sights; day pass: B75. Call to confirm tours to Koh Kret (9am-4.30pm Sun, B300, B250 children) or Bang Pa-In (7.30am-6pm Sun, B300-B390, B250-B300 children).

River ferries

Dumpy ferries (*kham fahk*) bob across the Chao Phraya river from many piers (every 5mins 5am-midnight, some until 9pm, daily) for just B3. River hotels have guest ferries to Tha Saphan Taksin, Tha Oriental and Tha Si Phraya (River City).

Cycling

Bangkok is flat and has canals, but this is no Amsterdam. Thai traffic and roads are brutal to cyclists, with few cycle lanes, but new roads must have cycle lanes. A cycle bridge links bike paths in Lumphini and Benjakitti Parks, which rents bikes out.

Spice Roads Bike Tour

14/1-B Promsri Soi 2, Sukhumvit (0 2712 5305/www.spiceroads.com). Phrom Phong BTS. **Open** 9am-6pm Mon-Fri; 10am-3pm Sat. **Credit** MC, V. **Map** p251 G6. Trips to floating market, Ko Kret, countryside, plus custom and overnight tours (half day B1,000 per person, day trip B2,000 per person).

Walking

Walking can be a stressful, wearisome challenge. Vehicles trump pedestrians even at marked crossings. Pavements tend to strewn with stalls, stray dogs, motorcycles, café tables, beggars, parked cars and people. Anti-walking prejudice links to notions that darker skin from outdoor activity indicates lower status. Pedestrianisation has novelty appeal, but is permanent only at Thanon Khao San (*see p71*).

Travel advice

For current information on travel to a specific country – including the latest news on health issues, safety and security, local laws and customs – you should contact your home country's government department of foreign affairs. Most have websites with useful advice for would-be travellers.

Australia
www.smartraveller.gov.au

Canada
www.voyage.gc.ca

New Zealand
www.safetravel.govt.nz

Republic of Ireland
http://foreignaffairs.gov.ie

UK
www.fco.gov.uk/travel

USA
http://travel.state.gov

Directory

Resources A-Z

Addresses

Bangkok addresses are notoriously complicated and take quite a lot of getting used to – even hardened locals can have difficulty pinpointing a location from its address alone. Addresses typically start with the building's street number. Any digits following an oblique slash represent the subdivision of a plot, ie 49/16, but plots are often numbered by order in which they were developed, rather than by their location. Next comes the room/unit/floor number (confusingly mixing UK and US systems, so you may enter on either the first or ground floor), building name and, outside Downtown, any *moo* (estate) number/name. Then comes the *thanon* ('road') name, eg 346/2, Room 3B, Floor 2, Sri Bamrung Building, Moo 2, Thanon Srinakharin.

If it's on a named *trok* ('lane', which are rare) or *soi* ('sidestreet'), it may be followed by a *thanon*, eg Soi Phiphat, Thanon Silom. If it's on a numbered *soi* running off a *thanon*, it drops the word *thanon*, hence Silom Soi 4. If the numbered *soi* also has an oft-used name, Thais would write it as Sukhumvit Soi 21 (Soi Asoke), though variations include: Sukhumvit 21, Soi Asoke, Soi Sukhumvit 21 or even Sukhumvit Road Soi 21 or Asoke Road (English terms like Road, Avenue, Tower or Centre are often used, eg Beach Road, Pattaya). Long roads may use kilometre markers, eg km5 Thanon Bangna-Trad.

That's all followed by the subdistrict name (*khwaeng* in Bangkok, *tambon* in villages and towns), then district name (*khet* in Bangkok, *amphoe* upcountry) and province name (*jangwat*). There follows a five-digit postcode, roughly one for each district, starting with 1 in Bangkok (eg Lumphini, Pathumwan, Bangkok 10330). Each province shares its name with its capital whose district is always Amphoe Muang ('town district') followed by the province name.

Age restrictions

You must be 18 to drive, buy cigarettes and alcohol, or have sex (straight or gay), while under-20s aren't allowed in bars or clubs, which request picture ID of all customers.

Attitude & etiquette

Thailand is known as the 'Land of Smiles' and with good reason – the epithet does not mean one grin is thoughtlessly repeated, but refers to specific smiles according to the myriad social concepts that govern Thai behaviour and language.

Do's & don'ts

● Show respect for the monarchy, members of the royal family, Buddhism and the monkhood. Criticism causes universal offence and may be heavily penalised.
● Stand for the King's Anthem at the start of performances and the national anthem.
● The head is the highest part of the body spiritually and must not be touched or pointed at, particularly by the feet, the lowest part of the body. So never use feet to move, shut or point at things, nor step on a coin or banknotes (they bear the king's head). Sitting on the 'head' of a boat is also taboo.
● Treat Buddha images with respect. Don't point at them (especially with feet), hang anything on them or pose with them in photos.
● Inside temples, wear polite clothing (cover shoulders and knees). Sit with feet tucked back or cross-legged in front of monks/Buddha images.
● Monks are celibate and must not touch women, who give monks things via a male or by placing it down. *Mae chi* (nuns) are treated like secular women.
● Remove shoes before entering rooms in temples, palaces, homes and some museums. Step over, not on, door thresholds.
● Make a symbolic gesture to lower your head as you pass elderly/very senior Thais in a room.
● Avoid direct criticism of anyone or anything (including Thailand).
● Don't lose your temper. Anger is viewed (and avoided) as temporary insanity and prevents resolution of problems, often swapping culprit and victim in Thais' esteem. But jollying people along can accomplish great feats; Thais like to help.
● Presentable, clean clothing, footwear and hair gain you respect and help, particularly from officials.
● Eat and pass things with your right hand as the left is used for cleaning after defecating.

Business

Conventions & conferences

Impact Exhibition Centre *99 Thanon Popular, Thanon Chaengwattana, Nonthaburi Province, Outer North (0 2504 5050/www.impact.co.th).*
Queen Sirikit National Convention Centre *60 Thanon Ratchadaphisek Tud Mai, Sukhumvit (0 2229 3000/www.qsncc.com).*
BITEC (Bangkok International Trade & Exhibition Centre) *8 km1 Thanon Bangna Trad, East (0 2749 3939-60/www.bitec.net).*

Couriers & shippers

DHL Express *7th-8th floors, Sathorn City Tower, Thanon Sathorn Tai, South (0 2345 5000/ www.dhl.co.th).* **Open** 24hrs daily. **Credit** AmEx, MC, V. **Map** p251 J4.
Federal Express *8th floor, Green Tower, Thanon Rama IV, Sukhumvit (1782/www.fedex.com).* **Open** 8am-11pm Mon-Fri; 9am-5pm Sat, Sun, public holidays. **Credit** AmEx, MC, V. **Map** p251 J7.
TNT Express Worldwide *599 Thanon Chua Phloeng, Bangrak (0 2249 0242/www.tnt.com).* **Open** 24 hrs daily. **Credit** AmEx. **Map** p250 F7.

Office hire & services

Mr Centre *43rd floor, United Centre Tower, 323 Thanon Silom, Bangrak (0 2631*

*0330/www.mrcentre.org). Saladaeng
BTS/Silom MRT.* **Open** 8am-5.30pm
Mon-Fri. **Credit** AmEx, MC, V.
Map p250 F7.
Offices for monthly rental, plus
phone, fax, mail and secretarial
services up and running instantly.

Women Secretaries' Association

*6/2 Thanon Phichai, Dusit (0 2241
5555/www.secretarythai.and.org).*
Open 8.30am-4.30pm Mon-Fri, by
appointment.
A service designed to find secretaries
according to the professional
qualities you specify.

Translators & interpreters

Bangkok Translation Services

*562 Thanon Ploenchit, Pathumwan
(0 2251 5666). Ploenchit BTS.*
Open 8am-5pm Mon-Fri; 8.30am-
4.30 Sat. **Map** p251 H5.
Between Thai and other languages
for serious documentation needs.
Price and time vary by language.

Interlanguage Translation Centre

*501 Thanon Samsen, Dusit (0 2243
2018/2109/www.itctrans.com).*
Open 8.30am-5pm Mon-Fri;
8.30am-4pm Sat. **Map** p248 C2.
Official standard translations
between all major languages. Cost
depends on subject and language.
Other locations: 554 Thanon
Phloenchit, Pathumwan (0 2252
4307); 1 Sukhumvit Soi 1, Sukhumvit
(0 2252 3877); 57/3 Thanon Witthayu,
Pathumwan (0 2650 7831).

Useful organisations

**American Chamber of
Commerce** *18th floor, Kian Gwan
2 Building, 140/1 Thanon Witthayu,
Pathumwan (0 2254 1041/www.
amchamthailand.com).* **Open**
8.30am-5pm Mon-Fri. **Map** p251 H5.
**Australian-Thai Chamber of
Commerce** *Unit 203, 20th floor,
Thai Chamber of Commerce Tower,
889 Thanon Sathorn Tai, South
(0 2210 0216-8/www.austcham
thailand.com). Surasak BTS.* **Open**
9am-5pm Mon-Fri. **Map** p251 G7.
British Chamber of Commerce
*7th floor, 208 Thanon Witthayu,
Pathumwan (0 2651 5350-3/
www.bccthai.com). Ploenchit BTS.*
Open 8.30am-4.30pm Mon-Fri.
Map p251 H5.
**Canadian Chamber of
Commerce** *9th floor, Set Thi One
Building, Thanon Pan, Bangrak (0*

*2266 6085-6/www.tccc.or.th). Chong
Nonsi BTS.* **Open** 9am-5pm Mon-Fri.
Map p250 E7.
**New Zealand-Thai Chamber of
Commerce** *9th floor, ITF Tower,
140/11 Thanon Silom, Bangrak
(0 2634 3283/www.nztcc.org).
Saladaeng BTS/Silom MRT.*
Open 9.30am-5pm Mon-Fri.
Map p250 F7.
Thai Chamber of Commerce *150
Thanon Ratchabophit, Phra Nakorn
(0 2622 1860-76/www.tcc.or.th).*
Open 8.30am-4.30pm Mon-Fri.
Map p248 B4.

Consumer

Some shops might refund
or exchange faulty goods
(unlikely if you lose your
temper). Refer complaints
to the **Office of the
Consumer Protection
Board** (hotline 1166/0 2629
8262-4, www.ocpb.go.th) or
the **Food & Drug
Administration** (hotline
1556, www.fda.moph.go.th).

Customs

On arrival, fill in Passenger
Declaration Form 211 for
Customs (hotline 1164,
www.customs.go.th). Duty-free
import limits include 200
cigarettes or 250g of cigars/
tobacco; 1 litre of spirits;
1 litre of wine; B10,000 of
perfume; B10,000 of effects for
personal or professional use.
Prohibited imports/exports
include drugs, pornography,
protected wild animals or
related products.
Goods requiring a permit
for import/export include
firearms, ammunition,
explosives (**National Police
Office** 0 2205 1000, 0 2354
6510); Buddha images,
artefacts and antiques (**Fine
Arts Department** 0 2221
7811); radio transceivers/
telecom equipment (**Post &
Telegraph Department**
0 2271 0151-2); plants/
agricultural materials
(**Agriculture Department**
0 2579 0151-7); live animals/
animal products (**Live Stock
Development** 0 2653 4550-3);

medicines and chemical
products (**Food and Drugs
Administration** 0 2590 7000).

Disabled

Despite general compassion
there's mixed treatment of the
disabled, who tend to be kept
hidden, partly due to karmic
belief, face and prejudice about
appearance. The Thai deaf
subculture's sophisticated
signing is visible among deaf
vendors. Maimed/leprous
beggars are mostly Khmer
amputees enslaved by mafia.
For further advice, contact
the **Association of the
Physically Handicapped**
(0 2951 0445/0447,
www.apht.or.th/www.
flyingwheelchairs.org).

Drugs

Punishment for possession of –
and particularly for dealing or
trafficking in – illicit drugs is
severe, with the death penalty
enforced. Nightclubs and even
schools get raided with urine
tests on all to find ecstasy,
cocaine and the amphetamine
yaa baa ('crazy drug'). Those
in possession face one to
ten years' jail and fines of
B10,000-B100,000.

Electricity

The standard current is 220V,
50 cycles/sec, but plugs are
unearthed two-pins (round
or parallel flat), so beware
of shocks.

Embassies & consulates

American Embassy

*120-122 Thanon Witthayu,
Pathumwan (0 2205
4000/www.usa.or.th).* **Open** 7am-
4pm Mon-Fri. **Map** p251 H5.

Australian Embassy

*37 Thanon Sathorn Tai, South (0
2287 2680/www.austembassy.or.th).*
Open 8.30am-4.30pm Mon-Fri.
Map p251 G7.

Directory

British Embassy

1031 Thanon Witthayu, Pathumwan (0 2305 8333/www.britishembassy. gov.uk/thailand). Ploenchit BTS. **Open** 8am-3.30pm Mon-Thur; 8am-noon Fri. **Map** p251 H5.

Canadian Embassy

15th floor, Abdul Rahim Place, 990 Thanon Rama IV, Bangrak (0 2636 0540/ www.bangkk.gc.ca). Saladaeng BTS/Silom MRT. **Open** 7.30am-4pm Mon-Thur; 7.30am-1pm Fri. **Map** p251 G7.

EU Delegation

19th floor, Kian Gwan Building II, 140/1 Thanon Witthayu, Pathumwan (0 2305 2600/ www.deltha.ec.europa.eu). **Open** 9am-5pm Mon-Thur; 9am-2pm Fri. **Map** p251 H5.

New Zealand Embassy

14th floor, M-Thailand Building, 87 Thanon Witthayu, Pathumwan (0 2254 2530/www.nzembassy. com/thailand). Ploenchit BTS. **Open** 8am-noon, 1-4.30pm Mon-Fri. **Map** p251 H5.

Emergencies

First ring the responsive, English-speaking **Tourist Police** (24-hour hotline 1155) or **Tourist Assistance Centre** (0 2281 5051). If necessary, try the 24-hour **Police Hotline** (191) or police stations (*see p233*). For utilities crises call the **Bangkok Metropolitan Administration Call Centre** (hotline 1555). For Bangkok hospitals, *see p231*; for helplines, *see p231*. Most embassies (*above*) have duty staff outside office hours.

Gay & lesbian

Help & information

Bangkok Rainbow

08 6607 1069/www.bangkok rainbow.org.
Part of the Asian Rainbow network, this group promotes understanding and provides counselling for gays.

Lesla

0 2618 7191-2/www.lesla.com.
Thailand's biggest lesbian organisation also runs socials.

Long Yang Club

PO Box 1077, Silom, Bangkok 10504 (0 2266 5479/www.long yangclub.org/thailand).
Global East-West gay social club.

Health

Accident & emergency

Road casualties often get picked up by Chinese charities, such as Poh Tek Tung; many end up in the **Police Hospital** or **Bangkok Hospital** (for both, *see p231*).

Erawan Centre

514 Department of Medical Services, Bangkok Metropolitan Administration, Thanon Luang, Phra Nakorn (0 2223 9401-3/ hotline 1646/1554). **Open** 24hrs daily. **Map** p248 C4.
Free emergency medical treatment and distribution of ambulances and doctors, plus health advice.

International SOS Services Thailand

11th floor, Diethelm Tower, 93/1 Thanon Witthayu, Pathumwan (0 2205 7755/www.international sos.com). **Open** 24hrs daily. **Map** p251 H5.
Tackles any emergency, emphasising speedy ambulances and police contact.

Before you go

It's wise to get vaccinations for hepatitis A and B, polio, rabies, typhoid and tuberculosis, but cholera shots are widely discredited. Also ensure full immunisation for tetanus, diphtheria, measles, mumps and rubella. Arrivals from Africa or Latin America must be vaccinated for yellow fever. For bird flu, seek ongoing advice.

Some vaccinations require widely spaced shots up to six weeks before departure. Avoid wading in floodwater, which may be infectious from rat urine, etc.

Malaria is only an issue on the Burma, Laos or Cambodia borders and in remoter forests, visitors to which should consult specialists, like **Travel Doctor** (www.traveldoctor. com.au). Tropical medicine experts often caution against malaria prophylaxis due to resistant strains and side effects (particularly from Larium). Avoiding bites is best, so wear white and use insect repelling lotions (Jaico is reliable), sprays, coils and electric tabs. Most rooms have screens or nets.

That's also the only defence against haemorrhagic dengue fever (*kai leuad ok*), which has increased lately, notably in cities during rainy season. Passed on by the daytime, striped-legged Aedes mosquito, dengue has similar symptoms to malaria, but no prophylaxis or cure. It is most serious in children, the elderly and repeat sufferers. Seek early diagnosis (before the rash).

Contraception

Condoms in various brands, sizes and flavours (durian-flavoured rubber, anyone?) are sold alongside lubricants and feminine products from corner shops, drug stores and supermarkets countrywide.

Population & Community Development Association (PDA)

8 Sukhumvit Soi 12, Sukhumvit (0 2229 4611-28/www.pda.or.th). Asoke BTS/Sukhumvit MRT. **Open** 8am-4.30pm Mon-Fri. **Map** p251 J5.
Founded by ex-minister and social campaigner Senator Mechai 'Mr Condom' Viravaidhya, PDA advises on family planning, AIDS and unplanned pregnancy; supplies morning-after pills and contraceptives, and promotes sustainable development.

Dentists

Asavanant Dental Clinic *58/5 Sukhumvit Soi 55, Sukhumvit (0 2391 1842/www.asavanant.com). Thonglor BTS.* **Open** 9am-8pm Mon-Fri; 9am-5pm Sat, Sun. **Credit** AmEx, MC, V. **Map** p252 M5.
Dental Hospital *88/88 Sukhumvit Soi 49, Sukhumvit (0 2260 5000-15/www.dentalhospitalbangkok.com).* **Open** 9am-8pm Mon-Sat; 9am-4pm Sun. **Credit** AmEx, DC, MC, V. **Map** p252 L6.
Glas Haus Dental Centre *Glas Haus (Baan Chiang), Sukhumvit Soi 25, Sukhumvit (0 2260 6120-1). Asoke BTS/Sukhumvit MRT.* **Open** 10am-6pm Mon-Sat. **Credit** AmEx, MC, V. **Map** p252 K6.

Complementary medicine

Buteyko Breathing Asia

Jac Vidgen (0 2253 2614/www. buteykoasia.com) & Chris Drake (08 7938 1345/www.learnbuteyko.com).
Respiratory Health Institute practitioners Vidgen and Drake teach

five-day workshops in the Buteyko breathing technique. Reducing medication dependency, it aids sports performance and can improve many conditions, from asthma, allergies and sleep apnoea to stress, obesity, migraine and hangovers.

Holistic Health Systems

438/13 Thanon Ekamai, Sukhumvit Soi 63, Sukhumvit (08 1627 0312/0 2711 5102/ www.thailandchiropractor.com). Ekamai BTS then taxi. **Open** 8am-7pm Mon-Thur, Sat, Sun; appointment required. **No credit cards.**
Dr Mark Leoni's homely chiropractor clinic.

Doctors & hospitals

State hospitals range from the humble to teaching institutions. Private hospitals have English-speaking doctors in outpatient clinics, which also dispense medication. Beware of over-prescription. The efficient, luxurious, private **Bangkok, Bumrungrad, BNH** and **Samitivej Hospitals** all have multilingual clinics and rank among the best in Asia.
Bangkok Hospital *2 Soi Soonvijai 7, North-east (0 2310 3000/www.bangkokhospital.com).* Map p252 M4.
BNH (Bangkok Nursing Home) Hospital *9/1 Thanon Convent, Bangrak (0 2682 2700/www. BNHhospital.com). Saladaeng BTS/Silom MRT.* Map p250 F7.
Bumrungrad Hospital *33 Sukhumvit Soi 3, Sukhumvit (0 2667 1000/www.bumrungrad. com). Nana BTS.* Map p251 J4.
Police Hospital (state) *492/1 Thanon Ratchadamri, Pathumwan (0 2252 8111-25/www.policehospital. go.th). Chidlom/Ratchadamri BTS.* Map p251 G5.
Samitivej Hospital *133 Sukhumvit Soi 49, Sukhumvit (0 2711 8000/ www.samitivej.co.th).* Map p252 K6.
Sirirat Hospital (state) *2 Thanon Prannok, Thonburi (0 2419 7000/ www.si.mahidol.ac.th).* Map p248 A3.

Opticians

Hospitals also have eye clinics, notably **Samitivej** (*see above*).

Laser Vision Lasik Centre

49/1 Viphavadee Rangsit Soi 38, North (0 2939 5494/www.laser vision.co.th). Morchit BTS/Chatuchak Park MRT. **Open** 8am-8pm Mon, Tue, Thur, Fri; 8am-6pm Wed, Sat.

Credit AmEx, DC, MC, V. Map p249 & p250 F4.

Rutnin Eye Hospital

80/1 Thanon Sukhumvit Soi 21, Sukhumvit (0 2639 3399/www. rutnin.com). Asoke BTS/Sukhumvit MRT. **Open** 8am-8pm Mon-Sat; 8am-7pm Sun. **Credit** AmEx, DC, MC, V. Map p252 K5.

Pharmacies & prescriptions

Hospitals dispense in-house at inflated prices. Medicines are also sold from any *kai yaa* (pharmacy) without prescriptions, except those with major physiological, mental or narcotic impact. This has prompted indiscipline with drugs like antibiotics, which reduces their effectiveness.

Community Pharmacy Laboratory

22 Thanon Phayathai, Pathumwan (0 2218 8428-9/www.phar.chula. ac.th/osotsala). National Stadium BTS. **Open** 8am-7pm Mon-Sat. Map p249 & p250 F4.
Pharmacists and trainees from Chula Uni advise on symptoms and sell drugs cheaply without prescription.

Plastic surgery

Thai plastic surgery is world-famous, particularly beautification and sexual reassignment. It's regulated by the **Society of Plastic & Reconstructive Surgeons** (0 2716 6214, www.plasticsurgery.or.th).

Yanhee General Hospital

454 Thanon Charan Sanit Wong Soi 90, Thonburi (0 2879 0300/ www.yanhee.net).
Renowned for plastic surgery and sex changes (sex change $6,500-$7,500, Adam's apple removal $650).

STDs, HIV & AIDS

The **PDA** (*see p230*) has been pivotal for HIV/AIDS prevention, though Thailand's lauded pioneering efforts have recently regressed.

Anonymous Clinic

1871 Thanon Ratchadamri, Pathumwan (0 2256 4107-9/www. redcross.or.th). Ratchadamri BTS. **Open** noon-6pm Mon-Fri; noon-4pm Sat. Map p251 G5.
Thai Red Cross HIV/AIDS testing, information, counselling and treatment.

Division of Venereal Disease

Bangrak Hospital, 189 Thanon Sathorn Tai, South (0 2286 0108/ 0431/www.sti-thai.org). **Open** 8.30am-4.30pm Mon-Fri. Map p250 F7. Information and cures for STDs.
Other locations: Bang Kaen, North-east (0 2972 9606).

Médecins Sans Frontières

311 Lad Phrao Soi 101, North-east (0 2375 6491). **Open** 8.30am-5pm Mon-Fri.
Worldwide charity. Nurses offer data, advice and initial treatment for HIV/AIDS, then patient home visits.

Helplines

Alcoholics Anonymous

Holy Redeemer Church, 123/119 Ruam Rudi Soi 5, Pathumwan (0 2256 6157). **Meetings** 7-8pm Mon, Wed, Fri, Sun; 5-6pm Tue, Thur; 4.30-5.30pm Sat. Map p251 H5.

Narcotics Control Board (ONCB)

5 Thanon Din Daeng, North-east (0 2247 0901-19/www.oncb.go.th). **Open** 8.30am-4.30 Mon-Fri.
Info on all narcotics, plus advice on quitting and treatment.

New Community Services

230/60 Soi Thai Chamber of Commerce University, Thanon Wiphawadi Rangsit, North-east (08 1692 2981/0 2275 6762/ www.ncs-counselling.com). **Open** 9am-5pm Mon-Fri.
Thai and non-Thai counselling on any problem (family, addiction or anxiety, cross-cultural adjustment), group therapy, training and seminars.

Quit Line

Hotline 1600.
Service offering help coping with mental problems and quitting tobacco.

Samaritans of Thailand

PO Box 63, Por Nor For Santisuk, Bangkok 10113, South (0 2713 6793/ www.geocities.com/samaritansthai). **Open** Helpline noon-10pm daily.
Trained volunteers provide a friendly ear to those with emotional and mental problems.

ID

If possible, always carry your passport or photocopy,

Directory

especially for hotel check-ins, cashing travellers' cheques or exchanging more than $500. Store copies off your person. Nightlife venues now insist you show picture ID (passport or ID card).

Insurance

It's advisable to bring travel insurance, including health cover; otherwise try **American International Assurance** (0 2634 8888, www.aia.co.th) or **Ayudhya Allianz CP Life** (0 2305 7000, www.aacp.co.th).

Internet

Many shops stock prepaid online packages, including **CS Loxinfo** (0 2263 8222, www.csloxinfo.com), **KSC** (0 2979 7000, www.ksc.net), **Pacificnet** (0 2618 8088/ 8688, www.pacific.net.th) and **Qnet** (0 2377 0555, www.qnet.co.th). Terminals are common in business and tourist areas, most cheaply in Banglamphu, while **CATNET** at selected post offices costs B0.12 per minute using CATNET cards (B100, B300, B500). The following centres and cafés provide net access:

Amazing Cyber *925/6-8 Thanon Rama I, Pathumwan (0 2216 6236-7/www.bossapparels.com). National Stadium BTS.* **Open** 9am-8.30pm daily. **Rate** B50 per hr. **Map** p249 & p250 F4.

Olavi Internet Service *53 Thanon Chakrabongse, Phra Nakorn (0 2629 2228-9/www.olavi.com).* **Open** 10am-8pm. **Rate** B40 per hr Mon-Sat. **Map** p248 B3.

Time Internet Café *2nd floor, Times Square, Sukhumvit Soi 12, Sukhumvit (0 2653 3636-9). Asoke BTS/Sukhumvit MRT.* **Open** 9am-midnight Mon-Sat; 10am-midnight Sun. **Rate** B1 per min. **Map** p251 J5.

Left luggage

Airports *(Suvarnabhumi 0 2134 7795-6/Don Muang to be announced).* **Open** 24hrs daily. **Rates** B100 per piece per day.

Train *Hualumphong Station, Thanon Rama IV, Chinatown (0 2224 6165).* **Open** 4am-11pm daily. **Rates** B20 per piece per day; B100-B150 per bicycle/motorcycle. **Map** p249 & p250 D5.

Legal help

In legal difficulties, immediately inform your embassy, then a lawyer. The following firms are English-speaking. Some may not take criminal cases.

Baker & McKenzie *22nd-25th floors, Abdul Rahim Place, 990 Thanon Rama IV, Bangrak (0 2636 2000/www.bakernet.com). Saladaeng BTS/Silom MRT.* **Map** p251 G7.

Legal & Commercial Services International *Suite 1703-4, 17th floor, Two Pacific Place, 140 Thanon Sukhumvit Soi 4, Sukhumvit (0 2255 4941/www.legalcommercial services. com). Nana BTS.* **Map** p251 J5.

Tilleke & Gibbins *64/1 Soi Ton Son, Ploenchit, Pathumwan (0 2263 7700/0 2254 2640-58/www.tilleke andgibbins.com). Ploenchit BTS.* **Map** p251 M5.

Vovan & Associés *17th floor, Silom Complex, 191 Thanon Silom, Bangrak (0 2632 0180/www.vovan-associes.com). Saladaeng BTS/Silom MRT.* **Map** p250 F7.

Libraries

Most libraries are members-only, but allow reading on site. Photocopying is allowed in the **National Library** (*see p82*), **Siam Society Library** (*see p96*) and university libraries. The **British Council** (*see p93*) library also rents UK videos.

Neilson Hays Library

195 Thanon Surawong, Bangrak (0 2233 1731/www.neilsonhays library.com). Saladaeng BTS. **Open** 9.30am-5pm Tue-Sun. **Map** p250 E7.
A beautiful old building with the best range of English reading in town, plus exhibitions in the Rotunda. Entry for non-members is B50.

Lost property

Quickly report losses to the police (*see p233*) to get a statement for insurers.

Airport

Suvarnabhumi 0 2132 3888.
Don Muang to be announced.
For lost tickets, contact the airline directly.

Public transport

BMTA Bus Operation Division *Hotline 184/0 2246 0973/0339/ www.bmta.co.th*
BTS *0 2617 7141/ 7142/www.bts.co.th.*
MRT *0 2690 8200/www. bangkokmetro.co.th*
Train Hualumphong Station *24hr hotline 1690.*

Taxis

Jor Sor Roi (JS100) Radio Station *100FM (hotline 1137).*
Ruam Duay Chuay Kun Community Radio Station *96FM (hotline 1677).*
Drivers often tune into these Thai-language radio stations, which broadcast lost items and traffic news. Reports to police should note the taxi's colour (ie company) and number (printed inside and out).

Media

Newspapers & magazines

A locally printed *International Herald Tribune* edition joins two high-quality English daily newspapers, *Bangkok Post* and the feistier *Nation*, publishing local and international news and current affairs, with event listings in Friday supplements. Trendy weekly listings magazines *BK* and *GuRu* are free from venues (*GuRu* also in Friday's *Bangkok Post*). *Art Connection* is a free monthly map of exhibitions. Thai monthlies in English include *Big Chilli* (expats), *Untamed Travel* (formerly *Farang*, for backpackers), and *Thailand Tatler* (high society). Of the free tourist monthlies, *Bangkok 101* is the classiest. Papers, listings mags and free booklet *Shakers & Movers* carry classified ads, as does the **Villa Market** (*see p149*) expat noticeboard.

Radio

FM and AM broadcasts in Thai and English tend to play mainstream music with news bulletins. The army tries to keep control of most frequencies and **Radio Thailand**'s official pronouncements override 95.5FM, 105FM and 918AM at 7-8am, noon-1pm, 7-7.30pm and 8-8.30pm daily. English language stations include:

Chulalongkorn University
101.5FM. 9.35pm-midnight daily.
Classical.
Eazy FM 105.5FM. 6am-midnight
daily. Easy listening.
Virgin Hitz 95.5FM. 5.30am-
midnight daily. Pop dance and hits.
Get Radio 102.5FM. 24hrs daily.
DJs' choice, from retro and pop rock
to indie and dance.
Smooth 105FM. 5am-midnight
daily. Easy listening.
Voices of Thailand 95.5FM & 105
FM, 8.15am-8.30pm daily. Features.

Television

Of the six stations, two are
commercial: **Channels 3** and **7**
show mass market soaps, game
shows and so on. **Channels 5, 9** and
11 are government/army-controlled
and broadcast news, documentaries
and fewer entertainment shows.
Independent Television (**ITV**) was
set up to do investigative news, but
is in limbo after its sale by Thaksin's
family to Singapore, and massive
fines. Many hotels offer satellite/
cable channel **UBC** (0 2271 7171,
www.ubctv.com), offering BBC,
CNN, CNBC, Channel [V] and
international movie, sport and
entertainment channels, mostly
in English. MTV Asia is carried
on other cable channels.

Money

Thailand's currency is the *baht*
(B). B1 equals 100 *satang*. B1,
B2 (newly minted) and B5
coins are silvery; B10 coins
are copper with a silvery rim;
25 and 50 *satang* coins are
copperish. Bank notes are B20
(green – the most used note),
B50 (blue), B100 (red), B500
(purple) and B1,000 (grey).
At press time, £1=B69,
US$1=B35.

ATMs, banks & exchange

ATMs are plentiful at banks, malls,
petrol pumps and many shops.
They're open 24 hours, and most
accept credit cards.
  Banks generally open 8.30am-
4.30pm Mon-Fri, except bank
holidays. Some in department stores
may open 10am-8pm daily; banks
in Chatuchak Weekend Market
open 7.30am-8pm Sat, Sun; airport
branches open 24hrs. Bureaux de
change are found in tourist areas,
usually open 8.30am-9pm daily.

Credit cards

Most hotels, restaurants, shops and
department stores catering to
foreigners or middle-class Thais
accept credit cards. Visa, MasterCard
and American Express are more
widely accepted than Diners Club.

Missing credit cards

All are open 24 hours daily.
American Express 0 2273
5500/5522.
Diners Club 0 2238 3660.
**MasterCard ASEAN countries
hotline** 001 800 11 887 0663.
Visa Contact home country
issuing bank.

Police

The **Tourist Police** at
Tourist Information, 4
Ratchadamnoen Nok Avenue,
Dusit (0 2678 6801-9, national
hotline 1155) are best for
English skills, perseverance,
efficiency and familiarity with
non-Thai concerns. Most other
police speak little English,
with procedures that may add
to stress. Stations come under
the **Metropolitan Police
Bureau**, 323 Wang Parus,
Thanon Si Ayutthaya, Dusit
(hotline 191/0 2280 5060-4,
www.police.go.th).
Bangrak Police Station 50
*Thanon Naret, Bangrak (0 2234
0242/0 2631 8014-7/0 237 2601).*
Map p250 F7.
Chakkrawat Police Station 324
*Thanon Chakkrawat, Chinatown (0
2226 2131).* **Map** p249 & p250 D3.
Chanasongkram Police Station
*74 Thanon Chakrabongse,
Banglamphu (0 2282 2323).*
Map p308 B3.
Dusit Police Station 75 *Thanon
Rama V, Dusit (0 2241 2361-
2/4399).*
Pathumwan Police Station
*1775 Thanon Rama VI, Pathumwan
(0 2215 2992-3).* **Map** p251 G5.
Thonglor Police Station 800
*Sukhumvit Soi 55, Sukhumvit
(0 2390 2240-3).* **Map** p252 M6.

Postal services

Letters not over 20g cost B3
within Thailand; postcards
and letters abroad B12-B19;
aerogrammes B15. Newly
revamped **Post Offices**
(hotline 1545) have parcel

packaging, express and
registered mail, and CATNET
terminals (*see p232*), usually
opening 8.30am-4.30pm Mon-
Fri, 9am-noon Sat. The CPO
holds **Poste Restante** mail
for up to a month (bring ID,
fee payable). Stamps are sold
at convenience stores and
souvenir shops.

Central Post Office (CPO)

*Thanon Charoen Krung, at Sois
32-34, Bangrak (0 2233 1050-80).*
Open *Packing* 8am-4.30pm Mon-Fri;
9am-noon Sat. Post 8am-8pm Mon-
Fri; 8am-1pm Sat, Sun. *Postal orders
& money services* 8am-5pm Mon-Fri;
8am-noon Sat. *Poste Restante* 8am-
8pm Mon-Fri; 8am-1pm Sat, Sun.

Prohibitions

Draconian new rules prohibit
smoking in all air-conditioned
buildings and public places
(including streets, parks,
transport, hotel lobbies and
restaurants), except bars,
clubs, and places with signed
smoking rooms or zones (fine
B2,000). The B2,000 littering
fine has greatly cleaned up
Bangkok. Jaywalking on
designated congested roads
carries a minimum B200 fine.
For drug policy, *see p229*.

Religion

Anglican

Christ Church 11 *Thanon Convent,
Bangrak (0 2234 3634/0 2233
8525). Saladaeng BTS/Lumphini
MRT.* **Open** 8.30am-4.30pm Mon-Fri.
Map p251 G7.

Baptist

Calvary Baptist Church 88
*Sukhumvit Soi 2, Sukhumvit (0 2251
8278/www.thai-info.net/churches/
calvary). Nana BTS.* **Open** 8am-
5pm daily. **Map** p251 J5.

Buddhist

Thai Theravada Buddhist temples
typically open 6am-8pm daily; *bot*
(ordination halls) may open 9am-5pm
daily or require permission. Daily
services, in Thai, are generally 7-9pm
or longer, with prayer, *dharma*
(sermons) and meditation. Wat
Suthat is a model example.
Wat Suthat 146 *Thanon Bamrung
Muang, Phra Nakorn (0 2224 9845/*

0 2222 9632/www.watsuthat.org).
Open 8.30am-9pm daily. **Map**
p248 C4.

Catholic
Holy Redeemer Catholic
Church 123/19 Soi Ruam Rudi 5,
Pathumwan (0 2256 6305/6422).
Open 8.30am-8.30pm daily.
Map p251 H6.

Jewish
Even Chen Synagogue 4th floor,
Chao Phraya Tower, Shangri-La
Hotel, Soi Wat Suan Plu, Bangrak
(0 2236 7777). **Open** 6pm Fri;
9am-6pm Sat.

Muslim
Darul Aman Mosque Phetchaburi
Soi 7, North (0 1325 1617).
Map p250F3.

Safety & security

Bangkok is about as safe as
metropolises get. Some foreign
women urbanites live here
because it's so unthreatening,
even at night, with minimal
hassle from men. Muggings
and rapes of foreigners are
rare (but well publicised).
  Still, it pays to remain
cautious and guard against
pickpocketing, theft, scams,
credit card fraud and planting
of contraband in your bags.
Ignore touts, gem scammers,
predatory tuk-tuk drivers or
approaches by private guides.
Avoid walking in very quiet or
dimly lit areas at night. Avoid
involvement in narcotics,
gambling, prostitution or
illegal activities. Keep
passport, credit cards,
insurance, air tickets or ID
separate, with copies.

Smoking

Smoking is almost banned (see
above **Prohibitions**). Local
and some global brands are
legally on sale, but cannot
be displayed.

Study

Thai language classes

Jentana Personal Tutors 5/8
Sukhumvit Soi 31, Sukhumvit (0

2260 6138-9/www.thai-lessons.com).
Phrom Phong BTS. **Map** p251 K6.
Nisa Thai Language School
32/14-16, Thanon Yen Akat,
South (0 2671 3343-4). **Open**
8am-7pm Mon-Fri, 9am-5pm Sat.
Map p251 H8.
Siri-Pattana Thai Language
School 9th floor, YWCA, 13
Thanon Sathorn Tai, South (0 2213
1206). Lumphini MRT. **Open** 9am-
5pm daily. **Map** p251 G7.

Tax

VAT of 7 per cent is included
on most shop and restaurant
prices, but vendors avoid
paying it. Hotels and top
restaurants add 10 per cent
service plus VAT (known as
'plus plus' or '++'). You can
fill in VAT refund forms for
purchases over B2,000+VAT
(and totalling over B5,000+
VAT) at participating stores.
You collect the rebate at **VAT**
Refund Tourist Office (0
2272 9387-8/www.rd.go.th/vrt)
desks in airports, including
Suvarnabhumi Airport,
4th floor, West wing (0 2134
0675-6), East wing (0 2134
0677-8) and **Phuket Airport**
(0 7632 8267).

Telephones

Dialling & codes

You must dial the area codes in
Thailand, even within the same
area. So Bangkok's 7-digit landline
numbers are prefixed with an 0 2
code, and provincial 6-digit numbers
with 3-digit codes (Samui 0 77).
Local calls cost B3 (unlimited time).
Dialling upcountry (that is, not 0 2
numbers) is expensive, but cheaper
if you dial 1234 before the 0. Long-
distance is also better value via
mobile phones, which now have 10
digits, starting with prefixes 08 1,
08 5, 08 6, 08 7 or 08 9, followed by
a 7-digit number.
  To dial Thailand, dial the country
code 66, omit the 0, then dial the
remaining 8 digits (or 9 digits for
mobile phone).

Public phones

Call boxes require B1, B5 or B10
coins and/or a phone card. Some
accept credit cards for international
calls. Calling within the Greater

Bangkok 0 2 area, the minimum price
is B1 for 3mins, from B5 for 15mins.
Dialling a mobile costs B3 for 1min.
Buy phone cards at post offices or
convenience stores.

Operator & directories

For operator assisted calls, dial 100
and let the operator call (includes
surcharge of 3mins cost before you
start speaking).
Directory inquiries Hotline 1133
Bangkok; 183 regional. 24hrs; free.
Talking Yellow Pages Hotline
1188. 24hrs; B6 per min.

Mobile phones

Thailand is addicted to meur teur
(mobile phones) and their
customisation with ringtones,
animated displays, multicolour
re-casings, cute accessories and
numbers with auspicious digits.
Subscriber penetration is immense,
with great benefits (and new costs)
for remote locations, villagers,
vendors, drivers, etc. Liberalisation
has been limited, and competition
restricted. Visitors can use global
roaming, buy a cheap local phone
(from B3,500 including some calls),
or, if sharing the Thai GSM 900 or
1800 systems, buy a local prepaid
SIM card. Sold at some corner stores
or any phone shop (in most malls),
rechargeable SIM cards include a
number and some free calls, from
AIS One-2-Call, DTAC's D-Prompt,
True Move or Hutch's Say Prepaid.
Americans using 1900 GSM should
consult their service provider.

Time

Thailand is seven hours ahead
of Greenwich Mean Time, 12
hours ahead of US Eastern
Standard Time, and three
behind Sydney. The Thai
calendar is 543 years ahead
of the Gregorian calendar,
starting at the Buddha's
enlightenment; hence 2005 AD
is 2548 BE (Buddhist Era).

Tipping

In this hierarchical culture,
service is not a professional
calling, but a role (sometimes
temporary; even a poor diner
gets to summon a waiter as
nong, 'younger sibling'). Hence

tips are a small B20 (maximum B50), though *farang* often leave 10 per cent. Taxi drivers might round down a metered fare, such is the Thai heart, but passengers typically round up to the nearest B5.

Tip guides, maids and drivers, but not hairdressers or food vendors. Masseurs get low piece rates and rarely a salary, so tip them well. To Thais, generosity breeds good karma.

Toilets

A campaign to improve *hong nam* or *suka* has had some results. Public conveniences are rare, so use those in gas stations, department stores, hotels, temples or (asking politely) pubs, restaurants or shops where you're not a patron. You literally have to spend a penny (B2) at WCs in markets, stations and public places. Mobile toilet buses are provided at large events. Squat pans are common, with a plastic dipper and a water trough for cleaning yourself and flushing. Flush toilets usually have a spray hose. Tissue paper is often not provided (carry some) and must go in the basket so that it doesn't block the pipes.

Tourist information

Bangkok Tourist Bureau
17/1 Thanon Phra Athit, under Phra Pinklao Bridge, Phra Nakorn (0 2225 7612-5/www.bangkoktourist. com). Open 9am-7pm daily. **Map** p248 B2/3.
BTB handles Bangkok tourism, offering decent information on attractions, tours and BTB's own rewarding trips. The white BTB booths are numerous and easy to spot, found at tourist, hotel and shopping areas.

Tourism Authority of Thailand (TAT)
TAT Building, 1600 Thanon Petchaburi Tud Mai, North (0 2250 5500/www.tat.or.th). Open 8.30am-4.30pm Mon-Fri. **Map** p251 J4.

TAT's head office publishes useful leaflets that are not always to be found at TAT offices nationwide. However, the latter can often provide local insights – although they can't recommend particular companies or hotels.
Other locations: 4 Thanon Ratchadamnoen Nok, Dusit (0 2282 9773); Don Muang Airport (to be announced); Suvarnabhumi Airport (switchboard 0 2132 1888).

Visas & work permits

US, UK, Australasian and most European nationals can get a visa on arrival for 30 days, extendable twice to a maximum of 90 days in any six months, enforcing a 90-day gap before returning, due to a clampdown on illegal workers that collectively punishes innocent long-stay visitors and limits Thai tourism. Royal Thai embassies and consulates abroad may grant various visas for frequent or long-stay tourist or business visits.

Work permits (and tax returns) are required for those seeking paid work in occupations not restricted to Thais, and require the correct business visa and paperwork. Certain workers are eligible for the faster visa/work permit via the **One-Stop Service Centre** 16th floor, Rasa Tower 2, 555 Thanon Paholyothin, North-east (0 2937 1155, www.boi.go.th).

Immigration Department
507 Soi Suan Plu, Thanon Sathorn Tai, South (0 2287 3101-10/www. imm.police.go.th). Open 8.30am-4.30pm Mon-Fri. **Map** p251 G8.

Water & hygiene

Drink more water than you're used to. In fact, drink even if you're not feeling thirsty. If, however, you should get dehydrated, take a mixture of glucose and mineral salts with your water (this is why Thai fruit and juices often come

with salt/sugar as dips/mixers). Sea or rock salt is best. Coconut juice is an all-round replenisher and, when drunk directly from the shell, a safe source of uncontaminated liquid. The tap water in Bangkok and other major cities is filtered and chlorinated, but that doesn't make it good for drinking. Bottled and filtered water is everywhere (clear bottles signify more filtration than white bottles). Ice cubes (or rings) are frozen filtered water, shaved ice often is not.

Peel fruit, check expiry dates and in street eateries wipe plates and cutlery (as the Thais do) with the otherwise uselessly tiny napkins.

Weights & measures

The metric system predominates in weights, volumes, distance and fabric. Distance is measured in mm, cm, m and km; food in kg or g; liquids in litres. Fabric is measured in metres (or yards), but there's a Thai measurement for land: 1 *wa* = 2sq m; 1 *rai* = 4 *ngan* or 400 *talang wa* (square wa); 1 *rai* = 1,600sq m; 1 acre = 2.5 *rai*; 1 hectare = 6.25 *rai*. Gold comes not in ounces, but non-monetary *baht* (15.2g) and *saleung* (25 *satang* = 0.25 *baht*) weights.

What to take

Thailand is tropically humid, so pack loose, lightweight clothes. Tops that hang outside belts cool you by convection. Clothes and shoes are cheap and fashionable to buy, but rarely in large sizes. White deflects solar heat (and deters mosquitoes). Winter nights (and malls and cinemas) can be chilly, so bring layers and a light jacket or long-sleeve top. Lace-up shoes are a

Directory

chore as you must shed shoes continually. Velcro strap-sandals are practical, but say you're a tourist. Trekkers need boots with ankle support, and maybe a sleeping bag. Have one smart-ish ensemble for bureaucratic or social situations. Neatness and cleanliness are prized by Thais, who severely judge unkempt *farang kee nok* ('birdshit Westerners').

On arrival, buy a sarong; not so much to wear, but as a multi-purpose cloth to change in, lie on, picnic upon, wrap or carry things, cover dirty surfaces or burnt shoulders, or fold into a cushion. Many find wrap-around *gahng-gaeng talay* (fisherman's trousers) ideal at beaches or leisure, but look crass in Bangkok (where Thai ensembles look hip only if done with panache).

In urban/tourist areas, most medicines are notoriously easily obtainable without prescription (except very strong ones), so only bring specialised personal medication. Other essentials include door and luggage locks, a money belt, insect repellent, photocopies of documents, sunscreen (minimum SPF 15), spare batteries and an electrical adaptor. You might also want candles, a phrasebook, a torch, a penknife (not packed in hand-luggage or it will be confiscated), a teaspoon, toiletries, sanitary towels and an umbrella.

When to go

Thailand is tropical but has various climate zones. It stretches north to Himalayan foothills and south to a near-equatorial, rainforested peninsula with different monsoons in each ocean causing rains intermittently year round; most severe in late Oct-Dec in the Thai Gulf (Pacific Ocean) and June-Oct in the Andaman Sea (Indian Ocean), most pleasant in May-Oct and Nov-Mar respectively.

Bangkok sits in the hotter, humid, less breezy central plain, which, like the east coast, follows clear seasons. It's the world's hottest city since it doesn't vary hugely by hour or season from an average 27.8°C (81°F) and 77% humidity. Get forecasts from the **Meteorological Department** (0 2399 4012-4, hotline 1182, www.tmd.go.th).

Seasons

Hot mid Feb-mid May, hottest in Apr (hitting 40°C/104°F), windiest in Mar.

Rainy May-Oct, starting with erratic downpours (till June), then regular rain in late afternoon or evening from July, with Sept being wettest, Oct most prone to floods.

Cool Nov-mid Feb, when days are sunny, clear and fresh, and nights balmy. This is the tourist high season, when it's fine across most of Thailand.

Public holidays

New Year's Day 1 Jan.
Makha Bucha Day Jan-Mar (lunar).
Chakri Day 6 Apr.
Songkran (Thai New Year) 13-15 Apr.
National Labour Day 1 May.
Coronation Day 5 May.
Royal Ploughing Day (officials only) 9 May.
Visakha Bucha Day May-June (lunar).
Khao Phansa (Buddhist Lent) July (lunar).
HM The Queen's Birthday (Mother's Day) 12 Aug.
King Chulalongkorn Day 23 Oct.
Ok Phansa (end of Buddhist Lent) Oct (lunar).
HM The King's Birthday (Father's Day) 5 Dec.
Constitution Day 10 Dec.

Women

National Council of Women of Thailand
Baan Manangkasila, 514 Thanon Lan Luang, Dusit (0 2281 0081/ www.thaiwomen.or.th). **Open** 8.30am-4.30pm Mon-Fri. **Map** p249 & p250 D3.
Aims to improve women's status in every field.

Average monthly climate

Month	High temp (C°/F°)	Low temp (C°/F°)	Rainfall (cm)
Jan	33/92	25/77	0.72
Feb	34/94	25/77	1.37
Mar	33/92	26/79	3.25
Apr	36/98	28/82	5.83
May	33/92	26/79	17.08
June	33/92	26/79	11.25
July	33/92	27/81	11.81
Aug	33/92	26/79	16
Sept	34/94	26/79	25.25
Oct	33/92	25/77	20.73
Nov	32/90	23/73	3.24
Dec	32/90	23/73	0.33

Directory

Vocabulary

Though daunting, attempting Thai is useful and delights locals. The Thai language expresses cultural contexts of hierarchy, social obligation and the culture's multiple origins. Many words boast a lineage from Indian Sanskrit and Pali. Modern nouns such as *torasàp* ('telephone') are assembled from these Asian classical cousins to Latin and Greek, forming one tenuous link to European tongues; the other is a smattering of English, French and Portuguese words. Otherwise, Thai is utterly alien to Romance, Teutonic or Slavic speakers, using an Indianised script without word spaces. Hailing from Chinese are monosyllables, numbers, many words and the notorious five tones (low, falling, flat, rising and high) that turn the same sound into different words. Meanwhile, regional dialects demonstrate the influence of Mon, Khmer, Burmese, Lao or Malay or Sinified Tibeto-Burman tongues.

Central Thai is the standard, but – just as Londoners range from 'BBC English' to dropping their Cockney Hs – Bangkokians enunciate special languages to address royalty, nobility or monks, even though many 'drop' their Rs in a vernacular that turns Rs into Ls and Ls into Ns, especially in Bangkok's slightly Sinified accent. Be careful who you learn from: talk *pàk tàlàad* ('market speak') and you won't get far in society.

Politeness is ingrained in different layers of personal pronouns, in closing each sentence with *khâ* for females or *krúb* for males (which is like saying 'please'), in opening requests with *khŏr* ('I would like'), and in multilevel words such as the verb 'to eat'. In everyday lingo it's *kin, than* is

more polite, *rápprathan* formal, *chan* only with monks, and *sawŏey* just with royalty.

Transliteration & grammar

Many contradictory systems are used, partly because monosyllables lead to conglomerate words being separated out, partly as there are more consonants and vowels than ways to write in them in English, with several Ks, Ts, Js, Ps, As, Ss, Us, Ts, etc. An H following a T, P, K or B softens and aspirates it, those without are harder, explosive, sounding more like DT, BP, G or P; hence Phuket is not Fookhet but Pooget. Even academic spellings require phonetic letters to approximate Thai sounds, so accept the many anomalies. While wrong tones may possibly be understood through context, mistaking a long or short vowel is fatal to comprehension. Grammar has no articles or tenses; adjectives follow the noun; the name of a road, canal, hotel etc follows its generic noun (eg Thanon Silom, Tha Chang, Rong Raem Sukhothai), but numbers go before the 'generic counter' of any quantity, hence *sóm-ò sŏng lûuk* (two rounds of pomelo) or *baeb form săm bai* (three sheets of forms), with *un* (small thing) being a multi-purpose counter. Consonants often change sounds, whether at the end of a word or when put together. Thais can't pronounce most combinations of two consonants together without putting a sound in between, and some spellings reflect that: *pŏllámái* (fruit) is said *pŏnlámái; stàng* (cent) is pronounced *satàng; spaghéttî* is rendered *'sapaa-gét-tîî'*. Grasping such 'Thainglish' pronunciation of foreign words is a good first step.

Consonants

bh as in peace
j is like ch, often spelled ch or tch
kh as in camel
k like g in began, not George
ll in mid word becomes -nl-
ng as in sing without the 'si'
p like bp, as in explode
ph as in pine, not f
r is trilled, or slurred to l
ss in mid word becomes -ts-
t like dt, as in bottle
th as in Thai, not 'the'/'three'
v is like w
When ending a word or syllable: **-j, -ch** and **-s** becomes **-t; -r** often becomes **-orn; -l** becomes **-n; -tr** becomes **-t;** and **-se** and **-ha** are usually silent.

Vowels

a as in upon
aa as in barn, with no r
ae as in air, with no r (also used for a as in cat)
aew as in air-uw with no r
ai as in high
ao as in how with no w
aw as in awe with no w or r
e as in hay
eu as in urban, but flatter
eua as above with a rising a
i as in hit
ii as in teeth
o as in hot
oe as in earn with no r
oh as in so
oo or u as in book
uu as in fool
uay as in oo-way with no w

Tones

There are five tones, signified thus: high (ó), falling (ô), neutral (no mark), rising (ŏ), low (ò).

Thai names

Thais have at least three names. Formal first names are words with auspicious meanings, followed by a family name. Every Thai person gets a nickname from birth, sometimes later; they're often descriptive like Daeng (red), Nèung (one), Lék (small), Yài (big) or amusing, such as Mõo (pig), Ódd (tadpole), Gòp (frog) or Maew (cat), even fashionable: Bénz, Gòlf or Neòn. Monks get a special name on ordination.

Vocabulary

Basics

hello *sàwàsdee*; **goodbye/see you later** *la kòrn/láew jeur kun*; **good luck** *chôk dee*; **what's your name?** *khun chêu arai (khâ/krúb)*; **my name is...***chán/phõm chêu ...* **I** *chán (female)/phõm (male)*; **Mr/Mrs/Miss/you** *khun*; **he/she** *khão*; **girl/boy friend** *faen*; **friend** *puêan*; **wife** *mia*; **husband** *samee*; **minorwife** *mia-nói*; **monk** *luang phõr*; **child/boy/girl** *dek/dekchai/dekying*; **man** *phûchai*; **women** *phûying*; **gay** *gay*, **ladyboy** *kàtoey*; **lesbian** *tom-dêe*. **yes** *châi*; **no** *mâi chái*; **can** *dâi*; **cannot** *mâi dâi*; **please** *pròd, gàrúna*; **thank you** *khòb khun khâ (female)/krúb (male)*; **excuse me** *kõr thôd khâ/krúb*; **I'm sorry** *chán /phõm sìa jai (khâ/krúb)*; **never mind** *mâi pen rai*. **ask/can I have...** *chán /phõm kõr...*; **excuse me** *kõr thôd (khâ/krúb)*; **please help me** *dâi pròd chûay chán/phõm nòi*; **wait a moment** *ror sàk khrù (khâ/krúb)*. **what is this in Thai?** *Nîi rîak pen Thai wâh arai?* **do you speak English?** *khun phôod pasãa angìd dâi mái (khâ/krúb)?* **sorry, I can't speak Thai** *sìa jai, chán/phõm phôod pasãa Thai mâi dâi*; **I can speak Thai a bit** *chán/phõm phôod pasãa Thai dâi nìd nòi*; **I don't understand** *chán/phõm mâi khâo jai*; **speak more slowly, please** *pròd phôod chã nòi (khâ/krúb)*, **why?** *tham mai?*; **when?** *mûea rài?*; **who?** *krai?*; **what?** *arai?*; **where?** *têe nãi?*; **how?** *yàng rai?*, informal *yàng ngài?* **very** *mâak*; **and** *láe*; **or** *rue*; **with** *dûay*; **without** *mâi meeopen pèrd*; **closed** *pid*; **what time does it open/close?** *pèrd/pid kèe mong?* **I want/would like...** *chán/phõm tõng karn...(I want...)*; **how many would you like?** *khun tõng karn thâo rai?* **I like...** *chán/phõm chôrb...*; **I don't like...** *chán/phõm mâi chôrb...*; **OK/fine** *OK*; **that's enough** *por láew*. **price** *raakha*; **rent/hire** *châo*; **free** *free*; **discount** *lód raakha*; **how much?** *thâo rai (khâ/krúb)*; **could you discount?** *lód raakha dâi mái (khâ/krúb)*; **that's expensive/**

cheap *paeng mâak/tòok mâak*; **the bill/check, please** *chék bin (khâ/krúb)*; **do you have any change?** *khun mee torn mái (khâ/krúb)*. **what's that?** *nân arai?*, **where is...?** *...yòo têe nãi?*, **I'm going to...** *chán ja pai*. **good** *dee*; **bad** *mâi dee*; **big** *yài*; **small** *lék*; **little** *nói*; **entrance** *thang khâo*; **exit** *thang òkk*; **painful** *jèb*; **help** *chûay*; **dangerous** *antarai*; **accident** *òobùtihèd*; **doctor** *mõr*; **medicine** *yaa*; **on one's own** *khon dêe-o*; **smile** *yim*.

Places

bridge *sàphan*; **canal** *khlong*; **main road** *thanõn*; **side road** *soi*; **alley** *tròk*; **expressway** *thang dòuan*; **river** *mãe nám*; **pier** *thâ*; **station** *sàtãanee*; **gaan ká*; **temple** *wát*; **bank** *thána karn*; **post office** *prai sa nee*; **restaurant** *ráan ar-hãrn*; **...hospital** *rong phaya bâan...*; **...palace** *wang*; **house** *bâan*; **housing estate** *mòo bâan*; **town** *meuang*; **island** *kò*; **beach** *hàad*; **bay** *ào*; **mountain** *khão*; **forest** *pà*; **market** *talàd*; **embassy** *sàtãan tôot*; **province** *changwàt*; **district** *amphoe* (in Bangkok *khet*); **sub district** *tambon* (in Bangkok *khwãeng*); **country** *prathêt*; **where's the toilet?** *hông nám yoo nãi (khâ/krúb)*.

Transport

Bicycle *rót jàkràyan*; **boat** *ruea*; **bus** *rót may*; **car** *rót*; **express boat** *ruea dòuan*; **ferry** *ruea khâm fàk*; **long-tailed boat** *ruea hãang yao*; **motorcycle** *motersài*; **taxi** *táirk-sîi*; **train** *rót fai*; **skytrain** *rót fai fáh*; **subway** *rót fai tâi din*; **pickup bus** *sõngtãew*; **plane** *krêuang bin*; **platform** *charn cha la*; **ticket** *tua*; **one way** *têo dii-o*; **bus stop** *pâai rót may*. **do you know the way to...?** *khun róo thang pai...máii (khâ/krúb)?* **to the end of the street/lane** *sòod thanõn/soi*; **near** *klâhy*; **far** *klaii*; **right** *khwã*; **left** *sáai*; **stop** *yùut*; **stop here/there** *yùut tîi-nîi/tîi-nán*; **return** *pai klàb*; **turn** *lii-o*; **u-turn** *lii-o klàb*; **opposite** *trong khâm*; **beside** *khâng khâng*; **the next stop** *paai nâa*.

Accommodation

...hotel *rong raem...*; **room** *hông*; **with/without bathroom** *mee hông nám/mâi mee hông nám*; **shower** *fàk bua*; **air-conditioned** *hông air*; **fan-cooled** *hông phát lom*; **double bed** *tiang khòo*; **breakfast included** *ruam ar-hãrn cháo*; **lift** *lif*; **swimming pool** *sà wâi nám*; **an**

inside/outside room *hông dâan nai/hông dâan nôk*. **do you have a double/single room for tonight/one week?** *khun mee hông khõo/hông dêow s_mrúb kheun nii/nèung aa-thít*; **we have a reservation** *rao jong hông láew*; **where is the car park?** *tîi jòrd rót yoo tîi nãi*.

Time

morning *torn cháo*; **midday** *klang wan*; **noon** *thîang wan*; **afternoon** *torn bàì*; **evening** *torn yen*; **night** *torn klang kheun*; **midnight** *thîang kheun*; **early** *cháo*; **late** *sãi*; **week** *aa-thít*; **weekend** *wan sòod sàb da*; **now** *torn nii*; **later** *pai lãng*; **today** *wan nii*; **yesterday** *mêua wan nii*; **tomorrow** *wan prôong nii*; **delayed** *lãa chãa*. **what's the time?** *kèe mong*; **hour** *chûamong*; **in an hour** *iik nèung chûamong*; **last 2 hours** *chãi way-la sõng chûamong*; **at 8am** *pàed mong cháo*; **at 1pm** *bài mong*; **at 2pm** *bài sõng mong*; **at 7pm** *nùeng thûm*; **at 8pm** *sõng thûm*. **day** *wan*; **Monday** *wan jun*; **Tuesday** *wan ankarn*; **Wednesday** *wan phúd*; **Thursday** *wan pàrêuhàssàbordii*, *wan pàrêuhàt*; **Friday** *wan sùk*; **Saturday** *wan são*; **Sunday** *wan athít*. **Month** *deuan*; **January** *mókkàrakhom*; **February** *koomphaphan*; **March** *meenakhom*; **April** *maesãyon*; **May** *prúedsàphakhom*; **June** *míthùunayon*; **July** *kàràkàadakhom*; **August** *singhãkhom*; **September** *kunyayon*; **October** *tùlakhom*; **November** *prúesàjikayon*; **December** *thanwakhom* **summer** *réudoo rórn*; **rain** *réudoo fõn*; **winter** *réudoo nãow*; **year** *pii*.

Slang

handsome *lòr*; **cute** *nâa-rák*; **beautiful** *sũay*; **delicious** *aa-ròi*; **cool** *jeng*; **lousy** *hûay tàek*; **international** *inter*; **modern** *dêrn*; **going out** *pai tîi-o*; **ticklish** *jàkkàjîi*; **exclamation sound** *oõ-ii*.

Numbers

0 *sõon*; **1** *nèung*; **2** *sõng*; **3** *sãm*; **4** *sìi*; **5** *hâa*; **6** *hòk*; **7** *jèd*; **8** *pàed*; **9** *kão*; **10** *sib*; **11** *sib-èt*; **12** *sib-sõng*; **13** *sib-sãm*; **14** *sib-sìi*; **15** *sib-hâa*; **16** *sib-hòk*; **17** *sib-jèd*; **18** *sib-pàed*; **19** *sib-kão*; **20** *yî-sib*; **21** *yî-sib-èt*; **22** *yî-sib-sõng*; **30** *sãm-sib*; **31** *sãm-sib-èt*; **32** *sãm-sib-sõng*; **40** *sìi-sib*; **50** *hâa-sib*; **60** *hòk-sib*; **70** *jèd-sib*; **80** *pàed-sib*; **90** *kâo-sib*; **100** *nèung rói*; **101** *nèung rói nèung*; **200** *sõng rói*; **1,000** *nèung phun*; **10,000** *nèung mèun*; **100,000** *nèung sàen*; **1,000,000** *nèung láan*; **1st** *tée nèung*; **2nd** *tée sõng*; **3rd** *tée sãm*; **last** *tîi sòod*.

Further Reference

Books

Fiction

Bunnag, Tew *Fragile Days: Tales form Bangkok* Poised, poignant vignettes from every social strata, rich with cultural colour.
Burdett, John *Bangkok 8, Bangkok Tattoo* Benchmark of the 'Bangkok underworld novels' genre.
Lapcharoensap, Rattawut *Sightseeing* Multi-prizewinning young writer fillets Thai life in dazzling short stories.
Masavisut, Nitaya *SEAwrite Anthology of Thai Short Stories and Poems* A sampler by prize-winning writers.
Needham, Jake *The Big Mango* Bangkok's Elmore Leonard gives the usual suspects unusual panache.
Pramoj, Kukrit *Si Phaendin (Four Reigns)* Life under Ramas V-VIII by a noble late PM of deep wisdom.
Somtow, SP *Jasmine Nights* Bangkok coming-of-age tale, written with edge, beauty and wit.
Srinawk, Khamsing *The Politician & Other Stories* Scathing progressive prose fables of modern village life.
Sutham, Pira *Shadowed Country* An Isaan villager turned Sussex expat dissects the roots of corruption.

Non-fiction

Books also get mentions in the **History, Galleries, Restaurants, Gay & Lesbian** and **Mind & Body** chapters.
Cornwel-Smith, Philip *Very Thai: Everyday Popular Culture* Zesty insight into streetlife. Pop Bangkok Modern indie culture distilled.
Ekachai, Sanitsuda *Keeping the Faith* Thai beliefs.
Fellowes, Warren *The Damage Done* Excoriating exposé of Thai prisons by a former inmate.
Jackson, Peter *Dear Uncle Go: Homosexualities in Thailand*; Ladyboys-Tomboys-Rentboys Gay Thai ways teased out by a lucid academic.
Jotisalikorn, Chami *Classic Thai* Traditional arts and design.
Kerr, Alex *Bangkok Found* A lyrical journey through Thai culture by the Asian arts expert.
Klausner, William *Transforming Thai Culture* Third volume of the anthropologist's penetrating view.
Mertens, Brian *Bangkok Design; Architecture of Thailand* The creation of forms old, new and eternal.

Odzer, Cleo *Patpong Sisters* A window on Thai prostitution.
Pannapadipo, Phra *Peter Phra Farang*; Little Angels Temple tales by an English monk.
Phongpaichit, Pasuk & Baker, Chris *Thaksin: The Business of Politics in Thailand*; Thailand's Boom and Bust Revelations about Thai power.
Rajadhon, Phya *Anuman Essay on Thai Culture* Definitive wisdom on the way things were.
Van Beek, Steve *Bangkok Then and Now* A century recorded in clippings. Plus his waterways tomes.
Warren, William *Bangkok* Informed long-time reflections.
Wyatt, David *Reading Thai Murals* Acclaimed historian reveals what pictures say.
Ziv, Daniel & Sharrett, Guy *Bangkok Inside Out* Quirky, realistic portrait of the Big Durian.

Music

Classical/phiphat

Bangkok Symphony Orchestra *Mahajanaka Symphony* (BSO Foundation) The pastiche by SP Somtow that launched an opera house.
Fong Naam *Jakajan* Bruce Gaston's compositions and/or arrangements for phiphat, plus rock/jazz ensemble.
Kangsadan *Golden Jubilee Overture* (Pisces) Modern phiphat ensemble outdoing the Latin, jazz and lounge fusion of labelmates Boy Thai.
Harvey, Richard *The Spirit of Suriyothai* (Asian Music International) Elaboration of his film score.

Luuk thung/morlam

Amphipong, Siriporn *Greatest Hits Vols 1-5* (MGA) Vol 3 is easiest on Western ears (feels like the blues).
Duangjan, Phomphuang *Through the Years, Vol 1 & 2* (Topline) The Thai equivalent of Hank Williams versus modern C&W.
Poonlarp, Jintara *Greatest Hits Vols 1 & 2* (MGA) Over 30 CDs, so pick this collection from Grammy's Nashville/Khorat division.

Indie/dance

A Mosquito *This is Asia* (Red Beat) Peculiarly loopy Thai dance music.
Apartment Khunpa *Romantic Comedy* (Sexy Pink Studio) Definitive indie band.

Futon *Never Mind the Botox* and *Love Bites* Outrageous Thai-Brit group pit witty lyrics to electrotrash.
Joey Boy *Anthology* (Bakery Records) From funkfest 'Chinese Connection' to 'Fun Fun Fun'; plus any of the Gancore releases.
Modern Dog *That Song* (Bakery) Produced by Tony Doogan, the indie nu-metal heroes' best album since Café.
Pru *From Hero to Zero* Arty prog rock from indie's first family.

Pleng puer cheewit

Carabao, Ad *Best of* (Warner) Splendid gold-covered primer.
Caravan *Best of: Vol 1* (UPL) Rootsy 70s folk that sparked a revolution.
Khampee, Pongsit *Best of... 2530* (ATO) Sweet-voiced, thinking rebel.
Marijuana *Buppha Chon* (Milestone/MGA). The mellow Deadhead side of *pleng puer cheewit*.

T-Pop

Labanoon *The Very Best of* (Grammy) Stirring, wistful Muslim-Thai rock ballads of rare craft.
LoSo *The Red Album* (Grammy) Testosterone power ballads and raunchy rock. *For God's Sake* is Sek Loso's debut in English.
McIntyre, Thongchai 'Bird' *Faen Jaa* Perennial pop fusionist enlists rap and folk to zeitgeisty effect.
Palmy *Palmy* (Grammy) Hook-laden, non-stop hip-sway grooves in a hippie-dippy trip-hop-lite mode.
Young, Tata *I Believe* (BEC Tero) Kid star turned 'Sexy, Naughty, Bitchy' pop-dance vamp. Her *Temperature Rising* album is in English.

Websites

www.bangkokpost.net Online paper of record.
www.bangkokrecorder.com Hip, clubby web mag.
www.ethaimusic.com Ingeniously teaches Thai using hit songs.
www.eThailand.com Portal with community emphasis.
www.nationmultimedia.com On-the-ball news coverage.
www.thai-blogs.com Selected postings on things Siamese.
www.thailandlife.com Gor's inspiring honest take on life, youth, language, drugs and jail.
www.travelfish.org By and for independent travellers.

Directory

Index

Advertisers' Index

Place of interest and/or entertainment	▭
Railway & bus stations	▭
Parks	▭
Hospitals/universities	▭
Neighbourhood	DUSIT
Subway station	🅄
Subway route	—
Skytrain route	=
BTS/BRT route	—
Skytrain station	Ⓢ
Temple	⛩

Maps

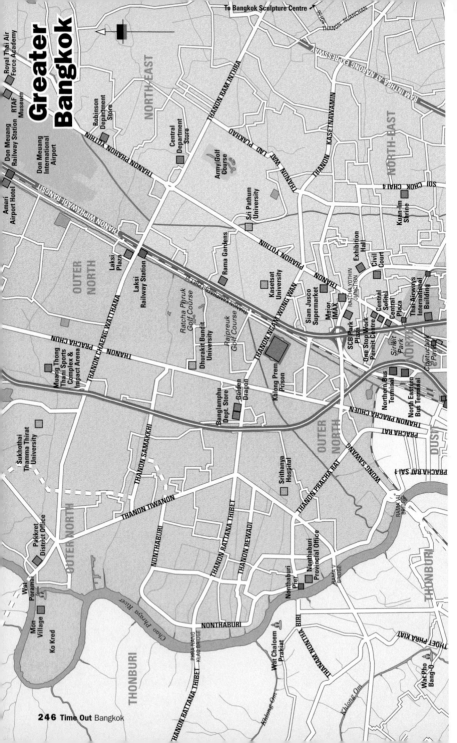

Greater Bangkok

To Bangkok Sculpture Centre

THANON HUACHIN

RAM INTHRA AT NA YONG EXPRESSWAY

Royal Thai Air Force Academy

RTAF Museum

Don Meuang Railway Station

Don Meuang International Airport

Amari Airport Hotel

Robinson Department Store

Central Department Store

Army Golf Course

Sri Pathum University

Rama Gardens

Kasetsat University

Exhibition Hall

Civil Court

Kuan-Im Shrine

NORTH-EAST

NORTH-EAST

THANON PHAHON YOTHIN

THANON RAM INTHRA

THANON WAT LAD PLAKHAO

KASETNAVAMIN

SOI CHOK CHAI 4

THANON VIPHAVADI RANGSIT

OUTER NORTH

Laksi Plaza

Laksi Railway Station

Ratcha Phruk Golf Course

Rajpreuk Golf Course

Dhurakit Bundit University

PHAHON YOTHIN JUNCTION

RACHA YOTHIN

Siam Jusco Supermarket

Major IMAX

SCB Park Plaza

One Stop Work Permit Centre

Central Sofitel

Central Plaza

Thai Airways International Building

Sirikit Park

Chatuchak Park

THANON CHAENG WATTHANA

THANON PRACHA CHUEN

Muang Thong Thani Sports Complex & Impact Arena

OUTER NORTH

Golden Dragon

Banglamphu Dept. Store

Khlong Prem Prison

Northern Bus Terminal

North Eastern Bus Terminal

DUSIT

THANON NGAM WONG WAN

THANON NONTHABURI PRACHA CHUEN

PRACHA RAI

WONG SAWANG

PRACHA RAI SAI 1

Sukhothai Thamma Thirat University

Srithanya Hospital

THANON SAMAKKHI

THANON TIWANON

THANON RATTANA THIBET

THANON REWADI

THANON PRACHA RAI

RAMA VII BRIDGE

Pakkret District Office

OUTER NORTH

Nonthaburi Provincial Office

Nonthaburi Pier

RAMA V BRIDGE

THONBURI

Wat Poramai

Mon Village

Ko Kred

Chao Phraya River

PHRA NANG KLAO BRIDGE

THONBURI

NONTHABURI

Wat Chaloem Prakiat

THANON NONTHABURI

THONBURI

THANON RATTANA THIBET

THANON NONTHABURI 1

THOET PHRA KIAT

Wat Pho Bang-O

Khlong Om

Khlong Om

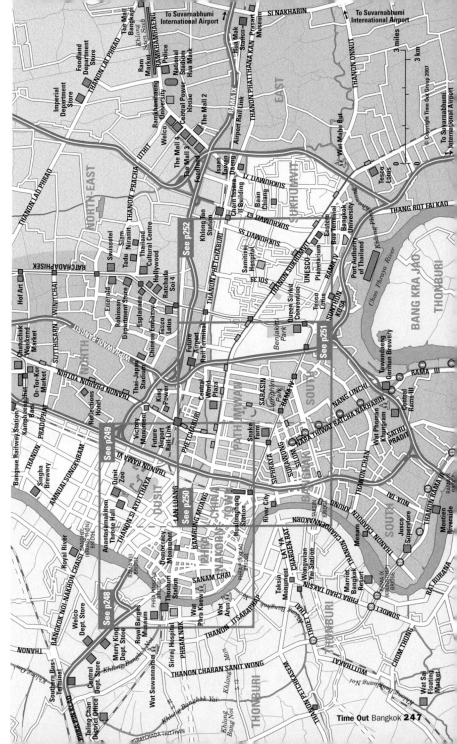

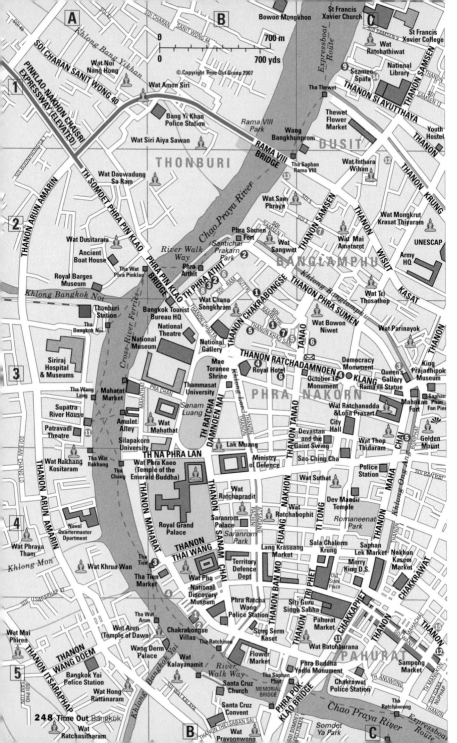

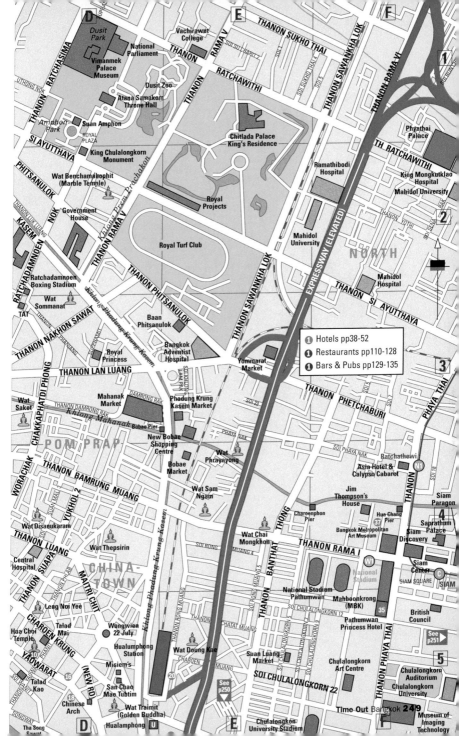

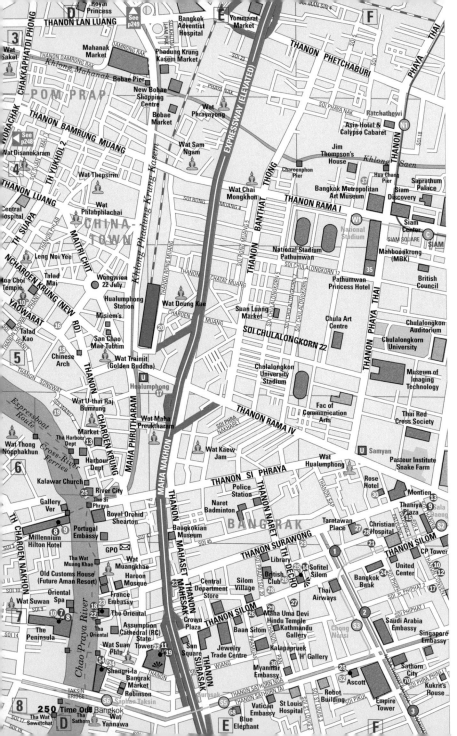

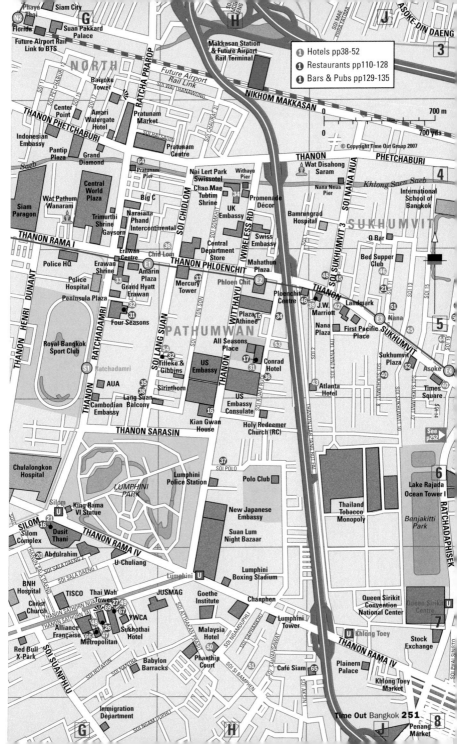

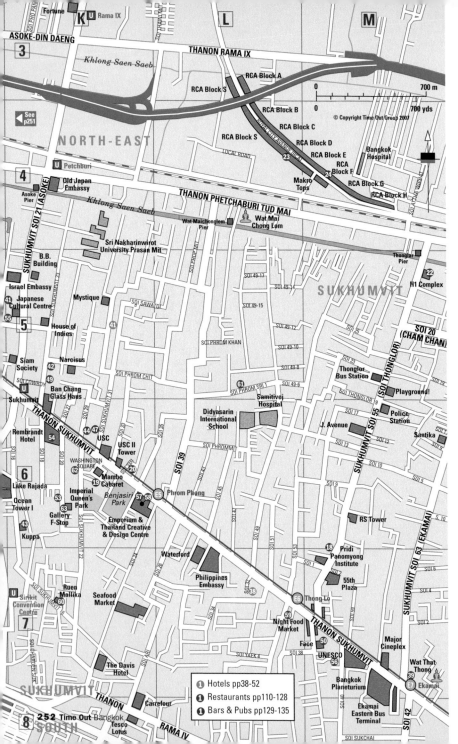

Street Index

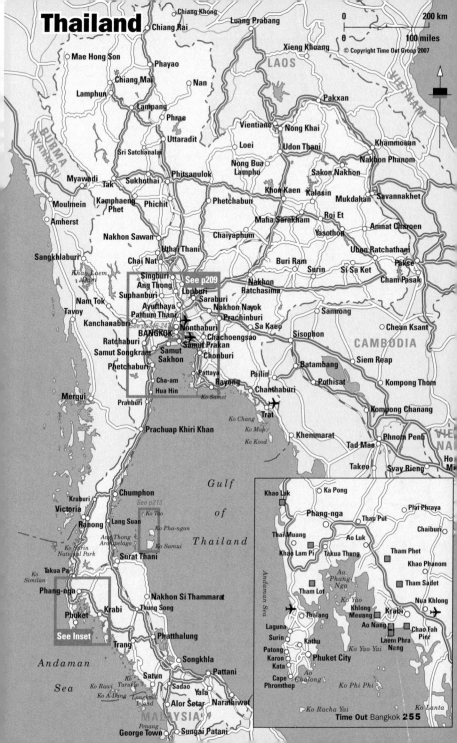

Thailand

Chiang Khong
Chiang Rai
Luang Prabang
Xieng Khoang
Mae Hong Son
Phayao
Chiang Mai
Nan
LAOS
Lamphun
Lampang
Phrae
Pakxan
Myawadi
Tak
Uttaradit
Vientiane
Nong Khai
Khammouan
Sri Satchanalai
Loei
Udon Thani
Nakhon Phanom
Moulmein
Kamphaeng Phet
Sukhothai
Phitsanulok
Nong Bua
Lamphu
Sakon Nakhon
Savannakhet
Amherst
Phichit
Phetchabun
Khon Kaen
Kalasin
Mukdahan
Sangkhlaburi
Nakhon Sawan
Maha Sarakham
Roi Et
Amnat Charoen
Khao Laem Dam
Uthai Thani
Chaiyaphum
Yasothon
Ubon Ratchathani
Chai Nat
Singburi
See p209
Nakhon Ratchasima
Surin
Si Sa Ket
Pakse
Ang Thong
Lopburi
Cham Pasak
Nam Tok
Suphanburi
Saraburi
Ayutthaya
Nakhon Nayok
Samrong
Tavoy
Pathum Thani
Prachinburi
Kanchanaburi
See p246-24
Nonthaburi
Sa Kaeo
Chean Ksant
BANGKOK
Chachoengsao
Ratchaburi
Samut Prakan
Sisophon
CAMBODIA
Samut Songkram
Samut Sakhon
Chonburi
Phetchaburi
Pattaya
Rayong
Pailin
Batambang
Siem Reap
Kompong Thom
Cha-am
Hua Hin
Ko Samet
Chanthaburi
Pothisat
Kompong Chanang
Prahburi
Ko Chang
Ko Mak
Trat
Khemmarat
Phnom Penh
Prachuap Khiri Khan
Ko Kood
Tad Mao
Takeo
Svay Rieng

Gulf
of
Thailand

Chumphon
Ka Pong
Kraburi
Victoria
Ranong
Lang Suan
See p213
Ko Tao
Ko Pha-ngan
Ang Thong
Archipelago
Ko Samui
Ko Surin
National Park
Surat Thani
Ko Similan
Takua Pa
Phang-nga
Nakhon Si Thammarat
Phuket
Krabi
Thung Song
See Inset
Patthalung
Trang
Andaman
Songkhla
Pattani
Sea
Satun
Sadao
Yala
Ko Rawi
Tarutao
Ko A-Dang
Langkawi
Island
Alor Setar
Narathiwat
Penang
MALAYSIA
George Town
Sungai Patani

Inset

Khao Lak
Ka Pong
Phang-nga
Thap Put
Plai Phraya
Thai Muang
Ao Luk
Chaiburi
Khao Lam Pi
Takua Thung
Tham Phet
Khao Phanom
Andaman
Sea
Ao
Phang
Nga
Tham Lot
Tham Sadet
Ko Yao
Nua Khlong
Thalang
Khlong
Meuang
Krabi
Laguna
Ko Yao
Surin
Ao Nang
Chao Fah
Kathu
Laem Phra
Pier
Patong
Nang
Karon
Phuket City
Kata
Ao
Ko Yao Yai
Chalong
Cape
Phromthep
Ko Phi Phi
Ko Racha Yai
Ko Lanta

0   200 km
0   100 miles
© Copyright Time Out Group 2007

Bangkok Transport

© Copyright Time Out Group 2007